Women Creating Lives

Vera Brittain. *(From the Vera Brittain Papers, the William Ready Division of Archives and Research Collections, McMaster University Library, Hamilton, Canada.)*

WOMEN CREATING LIVES

Identities, Resilience, and Resistance

edited by
Carol E. Franz
Williams College
Abigail J. Stewart
University of Michigan

Westview Press
Boulder • San Francisco • Oxford

Paperback cover photos provided courtesy of (from top): Sarah F. Colt; Vera Brittain Papers, The William Ready Division of Archives and Research Collections, McMaster University Library; National Archives; Brad Hess and Suzanne Hiatt; and Sarah F. Colt.

Published in 1994 in the United States of America by Westview Press, Inc., 5500 Central Avenue, Boulder, Colorado 80301-2877, and in the United Kingdom by Westview Press, 36 Lonsdale Road, Summertown, Oxford OX2 7EW

Design and Composition by Westview Press, Inc.

Library of Congress Cataloging-in-Publication Data
Women creating lives : identities, resilience, and resistance / edited
  by Carol E. Franz, Abigail J. Stewart.
    p.   cm.
  Includes bibliographical references and index.
  ISBN 0-8133-1872-6 (hc.) — ISBN 0-8133-1873-4 (pbk.)
    1. Women—Psychology.   2. Women—Social conditions.   I. Franz,
Carol E.   II. Stewart, Abigail J.
HQ1206.W87445   1994
305.42—dc20   93-48990
                                                                     CIP

Printed and bound in the United States of America

∞   The paper used in this publication meets the requirements
     of the American National Standard for Permanence of Paper
     for Printed Library Materials Z39.48-1984.

10   9   8   7   6   5   4   3   2   1

Contents

PART FOUR
One Life Among Many: Cases Drawn from Group Studies

PART FIVE
Lives in Contrast: Comparative Case Studies

Acknowledgments

Working on this book has been rewarding to us for many reasons. It has offered us a chance to explore the role of case studies of women in the field of personality in a sustained way. Our own lives have been enriched by "getting to know" the women whose stories are told in this book. Perhaps most of all we have had a chance to collaborate with colleagues whose work we admire and whose intellectual company—and friendship—we cherish.

Several institutions and individuals played special roles in supporting the work of this book. The Henry A. Murray Research Center at Radcliffe College fostered the book's beginnings by sponsoring a conference on methods for studying women's lives, at which two papers were presented that subsequently became chapters in this book. Ravenna Helson encouraged us to develop the book after reading one of the papers, and Faye Crosby and David Winter provided important support and feedback along the way. The University of Michigan and the Institute for Personality and Social Research at the University of California at Berkeley provided supportive work environments for this project. Joan Ostrove provided us with sage editorial advice and expert indexing and exhibited amazing problem-solving talents in locating and acquiring photographs to accompany many chapters. Several people were exceptionally helpful in providing information and advice about photographs: Deborah Belle, Alison Cheek, Emily Hewitt, Sue Hiatt, Jane Knowles, Patricia Frazer Lamb, Brinton Lykes, Susan Quinn, and Charlotte Stewart-Murphy. We were fortunate throughout the process of working on the book in having the assistance of Nancy Carlston, Shena Redmond, and Meredith Sund at Westview Press. We are especially grateful for Nancy Carlston's commitment to (and success at) finding reviewers who would offer us sympathetic and critical feedback throughout the process, and for her own enthusiasm, judgment, and advice.

We are also grateful to those psychologists and feminists who pointed to the possibilities and benefits of doing case studies and studying women's lives, and who provided inspiration at the beginning and along the way. These include Mary Catherine Bateson, Rae Carlson, Carolyn Heilbrun, Ravenna Helson, W. MacKinlay Runyan, and Robert White.

Our deepest thanks go to the women whose stories are told in this book and to the authors who studied and wrote about their lives. We are grateful for their time, energy, honesty, and courage in letting their voices be heard in this way.

Carol E. Franz
Abigail J. Stewart

1

Introduction:
Women's Lives and Theories

CAROL E. FRANZ & ABIGAIL J. STEWART

CURRENT VOICES in the scholarship on women remind us that existing psychological theories do not permit the construction of women's lives on the women's own terms. Instead, some theories simply ignore women; some formalize men's fantasies about women into theories of women; and some assume that women's lives are like men's. In this book we offer accounts of women's lives that should provide useful material for better psychological theorizing about women's lives.

Psychological theories have not been constructed much in terms of lives at all. Therefore, one goal we have in this book is to attend to what Robert White (1966) called the "gap in the center of our knowledge about personality"—an understanding of psychological development over long periods of time in ordinary circumstances. White suggested that "the searching eye of scientific research has barely glanced at everyday lives in progress, to say nothing of lives marked by unusual happiness or major social contributions" (White, 1966, p. 23). More recently, Carlson (1985) and Runyan (1982; 1988) urged that more attention be paid to the study of the person to avoid the convenient oversimplifications that are often a consequence of nomothetic research. According to Carlson (1985), the study of persons will ultimately revise our "ideology of science," force us to focus on "human being" theory rather than personality theory, and help us to develop personality theory (and research) that better reflects the complexity, heterogeneity, and diversity of lives and personalities. In recent years, we have witnessed some serious attention in psychology to the study of individual lives (e.g., Josselson and Lieblich, 1993; McAdams and Ochberg, 1988; Rosenwald and Ochberg, 1992; Runyan, 1982); we offer this book as an addition and also to help fill the gap in psychological understandings of women.

The studies of lives that have been done in psychology have tended to be studies of men. Feminist scholars in other fields have produced wonderful, rich collections of *women's* lives (e.g., Bateson, 1989; Brodzki and Schenck, 1988; Gluck and Patai, 1991; Personal Narratives Group, 1989). Within psychology, though, such studies are very few, and they tend to be limited to particular topics or domains. For example, Grossman and Chester's (1990) valuable collection of qualitative studies focused on women's work lives. Similarly, Josselson's books on women's identity (1987) and on intimacy (1992) contain many case accounts, but they were intended to illustrate particular issues, rather than "lives." Most recently, Rosenwald and Ochberg (1992) included quite a few accounts of women, but the focus of the book is less on lives and more on the process of story-telling about experiences in one's life.

This book, then, provides an opportunity to study lives and broad concerns of particular women—women who vary in age at the time of study, race/ethnicity, social class, and historical period. Some of the women came from backgrounds of great hardship—poverty, exile, abuse; others experienced great opportunities—wealth, talent, education. The authors who have written about each woman's life necessarily tell us one (or at most a few) of many possible stories about even that one life. In telling their stories, the authors have tried to avoid use of technical language and have quoted directly from the women themselves as much as possible. They have, moreover, organized their accounts according to themes and issues that seemed to them most pertinent and relevant to the particular woman's life. We are indebted not only to the authors, but also to the women who contributed their lives to this project; we agree with Santayana that "Nothing requires a rarer intellectual heroism than willingness to see one's equation written out" (quoted in White, 1966, p. v).

Although the authors were not constrained to any particular content or perspective, several themes emerged that cut across the diverse chapters. They include the theme of struggle: for identities, understanding, self-expression, and survival under potentially crippling social or internal conditions. Most of the women grappled with a marginal social position. Coming so close to these struggles through the case study approach, the reader gains intimate knowledge of the women and their modes of resilience, coping, and resistance. Through the cases we observe the ways in which racial, class, and gender inequalities constrained women's lives, but we also see the ways in which women variously played the hands they were dealt. The ways in which women endured and transcended the difficulties in their lives inform us about the obstacles in their path as well as their inventive strategies for removing or circumnavigating them.

Instead of organizing the chapters thematically (since so many themes cut across chapters) or by categories or types of women, we have left it for readers to identify themes and patterns themselves. We will, however, outline some possible approaches to using the chapters in this book, particularly for teaching, in the final section of this chapter.

The Organization of the Book

The book is organized into five sections. In Part One, three chapters address broad methodological, philosophical, and ethical issues that arise in the course of trying to study or "recreate" women's lives. Some of these issues, once raised, seem to apply with equal force to studying men's lives, but it is probably no accident that they first came into sharp focus when psychologists began to theorize about women's lives and experiences.

In the first chapter in this section, Stewart suggests that feminist theory can provide some useful guidelines for the student of women's lives. She illustrates how these guidelines can be used to illuminate a life—and the limitations of the researcher—by describing her own analyses of the life of the feminist author Vera Brittain. In the following chapter, Belle reflects on the complex situation of the psychologist "studying" other women's lives through contemplation of the meaning of social class for her as a researcher, for her less privileged research participants, and in their exchanges. She illustrates how the process of studying women's lives is a transaction in which the women studied can transform the researcher's understandings. Finally, Hornstein poses questions about the process of writing about another woman's life. Here, too, aspects of the relationships between the author, her "subject," and her readers are central. In thinking about those relationships, Hornstein confronts issues of truth, loyalty, and responsibility that are often prominent in the thinking of case study writers as they do their work, but are rarely discussed in detail. These three chapters raise epistemological, ethical, and methodological issues that are then illustrated and examined in various ways in the subsequent chapters.

In the next two sections, each chapter presents one woman's life. In Part Two, researchers were able to interview the women they studied and to invite the women's collaboration in thinking about their lives. In Part Three, researchers were forced by the death, geographic distance, or fame of the women they studied to think about these women's lives without the opportunity for dialogue with the woman herself. Across the two sections, the researchers used a variety of materials to help them understand the women's lives: interviews with the women and with others in the women's communities, published diaries and interviews, films, private correspondence, and the poetry and theories these women produced. Regardless of the scholar's method, the fascination of the researcher is with the particular woman as a special individual, her unique ways of patterning and creating a life for herself. The stories and contexts vary widely—from an émigré psychiatrist to Madonna to a Maya woman in exile to a Black social worker—and so they should vary, since one important function of the case study is to illuminate those characteristics that make a person distinctive. Across the differences in the cases, however, run some common threads: women negotiating identities; enduring, resisting, and overcoming social forces, societal standards, and personal misfortune; and finding resources for personal resilience.

The five cases in Part Two involved the kind of personal interaction that Belle described—an interaction between the psychologist and the person she studied that was influential in shaping the psychologist's thinking. Grossman and Moore elaborate a model of resiliency as they tell the story of a woman who survived childhood sexual and physical abuse. Their portrait is enriched by their account not only of their interactions with her but also of her reactions to their description of the interviewing experience. Ceballo describes the life of a social worker, now in her seventies, who confronted racism and sexism in many different forms in her struggle to develop professionally and psychologically. Ceballo also reflects on what this story can and does mean to another generation of young women of color pursuing professional careers.

The theme of struggle with social forces is powerfully present in Lykes's story of an exiled Maya woman's resilience and transformation in the face of ongoing violence and war, personal pain, and loss. The experience of a Japanese-American woman interned during World War II provides the focus for Nagata's sensitive examination of coping and racism in a very different context. Recounting Sachi Kaneshiro's experience, Nagata also articulates her own complex feelings as she aims to understand the experience of a previous generation of Japanese-Americans: curiosity, a longing to understand and connect, respect for privacy, and a desire not to bring new pain. Finally, Schulz describes a Navajo woman's struggle to develop and retain a connected but autonomous sense of self as she negotiates two sociocultural systems. Crises in Anne's relationships with her parents, her husband, and her son—as well as her larger community—are key events in Anne's own personality development. There is, too, in all of these chapters, a strong sense of relationship with the reader; in different ways, both the authors and the women written about in these five case studies see themselves as bearing witness to both the terrible things they have experienced and the possibility of surviving and overcoming these events.

In Part Three, the case study writer must operate "at a distance" from the woman being studied, since these four cases are based almost entirely on archival materials. Nevertheless, as both Stewart's discussion of Vera Brittain and Hornstein's of Frieda Fromm-Reichmann anticipated, aspects of the relationship between author and "case" are still present. For example, Layton deepens our understanding of women and identities in her analysis of the public and private personalities of Madonna, in part by conceding her own ambivalent fascination with Madonna.

In other studies, we are shown something important about a woman's personality through examination of her relationships with people in her life. McAdams highlights a novel approach to studying identities through his examination of Karen Horney's life narrative as one of struggles with conflicting themes of agency and communion. He concludes with an analysis of the way Horney's relationships with her daughters allowed her partially to express undeveloped and suppressed aspects of her own identity. The letters of Patricia Frazer Lamb provide Paul with an unusual opportunity to explore the transactional process of two interpersonal relationships. Paul shows how those relationships played an important role in Lamb's personality development in her early adult years. Espin also draws on a lengthy correspondence, in this case between a teacher and former student. She examines the development of a young Latin American woman (V.) through adolescence in the midst of political upheaval that resulted in separation from her parents and exile. Espin cites V.'s recognition of the importance of her relationship with her teacher: "I realize now that I started changing my ways of being with people the moment you started to be concerned about my things. I think that has been decisive in my life."

In the cases presented in the next two sections, each woman's individuality is explored in an explicitly comparative context. In each chapter in Part Four, one woman's life and experience is examined against the backdrop of a larger study of many women; the authors in Part Five each compare a few women directly.

Cartwright examines the personal and professional development of a distinguished and controversial woman physician in the context of a larger study of the lives of an unusual cohort of women doctors. In this case, as in several others in this volume, costs and benefits of maintaining nontraditional identities are examined. Franz describes a white 1960s activist's ongoing struggle for autonomy and connectedness and the role the social movements of the 1960s played in her struggle. She assesses the ways in which quantitative findings from the larger sample of young adults who came of age during that decade both illuminate and conceal important aspects of Lydia's experience. Tomlinson-Keasey traces the life of a woman who was studied from ages ten to eighty as part of Terman's Genetic Studies of Genius. She shows how a "clandestine intellectual" coped with a life full of external and internal obstacles, including the struggle to be appreciated for her intellect.

In each chapter in the next section, a few individual women are described in comparison with each other and against the backdrop of a larger study. Drawing from her study of three generations of lesbians, Stein compares the constructions of lesbian identity of three women who came to a lesbian consciousness during the early 1970s. She shows both some common features of identity construction among lesbians in this cohort and the unique structures created by each woman's life, experience, and personality. Gold-Steinberg compares two women's experiences with legal and illegal abortion, enriching our understanding of her broader based findings about women's experiences in coping with unanticipated and unwanted pregnancies in different legal contexts. Litzenberger explores themes of marginality, "coming out," personal vocation, spirituality, and struggle for survival in the lives of two lesbian priests. The theme of "being different" arises once again in the chapter by Ostrove and Stewart. In cases drawn from a study of Radcliffe graduates, Ostrove and Stewart explore how both a woman from a working-class background and one from an upper-class background experienced their social class as a "marginalizing" identity, whereas two middle-class women did not. Finally, Cole compares two African-American women's experiences of identity and community as political activists at the University of Michigan during two historical periods. She highlights the similar and different ways in which the two women constructed themselves and their activism in relation to their communities.

Ways to Read This Book

We hope different readers will approach this book in different ways. Some might simply read the narratives in the order we placed them and perform their own thematic analyses as they go along. Others, though—for their own purposes or for their students—may want to structure the chapters to explore a particular issue or topic. We have found that new aspects of a chapter emerge when we think about it in the context of particular other chapters. For example, we are drawn to methodological issues involved in analyzing archival materials if we read Paul's study of Lamb's correspondence along with Espin's study of V.'s correspondence with her teacher; reading those two chapters together also nicely highlights issues of identity in adolescence versus early adulthood. However, if we read Espin's chapter along with Lykes's account of a Maya woman in exile, themes of violent social change and exile are much more prominent. Similarly, if we read Paul's study alongside Layton's on Madonna, we notice how one focuses on identity formation as reflected in a close relationship, whereas the other explores Madonna's self-construction in public. We have found the process of reading the cases against one another enormously generative; for that reasons we encourage readers to do just that. We also here outline a few ways this book could be used to explore particular issues.

One group of chapters can be considered as taking a "life course" perspective, that is, they follow a life over a very long period of time and show something of its overall shape and structure. These include accounts of a Nisei internee (Nagata), an émigré psychiatrist (McAdams), two lesbian priests (Litzenberger), a Maya woman returned from exile in Mexico (Lykes), a physician (Cartwright), a Black social worker (Ceballo), a clandestine intellectual (Tomlinson-Keasey), a Navajo (Schulz), a 1960s activist (Franz), and a survivor of sexual abuse (Grossman and Moore). By reading some or all of these chapters together, certain interesting themes emerge: Although "gender" shaped all of these women's lives, the diversity of meanings of gender in the life course is striking. Similarly, all of these women faced serious difficulties in their life, but the kinds of difficulties and their timing varied greatly, as did the kinds of resources the women brought to them.

Another group of chapters explicitly explores cases drawing on existing psychological and feminist theories. These include most clearly Espin's use of Erikson's theory of adolescent development, Layton's use of both object relations and postmodernism, and McAdams's own integrative theory of the life story model of identity. Several others draw more loosely from theories; for example, Tomlinson-Keasey examines the utility of developmental models used in research on men (Vaillant, Levinson) and for women (Gilligan, Bateson).

Other groupings of chapters focus on a topic, a period, or an event. Readers with a special interest in *identity* in women would find much of value in most of the chapters. Taken together, the chapters by McAdams, Espin, Schulz, Paul, Litzenberger, Lykes, and Layton form a set that permits exploration of developmental, social contextual, and relational aspects of women's identities. Similarly, most chapters illustrate aspects of *resilience* at different points in the life course; however, creative transcendence of difficulties is especially central in the chapters by Belle, Cartwright, Ceballo, Espin, Franz, Gold-Steinberg, Grossman and Moore, Litzenberger, Lykes, Nagata, Schulz, and Tomlinson-Keasey. Women's *resistance* to the various forms of oppression and discrimination in their lives is also explored in many chapters; forms of oppression are varied, as are the strategies of resistance. Gold-Steinberg explores women's responses to the dangers of illegal abortions, and Grossman and Moore (and Layton, to a lesser degree) explore responses to sexual abuse. In addition, resistance to a variety of other social structures is evident in virtually every chapter. It is especially salient for social class in Belle, Ceballo, and Ostrove and Stewart; for race and ethnicity in Ceballo, Nagata, Schulz, Franz, and Lykes; and for sexuality in Litzenberger and Stein.

Several chapters address women's *political activity* (Cole, Ceballo, Franz, Lykes, Stewart), whereas others explore *meanings of religion* in women's lives (Espin, Litzenberger, Franz, Schulz). A number of chapters explore the centrality of *relationships* in women's lives and identities (especially Paul and Espin), and many of these also explore the meaning of *community* as well (Nagata, Cole, Litzenberger, Lykes, Ceballo, and Schulz). Some of the authors bring the *historical context* of the case to the foreground: Ceballo, Cole, Espin, Franz, Litzenberger, Lykes, Nagata, Schulz, Stein, and Tomlinson Keasey. In fact, a number of these chapters really focus on aspects of *the late 1960s and early 1970s*, in which the women's movement, civil rights, and the Vietnam War were all important contextualizing events (Cole, Franz, Gold-Steinberg, Ostrove and Stewart, Paul, and Stein). Finally, quite a few authors bring *methodological issues* into focus, including the author's place and voice in the creation of the life history (Belle, Grossman and Moore, Franz, Hornstein, Layton, Lykes, Nagata, Stewart).

However the accounts in this volume are read, we believe that together they show that the diversity, richness, and complexity of women's lives can be brought to the surface by looking at individual lives. In turn, that diversity, richness, and complexity opens new avenues for the development of theories of lives that reflect and incorporate women's experiences; these notions are explored in a concluding chapter by Franz, Cole, Crosby, and Stewart. In the pages ahead, we see women suffering in some of the ways familiar to us in psychology. We also see some much less familiar things—women inventing, bypassing, overcoming, creating, transcending, and challenging. The resilience and creativity of these women (along with their pain) reminds us that "a person serves to some extent as a transforming and redistributing center, responding selectively to create a new synthesis" (White, 1966, p. 365).

References

Bateson, C. (1989). *Composing a life.* New York: Plume.

Brodzki, B., & Schenck, C. (1988). *Life/lines: Theorizing women's autobiography.* Ithaca: Cornell University Press.

Carlson, R. (1985). Masculine/feminine: A personological perspective. *Journal of Personality, 53,* 296–311.

Gluck, S. B., & Patai, D. (1991). *Women's words: The feminist practice of oral history.* New York: Routledge.

Grossman, H., & Chester, N. L. (1990). *The experience and meaning of work in women's lives.* Hillsdale, NJ: Erlbaum.

Josselson, R. (1987). *Finding herself: Pathways to identity development in women.* San Francisco: Jossey-Bass.

———. (1992). *The space between us: Exploring the dimensions of human relationships.* San Francisco: Jossey-Bass.

Josselson, R., & Lieblich, A. (1993). *The narrative study of lives* (Vol. 1). Newbury Park, CA: Sage.

McAdams, D. P., & Ochberg, R. L. (Eds.). (1988). *Psychobiography and life narratives.* Durham, NC: Duke University Press.

Personal Narratives Group. (1989). *Interpreting women's lives: Feminist theory and personal narratives.* Bloomington: Indiana University Press.

Rosenwald, G. C., & Ochberg, R. L. (1992). *Storied lives.* New Haven: Yale University Press.

Runyan, W. M. (1982). *Life histories and psychobiography: Explorations in theory and method.* New York: Oxford University Press.

———. (1988). Progress in psychobiography. *Journal of Personality, 56,* 295–326.

White, R. W. (1966). *Lives in progress* (2d ed.). New York: Holt, Rinehart & Winston.

PART ONE

Psychologists (Re)Creating Women's Lives

(Photo by Sarah F. Colt.)

2

Toward a Feminist Strategy for Studying Women's Lives

ABIGAIL J. STEWART

SINCE THE BEGINNING of the second wave of feminism, or at least since 1970, feminist theorists have been exploring the ways in which social and "natural" scientists ground their research in a theory of knowledge and a method that is limited and inherently exclusionary (see, e.g., D. E. Smith, 1974b; Weisstein, 1971). In the past few years the critique has grown more profound and paralyzing to many feminist natural and social scientists (see Fine and Gordon, 1989; Harding, 1986; Harding and Hintikka, 1983; Hartsock, 1987). Some of the analyses by feminist critics begin with observations and arguments that have been made by other critics of positivism and the scientific method (Habermas, 1971; Lyotard, 1984; Rorty, 1979; Sampson, 1978): for example, the observation that scientific methods so narrow researchers' focus that critical facets of a problem may be out of the picture and the recognition that all scientific investigations proceed from a series of assumptions that define a "standpoint" or position and that in this sense no science can ever be—even in principle—completely "objective." Feminist theorists have brought, though, a specific perspective to these observations: a sensitivity to the ways in which gendered features of our world are taken for granted and therefore invisible and an awareness that this invisibility serves those with more power and resources and not those with less. Thus, feminist theorists have examined the specific ways in which traditional scientific methods permit or require the systematic exclusion of some knowledge, particularly knowledge about things important to women and knowledge of the ways in which taken-for-granted aspects of our world are in fact gendered.

My purpose is not to add to the many, convincing critiques of the scientific method; nor is it my purpose to present further evidence that the scientific method has been inadequate as a tool for generating knowledge about women and gender—though I believe it has been. Instead, my purpose is to try to derive from feminist theory a set of strategies that those of us who want to study women's lives can use to help us avoid the errors our sometimes innocent predecessors made. Some or all of the seven strategies discussed in this chapter have been used by individual students of lives with or without an explicitly feminist purpose. I do not claim that these strategies are *unique* to a feminist perspective, but each of them has arisen from feminist theory and is, I think, usefully considered within that context.

In deriving these strategies, I draw quite freely from arguments and analyses made from a variety of theoretical stances. It is important to emphasize, I think, that feminist theorists have mostly not seen it as their problem to figure out how "science" can be done better, and therefore feminist theorists themselves have only rarely tried to generate guidelines of the sort I have (see Cook and Fonow, 1990; Fine and Gordon, 1989, for exceptions). Moreover, many of the discussions of feminist methodology, as well as feminist critiques of science, have been quite abstract and difficult to translate into procedures in any discipline. It is the task of those who stubbornly hope to study things to take account of the criticisms of our methods and try to develop better ones.

Because I want to emphasize the *pragmatic* value of feminist theory for studying women's lives, I offer these recommendations and mention a few of their sources in feminist theory. These recommendations are offered both to those who are writing about women's lives and to those who read about them. In both writing and reading, the strategies may serve as a guide to what should be there, at least from several feminist theoretical perspectives. I present the strategies in roughly chronological order as they have emerged from feminist theorizing over the past twenty years. The strategies are: look for what's been left out, analyze your own role or position, identify agency in the context of social constraint, use the concept of gender as an analytic tool, treat gender as defining power relationships and being constructed by them, explore other aspects of social position (such as race, class, and sexuality), and avoid the search for a unified self. After describing each strategy, I try to illustrate its use by referring either to reasonably well known studies or to my own evolving study of Vera Brittain. To make those examples more intelligible, I begin by briefly describing Brittain herself and what I have done and am doing in my work.

Studying Vera Brittain's Life

Vera Brittain was an English feminist and pacifist activist and novelist born at the end of the nineteenth century. She is best known for writing the autobiographical account called *Testament of Youth* (1933/1970), which was serialized on public television as a Masterpiece Theater offering some years ago. That book, written when she was about forty, was her account of her adolescent experience of the period before, during, and after World War I and an extended argument against war. World War I shaped her pacifist ideology and became the central social and personal experience of her life. Efforts to prevent, and then to end, World War II dominated all of her activities from 1918 to 1945, even her novel writing.

Perhaps the second best known aspect of Vera Brittain is her close and moving friendship with the novelist Winifred Holtby, who died when only in her middle thirties, leaving Brittain quite bereft. Brittain composed a biography of Holtby, which includes a rich account of their relationship, in *Testament of Friendship* (1940/1981b), one of the first accounts of female friendship and still a powerful one.

My own work on Brittain has focused on the impact of her losses in the war on her identity formation and the connections between those adolescent identity-forming experiences and her midlife efforts to cope with the threat of World War II (Peterson and Stewart, 1990; Stewart, Franz, and Layton, 1988; Stewart and Healy, 1986). In discussing the strategies I've generated, though, I will be talking not so much of the work I've done, but of the ways in which these guidelines can influence the work I can do.

Feminist Strategies for
Studying Women's Lives

1. **Look for what's been left out.** Feminist theorists' earliest observation about the inadequacy of the traditional scientific method was that it permitted women and central features of women's lives and experience to be "left out" of both theory and research about "people." Naomi Weisstein (1971) pointed out in the early 1970s that until then psychology researchers completely overlooked women as subjects, and when they did "construct the female," they focused exclusively on "Kinder, Küche, Kirche" [children, kitchen, and church] as domains of female activity. In a parallel development in sociology, Marcia Millman and Rosabeth Kanter (1975) pointed out that "most of what we have formerly known as the study of society is only the male study of male society" (p. viii). They argued that not only had women been left out of sociology but in general the "unofficial, supportive, less dramatic, private and invisible spheres of social life and organization" (p. x) had been unconceptualized. Both fields, and the social sciences generally, have in the past twenty years made progress in defining women and women's lives as legitimate subjects of study and new topics (sexual harassment; gender dynamics in small groups; marital violence; intersections of gender, race, class, and sexuality; etc.) as important domains for analysis (see Lykes and Stewart, 1986, for a review in psychology). Feminist scholars have succeeded in moving the study of women's lives and identities, sex roles, domestic violence, abortion activism, comparable worth, and affirmative action from the margins closer to the center of social science disciplines.

For my purpose here, though, the importance of this argument within feminist theory is the strategy it offers: the strategy of resisting the "canon," or currently accepted definition of what are the necessary and sufficient subjects of inquiry (Lauter, 1985; Robinson, 1985). In the first instance, this means studying women:

choosing individual women—who were, by definition, always less "important" than male counterparts—as worthy of study. This is precisely what both Quinn (1987), in choosing to study the "minor psychoanalytic theorist" Karen Horney, and Scarborough and Furumoto (1987), in choosing to study the first generation of women academic psychologists, did.

More deeply, though, it means that in our studies of the women we define as "important" we look for what has been overlooked, unconceptualized, and not noticed, but may be very central to women's experience (see Fine and Gordon, 1989). This may mean, in the case of the nearly canonical Virginia Woolf, for example, considering the impact of childhood sexual abuse, as Louise DeSalvo (1989) did in contrast to most previous biographers and critics. In a different vein, it may mean stressing the psychological significance of world events to an individual woman, even an intensely private one like Virginia Woolf. Thus, Carolyn Heilbrun (1983) argued that Woolf's suicide may have been deeply stimulated by and connected with her feelings of helplessness and hopelessness about war. In the case of Vera Brittain, it has meant—both to Carolyn Heilbrun (in her Introduction in Brittain, 1940/1981b) and to Jean Kennard (1989)—focusing on the role of the long-term friendship with Winifred Holtby in Vera Brittain's life as a married woman with children.

There is much left to be done. For example, feminist theorists (such as Hartmann, 1981; Miller, 1986; Rich, 1976) have increased our understanding of the ways in which individual women struggle with their social devaluation and powerlessness within their families—both their families of origin and their adult families. Individual studies of lives have not yet fully reflected this political understanding of women's family lives, though some biographies have incorporated it to some degree (e.g., Glendinning, 1983, on Vita Sackville-West). In Vera Brittain, for example, we have an individual whose feminism was deeply and consciously derived from her experience of a patriarchal household structure. She bitterly resented her father's authority and her brother's advantages (see, e.g., Brittain, 1933/1970, p. 59) and explicitly based her feminist ideology on her analysis of the injustice she observed closely at home. In fact, she developed an explicit theory of egalitarian marriage and published a book on it during the early years of her own marriage (Brittain, 1929). She also published an autobiographical volume about her "honeymoon" and early years of marriage without children (1938) and wrote many articles about women's difficulties combining career and family (see Berry and Bishop, 1989). Nevertheless, we have so far seen little examination of her own marriage in studies of her life (see Paul, 1991, for an exception) for two reasons: She eventually seemed to emotionally disengage from it; and the conventional ways of thinking about marriage in women's lives do not readily apply. It was not, for example, a marriage in which the husband clearly had the upper hand in financial, educational, occupational, or status resources, nor was it a deeply satisfying, intimate companionship, at least during the best-documented years. It is, I think, important that we study the course of this relationship, then, not in the conventional terms given to us (courtship, honeymoon, intimacy, sexuality), but

Vera Brittain and her brother, Edward. *(From the Vera Brittain Papers, the William Ready Division of Archives and Research Collections, McMaster University Library, Hamilton, Canada.)*

Vera and her husband, George Catlin, 1928. *(From the Vera Brittain Papers, the William Ready Division of Archives and Research Collections, McMaster University Library, Hamilton, Canada.)*

Vera, Winifred Holtby, and Vera's son John. *(From the Vera Brittain Papers, the William Ready Division of Archives and Research Collections, McMaster University Library, Hamilton, Canada.)*

in the terms dictated by Vera Brittain herself and through the lens of feminist theory. As Brittain (1933/1970) put it, "Marriage, for any woman who considered all its implications ... could never mean 'living happily ever after'; on the contrary, it would involve another protracted struggle, a new fight" (p. 654).

In Brittain's case, her marriage involved the constant need to negotiate and renegotiate financial, residential, and domestic roles. During an early period, she understood her private marital contract to include a commitment to equally shared domestic responsibility, fidelity, and equal importance of both individual's careers (see, e.g., Brittain, 1957/1981a, pp. 17–41), and indeed that contract seemed to work for a while. Over time, each of these areas was renegotiated more than once, including a period during which the household included Winifred Holtby as a part-time member. Analysis of the ways in which both Brittain and her husband, separately and together, struggled with external expectations and demands based on a traditional conception of marriage, as well as their internal and relational expectations, demands, and history of conflict and disappointment, can and should inform our understanding of her life. It is more likely to if we think about what has been overlooked or unconceptualized.

Naturally it is always difficult to figure out what is missing when we look at a life or anything else; but generally feminist theory would lead us to expect that the things that will be missing will be things that those who are not women are not likely to be able to know and things that those who have a stake in the status quo are unlikely to want to know. In the end, then, this strategy begins with a recognition that the knower or researcher is *involved* in the process of knowing; that recognition has developed and deepened in more recent feminist theory, but it has always been at the center of feminist strategies for studying women's lives.

2. Analyze your own role or position as it affects your understanding and the research process. From an early point, feminist analyses of the biases in mainstream social science included a recognition that an important part of the problem was that traditional scientific methodology required belief in the irrelevance of the researcher's characteristics (Fee, 1983; Sherif, 1979). The hallmark of "good science" was thought to be replicability by *any other scientist:* thus, one's gender, race, or social class were or should be completely irrelevant to the conduct of one's research. Feminist critiques of traditional science, though, demonstrated the myriad ways in which the characteristics of scientists had nevertheless influenced the questions they asked, the methods they used to ask them, and their interpretations of what they found (Grady, 1981; Parlee, 1975; Stanley and Wise, 1983). This left feminist researchers in the position of suspecting that it would be impossible to leave their demographic or ideological characteristics outside of research (see, e.g., Eichler, 1980; Reinharz, 1979; Westkott, 1979). Many feminist social scientists have viewed this observation as exciting in that it makes it possible to envision a social science that can be "for women" (as Nancy Henley, 1974, and Mary Parlee, 1975, put it), not merely "about," and surely not "*against*" women (as much traditional social science has been). On the other hand, taken to an extreme this position suggests a complete relativism of knowledge and the impossibility of ever evaluating any interpretations as better than others; all interpretations could be viewed as equally valid, because equally dependent on the interpreter's position or standpoint. Clearly this radical relativism will not do if we are to think of ourselves as in any sense generating "knowledge," even of the most limited sort (for example, about a single case). A reasonable strategy, I think, is to consider consciously and systematically the ways in which one's demographic and ideological characteristics may influence one's work: to bring the researcher inside the investigation (D. E. Smith, 1974a,b; 1979). Self-reflection of this sort can provide new insight into aspects of the life being studied.

Erikson (1969) engaged in something like this sort of self-reflective activity when he examined his own motives for ignoring or minimizing Gandhi's abusive treatment of his wife and other women. Howard Feinstein (1991) did, too, when he observed that he had underestimated the role of Alice James in William James's life because of his own painful and troubled relationship with a sick sister. In a more explicitly feminist analysis, Ann Oakley (1981) discussed the ways in which she was viewed by the pregnant women she interviewed as a resource and support and not as a "neutral" data collector. Interestingly, Erikson and Feinstein were forced to analyze these issues without benefit of conversation with the person they were studying, and in fact both engaged in a sort of "dialogue" with the reader about their position with respect to the person. In contrast, Oakley was in a position to discuss her role and herself with the women she interviewed. Similarly, Lykes (1989) explored the complex negotiations about the meaning of "informed consent" with a Guatemalan Indian woman she interviewed (see also Anderson, Armitage, Jack, and Wittner, 1990). When dealing with historical figures it is different—though, I argue, not precisely "worse" or more problematic—because we may fail to comprehend crucial aspects of their situation and they cannot point out our failure. We must be careful when we interview living women to build in opportunities to tell them what we are thinking so they can tell us how they see us and where we have gone wrong. When we study the lives of women who are no longer living, we must make extra efforts to build our analyses on the basis of multiple sources of information—sources that can be used to raise questions about each other.

In my work with Vera Brittain, it has occurred to me often that it is probably no accident that during the thirteen-year period in the 1970s and 1980s in which my academic husband and I worked out a more or less tolerable commuting arrangement, I found the vicissitudes of Brittain's "semi-detached" commuting marriage to the academic George Catlin in the 1920s fascinating, if disturbing. It is a little embarrassing to realize how directly one's personal concerns are involved in one's work, but I think the important thing is that I could better *use* that awareness to understand the failure of the Brittain-Catlin experiment with commuting—across the Atlantic Ocean—than could someone without personal experience of a commuting marriage. In this case, early on I romanticized Brittain's struggle and failed to understand the deep conflicts emerging in her marriage because of my own hopes for success in the same enterprise. Only by a process of self-examination did I begin to see how much I longed for a model and feared her failure and what I therefore missed in her experience. My own needs did not merely blind me to some aspects of Brittain's experiment—they also made me attend closely to other aspects. Moreover, my own experience of the complex structures of resentment in a commuting marriage and the painful and ironic struggles over *both* too much autonomy when apart *and* too much closeness when together helped me sort out some of what was simply part of the situation in the Catlin-Brittain marriage and what was informative about the partners' private responses to it.

Other circumstances of Brittain's life echo circumstances of mine; in some of these, I think the similarities have made me a better listener. For example, she had a gifted, slightly younger brother with whom she shared real companionship, as I do; and she felt as an adolescent that her family was more invested in his success than in hers, as I did. There certainly were important differences in our experience, but this similarity sensitized me to the possible depth of meaning this relationship might have had for her, even though her brother died when they were both very young and mine did not.

Having the meaning of Brittain's relationship with her brother in mind helped me understand several incidents she described in her autobiography. At several points during the war, there were exchanges of letters among various family members about the need for Vera to go home to help the parents. In those exchanges it was clear that her brother Edward supported Vera's autonomy and attempted to fend off their parents' demands on her. In her earlier conflict with her parents over her education, she had also been grateful for his support for her aspirations and her rights. In both cases, then, it is clear that although the parents privileged Edward over her, he was uneasy with his privilege and willing to use it to benefit her. She wrote of this period in retrospect, "Only to Edward could I express the explosive misery caused by my dilemma, and he responded with his usual comprehending sympathy" (Brittain, 1933/1970, p. 424). Focusing on these incidents, in which Vera was supported by her brother in conflicts with their parents over their ambitions and independence, it becomes clearer how much she lost an ally and support in her quest for freedom from her confining family role when he died. Further, we can see that she had experienced, and lost, a deeply trustworthy male ally, one willing to "renounce his privilege" for her sake.

There are also other, much later signs that Brittain's relationship with her brother was deeply meaningful to her. She took great pleasure in imagining her son to be just like him, a replacement (see, e.g., 1933/1970, p. 495). And even in midlife she noted the anniversary of his death in her diary every year (for example, on June 15, in 1942, she wrote "Twenty-fourth anniversary of Edward's death on the Asiago Plateau"; Bishop and Bennett, 1989, p. 154). More indirectly, her model of marriage as a sympathetic companionship of equals may have been based on her relationship with Edward. The resonance of Brittain's experience in this relationship with my own may have helped me see its importance for her—

particularly in creating her expectation of sympathetic alliance from men—which could have been easy to miss.

3. Identify women's agency in the midst of social constraint. Although feminist theory has always aimed to identify the ways in which norms, roles, institutions, and internalized expectations limit and constrain women's behavior, at the same time it requires affirmation of women's personal efficacy or control—agency—within those constraints (see Delmar, 1986). Subordination and oppression always have consequences, but feminist theorists have demonstrated that those features of women's lives are not and could not be wholly definitional—one is never *only* oppressed (see, e.g., King, 1988). Moreover, within the context of relative powerlessness, women—like all people in a subordinate status—make choices and resist oppression (Fine, 1987; 1989). Recognizing agency is sometimes complicated and difficult, but assuming it is there can help. Thus, for example, Michelle Fine and Nancie Zane (1989) have shown that for poor young women, dropping out of high school is sometimes the only way to resist the silencing of their growing race, class, and gender consciousness. It is particularly difficult to recognize agency in women's lives when they don't perceive it themselves. As Fine (1989) argued,

> Persons of relatively low ascribed social power ... cannot control those forces which limit their opportunities ... [but] they do assert control in ways ignored by psychologists. For many, taking control involves ignoring advice to solve one's problems individually and recognizing instead the need for collective, structural change. Taking control may mean rejecting available social programs as inappropriate to one's needs, or recognizing that one's social supports are too vulnerable to be relied upon. (p. 187)

Some of the earliest feminist scholarship focused on demonstrating how women's psychological symptoms could be understood as efforts to resist sexist constraints and hence as reflections of their agency. Arguments like these have been used to illuminate the behavior of Dora so clearly misunderstood by Freud (see Bernheimer and Kahane, 1985). The feminist theorist Charlotte Perkins Gilman (1892/1973) vividly portrayed the resistance expressed in "madness" in her novel *The Yellow Wallpaper*. More recently, Susan Bordo (1989) argued that anorexia can be seen as a complex condition combining both submission and resistance to traditional sex role standards. When conditions are right, agency and resistance can be manifest in less self-destructive forms, but still ones that are hard to recognize.

Vera Brittain saw herself in most ways as an active agent. Those who have studied Brittain for various purposes have described her adolescent "personality as characterized by intelligence and analytic ability, drive and ambition, a quest for work, rebelliousness and independence, a 'difficult' interpersonal style, idealism, and a commitment to social issues" (Stewart et al., 1988, pp. 47–48). Given this overall picture, the rare instances of apparent passivity are all the more striking and puzzling; if we try to identify the ways in which Brittain may be exercising agency in them, they may be valuably illuminated.

In April 1918, Brittain was working as a nurse very close to the front in France. As she described it,

> For nearly a month the camp resembled a Gustave Doré illustration to Dante's *Inferno*. Sisters [meaning nurses] flying from the captured Casualty Clearing Stations crowding into our quarters; often completely without belongings they took possession of our rooms, our beds, and all our spare uniform. ... The wards were never tidied and the work was never finished; each convoy after staying its few hours was immediately replaced by another, and the business of dressing wounds began all over again. (1933/1970, p. 412)

In this situation she received a letter from her father saying that her mother had "crocked up" and had gone into a nursing home as the result of a "complete general breakdown." He concluded, "As your mother and I can no longer manage without you it is now your duty to leave France immediately and return to Kensington" (1933/1970, p. 421).

Brittain knew that it would not be so easy for her to leave her post. In fact she was not granted a formal leave, but was forced to resign, which would necessitate her signing up again and again working her way up the nursing hierarchy from the bottom. What is interesting to me is that she described her situation as one of complete helplessness to resist the demands of her family. However, there are signs in her account that some other factors may have been relevant.

After receiving her father's letter, Brittain kept hearing a recurring sentence in her mind—"The strain all along is very great"—but had difficulty locating the reference for the sentence. Who said it? What was it said of? She considered and rejected the possibility that it was herself:

> The enemy within shelling distance—refugee Sisters crowding in with nerves all awry—bright moonlight, and aeroplanes carrying machine guns—ambulance trains jolting noisily into the siding, all day, all night—gassed men on stretchers clawing the air—dying men, reeking with blood and foul green-stained bandages, shrieking and writhing in a grotesque travesty of manhood—dead men with fixed, empty eyes and shiny, yellow faces... Yes, perhaps the strain all along *had* been very great.
>
> Then I remembered; the phrase came out of my father's letter, and it described, not the offensive in France, but the troubles at home. (p. 423)

The next day Brittain did indeed break her contract and go home, believing she was simply yielding to her family's demands.

I wonder. Perhaps Brittain knew, as she both revealed and denied in the passage above, that for *her* "the strain all along [was] very great." Once she got home she experienced a profound depression. She said she "found it excruciating to maintain even an appearance of interest and sympathy" (p. 431), felt "marooned in a kind of death-in-life" (p. 430), and experienced "irritable impatience" and "moods of black depression" (p. 432). No doubt these symptoms were in part, as Brittain saw them, the result of her forced withdrawal from an arena of competence and importance to one she saw as trivial and in which she had no role she valued. But it seems to me, too, that when she received the letter from her father

Vera as war nurse (V.A.D.) with soldiers, in Malta, 1916. *(From the Vera Brittain Papers, the William Ready Division of Archives and Research Collections, McMaster University Library, Hamilton, Canada.)*

Brittain *was* aware of a psychological toll being taken by her wearing service at the front, and far from being passive, she may have internally embraced—however unconsciously and guiltily—an opportunity for a healing respite from the strain.

4. Use the concept of "gender" as an analytic tool. Feminist theorists in many disciplines have increasingly argued for the importance of understanding that gender is a *social* construct (Fine and Gordon, 1989; Keller, 1987; Scott, 1988b). These theorists suggest that biological sex, if it even can be defined in entirely physical terms, is in any case in no way coextensive with gender, or the social definition of what a woman—or a man—is. Moreover, these theorists argue that there is no universal social definition of gender. Theorists advocating this sort of analysis are not merely saying that sex role definitions vary, or that the implications of biological sex vary, or that the definition of the ideal woman varies, but that the very concept of what it is to be a woman (or man)—good or bad—varies. The importance of this concept in turn is that it shapes who we actually experience ourselves to be. Thus, if we do not understand a woman's underlying conception of gender, as well as the conceptions current in her social world, we cannot comprehend her.

If, for example, a woman believes that it is in the nature of women "in sorrow ... to bring forth children" (Genesis 3:16) that belief, in herself and those around her, will shape her experience of having babies. If, instead, she believes that "Labor ... can be a fulfilling experience—potentially one of the most fulfilling life has to offer" (Jones, 1987), that too will shape her experience. This is not to say that she cannot experience birth in ways running counter to those beliefs; these beliefs do not completely control her, but they do define the framework within which she responds. If she expects birth to be a catastrophic, painful, and humiliating experience and it is not, then she may feel herself to be particularly blessed and fortunate. If she expects it to be the most beautiful moment in her life and she finds it painful, frightening, or exhausting, she may feel inadequate or deficient. The point is not that the beliefs, and the language we use to describe our experience, wholly create our experience, but they do define the terms of it and give it its form.

This means, then, that in studying a woman's life we must always inquire into her understanding of gender, as well as the consistencies and inconsistencies between her understandings and those of the people closest to her and in the wider culture affecting her at the time. If we use this strategy to study Vera Brittain we can illuminate some tensions and paradoxes in her feminist ideology and her life choices. First, it is clear that Brittain's conception of "womanhood" was at odds with many aspects of broader cultural conceptions: At most times in her life, she believed that women's competence and intelligence were the equivalent of men's; that women could perform at the same level as men in occupations as well as government; that women had a human right to economic independence (see Brittain, 1953; Stewart and Healy, 1986). As she put it in 1927, "Woman herself, long conscious of complete humanity, today desires only that others shall recognize it and honestly accept the implications of such recognition" (Berry and Bishop, 1989, p. 99). It was her view, then, that the definition of a woman was most centrally the definition of a "human." In this sense, she denied that people's abilities and public roles are inherently gendered. She also believed, more in tune with general beliefs at the time, that sexuality was a biological need demanding expression in both men and women (see, e.g., Brittain, 1933/1970, pp. 578ff) and that motherhood was a necessary component of fulfillment as a woman (Brittain, 1933/1970, p. 580).

These beliefs combined to sharpen her dilemma when, after the death of so many men of her generation in World War I, she joined the ranks of those officially known in England as "surplus women." Despite her feminist ideology, and the fact that she had established a deeply satisfying friendship and household with Winifred Holtby, Brittain was profoundly concerned about finding a husband and having a family. She sometimes denounced this preoccupation in principle, expressing the strong view that women's value did not depend on their attachment to a man by marriage. In 1921 she wrote to Holtby that "personally I haven't the least objection to being superfluous as long as I am allowed to be useful" (1933/1970, p. 578). Nevertheless, she engaged in a vigorous search for an acceptable male life partner, even agreeing to meet a "fan" of her first novel, who eventually became her husband (1933/1970, pp. 606–610). She struggled with her initial dislike of this man as well as with her awareness that marriage would probably compromise and would certainly complicate the work life so fully supported by her arrangement with Holtby. No doubt there were many factors contributing to Brittain's search for a marriage partner, but one of them was her beliefs about the "nature" of women's needs for sexual expression and motherhood. Only by exploring in detail Brittain's conception of gender can we use an understanding of the tension between it and the wider culture's conception to illuminate her personal choices and her work.

5. Explore the precise ways in which gender defines power relationships and in which power relationships are gendered. Recent feminist theorists (see, e.g., Fine and Gordon, 1989; Keller, 1987; Scott, 1988b) have stressed the way in which gender appears to be a construct "located" in the body and thereby most closely associated with sexuality and reproduction, but is actually located in power relationships, which in turn define sexuality and reproduction. As Catharine MacKinnon put it,

> on the first day that matters, dominance was achieved, probably by force. By the second day, division along the same lines had to be relatively firmly in place. On the third day, differences were demarcated, together with social systems to exaggerate them in perception and in fact, *because* the systematically differential delivery of benefits and deprivations required making no mistake about who was who. Comparatively speaking, man has been resting ever since. *Gender might not even code as difference, might not even mean distinction epistemologically, were it not for its consequences for social power* [emphasis mine]. (MacKinnon, 1987, p. 40)

Although not all feminist theorists agree that dominance is primary, that is, precedes "difference," there is consensus that a critical aspect of gender requiring analysis is power. In studying women's lives, then, we must understand the ways in which particular power relationships women experience are gendered, as well as the ways in which the relationships in which gender may seem primary are also complex power struggles.

I have already pointed to the power struggles in Brittain's marital relationship and the way in which they were gendered. Throughout the years of most active engagement in the marriage, negotiating their individual responsibilities as parents was one focus of those struggles. In the early years, Brittain and Catlin's conflicts mirrored those of contemporary couples who find their previously egalitarian and companionate marriage suddenly sex differentiated when children arrive. In fact, in her book on marriage, Brittain (1929) asserted that "parenthood in the twentieth century appears to have been one of the chief sources of marital misery and disruption" (p. 49). The desire to recapture shared and identical roles gradually yielded to a desire to find some fair and practical modus vivendi. It is clear that Brittain held on to the hope of reinstating shared and identical roles far longer than Catlin did and that she saw herself as victimized by his abandonment of their shared vision and marital contract. On April 4, 1931, she wrote to him,

> Why must I always be considering *your* career when as it is I get at most two hours a day in which to further my own? Most people, I think, would say that considering I free you completely from all responsibility for the children, including financial responsibility, this is a very major contribution to your career and about as much as I

could be expected to make. The majority of men are continually hampered in their ambitions by having to provide for their families and put aside for their education; all this you are spared. I think you often forget it. (unpublished letter)

Over time, the effort to identify an equitable, equal arrangement gradually resulted in a transformed discourse: Instead of talking about relationships and tasks, they talked about money, in part because it was money that purchased services that produced some sense of equity. It is quite clear that at certain points in their marriage, Brittain used her greater financial resources as a weapon in her struggle with Catlin. Precisely what they were fighting about and what money signified in that fight can only be understood if we explore how each of them understood the connections among money, power, and gender. For Brittain financial independence was a defining feature of full humanity. She wrote, for example, that young women after the war accepted "the idea of self-support as a moral principle, a duty as obvious as it has hitherto been for men. ... To live on money entirely supplied by someone else is ignoble and humiliating, however socially useful one's activities may be" (Berry and Bishop, 1989, p. 106). This view must be considered when we review her correspondence with Catlin during the years when it became clear that Catlin could not secure an academic post in England and that to leave his position in the United States at Cornell University would leave him financially and professionally insecure. Eventually Brittain argued that Catlin's obligation to co-parent with her must be primary. But we can see the cost—to her respect and commitment to him when *from her point of view,* first he deserted their ideal vision of perfect companionship (by remaining in the United States when their child was born), and then he became a financial burden (when he eventually gave up his position at Cornell and moved to England). It is equally clear that to fully understand this whole process, we must take account as well of Catlin's understandings of money, power, and gender.

There are many less intimate features of a woman's life that can also be illuminated by an understanding of gender as dominance or power. *Many* aspects of women's experience that are "gendered"—that is, associated with maleness or femaleness—are also experiences of subordination and can be understood better in those terms. A consciousness of marginality is a central aspect of many features of women's experience of subordination. It is captured in the title Brittain proposed for her book about her early years of marriage in the United States, "Thrice a Stranger," as well as in her account of participating in organizations with both male and female members. She argued that quite often these groups

are conducted on the assumption that the women members will not be worth hearing, and are to be tolerated, should they venture to express themselves, only out of politeness. [One such group] specialized in after-dinner speeches followed by debates. Never, throughout the period of my membership, was the set speaker a woman, and during the debate, according to conventional procedure, the women present remained silent until, late in the evening, the chairman remarked with a bland smile, "Perhaps one or two of the ladies would like to contribute to the discussion."

Once, with a tremendous exercise of courage, I forestalled this weighty permission in order to correct the misstatements of a speaker ... [who heard me out with] affronted courtesy. (Berry and Bishop, 1989, pp. 115–116)

By focusing on the gendered power relationships Brittain observed and experienced, we can achieve an understanding of the ways in which she experienced herself as marginal and powerless, even as we also see her as a vigorously successful, effective activist.

6. Identify other significant aspects of an individual's social position and explore the implications of that position. The critique of early second-wave feminist theory by feminist women of color such as Bonnie Thornton Dill (1983), Patricia Hill Collins (1989), and Maxine Baca Zinn (Zinn, Cannon, Higginbotham, and Dill, 1986) raised many white feminists' consciousness of the many other dimensions of social position that must be examined in addition to gender (see also A. Smith and Stewart, 1983; Spelman, 1988). Race, social class, and sexual orientation are the features of individuals so far best understood as filled with consequences, including consequences for the experience of gender. In the case of Brittain, her middle-class privilege and elitism have been recognized by a number of writers, though they have been identified more as embarrassments or "problems" than explored for their implications. For example, Brittain's preoccupation with the difficulties of combining career and marriage clearly provided a rather limited focus for her feminist activism in a society in which very few women had the education or advantages to pursue a career. It is important to identify her "blind spots" and the failures in her understanding, but it is most illuminating to do so by examining the sources of those failures, rather than merely naming them.

In the prosperous, middle-class world Brittain inhabited, servants occupied a very specific role and provided her only direct knowledge of the lives of people of a different class. Throughout her life she depended on servants, particularly poignantly and openly during World War II when she and they shared the terrors of the Blitz. During that war, during the period when she and Winifred first began to live in London on their own, and during her earliest years of motherhood, Brittain often expressed her sense of inadequacy in the face of domestic chores, as well as her feeling of dependency on servants (see, e.g., Brittain, 1933/1970). In a very real sense, though, Brittain did not recognize at all that she was in a powerful position in relationships with her servants. Yet she understood very well that the servant's relationship was in principle a powerless one. She wrote, for example, "We are living still under the shadow of an age which made a woman the first servant of her parents, with the usual alternative of standing in the same relations to her husband, and later to her children" (Berry and Bishop, 1989, p. 121). Her desire to free "women" (meaning middle-class women) from the tyranny of the household led her to argue for the development of professionalized domestic and child care services (see, e.g., "I denounce domesticity!" [Berry and Bishop, 1989, pp. 139–144]), and at least in some places she saw this professionalization as increasing paid employment opportunities for women (Berry and Bishop, 1989, pp. 137–138). Much of the time, though, her perspective was narrowly focused on the middle-class professional woman's obstacles, and the difficulties of poor and working-class women were not discussed. Partly because servants "inhabited" her world in some limited sense—she certainly did not inhabit theirs—and partly because of a studied, class-based obliviousness to servants, she was free to assume a greater similarity between their experience and hers than would have survived any closer effort at connection.

However, in the service of a richer understanding of her own class and gender consciousness, I think it would be valuable to examine much more closely the fleeting references to servants in her diaries and letters. For example, she wrote two accounts of hearing the announcement of England's entry into World War II—one in her diary, which she eventually published (see Brittain, 1941); one in a letter to her husband. There is only one small, but possibly telling, difference in the accounts. In both she described herself as sitting between her two children, listening to the announcement on the radio with tears streaming down her face. To her husband she added, "Burnett [the chauffeur] slipped out discreetly to fetch me a handkerchief" (unpublished letter, September 3, 1939). Why did she leave that out of the published account of that moment? Why did she include it in her account to Catlin? I hesitate to interpret its meaning, but perhaps further comparisons of accounts in which the roles and activities of servants are included and excluded would help clarify the meaning to her both of servants and of her social class position.

In addition to the need for exploration of the meanings of social class in Brittain's life, both Brittain and Holtby deserve study in terms of their global consciousness and their commitment to what Brittain called the "liberation of subject races" (quoted in Berry and Bishop, 1989, p. 14). In the last years of her life, Holtby involved herself deeply in the struggle for a political voice for Blacks in South Africa. In 1930 she wrote in this context, "It seems as though no privileged minority can be trusted to treat with decency a subject class, sex or race" (Berry and Bishop, 1989, p. 188). A decade later Brittain both worked on behalf of the Indian independence movement and made efforts to build ties between the women's movement in India and in England. It is not clear how and why these two white, middle-class Englishwomen developed these commitments, but we cannot hope to truly understand their lives if we don't explore their race and class consciousness, as well as the implications of their race and class positions. There are, I should note, other important social status positions worthy of consideration; in the case of Brittain and Holtby, assumptions that they might be lesbians and regional identifications within England were sometimes quite significant in their own thinking and others' reactions to them. In the case of Karen Horney, Quinn (1987) made a convincing case for the relevance and importance of an "immigrant" status. The critical element of this strategy is exploration of the ways in which social structural characteristics shape a person's opportunities, relationships, activities, and ideology. In these explorations, as in using gender as an analytic tool, it is crucially important to examine those characteristics within an explicit historical framework. Further, the need for an explicit historical context applies not only to the person being studied, but to the scholar as well. It is important for me to reflect directly on the ways in which my own life has been shaped by the very different class, race and ethnic, and sexual consciousnesses of my time and place and to consider what those features make me likely to miss— or misinterpret—as I try to understand a very different woman's characteristics in a very different time and place.

On the other hand, I can use my experience as an educated, middle-class person who has often felt helpless in the face of mechanical failures to help me imagine the sort of anxious and resentful dependency Brittain may have felt in relationships with servants. It may be that that relationship and those feelings powerfully reevoked for her the frustration and sense of suffocation she experienced growing up in a restricted, provincial household. If so, her adult failure to recognize the oppression of those closest to her in her own household may be understood in part as the result of her own incomplete freedom from her earlier experiences of oppression. I cannot use my experience as a direct guide to hers, but in an area like this in which she had a mostly undeveloped consciousness, I can use it as a source of questions and I can look for answers to those questions in Brittain's diaries, and letters, and novels.

7. Avoid the search for a unified or coherent self or voice. Recently, feminist theorists have increasingly argued for the inadequacy of a conception of the person, or the self, as singular or stable (see Haraway, 1989; Nicholson, 1990). Some (Scott, 1988a) have based this argument on an extrapolation from the recognition of the instability of "texts," and the recognition that texts have multiple meanings that cannot be somehow "evaluated" and reduced to a "correct" meaning. Others (King, 1988; Spelman, 1988) have worked from an analysis of the social bases of identity and a recognition that we are differentially conscious of those social bases in different situations. This observation has been made most often about race, class, and gender; it is equally true, though, of many other socially defined aspects of identity. For example, my sense of myself as a psychologist is most salient when I am talking with my colleagues in women's studies from the humanities; but it is mostly taken for granted and out of awareness when I am with my colleagues in psychology. The fact that I am a feminist psychologist is similarly taken for granted in the Women's Studies Program, but not in the Psychology Department. Within psychology, there has also been increasing scholarship focusing on the diverse and multiple selves and identities included within a single person (see, e.g., Markus and Nurius, 1986; Higgins, Klein, and Strauman, 1985).

The women whose lives we study are unlikely to have more stable or monolithic identities than we do, but the effort to "tell a good story" and to summarize and define a person pushes us to represent them as unified persons and personalities. This effort to organize and structure the different voices and selves must be understood as an effort to control—literally to impose an order or unity on what is in fact multiple and even disorderly. (Moreover, the women themselves are no doubt moved, as we all are, by efforts to feel and appear coherent and consistent; see, e.g., Gergen, 1968; Greenwald, 1980.)

It is likely to be illuminating if we are able not only to notice inconsistencies but also to specify the times and places that particular identities are evoked. For example, Brittain *was* very self-conscious about benefiting from her middle-class privilege to send her children to safety in the United States during World War II (letter to Ruth Colby, June 3, 1940, quoted in Stewart and Healy, 1986, p. 25). She worried about balancing her personal obligation—and wish—to protect her own children with the moral bankruptcy of schemes that protected only the children of the rich. Why was her own class privilege so evident to her in this area and so invisible to her in so many others? I would speculate that because, as I argued earlier, motherhood was a critically defining activity for "womanhood" in Brittain's view, it was motherhood that Brittain felt she shared most with women of other classes. As a result, even though she had little empathy for the servants who shared her household, she could imagine the frustrated rage of an unknown poor woman who was unable to protect her own children watching the rich protect theirs.

There are many other inconsistencies in Brittain's personality that remain to be understood. She was capable of unusual intimacy and devotion in friendships with women, but there were also some bitter rifts. She was intense in her personal ambition, earnest and passionate about peace and social justice, yet often in the midst of world crises indulged her pleasure in buying lovely clothes and having her hair "done." She was preoccupied with large issues of women's status, of national and international policy; still, even when her finances were quite secure, her diaries and correspondence were filled with nearly endless discussions and complaints about household expenses and arrangements. These inconsistencies and complexities are all part of the woman who fascinated, irritated, and impressed her intimates—and me. It is important to notice the many different voices of the women we study for the same reason it was important to notice that women had something to say at all: Silencing voices always leaves us without knowledge. Listening will leave us with more.

Conclusion

There are few guidelines for studying lives in psychology (see Allport, 1942; Erikson, 1975; Runyan, 1982; White, 1975, 1981, for exceptions) and they offer no special help in thinking about women. The suggestions outlined here are derived not from psychology, but from twenty years of feminist theoretical critique of science. Serious consideration of the issues raised by feminist theorists, when translated into specific practices or methods, should enable us to study women's lives "better"—that is, in a way more likely to generate knowledge about women and gender. This will be true, I think, whether scholars adopt qualitative or quantitative methods. (There is increasing consensus among feminist critics that the presence or absence of numbers in our work is a poor guide to its epistemological and political stance; see Jayaratne and Stewart, 1991; Peplau and Conrad, 1989; Yllo, 1988.) In short, a frankly feminist strategy would help scholars render women's lives with respect for their agency, their complexity, and the constraints under which they operated. The seven guidelines offered here are a beginning.

Acknowledgments

A version of this paper was presented at a conference sponsored by the Henry A. Murray Research Center, "The Study of Individual Lives," at Radcliffe College, May 11, 1990. I am grateful to the staff at the Murray Center for this opportunity to develop these ideas in that context. I am grateful to Faye Crosby, Carol Franz, Ravenna Helson, Gail Hornstein, Joan Ostrove, George Rosenwald, and David Winter for many helpful and encouraging comments on various drafts of the manuscript.

I am also grateful to the staff of the William Ready Division of Archives and Research Collections, Mills Memorial Library, McMaster University, which houses the Vera Brittain Archive. Unpublished letters, diaries, and pamphlets and newspaper and magazine articles available there have been invaluable sources in studying Brittain's life. Quotations from unpublished letters are printed with the permission of the William Ready Division of Archives and Research Collections, McMaster University Library, Hamilton, Canada.

References

Allport, G. W. (1942). *The use of personal documents in psychological science.* New York: Social Science Research Council.

Anderson, K., Armitage, S., Jack, D., & Wittner, J. (1990). Beginning where we are: Feminist methodology in oral history. In J. M. Nielsen (Ed.), *Feminist research methods* (pp. 94–112). Boulder: Westview.

Bernheimer, C., & Kahane, C. (Eds.). (1985). *In Dora's case.* New York: Columbia University Press.

Berry, P., & Bishop, A. (1989). *Testament of a generation: The journalism of Vera Brittain and Winifred Holtby.* London: Virago, 1985.

Bishop, A., & Bennett, Y. A. (Eds.). (1989). *Wartime chronicle: Vera Brittain's diary 1939–1945.* London: Victor Gollancz.

Bordo, S. R. (1989). The body and the reproduction of femininity: A feminist appropriation of Foucault. In A. M. Jaggar & S. R. Bordo (Eds.), *Gender/body/knowledge* (pp. 13–33). New Brunswick, NJ: Rutgers.

Brittain, V. (1929). *Halcyon, or The future of monogamy.*

———. (1938). *Thrice a stranger.* London: Gollancz.

———. (1941). *England's hour.* London: Macmillan.

_____. (1953). *Lady into woman.* London: Andrew Dakers.

_____. (1970). *Testament of youth.* New York: Wideview. (Original work published 1933)

_____. (1981a). *Testament of experience.* New York: Seaview. (Original work published 1957)

_____. (1981b). *Testament of friendship: The story of Winifred Holtby.* New York: Wideview. (Original work published 1940)

Collins, P.H. (1989). The social construction of Black feminist thought. *Signs, 14,* 745–773. London: Kegan Paul.

Cook, J. A., & Fonow, M. M. (1990). Knowledge and women's interests: Issues of epistemology and methodology in feminist sociological research. In J. M. Nielsen (Ed.), *Feminist research methods* (pp. 69–93). Boulder: Westview.

Delmar, R. (1986). What is feminism? In J. Mitchell & A. Oakley (Eds.), *What is feminism?* (pp. 8–33). New York: Pantheon.

DeSalvo, L. (1989). *Virginia Woolf: The impact of childhood sexual abuse on her life and work.* Boston: Beacon.

Dill, B. T. (1983). Race, class and gender: Prospects for an all-inclusive sisterhood. *Feminist Studies, 9,* 131–150.

Eichler, M. (1980). *The double standard: A feminist critique of feminist social science.* New York: St. Martin's.

Erikson, E. H. (1969). *Gandhi's truth.* New York: Norton.

_____. (1975). *Life history and the historical moment.* New York: Norton.

Fee, E. (1983). Women's nature and scientific objectivity. In M. Lowe & R. Hubbard (Eds.), *Women's nature and scientific objectivity* (pp. 9–28). New York: Pergamon.

Feinstein, H. (1991). The meaning of truth in *Becoming William James.* In A. J. Stewart, J. M. Healy, Jr., & D. Ozer (Eds.), *Perspectives in personality* (Vol. 3B, pp. 183–195). London: Jessica Kingsley.

Fine, M. (1987). Silencing and nurturing voice in an improbable context: Urban adolescents in public school. In H. Giroux & P. McLaren (Eds.), *Schooling and the politics of culture.* Albany: SUNY Press.

_____. (1989). Coping with rape: Critical perspectives on consciousness. In R. K. Unger (Ed.), *Representations: Social constructions of gender* (pp. 186–200). Amityville, NY: Baywood.

Fine, M., & Gordon, S. M. (1989). Feminist transformations of/despite psychology. In M. Crawford & M. Gentry (Eds.), *Gender and thought* (pp. 146–174). New York: Springer-Verlag.

Fine, M., & Zane, N. (1989). Bein' wrapped too tight: When low-income women drop out of high school. In L. Weis, E. Farra, & H. G. Petri (Eds.), *Dropouts from school* (pp. 23–53). Albany, NY: SUNY Press.

Gergen, K. J. (1968). Personal consistency and the presentation of self. In C. Gordon & K. J. Gergen (Eds.), *The self in social interaction* (Vol. 1, pp. 299–308). New York: Wiley.

Gilman, C. P. (1973). *The yellow wallpaper.* New York: Feminist Press. (Original work published in 1892)

Glendinning, V. (1983). *Vita.* New York: Knopf.

Grady, K. E. (1981). Sex bias in research design. *Psychology of Women Quarterly, 5,* 628–636.

Greenwald, A. G. (1980). The totalitarian ego: Fabrication and revision of personal history. *American Psychologist, 35,* 603–618.

Habermas, J. (1971). *Knowledge and human interest.* Boston: Beacon.

Haraway, D. (1989). A manifesto for cyborgs: Science, technology, and socialist feminism in the 1980s. In L. J. Nicholson (Ed.), *Feminism/postmodernism* (pp. 190–233). New York: Routledge.

Harding, S. (1986). *The science question in feminism.* Ithaca: Cornell University Press.

Harding, S., & Hintikka, M. B. (Eds.). (1983). *Discovering reality: Feminist perspectives on epistemology, metaphysics, methodology and philosophy of science.* Dordrecht, Holland: D. Reidel.

Hartmann, H. (1981). The family as the locus of gender, class, and political struggle: The example of housework. *Signs, 6* (31), 366–394.

Hartsock, N.C.M. (1987). The feminist standpoint: Developing the ground for a specifically feminist historical materialism. In S. Harding (Ed.), *Feminism and methodology* (pp. 151–180). Bloomington: Indiana University Press.

Heilbrun, C. (1983). Woolf in her fifties. In J. Marcus (Ed.), *Virginia Woolf: A feminist slant* (pp. 236–253). Lincoln: University of Nebraska Press.

Henley, N. (1974). Resources for the study of psychology and women. *RT: Journal of Radical Therapy, 4,* 20–21.

Higgins, E. T., Klein, R., & Strauman, T. (1985). Self-concept discrepancy theory: A psychological model for distinguishing among different aspects of depression and anxiety. *Social Cognition, 3,* 51–76.

Jayaratne, T., & Stewart, A. J. (1991). Quantitative and qualitative methods in the social sciences: Current feminist issues and practical strategies. In M. M. Fonow & J. A. Cook (Eds.), *Beyond methodology* (pp. 85–196). Bloomington: Indiana University Press.

Jones, C. (1987). *Mind over labor.* New York: Pergamon.

Keller, E. F. (1987). The gender/science system: or, Is sex to gender as nature is to science? *Hypatia, 2* (3), 33–44.

Kennard, J. E. (1989). *Vera Brittain & Winifred Holtby: A working partnership.* Hanover: University of New Hampshire Press.

King, D. (1988). Multiple jeopardy, multiple consciousness: The context of a Black feminist ideology. *Signs, 14* (1), 42–72.

Lauter, P. (1985). Race and gender in the shaping of the American literary canon: A case study from the twenties. In J. Newton & D. Rosenfelt (Eds.), *Feminist criticism and social change* (pp. 19–44). New York: Methuen.

Lykes, M. B. (1989). Dialogue with Guatemalan Indian women: Critical perspectives on constructing collaborative research. In R. K. Unger (Ed.), *Representations: Social constructions of gender* (pp. 167–185). Amityville, NY: Baywood.

Lykes, M. B., & Stewart, A. J. (1986). Evaluating the feminist challenge to research in personality and social psychology: 1963–1983. *Psychology of Women Quarterly, 10,* 393–412.

Lyotard, J. F. (1984). *The post-modern condition: A report on knowledge.* Minneapolis: University of Minnesota Press.

MacKinnon, C. A. (1987). *Feminism unmodified: Discourses on life and law.* Cambridge, MA: Harvard University Press.

Markus, H., & Nurius, P. (1986). Possible selves. *American Psychologist, 41,* 954–969.

Miller, J. B. (1986). *Toward a new psychology of women* (2d ed.). Boston: Beacon.

Millman, M., & Kanter, R. M. (1975). Introduction to *Another voice: Feminist perspectives on social life and social science.* In S. Harding (Ed.), *Feminism and methodology* (pp. 29–36). Bloomington: Indiana University Press.

Nicholson, L. J. (Ed.). (1990). *Feminism/Postmodernism.* New York: Routledge.

Oakley, A. (1981). Interviewing women: A contradiction in terms. In H. Roberts (Ed.), *Doing feminist research* (pp. 30–61). Boston: Routledge Kegan Paul.

Parlee, M. B. (1975). Psychology. *Signs, 1* (1), 119–138.

Paul, E. L. (1991). Women's psychosocial development: The role of marriage and friendship in two lives. In A. J. Stewart, J. M. Healy, Jr., & D. Ozer (Eds.), *Perspectives in personality: Approaches to understanding lives* (pp. 197–232). London: Jessica Kingsley.

Peplau, L. A., & Conrad, E. (1989). Beyond nonsexist research: The perils of feminist methods in psychology. *Psychology of Women Quarterly, 13,* 379–400.

Peterson, B. E., & Stewart, A. J. (1990). Using personal and fictional documents to assess psychosocial development: A case study of Vera Brittain's generativity. *Psychology and Aging, 5,* 400–411.

Quinn, S. (1987). *A mind of her own.* New York: Summit.

Reinharz, S. (1979). *On becoming a social scientist.* San Francisco: Jossey-Bass.

Rich, A. (1976). *Of woman born.* New York: Norton.

Robinson, L. (1985). Treason our text: Feminist challenges to the literary canon. In E. Showalter (Ed.), *The new feminist critics.* New York: Pantheon.

Rorty, R. (1979). *Philosophy and the mirror of nature.* Princeton: Princeton University Press.

Runyan, W. M. (1982). *Life histories and psychobiography: Explorations in theory and method.* New York: Oxford University Press.

Sampson, E. E. (1978). Scientific paradigms and social values: Wanted—a scientific revolution. *Journal of Personality and Social Psychology, 36* (11), 1332–1343.

Scarborough, E., & Furumoto, L. (1987). *Untold lives: The first generation of American women psychologists.* New York: Columbia.

Scott, J. (1988a). Deconstructing equality-versus-difference: Or, the uses of poststructuralist theory for feminism. *Feminist Studies, 14* (1), 33–50.

———. (1988b). Gender: A useful category of historical anaysis. In *Gender and the politics of history* (pp. 28–50). New York: Columbia University Press.

Sherif, C. W. (1979). Bias in psychology. In S. Harding (Ed.), *Feminism and methodology* (pp. 37–56). Bloomington: Indiana University Press.

Smith, A., & Stewart, A. J. (1983). Approaches to studying racism and sexism in black women's lives. *Journal of Social Issues, 39* (3), 1–15.

Smith, D. E. (1974a). The social construction of documentary reality. *Sociological Inquiry, 44,* 257–268.

———. (1974b). Women's perspective as a radical critique of sociology. *Sociological Inquiry, 44,* 7–13.

———. (1979). A sociology for women. In J. A. Sherman & E. T. Beck (Eds.), *Prism of sex: Essays on the sociology of knowledge* (pp. 135–187). Madison: University of Wisconsin Press.

Spelman, E. V. (1988). *Inessential woman: Problems of exclusion in feminist thought.* Boston: Beacon.

Stanley, L., & Wise, S. (1983). *Breaking out: Feminist consciousness and feminist research.* London: Routledge & Kegan Paul.

Stewart, A. J., Franz, C., & Layton, L. (1988). The changing self: Using personal documents to study lives. *Journal of Personality, 56* (1), 41–74.

Stewart, A. J., & Healy, J. M., Jr. (1986). The role of personality development and experience in shaping political commitment: An illustrative case. *Journal of Social Issues, 42* (2), 11–32.

Weisstein, N. (1971). Psychology constructs the female. In V. Gornick & B. K. Moran (Eds.), *Women in sexist society* (pp. 207–224). New York: New American Library.

Westkott, M. (1979). Feminist criticism of the social sciences. *Harvard Educational Review, 49*, 422–430.

White, R. W. (1975). *Lives in progress.* New York: Holt, Rinehart & Winston.

———. (1981). Exploring personality the long way: The study of lives. In A. I. Rabin, J. Aronoff, A. M. Barclay, & R. A. Zucker (Eds.), *Further explorations in personality.* New York: Wiley.

Ÿllo, K. (1988). Political and methodological debates in wife abuse research. In K. Ÿllo & M. Bograd (Eds.), *Feminist perspectives on wife abuse* (pp. 28–50). Newbury Park, CA: Sage.

Zinn, M. B., Cannon, L. W., Higginbotham, E., & Dill, B. T. (1986). The cost of exclusionary practices in women's studies. *Signs, 11* (2), 290–303.

3

Attempting to Comprehend
the Lives of Low-Income Women

DEBORAH BELLE

WITHOUT PERSONALLY experiencing poverty it is difficult to comprehend the lives of poor women or view the world through their eyes. If we are economically secure ourselves, poor women often figure as problems of one sort or another. We contemplate the welfare problem or the teenage pregnancy problem or the alarming incidence of depression among poor women. We fail to see individual women confronting specific life circumstances and grappling with them in specific ways. Our own hidden advantages in life distort our perceptions of the lives of others. Our efforts at understanding are further hindered when the explanatory models we bring with us to the study of poor women are those developed through the study of men or the study of middle-class women. Our lack of comprehension then makes it easier to "blame the victim" of poverty and to attribute the problems she experiences to deficits of character or intelligence.

I don't want to argue, however, that such barriers to understanding are insurmountable. I think that even without the personal experience of poverty and even with the limitations and biases of existing research instruments and theories, we can come closer to understanding the lives of poor women. As a middle-class white woman, childless at the time of my research, I believe I gained some insights into the lives of African American and white women rearing children in poverty. Meeting regularly with two women I will refer to as Faye Eaton and Sally Becker showed me what immense variation is concealed behind the word "poverty" and indicated some of the dimensions by which this variation might be measured. My experiences with these women also changed many of my initial ideas about social support, stress, and coping.

I will argue that a useful tool for me in the analysis of these women's lives was my discovery of my own class position and my own life context as a middle-class white woman. Analyzing what I shared with each woman and what I did not share led me to a better understanding of each woman's life situation and helped me to revise my theories. My analyses were powerfully shaped by encountering these women in the context of an intensive study of poor women in which the women were treated as collaborators rather than solely as research subjects.

The Stress and Families Project was begun by Marcia Guttentag in 1976 to investigate the stresses that give rise to high rates of depression among low-income women with children and to study the implications of stress and depression for the mother-child relationship. In addition to its basic research goals, the study was designed to locate points at which interventions might be successful in protecting mental health and family functioning. The project, which was funded by the National Institute of Mental Health, was originally planned as a large-scale study of several hundred low-income mothers and their children in two urban sites. Earlier research findings on the epidemiology of depression and on the consequences for children of maternal depression laid the intellectual groundwork for the study. The larger women's movement of the time created the political and social context in which such a study could actually be funded and carried out.

Marcia Guttentag hired me as project director, and she and I assembled a young, multiracial, multidisciplinary research group. I had earned my doctorate only weeks before starting work on the project, one staff member was a tenured psychology professor joining the study during a sabbatical leave, and most of the other staff members were graduate students. Many of us had studied child development, and others came from backgrounds in social psychology, anthropology, and public health. The research team included never-married, divorced, and married women; women with children and those without; women who had grown up in middle-class households and in working-class households; and women who had been on welfare. Most of us would have described ourselves as feminists and many of us were concerned with economic inequalities, but our political and moral visions of the world were diverse.

Our first mission was to write a brief interview schedule measuring the key stress factors in the lives of low-income mothers. Coming from diverse disciplines and life histories, we found that we had conflicting ideas about the kinds of data we should collect. Were quantitative stress ratings sufficient? Did we need descriptive information about each respondent's living environment? Did we need to learn about women's strengths as well as their vulnerabilities? Should we collect the most rigorously objective data possible, or was it important to understand the way a woman construed her own life situation?

After reviewing the existing research on stress, depression, and women's lives, we began to fear that we did not yet know enough to design the brief interview schedule that was needed. We became critical of the research instruments then in use, as they seemed to miss so much about the experience of low-income women with children. Makosky (1980), for instance, pointed out the limitations of early research on life events stress for answering questions about the stress of women's lives. As she noted, most of these early stress studies focused on research populations that were exclusively or predominantly male: "Prisoners of war, football players, industrial employees, medical interns, physicians, and Navy personnel at sea, for example" (p. 114). Sex comparisons were rarely reported, and the standard inventory of stressful events included a disproportionate number that apply more often to men than women and excluded events that women are likely to experience. Thus, being drafted or being promoted at work often appeared on inventories of stressful events, but experiencing an abortion, a rape, or a change in child care arrangements generally did not.

Given our group's interest specifically in poor women, most early inventories of stressful life events also had a second limitation in that they tended to include events likely to happen to middle-class people, but exclude events common among the poor. Taking out a mortgage would rate stress points on many early stress inventories. Going on welfare would not. Using such scales many stresses in the lives of middle-class males are quite apparent; those of low-income women are almost invisible.

But once we ventured beyond the established instruments, we soon realized that many realms of life might contribute to the experience of stress. How could we call our study complete if we did not attend to women's work histories, experiences of discrimination, economic situations, parenting philosophies, or coping strategies? And if we did attend to such issues, often in the open-ended format that came to seem desirable, how could we possibly include them all in a study of hundreds of women?

As we vigorously debated our research direction, we also realized that we were not making decisions based simply on the official hierarchy of the research group. Although academic credentials and official position might lend weight to an argument, a researcher who had personally experienced poverty or motherhood or racial discrimination could also speak with authority. We moved away from our official hierarchy toward a self-consciously collaborative approach, with every staff member having an opportunity to influence others, and with most decisions made consensually. Our research group meetings were often long and turbulent, but they led to decisions that satisfied us and strengthened our commitment to the work.

We discussed the historical tendency of researchers to pathologize the behavior of oppressed or merely different people. We articulated a vision of research in which the women we interviewed would be seen as experts on their own lives and as contributors to, not subjects of, our research. We looked to them for wisdom as well as data. We made it our goal to examine critically our own assumptions and the assumptions of our disciplines. We were exhilarated to be women studying women and were aware of the opportunity to set right historic misunderstandings (as well as to create new ones). In all of this we reflected the emerging ideas and emotions of the larger women's movement in our society.

We soon decided to reshape the Stress and Families Project into an intensive, small-scale study that would explore in depth the lives of low-income women and their children, generating as well as testing hypotheses about sources of stress and depression, and thus paving the way for the large-scale study that had originally been envisioned. With the approval of our funding agency, we conducted an intensive study of forty-three low-income mothers (twenty-one African American women and twenty-two white women) and their children. Twenty of the women were single parents, twelve lived with their husbands, and eleven lived with boyfriends. Per capita annual household incomes for the families ranged from $500 to $4500, which meant that some families lived far below federal poverty lines and some lived just above poverty lines. Of the forty-three respondents, thirty-three received government welfare payments, and most of the remaining ten had received these benefits in the past or participated in other public assistance programs, such as food stamps. Educational attainments of the respondents ranged from fourth grade to graduate school, with a mean educational level of 11.8 years of schooling.

Each of the forty-three women worked with one interviewer and one observer for several months of weekly or twice-weekly meetings, and each woman was paid $150 for her work with us. Meetings generally took place in the respondent's home. An interviewer gathered information on the woman's mental health, recent life events, enduring life conditions, daily routines, childhood, employment history, experiences with social service and political institutions, experiences of discrimination, social relationships, coping efforts, and diet. An observer recorded six half-hour periods of mother-child interaction in the home, interviewed children about the parent-child relationship, and interviewed the mother about parenting philosophies and practices.

Marcia Guttentag died suddenly in the early months of our fieldwork. Because of the collaborative staff structure she had encouraged we were all involved in the plans for the remainder of fieldwork and data analysis, and we had a clear direction for our work. She also left us with the inspiration of her active and meaningful life and the strong desire to complete our work in a way that would honor her memory and justify her trust in us.

Although Marcia's death drew me into more administrative responsibilities, I did get to work as an observer in two research families. Both of the mothers I worked with were about my own age (late twenties), divorced, and had three children. One woman was white, the other Black.

Faye Eaton, an African American woman, lived in a public housing project, portions of which were boarded up and uninhabited. The shabbiness of the building and its style of construction announced clearly to visitors, "Poor folks live here." Finding the Eaton apartment required questioning neighbors, as all the nameplates had long since been torn off the mailboxes. Faye and her three children were squeezed into four small rooms with a minimum of furniture and few playthings for the children.

My relationship with Faye Eaton began dramatically. Arriving at her apartment, my research partner and I were met not only by Faye, but also by a representative of her community's research review committee who wanted to know our intentions, our methods, and our backers. This encounter spoke to my deepest fears that as a middle-class white woman I would be perceived as an enemy, one

likely to hurt Faye and others like her through my misunderstandings and deni-
gration of her life. Perhaps such a perception might even be correct, and my efforts to learn from Faye and her family would be futile. We did apparently satisfy
the committee member, however, because we did not hear further from her, and
Faye entered wholeheartedly into the research.

My research partner was a young Black woman who had grown up in the
South, as had Faye. The two quickly developed rapport, and the strength of their
relationship eased my own entry into the home. I was touched when on a very hot
day, Faye insisted on filling some empty orange juice concentrate containers with
ice water for us to drink while we waited for the bus to take us home. One afternoon several months into the study, I was interviewing Faye's daughter when Faye
flew into the room where we were. Her social worker was visiting, and Faye
wanted to tidy up the apartment. I realized then that I could be shown their apartment as it usually was. Such indications that I was cared for and accepted meant a
great deal to me.

Faye lived in a neighborhood with a high crime rate, and I took many precau-
tions to protect myself when I visited her. I traveled in daylight, and if possible,
with a colleague. I carried no handbag and concealed my tape recorder in a grocery bag. I was alert to those I passed on the street. Despite my wariness, I usually
enjoyed walking across the small, open park on the way from my bus stop to the
Eaton apartment. The park looked uncared for, but at least it had green grass and
a few fine trees. I began to wonder why I never saw the Eatons or other families
with children in the park, why everyone instead played in the project playground,
where broken glass made the jungle gyms and swings dangerous. I confess that in
my ignorance I actually thought that perhaps Faye and the other parents might
have overlooked the park in favor of the playground or been too lazy to go the
small extra distance to take advantage of it. When I finally got around to asking
Faye why she didn't take her children to the park, she told me, "People get killed
there. That's where the dope dealers hang out." This conversation and others like
it showed me that the world around us offered Faye fewer options than seemed
evident to a middle-class observer. This conversation, of course, also taught me
not to walk through the park!

In talking with Faye I was particularly interested in her relationships with
friends, relatives, and neighbors. Before beginning the study I had done a good bit
of reading about social networks and social support and I was eager to learn how
our respondents' social networks might act as support systems for them. I believed that isolation from supportive ties was a grave danger, but that involvement
in relationships could lead to many advantages. Residential mobility I saw as a
threat, because it tended to disrupt social ties, but staying in one apartment or
one neighborhood seemed to promise many benefits.

One day while walking around the housing project with Faye I asked her to tell
me how long she had known each of the people we met. At one point I turned to
her and remarked with satisfaction, "You've known most of these people five or
six years." To my way of thinking at that time, such stability augured well for the

Women playing with their children outside a housing project. *(Photo by Sarah F. Colt.)*

supportiveness of her social network. "Yeah," she said. "That's about how long it takes to get out of here." Her response opened my eyes to other implications of residential stability, which is not the same phenomenon in a public housing project as it is in a pleasant suburban town. When I discovered later that for the women in our study, living longer in a neighborhood was not associated with a more positive assessment of the neighborhood or with mental health advantages, I had some ideas about these "unexpected" findings.

Faye took great joy in the happiness of others. One of my vivid memories of her is of her laughingly lifting her cousin in a great bear hug and whirling her around the floor in shared pleasure at some good news this woman had received. Yet Faye was having serious problems with her physical health, with taking care of her three young children, and with her mental health. She suffered from many symptoms of depression and during a time shortly before the study she often drank enough to induce forgetfulness and dull her pain. Looking back on a year during which she completed a treatment program for her alcohol problem, she commented that her life is harder now "because I don't have the alcohol to blind me and help me to forget. I got to face reality, and it's horrible with no husband, no boyfriend, three kids, and the Welfare." As I became more aware of what she suffered, I tried to think through ways in which Faye's problems could be solved.

Perhaps a job was the solution, and in fact Faye often spoke longingly of her wish for employment, of her memories of a time before the children and before her marriage failed when she had enjoyed working. But what were her realistic options at this moment, without education beyond high school, without credentials or marketable skills, and with responsibility for three preschool children and no co-parent or convenient grandparent to help with their care? Virtually all the jobs she might have found would have paid less than the cost of the necessary day care for her children, and she would also have lost the state-provided medical insurance on which she and her family depended. Further training could have opened up better employment options, but how could Faye afford the costs of training as well as child care? In addition, her physical health was poor, as was that of many of the most stressed women in our study, and this further limited the types of employment that made sense for her.

If a job or job training were not possible at this time in her life, I wondered if she could at least ease her financial condition through help from other members of her family. But Faye had no one at all in her entire family circle with greater financial resources than she. In fact, she had provided a temporary home in her small apartment for her brother, and on other occasions, for her mother, who moved up from the South so that Faye could nurse her when she became ill. Far from being able to look to others for financial help, Faye was further strained by helping out members of her family in even greater financial distress than she. Faye's friends were mostly women in circumstances similar to her own, who were also struggling to make ends meet on an allotment from AFDC. The articles I had read on social support emphasized the advantages obtained through membership in a social network of mutual obligation and mutual assistance. Thinking about Faye Eaton's life made me aware of the stresses associated with such a network, particularly when one is called on to provide more economic and instrumental assistance than one receives.

Faye was not without resources in her struggles. She had a rich sense of humor and the capacity to connect with others. She had successfully found advocates and mentors among her professional helpers, and she had developed strong friendships with other women who did not let her down in times of need. When she found herself temporarily overwhelmed with the responsibility of caring for her three children, she had a friend who was willing to take good care of one of the children for several weeks. One social worker had become godmother to yet another of the children. The limitations in Faye's coping strategies did not seem to reflect any limitation in her thoughtfulness or skill, but rather limitations in the economic and social resources available to her and those around her.

My affection for Faye and my sorrow over her many trials in life made me wish strongly to do something for her. I felt guilty each time I headed home out of her neighborhood and my body relaxed as I moved away from the danger and pain that she lived with from day to day. Like virtually all of the other researchers on the study, I sometimes questioned the morality of my role in Faye's life, wondering how I could gain so much from her and offer so little in return. I seized on opportunities to bring small presents to her or the children, and I hoped that my work would lead to something positive for them and others in similar situations.

Taking leave of Faye at the end of the study was also difficult, although our research group had discussed and planned for these departures months in advance.

When Faye was asked what she had liked and not liked about the study, she said that meeting the interviewer and the observer was the best thing and showed her that "there are still some decent people in the world." However, she recommended that in future work with families we "don't be too friendly or get too close. Parting is such sweet sorrow." I shared her sense of loss, compounded with regret that so little had changed to make her life easier.

Meeting my second respondent, Sally Becker, was in some ways more disconcerting than meeting my first. Sally Becker was a low-income woman with young children, but she was also a great deal like me. I was a white woman, and so was she. I had gone to college, and so had she. My mother had hired a cleaning woman, and so had Sally's mother. Sally had a background as privileged as mine, and yet she had somehow fallen into poverty, following a marriage disapproved of by her parents and then a divorce. At the time I met Sally, I had barely completed my graduate studies and had only the most tenuous hold on a professional career. My encounter with her focused my attention on the omnipresent threat of downward mobility for most women.

Sharing so much in class background, race, and education, Sally and I had few obvious impediments to mutual understanding. Yet our very similarities created some awkwardness, since our roles in the study were so different. I think I might have felt more uncomfortable in the situation if I were not so aware of my own childlessness and Sally's happiness and competence as a mother of several children. I remember that Sally had a framed print in her living room showing a nun walking by a mother with several young children. The title of the picture was something like "Heaven on Earth" and suggested that the mother in the picture was the one supremely fulfilled. Although my curiosity about Faye Eaton's life had focused on her difficult life circumstances, my personal curiosity about Sally Becker centered on her mothering. In her evident pleasure with her children I hoped to catch glimpses of my own future joys, and in her marvelous parenting abilities I hoped I saw my own future competence as a parent prefigured.

I was particularly impressed with Sally's ability to respond to her children and maintain connections with them even as they pursued divergent tasks and needed her attention in different ways. During one of my observations of the family, Sally was in the kitchen, attending to her infant daughter and talking with a friend who had dropped by. Her seven-year-old son was at the dining room table addressing Valentine's Day cards for his classmates, and her oldest child was watching television in the living room. From time to time the seven-year-old would despair of getting a card right or would complain that he had run out of room before finishing someone's name or that the point on his pencil had broken. Sally responded to him calmly and helpfully, suggesting alternative strategies and keeping him encouraged. I watched as he completed his pile of cards and Sally nursed her baby and talked with her friend. Everyone in the house was satisfied, and each of Sally's children received from her what was needed at that time.

On another occasion, I arrived to do an observation, and the seven-year-old I was to observe had not yet come home from school. On that particular day he was to have taken a taxi from school to his house. Sally had arranged with the taxi company beforehand, and it should have been a straightforward matter. As the minutes ticked by and the boy did not arrive home, I began to imagine a number of terrible things that might happen to a young child on the way home in a taxi. As the sky darkened and he still did not arrive, I began to worry in earnest. Sally made several phone calls to track down her son; these produced no positive results, but she remained calm. Her son walked into the house an hour late with a perfectly reasonable story of missed communication and confusion. He was fine, Sally was fine, and only I had become a nervous wreck. I marveled at the apparent difference in our reactions and wondered whether I would be able to summon up at least the appearance of calm in a comparable future situation.

When I compared Sally Becker to Faye Eaton I realized that although Sally was poor, she had tremendous resources for dealing with her situation that were not available to Faye. Sally's family and many of her friends were people with extensive economic and social resources, which she could draw on in times of need. Although still estranged from her parents, Sally did accept from them gifts for her children. She also had the knowledge that her parents would help to provide higher education for her children and would help the family more substantially if things became quite desperate. In addition, Sally's brother, with whom she remained on good terms, owned and managed a small retail business in a nearby town. It might be possible for Sally's children to find part-time work there in the future, and cash loans from this brother were always a possibility. Certainly none of the members of Sally Becker's extended family were likely to need money or housing from her.

Unlike Faye Eaton, Sally Becker lived in a reasonably safe neighborhood in a privately rented apartment she had heard about through a friend of a friend. An African American family would have had great difficulty in renting an apartment in that neighborhood or in living there without harassment. Multifamily houses and small apartment buildings stood on short streets and cul-de-sacs, some buildings facing away or at oblique angles to the roads themselves. The resulting pattern created interesting public and private spaces. Sally's building, although somewhat dilapidated, seemed soundly constructed, and her apartment was comfortably furnished. Some of the Beckers' possessions may well have dated from the earlier era in Sally's life when she was married and comparatively affluent, and some of their belongings, particularly the children's toys and clothes, were gifts from Sally's parents. Sally's boyfriend lived with the family, and his modest income also contributed to the comfort of the family.

Sally's college degree meant that reasonably well paying jobs were at least a possibility for her. She had set her sights on a particular career and was currently taking classes part-time, planning to be able to work when her children were older. She had found programs that provided financial assistance to her during this period and made child care costs affordable. With many of her friends in positions of responsibility in the community and therefore well placed to hear news of programs that might be of assistance, Sally had a social network rich in resources she could tap.

In addition to all these advantages and buffers to her stresses as a low-income mother, Sally spoke middle-class English, looked middle class, and had a middle-class sense of entitlement. When her welfare worker gave her a hard time, she walked into the supervisor's office and demanded fair treatment. When she was told that her youngest child would have to have a social security number in order to continue receiving AFDC benefits, she was outraged and plotted strategies to avoid what she regarded as an affront. When people looked at her askance in the supermarket because she was buying her groceries with food stamps, she could stare them down with the inner conviction that she was as good as they were, that welfare benefits were a right not a privilege, that any woman might find herself poor one day, and that poverty itself was not a shameful thing. In that long, early, privileged portion of her life, Sally had learned to respect herself and to believe that society respected her. In her current difficulties she could believe that her future was full of promise.

We had hypothesized before the study began that women who had fallen into poverty out of the middle class would be more depressed than those who had always been impoverished, basing our hunch on ideas of loss and relative deprivation. We discovered, however, in our sample of forty-three women virtually the opposite was true: Lifelong poverty was a much greater risk factor than a descent into poverty during adulthood. Once again, by the time we had these findings we also had many plausible explanations for them.

Both Faye Eaton and Sally Becker sometimes made me feel afraid. The fear I felt with Sally, I discovered when I analyzed it, was mostly a fear for myself. If poverty could befall Sally, how could I believe myself immune? Talking with her, I imagined myself using food stamps and arguing with welfare workers. I realized I wouldn't be able to afford many things I took for granted and I doubted I would be as resilient as Sally Becker.

The fear I felt with Faye Eaton was more terrible and less self-focused. The more I talked with her about her situation, the less hope I could see for improving it. Without relatives or friends with money or with clout; without education or credentials; speaking English like the Southern-born, poor Black woman she was; having no long-nourished sense of entitlement to something better than she was now experiencing, Faye had few resources to shield her from the worst our society has to offer.

The contrast between these two women conveyed to me the variation concealed by the single word "poverty." Both Faye Eaton and Sally Becker had low incomes and received AFDC benefits. Yet the poverty of Faye Eaton was so unlike the poverty of Sally Becker. Although the sheer amount of income is an important component of poverty, and one of Sally's advantages was a higher household income, I now believe that assessments of poverty are incomplete without measures of educational level and class background, the social and economic resources of friends and relatives, accents of speech (as these convey class status), and the personal history that provides or fails to provide a sense of entitlement to the resources U.S. society has to offer.

Sally Becker and Faye Eaton also taught me something about social networks as protective factors for women in poverty. Although Faye's friendship and kinship network was able to provide emotional support and crucial child care assistance, her network did not have the resources to enable her to rise up out of poverty. On the contrary, her relatives and friends were often in situations more dire than her own. Sally's network, on the other hand, could offer not only moral support and task assistance, but also substantial economic help, information, and expert advice, and thus enable Sally to find the education and career that would free her from the indignity of welfare and poverty. Although a humanistic approach has emphasized the emotionally sustaining functions of social networks, meeting these two women reminded me that networks are also the conduits for powerful social and economic resources that make profound differences in people's lives.

I had begun this research concerned about the limitations of existing research on stress and coping. Meeting Faye Eaton and Sally Becker heightened my concerns. Stress research at the time of the study tended to focus on isolated events, missing the complex of chronic, ongoing, and interrelated stressors that so clearly differentiated Faye's situation from Sally's. Yet it seemed precisely the interplay between problems that was important. A health problem by itself was one thing, but when the health problem made it difficult to hold a job or was exacerbated because prescribed medications and diet could not be afforded, the stress that resulted seemed more than additive. And lack of money seemed to intensify just about any other problem. When we analyzed our quantitative data on chronic stress factors we found that financial problems were associated with problems in many other realms of life in a way that no other types of problems were (Makosky, 1980).

Getting a glimpse of the tangible and intangible resources Sally Becker had and Faye Eaton lacked also made me leery of research that takes an individual's coping strategy as the *starting point* for inquiry. How could one study coping without first learning a great deal about the resources and options actually available to specific individuals? In most studies, Faye Eaton and Sally Becker would be characterized as low-income, unemployed, single welfare mothers with three children. Differences in their coping strategies would be assumed to reflect differences in their character or coping style. Since Faye experienced a high level of depressive symptoms and Sally exhibited virtually none, Faye's coping strategies would be considered unsuccessful and Sally's would be applauded. By ignoring dramatic differences in their actual life contexts we could attribute their differences to personal factors alone, once again pathologizing the psychological outcomes of oppression.

My experiences with Faye Eaton and Sally Becker also inevitably made me think about the significance of race in women's lives and made me more aware of the complex ways in which race in the United States reflects the tragic history of our nation and has implications for virtually every facet of life.

Many of Sally's advantages seemed connected to her status as a white woman, and many of Faye's problems also seemed intertwined with her race. Sally received food stamps and welfare benefits, but many of her neighbors, friends, and relatives were economically secure. Faye lived in poverty, and so did virtually her entire social network. Recent research has shown that the neighborhoods of poor Blacks and poor whites tend to differ in just this way. In 1980, for instance, 38 percent of all poor Blacks in the ten largest U.S. cities lived in census tracts in which at least 40 percent of the people lived below the poverty line, although only 6 percent of poor non-Hispanic whites lived in such "hyperghettoes" (Wacquant and Wilson, 1989). As Wilson (1987, 1991) argued, the experience of such concentrated poverty limits the opportunities and diminishes the efficacy of individuals even beyond the impact of family poverty. The residential patterns of poor African Americans and poor whites must in turn be understood in the context of historical and contemporaneous housing discrimination.

Faye regretted the absence of a husband or boyfriend in her life, and even in this realm her race disadvantaged her. Marriage and remarriage rates among Blacks have fallen precipitously as Black men have lost jobs and earning power (Wilson, 1987). The factory jobs that once enabled men without advanced education to support a family have disappeared, particularly from inner-city areas. Nonwhite women now outnumber employed nonwhite men by ratios as high as two to one (Wilson, 1987). Men and women who live in hyperghettoes have even less opportunity for gainful employment and for marriage or remarriage to a stably employed mate than those who live elsewhere (Wilson, 1991).

At the outset of our study we decided to include equal numbers of African American and white women, and we attempted to recruit Black and white women who were approximately matched on factors like income, education, marital status, and numbers of children. This attempt showed us immediately that the world is not arranged in this way. It was quite difficult, for instance, to find white women who were married or living with boyfriends and yet had incomes low enough to qualify for our study. The earnings of white men were just too high.

We later discovered other unanticipated ways in which the white and African American women in the study differed. Most of the white respondents had grown up in the Boston area, but many of the African American women had grown up like Faye Eaton in the South. These women took part in a great Black migration northward and into large cities (Lemann, 1991), and their family networks were often split between North and South. The African American women in the study also came from larger families and had more brothers and sisters, not surprising given the rural, agricultural background of many of these families. These network characteristics in turn meant that Black women and white women tended to inhabit different sorts of social worlds, with different opportunities for support and stress from network members.

White women are now likely to seek employment while they are rearing children and to be single parents. African American women were often employed mothers and single mothers in earlier generations, and many of our Black respondents grew up with employed or single mothers. During our interviews, both white and Black women reported painful incidents of discrimination based on their poverty and single-parent status, but the Black women reported that discrimination based on their race was the most potent type of discrimination they faced. We learned of several violent episodes, some involving attempts to terrorize Blacks who were attempting to live in predominantly white neighborhoods. Such profound differences in so many realms of life suggest that race is not fully understood when it is simply conceptualized as a variable on which individuals may differ.

I think I learned a great deal from my time with Faye Eaton and Sally Becker, but I would not want to inflate the gains that are possible with such intensive encounters or to denigrate other methods of research. What I learned from these two women cannot, for instance, be generalized to draw conclusions about all African American women versus all white women. The larger study in which Faye and Sally participated demonstrated that many Black women were like Sally in possessing a strong sense of entitlement and many social resources for coping with poverty, while many white women lacked these advantages.

Meeting Faye Eaton and Sally Becker did affect my interpretations of the results we found in the larger project in which they participated, as I believe will be evident to those who read the book my colleagues and I wrote about this research (Belle, 1982a). Stimulated in part by thoughts about Faye and Sally, I wrote one essay exploring the potential costs of social ties for women (Belle, 1982b) and another discussing the impact of poverty on social ties and social supports (Belle, 1983). My contrasting memories of Faye and Sally contributed to my curiosity about the history of Blacks and whites in the United States and my interest in recent research on the spatial organization and temporal persistence of poverty. My encounters with Faye and Sally also seem to have addicted me to research that allows me to talk with people, learn from them, and hope that I can begin to see the world through their eyes.

Acknowledgments

I am grateful for comments on earlier drafts of this chapter from Carol Franz, Elizabeth Greywolf, Lou-Marie Kruger, Maureen Reese, Eve Rittenberg, Abby Stewart, Vicki Steinitz, Lisa Sutton, Barbara Trachtenberg, and Robert Weiss.

References

Belle, D. (1982a). *Lives in stress: Women and depression.* Beverly Hills, CA: Sage.

―――――. (1982b). The stress of caring: Women as providers of social support. In L. Goldberger & S. Breznitz (Eds.), *Handbook of stress: Theoretical and clinical aspects* (pp. 496–505). New York: Free Press.

―――――. (1983). The impact of poverty on social networks and supports. *Marriage and Family Review, 5* (4), 89–103.

Lemann, N. (1991). *The promised land: The great black migration and how it changed America*. New York: Knopf.

Makosky, V. (1980). Life stress and the mental health of women: A discussion of research and issues. In M. Guttentag, S. Salasin, & D. Belle (Eds.), *The mental health of women*. (pp. 111–127). New York: Academic Press.

Wacquant, L.J.D., & Wilson, W. J. (1989). The cost of racial and class exclusion in the inner city. *Annals of the American Academy of Political and Social Science*. Newbury Park, CA: Sage.

Wilson, W. J. (1987). *The truly disadvantaged: The inner city, the underclass, and public policy*. Chicago: University of Chicago Press.

_____. (1991). Studying inner-city social dislocations: The challenge of public agenda research. *American Sociological Review, 56*, 1-14.

4

The Ethics of Ambiguity:
Feminists Writing Women's Lives

GAIL A. HORNSTEIN

I AM IN THE BAR of a hotel in Philadelphia, surrounded by psychoanalysts, talking to a feminist known for writing lives. She introduces me to a passing acquaintance as "Frieda Fromm-Reichmann's biographer."[1] Wincing, I suddenly begin a disquisition on the functions of history, designed to show that just because Frieda is the main character in my story doesn't make it biography. The distinction is lost on them. They have no idea why it seems to matter so much to me.[2]

I am trying to escape the limits of fact. The Frieda in my book is as much the vehicle for the story as the Frieda her friends and patients remember and need. My Frieda is based on theirs, but part of her is mine. A person who actually lived is no more real than a character in a story that is true. Feminist biographers, having spent years "living and working inside another person's life," are understandably reluctant to admit this.[3] They want real to be more than believable. They want to resurrect their subjects, not turn them to narrative ends. My work looks just like theirs, so I keep having to explain how it could mean something so different to me. I'm trying to widen the space for invention, to write about Frieda as if she were real, which goes beyond describing who she was.[4]

In optics, there is a process called anamorphosis in which an image is "distorted so that it can be viewed without distortion only from a special angle or with a special instrument."[5] Nods to relativism notwithstanding, many of us cling to the belief that feminist empathy constitutes the clarifying lens. Even when the lives we illuminate are disappointing, deformed in ways we hadn't imagined, we reassure ourselves that at least we are seeing them for what they were.[6] We no longer write in the breathless prose of 1970—when we made it sound as if women's very existence were a fact worthy of note—but we still privilege feminist accounts, take them as better, more true, although we can no longer say very clearly what this means.[7]

Dr. Frieda Fromm-Reichmann

We need to give up these remnants of realism. Feminists cannot be less partisan than others who write lives. Our accounts are as transitory, as partial, as distorted by our own needs as the accounts we want to supersede. There are important differences between our stories and these others, but these differences are largely aesthetic. Having designed our choices—about what to include, what to leave out, what to emphasize—to appeal to the feminist eye, we take them as truth, but this is as much a statement of preference as anything else. What concerns me more is the implicit ethic of relationship we create between biographer and subject, an ethic that reflects our politics in ways we need to explore.[8]

1.

I was six years old when Frieda Fromm-Reichmann died. What could it mean to say that I know her? Is biography more than charades, an act of pretense in which a stranger brings a person to life for the amusement of other strangers? In fiction, the writer is on intimate terms with her characters and can anticipate their every move. Even those she finds irritating benefit at least from familiarity. Biographers are like people from another world—to be precise, we should call them anthropologists—who spend their time staring at stacks of notes, wishing that they would speak.

And yet biographers are the ones we trust. Novelists are allowed to dissemble, even commit fraud, so long as they do it well. Philip Roth once took a character he had killed in Chapter 1 and sent him to Israel to recover in Chapter 2.[9] Biographers, having nothing to offer but dispassion, keep more distance, which is why we trust them to tell the truth. The biographer who befriends her subject is suspect, like the juror who dates the defendant during a trial. Of course there are limits; we squirm at a writer who pins her subject to the mounting board. Detachment is not objectivity, in biography or anywhere else.

My problem is that I care so much about Frieda I have trouble writing about her. I am as concerned about hurting her as I am about telling what I know. It seems unnecessarily cruel to strip a person of every shred of privacy just because she is dead; to do this to someone who valued discretion above all else seems crueler still. Yet I feel as if I have no choice. I already know too many things about Frieda that she didn't tell her closest friends. To reveal them seems disloyal; not to do so seems worse. No one appointed me guardian of her memory. There are times when I feel her trying to pull me into the role—as she did others who preceded me—but this in itself cannot justify my taking it on.

Part of the seductiveness of writing a life is that it fosters the fantasy of perfect understanding. You start by imagining your subject as misunderstood and unappreciated, someone in need of rescue. Then you convince yourself that you are the first to recognize her, to see fully who she was. In a union that is more lamination than marriage, biographer and subject fuse their interests, allowing each other to speak in one voice. The more misunderstood the subject, the more intense her biographer's pleasure in slowly removing each veil. For a person like Frieda, rarely portrayed in any depth, the need for help seems acute. Dead only thirty-five years, she has already become an icon, an instantiation of an ideal, not someone who walked the dog. It seems an act of generosity to make her more real, to open places she could never show. But what if this is betrayal? Frieda spent her life cultivating opacity and remained unseen even to some of those who knew her best. Should I pretend not to know this? Or should I explain it away as defensiveness, her way of protecting herself from the greater pain of being misunderstood? If I swear not to misunderstand her, does this give me the right to say whatever I want?

These muddles thicken as I set loyalty to Frieda against my debts to her friends and patients. They are the ones who have told me much of what I know, in interviews that go on for hours and leave me mute with fatigue. I feel privileged to be meeting her colleagues, whose sensitivity, beyond attunement, lets them cherish patients so ill that even most psychiatrists despise them. There is something heroic about the stories people tell in these interviews, and I don't often get to hear that tone. But I am unnerved by the intensity of feeling about Frieda, especially when it ends up directed at me. I know I ask for it, always pressing harder on places no one has touched for thirty years. Most people are relieved to finally tell someone what they know. Others, grateful for my attentiveness, use it for self-aggrandizement, or reparation, or revenge. Most tell me what they take as truth, but there are those who can't bear it themselves or try to distract me with something else. Feelings fly around the room like trapped birds, and sometimes I have to struggle just to stay in my chair.

How do I calculate my debt to these people, who squeeze me into an hour between patients, take me home for dinner, or drive me where I need to go? Do I owe more to the ones who tell me everything than to those who hide? Some of these people won't live to see my book in print; does this mean I should worry less about how they feel? Sometimes I think everything will be fine so long as I don't use anyone's name. Yet some people want to be identified. Others have implied that they'd sue. No matter how admiringly I present Frieda, there are those who might feel betrayed. Can it be right to do this, even if what I am saying is true?

2.

In form, biography differs little from fiction. The subject is a character who has to be created, made to seem alive, moved about from scene to scene, and given things to do. The actuality of her existence functions for readers only as background, like the words "This is a True Story" at the start of a documentary. What makes biography good is not only accuracy—something few readers are in a position to judge—but believability. Truth that lacks the felicity of fiction seems untrustworthy.

Biography is believable when it draws us into a world that feels real, a world that novelist John Gardner called a "vivid and continuous fictional dream." So long as we are inside this dream, we "move among the characters, lean with them against the fictional walls, taste the fictional gazpacho, smell the fictional hyacinths." It is only "in bad or unsatisfying fiction," Gardner warns, that "we are abruptly snapped out of the dream, forced to think of the writer or the writing, as if a playwright were to run out on stage, interrupting his characters, to remind us that he has written all this."[10] A biographer who makes a life believable earns our trust, and we go along with whatever she says, even when it seems bizarre or utterly different from our own lives. The semblance of authenticity keeps us from asking "Is this really true?" or wondering how anyone could have known.

But to write a life you have to ask yourself these questions at every turn. Donald Spence talks of how "something may become true simply by being put into words. ... The construction not only shapes the past—it *becomes* the past."[11] Sometimes you literally see the image forming before you on the page. Things in Frieda's life that I could scarcely make out a year ago now seem sharp and clear, as if seeing consisted mainly in adjusting my eyes to the dark. Spence says there is no history independent of construction; instead we have "narrative fit," a truth of coherence.

Spence is speaking from the relative comfort of psychoanalysis, a form of collaborative biography in which the subject is still alive. Patient and analyst together create a narrative believable enough to be fact, and even when their efforts make things worse, they still have each other. Once they share the exquisite pleasure of hearing an interpretation plunk squarely into place, they never stop being astonished at what they are capable of doing. Biographers seldom have moments like these. Frieda stares straight out at me from the photograph on my desk and never says a word.

What's to stop me from inventing her out of my own need? "Life has no shape, artistically speaking," admitted Catherine Drinker Bowen after she had written four biographies, "any more than grief has a shape, or jealousy, or love, or any of those large angry things. It is for the writer to find a shape, find boundaries, a circumference within which he may freely move."[12] But what constrains this search or keeps it within bounds? Data from archives and interviews seem only the barest of tethers, preventing me, for example, from claiming that Frieda bore five children or traveled to Tunisia, but doing little to contain my imaginings about her inner life. Psychoanalyst and patient rely on each other to sift projection from reality. The biographer has little to prevent transference from becoming a free fall into her own need.

I don't want Frieda to end up more mine than real. But I have trouble sorting out what this means, since she feels most mine at precisely the moments when she seems most real. What I need most from Frieda is proof that she existed, and I need that so badly that sometimes I worry I have made her up. I find it difficult to interview people who have the same need; their images of Frieda get in the way of my own.

Elisabeth Young-Bruehl talks about the "lure of essence," the biographer's wish for the subject to "appear, like a voice at a seance, and speak into the pages of the biography his or her heart of hearts."[13] What a relief this would be, almost an absolution. I could claim that the story was Frieda's rather than mine, that I simply wrote it down, that the blind spots were hers. Even if we ended up colluding with each other in some folie à deux, I wouldn't be acting alone the way I am now.

But what if we take Young-Bruehl's remark in another way, as an ethical guideline rather than as a longing? To conjure up the subject and have her speak onto the page, the biographer has to render her in a form the subject can recognize. She need not agree with everything that is said—some of it will hurt her or make her angry—but she ought not to feel exploited or abused. We need a lodestar in biography, something to substitute for an objective standard of truth, and an ethical one might serve as well as any.

Having such a standard would force us to recognize that our relationships with our subjects are real, real in the psychoanalytic sense of being partly free from transference. This means, among other things, that we shouldn't treat our subjects in ways we wouldn't treat our friends. At a minimum, we ought not to say things about them in print that we would be ashamed to say to their faces. We can't omit material just because our subjects would find it damaging or because it would elicit their denial, but we can balance their right to privacy with the rights of our readers to know. A biographer who doesn't have at least that much loyalty to her subject probably shouldn't be writing; her book will be pathography, an act of hatred. Even scrupulous adherence to an ethical standard wouldn't protect a biographer from other failings, but it could help her to live with herself once the book was done.

Sometimes even transference, used homeopathically, can be beneficial. There is a great deal to be learned from moments when you feel estranged from your subject, or especially want to change her, or forget some crucial detail of her life. These lapses need not sabotage the work; seen properly, they can impel a deeper level of understanding. It would be odd if the biographical relationship had no periods of tension and discord; the task is not so much to prevent them as to find ways of making use of them when they occur.

No biographer can see into every corner of her subject's life. You can spend years snooping, ferreting out fragments that might someday prove useful, but you can never find it all. The same layers of need and identification that draw you to your subject serve equally to push you apart. Crevices open, barriers fall, but others form in their place. Leon Edel talks about the "delicacy" of biography, its quest to "evoke life out of inert materials."[14] But it is not only the difficulties of resurrecting a person from the detritus of grocery lists, torn envelopes, and unidentified letters that keep you from seeing her whole. There are also the ways she throws you off the track. Some people—Sigmund Freud was one—deliberately destroy crucial records to foil potential biographers. Others simply clean out their files every time they move or use old letters as scrap. The lives of millions of Europeans forced into exile during the war were all but erased, like tracks on a beach when the wind is blowing hard. Frieda was one of these. So little has survived from the first forty-six years of her life that I cried the day I found a prescription blank imprinted with her Heidelberg address. Imagine how I felt when I learned that most of her American papers had also been destroyed, not by Nazis, but by her friends, because of stipulations in her will or out of their own protectiveness.

I have a book titled *The Absence of the Dead Is Their Way of Appearing,* the testimonial of a woman whose daughter died too soon. Sometimes I wonder if this is how Frieda feels as I piece her together from a closetful of things her friends never found. She struggles to put me off, the way she put off ten others who set out to write her life. I resist. Her grief at being unseen fuses with my need to open the door. But other feelings stay shrouded, like the timidity she disguised as imperiousness and used to keep everyone at bay. We go back and forth; it's never clear who is gaining the upper hand. Frieda would have acknowledged that trying to remain invisible to a biographer is simply a mark of despair. But it is too late to bring back boxes of letters already burned, and I cannot force her friends to tell me what they know. I am left with Young-Bruehl's question: "What kind of biography will preserve my respect for what will always remain hidden to me?"[15]

3.

At least a year before her biography of Anne Sexton came out, Diane Wood Middlebrook made it known that she had relied heavily on tape recordings of Sexton's therapy sessions in writing the book.[16] Sexton's exhibitionism would have drawn an audience on its own, but Middlebrook's use of the tapes gave her account a voyeuristic cachet. By highlighting the ethical ambiguities of her method long before readers were in a position to judge its results, Middlebrook placed herself in a position that Sexton had compulsively occupied for her whole life.

Reviewers quickly made Middlebrook's disclosure about the tapes as central a part of the biography as Sexton's own indiscretions. Scott Vickers, writing in the *Bloomsbury Review,* quoted directly from the press kit the publisher sent around to create prepublication controversy about the tapes. Joyce Carol Oates focused on the book's content, but ended her *Washington Post* review by wondering whether it was "ethical, under any circumstances, for a psychiatrist to release material involving one his patients." Oates could not decide whether this was "dangerous precedent" or "merely another symptom of our era, in which the very nature of 'privacy' seems to be undergoing a radical reassessment."[17]

Alicia Ostriker, writing in the *Women's Review of Books,* was more certain. She presented Middlebrook as the unflinching feminist, willing to face up to the sordid truths of Sexton's life. To Ostriker, Middlebrook's critics—presumably even the feminist ones—are part of a "public that needs to be protected, needs not to know about the pain behind the veil of normal American family life." I find this an exceedingly odd view. So little of Sexton's family life appears "normal," even under contemporary standards, that Ostriker's strident defense of Middlebrook cannot be simply a desire for truth. By implying that Sexton's excesses—alcohol-ism, pathological narcissism, and the sexual abuse of her daughter—were just ex-treme adaptations to the constraints of prefeminist culture, Ostriker makes dis-closing the contents of a woman's therapy sessions seem to be the only way to avoid lying about her life.[18]

The question is not whether Middlebrook should have used the tapes. There can be no more useful source for biography than psychotherapy; it remains one of the few places in this culture where people commit themselves to tell the truth. Besides, much of what transpires today in therapy used to be recorded in diaries or letters, sources that have been, for centuries, the biographer's standard. Middlebrook's use of Sexton's therapy tapes—to which she had been granted full access by everyone legally empowered to provide it—cannot even be considered a choice; no biographer would have ignored such material were it offered to her. At issue is not whether Middlebrook should have used the tapes, but whether she should have justified doing so in the way she did.

When we choose to write about women who have behaved in problematic ways, we sometimes deal with our anger by scrupulously revealing every moment of their less than feminist lives. Middlebrook's book has this edge. She inundates us with intimate details—Sexton's masturbatory fantasies, verbatim excerpts from dozens of her therapy sessions, a precise description of the position of her body on top of her daughter's in bed. When asked whether any of this—especially the lengthy quotations from the therapy tapes—might constitute an invasion of Sexton's privacy, Middlebrook says that Sexton was an exhibitionist who wouldn't have cared. This is what I find disturbing. By using Sexton's pathology as a justifi-cation for her own actions, Middlebrook seems close to exploiting Sexton in pre-cisely the way her parents and husband seem to have done.

Women have always suffered from being psychiatry's primary patients, and the last thing they need is feminist biographers who treat them to more of the same. Anne Sexton's exhibitionism cost her her life. This is a tragedy, not some tidbit for dinnertime debate.[19] Sexton spent years fruitlessly searching for a therapist good enough to help her; in the end, her compulsive acting out and incessant demands were too much for them all. Middlebrook is quick to judge Sexton as untreatable. But I cannot see how the spectacular failings of these therapists—who either abandoned Sexton in various ways or sexually abused her—can be dismissed as easily as Middlebrook seems to have done. Sexton was enraging, but so were her therapists, and Martin Orne, in giving Middlebrook the tapes, may just have been getting his revenge in a different way.

Orne's self-serving introduction to Middlebrook's book reveals his loyalties, which are depressingly familiar. Having compromised Sexton's confidentiality by giving the tapes as well as all his private files to Middlebrook, Orne then goes to great lengths to protect the colleague who sexually abused Sexton, carefully not stating his name (in a later chapter Middlebrook reveals it to be Ollie Zweizung), and referring obliquely to the abuse as "a change in their relationship."[20] Orne's behavior is unsurprising—physicians are always more loyal to colleagues than to patients—but Middlebrook's requires explanation.[21] So does that of her reviewers, surprisingly few of whom see either Orne's behavior or Zweizung's as matters of note.[22]

Middlebrook had to have realized that using Sexton's pathology as justification would open her own actions to scrutiny, and this is presumably why she asked Orne to write a foreword to the book. But for Orne to give the benediction is like allowing codefendants to provide each other with alibis to a crime. By blaming Sexton for her craziness, Middlebrook and Orne collude in deflecting scrutiny onto her. Reviewers have made this process more pernicious by pumping up the claim that Middlebrook acted in accordance with Sexton's presumed wishes. Middlebrook simply asserts, "Everything I have learned about [Sexton] suggests that she would not have held back from the archive of her manuscripts and private papers the full collection of tapes. Sexton was not a person with a strong sense of privacy."[23] This phrasing makes clear that Middlebrook's claims are inferences, based on ten years of biographical research. Ostriker elides the distinction, calling Middlebrook's use of the tapes "exactly what the poet would have wanted." Grace Schulman, writing in *The Nation,* makes the further claim that "in releasing anything, Sexton's literary executor (her daughter Linda Gray Sexton) acted according to the poet's wishes."[24] But even Middlebrook admits that Sexton "made no reference to the tapes when writing her will," even though in other respects, she "dealt very professionally with the disposition of her literary estate."[25] Whether Sexton simply forgot about the tapes, as Middlebrook suggests, or took for granted that they were safe in Orne's confidential files is something we can never know.[26] As her biographer, Middlebrook is entitled to make whatever judgments she wants to about Sexton's life, but no one—even Linda Sexton, whose feelings about a mother who both loved and abused her are clearly conflicted—is in a position to speak in her name.[27] As readers, we are left with this uncomfortable question: By allowing Middlebrook to manipulate us into giving her the same kinky attention Sexton always got, are we unwittingly joining in abusing Sexton all over again?

4.

A few years after I began my work on Frieda Fromm-Reichmann, I went to Colorado to interview Joanne Greenberg, the patient who made her famous. Greenberg's memorial to their relationship—her autobiographical novel *I Never Promised You a Rose Garden*—turned "Deborah Blau" and "Dr. Fried" into sources of inspiration for millions of readers. Most of them didn't know the rest of Frieda's name, but it hardly mattered; the fictional portrait was so accurate that even Frieda's sister, reading the novel in translation, recognized her immediately. The story of Greenberg's dramatic recovery from schizophrenia spawned a controversy in psychiatry that continues to this day, and it took me several years to feel ready to wade through layers of myth to meet Greenberg on my own.

When I finally did, it transformed my story. The experience of sitting in Greenberg's house, seeing her as a 58-year-old writer/mother/wife—and not as the terrified sixteen-year-old of *Rose Garden*—made her real. I could no longer write about her simply as the vehicle for Frieda's success; she had to become a character in her own right. But to open a space for Joanne to be someone other than "Deborah Blau" meant letting the patient speak for herself, rather than in her doctor's voice, which is not something a training in the history of psychiatry teaches you to do.

Writing recent history is always messy; too many people with too high a stake in what happened are still there, looking over your shoulder. Greenberg became my private symbol for ethical murk when in a two-week period, I went from knowing her only as a character in a novel to having almost unconstrained access to information about her actual life. Following her recovery, Greenberg became a well-known novelist; her papers are being collected for an archive of U.S. writers, and she has allowed me to read them all. The profusion itself is painful—for every letter of Frieda's that is missing, there are twenty of Greenberg's, stuffed into folders, cataloged, and named. It has taken months to plow through the boxes, as competing images from the novel and from our talk in Colorado flash through my mind. I'm grateful for these materials, which are essential to my work; it's just that I can no longer find the line between doing history and reading someone else's mail.

Greenberg's letters let me decide for myself whether she was crazy. A generation of psychiatrists, frightened by the possibility that *Rose Garden* might be true, have tried to discredit its claims, and my whole view of Frieda depends on Joanne's having been cured. The debate in psychiatry concerns whether or not Joanne was schizophrenic, a question that seems to me to be beside the point. Frieda said she was, and most of her colleagues agreed. The seriousness of a person's mental disorder is mostly a measure of how removed she seems; the closer we feel to her, the less likely we are to think her insane. For Frieda to call Joanne "schizophrenic" meant she thought she was that far away. People who get that label today are farther gone, but our tolerance for insanity is also greater, so the distance is probably proportional to what it was between Frieda and Joanne in 1948.

My question is not whether Greenberg was "schizophrenic," but whether she was crazy enough for her recovery to count as a cure. The case records in themselves don't seem enough. Nor do the memories of hospital staff, so fogged by the haze of Greenberg's subsequent celebrity they can no longer tell me what I need to know. So I pore over her letters, looking for clues. The process is unspecific and hard to describe. Evidence of insanity appears more as a bad smell than as a smoking gun, a generalized sense that something is wrong. Most of the letters I have are from a much later period in Greenberg's life, and reading backward to find something so intangible makes it almost impossible to see.

What complicates writing about Frieda and Joanne even more is that they are so vivid in *Rose Garden* they can barely be imagined any other way. Biographers often struggle for a fresh view of subjects about whom much has been written, but trying to describe someone who already exists for millions of people as a fictional character is something else again. *Rose Garden* is highly accurate, but it's also a novel, a novel written by a patient who was astounded at her own recovery and needed to reassure herself that it was true.

That Frieda emerges as a saint in this narrative is unsurprising; the problem is to see beyond the glow. To dismiss a patient's admiration of her therapist simply as transference is as disrespectful as saying that the screams of battered women aren't real. Frieda did some extraordinary things, and they need to be given their due. But she evokes such intense feelings in anyone who tries to write about her that everything else fades from view. Frieda's would-be biographers—colleagues, followers, patients, even Greenberg herself—fill an entire folder in my files; their insightfulness and generosity inspire me, and my determination is a legacy of their own. But none was able to find a path through the thicket of loyalties that surround Frieda, and each gave up, with varying degrees of relief. I have the benefit of greater distance, in both emotion and in time, and these are enough for me to persevere. Like Greenberg, I've also come to appreciate the allure of a liminal truth. On the other hand, having had no personal contact with Frieda means I worry less about protecting her and am thus more vulnerable to the dangers of making her up. To an audience for whom she is already fiction I could say anything, and it might seem accurate enough.

Wanting to include Greenberg in my narrative layers the problem. She is as much a symbol as Frieda is, and I need to find a way of making her real. Having the letters helps. The physicality of archival work—the eyestrain, the mildew, the stiffness of bending and writing—combine with the inflexibility of the printed page to make Greenberg into a historical subject and therefore easier to describe. But I am constantly aware that she will read my book, as might those who wrote to her, and I question what right I have to know their names. I worry most about the patients. *Rose Garden* was published in 1964, and ever since, patients have written to Greenberg saying they know the story is true. She answers every single letter, even those that deform her experience in hideous ways. It feels voyeuristic to enter this scene. True, Joanne has invited me, but the others have not, and treating their importunities as data sometimes makes me ashamed. And yet my doing so serves larger purposes and may be the only way of allowing their stories to be heard.

What of my responsibilities to Joanne? Is access to her papers a license to rummage through the little that remains private in her relationship to Frieda after forty years? It feels sacrilegious to suggest an alternative to Dr. Fried. But it is presumptuous to want to protect Joanne from versions of Frieda other than her own, and at this point, the question is moot. I already know too much, most of which is likely to find its way onto the page. Frieda will inevitably end up looking different from the person Greenberg or any of the others knew. I keep hoping that at least this will make her less frozen, less an icon, cut off from contemporary psychiatry by a widening gulf. She has been Dr. Fried for so long—even to those who knew her best—that her life already seems more invented than real. Writing may be a construction, but we are still powerfully drawn to nonfiction, a genre defined only by what it is not supposed to be.

5.

Writing a life requires developing a relationship with one's subject, a relationship both transferential and real. Our side of the construction is easy to see; every biographer has some sense of the needs she is satisfying and the struggles they reveal. But what of the subject? She participates in the relationship just as we do, and even subjects who are long dead projectively recreate with us whatever dynamics were central to their psychic lives. Frieda, for example, related to almost all people as if they were patients, so this is who I become. I don't especially mind this—patients were the people she felt closest to, and they were intensely important in shaping her life. But feeling like her patient means I want to see only certain parts of her, and I have to struggle against protecting both of us from things Frieda didn't want to face.

There is more than repetition involved here. A biographer plays a special role in her subject's life, constellating whatever needs were left unfulfilled. Having spent sixty years caring for others, Frieda pulls for it to be her turn. But is it appropriate or possible to try to meet such a need? No matter how we frame an answer to this question, transference gets in the way. We press our subjects to be who we need them to be or remake them as versions of who we're afraid to become. The mutually constituting nature of the process is similar to what goes on in psychoanalysis; it's just that by being less explicit about it, we are more likely to be unconsciously acting out our own needs.[28]

Fantasies of fusion and the idealizations of gender make things worse. We construct our subjects as sisters in struggle and then expect them to show us how to live our lives. But if feminism has taught us anything in the last ten years, it is that gender takes no one form. Biography has to show us the range of possibilities and perversions that etch the surface of women's lives. We say we want this, and yet we still resent having to give up the pleasures of a feminism that simply celebrated these lives. When women we once admired are unmasked as banal, we don't know what to do. If they were really our sisters, they wouldn't betray us; every time they do, we have to decide all over again how to feel. Sometimes it's easier to attack their biographers for making us see.[29]

The feminist movement created an insatiable desire for women who can serve as models, and biography helps to slake this need. Yet imagining alternatives to what is currently possible cannot be based on distortions of what used to be. Every woman's life is a compromise, and we do her an injustice not to state its terms. Knowing this does not make it any less painful to do. I look at Frieda, for example, a forceful woman in so many ways, and I see a person struggling valiantly to unfortify her own mind. Burying her ideas inside the theories of great men, disclaiming even obvious accomplishments, Frieda acted as if independent thought were dangerous and could be allowed into her work only in disguise. I wish she had been bolder, that the loneliness of living too close to the edge hadn't made disapproval feel so much like abandonment to her. It saddens me that Frieda's legendary fearlessness turns out partly to have been defense; at the same time I know that like many women, she is ultimately a more powerful figure when she has room to be real.

Every biography has to find a form that naturally shapes itself to the contours of its subject's life. In this respect, Middlebrook succeeds: by writing exhibitionistically about Sexton's excess, Middlebrook pulls us deeper inside the deprivation that was her life. With someone like Frieda, who is so much more shadowed and harder to see, the temptation is to turn on the torchlights and illumine the scene. It was years before I understood that this was precisely the wrong thing to do. I kept wondering why I was so resistant to calling my work "biography," why I kept giving important roles to other people and writing chapters in which Frieda hardly appears. Finally it dawned on me that it was because this structure fit her; once I could see that, much more of her life became clear.

I might have caught on more quickly had I begun the work while Erich Fromm was still alive. He and Frieda had been briefly married in the 1920s, and they stayed close friends for the rest of their lives. I was puzzled by Fromm's refusal to cooperate with various of Frieda's would-be biographers and by his insistence that she would never have wanted anyone to write her life. Now I understand his worry: A standard biography would force Frieda into a shape clearly not her own.

6.

In *The Journalist and the Murderer,* Janet Malcolm provides an object lesson in the biographical relationship gone awry. The protagonists—neither of whom is especially appealing—happen in this case to be men: Jeffrey MacDonald, a physician convicted of the murder of his wife and two small children, and Joe McGinniss, author of *Fatal Vision,* a best-selling account of MacDonald's trial. McGinniss became close to his subject early on in the research—so close that he was made an official member of the defense team and given access to the most confidential files. McGinniss cried when MacDonald's conviction was read out in court, and after he was imprisoned, McGinniss visited him in jail, wrote him encouraging letters, and acted in every way as if he were on MacDonald's side. But when *Fatal Vision* was finally published, McGinniss made MacDonald out to be a psychopathic killer clearly guilty of his crime. Outraged by the betrayal, MacDonald sued McGinniss for fraud and breach of contract. The trial ended in a hung jury (although MacDonald later got a financial settlement), so it fell to Janet Malcolm to re-try the case where it really counted, in the pages of *The New Yorker* and then in her book.

With McGinniss as her foil, Malcolm accuses her fellow journalists of being "confidence men, preying on people's vanity, ignorance, or loneliness, gaining their trust and betraying them without remorse." It is hardly surprising, she argues, that such "treachery," "deception," and "perfidy" anger some subjects to the point that they sue. By keeping journalists "bound" to them through years of liti-gation, subjects get their revenge.[30] Malcolm acknowledges the irony of seeming to side with a triple murderer against a colleague in the case at hand, but in her view, McGinniss had clearly crossed the line.

To many journalists, however, Malcolm is the real suspect, and her skewering of McGinniss merely a subterfuge designed to throw everyone off the track. There is plausibility to this claim. During the months Malcolm spent documenting what she calls the "crude and gratuitous two-facedness of the MacDonald-McGinniss case,"[31] she was herself the defendant in a lawsuit filed by a former subject of hers, Jeffrey Masson, who claimed Malcolm attributed statements to him in print that he never said. Malcolm vigorously denies the suggestion that her indictment of McGinniss is essentially self-defense. In the glare of her recent trial on libel charges few readers believe this, but it seems to me useful that they are forced to try.[32]

The ambiguity of Malcolm's position derives in part from the fact that, as she herself points out, "the character called 'I' in a work of journalism ... is unlike all the journalist's other characters in that [s]he forms the exception to the rule that nothing may be invented: the 'I' character in journalism is almost pure inven-tion."[33] Nonfiction is a genre with narrative requirements of its own, and the writer is as much a part of the story as anyone else who appears. Her work is gov-erned by certain basic obligations—to represent faithfully the statements of her informants, to seek out a range of sources, to eschew oversimplification and rhe-torical excess. These values need not conflict with what Malcolm calls the right "to function as a writer rather than as a stenographer."[34] Unless there is some space for invention, there is no point in writing at all.

I have used my experience in writing about Frieda Fromm-Reichmann to ground the thinking in this chapter, but this does not mean the writer of that book is identical to the "I" who appears here. We cannot stand outside our own narratives, and what we say about ourselves cannot be taken more literally than what we say about anyone else. Admittedly, this limits our authority as writers, but that doesn't make it any less true.

The point of dragging Malcolm into this discussion is to further tangle its strands. By renouncing the disingenuousness of her profession—and here it makes no difference whether she herself is guilty of the same crimes—Malcolm forces all of us to lay our loyalties on the line. "The moral ambiguity of journal-ism," she writes, "lies not in its texts but in the relationships out of which they arise—relationships that are invariably and inescapably lopsided."[35] Biography is not journalism, but it is mired in the same inequities, and too few of us have squarely confronted this fact or made our allegiances clear.[36]

There is risk in doing this, as attacks on Malcolm ("the fallen woman of jour-nalism") reveal.[37] But I think that as feminists we have to take moral positions on these issues—however unpostmodern this sounds—because failing to distinguish between research and exploitation opens our subjects to abuse. Besides, why should we be less accountable for relationships with women we write about than for other relationships in our lives? If feminism risks its integrity, does it have a right to its own ground?

To see a dim star in a moonlit sky, you have to look away slightly to allow the image to clear. The biographical subject—fuzzy from any vantage point—requires a special kind of concentration to be visible at all. Intimate revelation in itself is not enough; used manipulatively, it can even deceive. Anne Sexton, elevating self-disclosure to an art form, called her style "faking it with the truth."[38] We owe it to our subjects not to do this to them, even if they could not help doing it themselves. And we owe it to each other not to deny our own needs. When I cross the lawn of Frieda's cottage late at night, after too many hours in the cramped basement files, I want to be held in the silent embrace of the mental hospital that was her home for twenty-two years.

Acknowledgments

For their generous, subtle readings of earlier drafts of this paper, I thank Ellen Keniston, Verlyn Klinkenborg, Frances Malino, Catherine Kohler Riessman, Jean Talbot, Elisabeth Young-Bruehl, members of the Women Writing Women's Lives Seminar at the NYU Institute for the Humanities, and the editors and reviewers of this book, especially Abigail Stewart, who can intuit what I need to write long before I can.

Notes

1. Frieda Fromm-Reichmann, M.D. (1889–1957) was a psychiatrist/psychoanalyst best known for her pioneering approach to the treatment of psychotic patients. Trained in Königsberg and Berlin and deeply affected by working with brain-injured soldiers during World War I, Fromm-Reichmann adapted classical psychoanalytic methods for use with even regressed, mute, and violent patients. Emphasizing the basic continuity in experience between therapists and their most seriously disturbed patients, she was critical of mainstream views in psychiatry that characterized psychosis as a brain disease for which only somatic treatments (e.g., shock, lobotomy, medication) were appropriate. Fromm-Reichmann spent the first half of her career working in sanitariums and hospitals throughout Germany; shortly after the Nazi takeover, she fled, arriving eventually at Chestnut Lodge, a small, private psychiatric institution in Rockville, Maryland. She lived and worked at the Lodge for the rest of her life, training a generation of younger psychiatrists in her methods and helping to make the institution one of few places in the world committed to treating psychotic patients with psychoanalytic methods. Most people know Fromm-Reichmann as the "Dr. Fried" of *I never promised you a rose garden* (New York: New American Library, 1964), a slightly fictionalized account of her most successful case, written after her death by the patient, Joanne Greenberg (writing as Hannah Green).

2. Throughout this chapter, I use "biography" and the "biographical relationship" as general terms for any form of writing lives. Psychologists are more likely to call their portraits "case studies" or "profiles," and there are substantive differences between these forms and others; these are beyond the focus of this discussion. Using the term "biography" here as the generic allows me to draw on a rich literature in that field and highlight the links between psychological portraits and other forms of writing lives.

3. This phrase is Gloria C. Erlich's, from her unpublished manuscript, "Whose life is it anyhow?" p. 2.

4. When I use locutions like "fact," "real," and "true," I am not positing objective description. These phrasings are largely ironic, intended to highlight how vivid realist assumptions continue to be. The fact that my own forays into nonrealist territory never fully succeed suggests that the ultimate irony of this chapter is that it stands on the same ground it seeks to erode.

5. *American heritage dictionary of the English language* (ed. W. Morris, Boston: Houghton Mifflin, 1973, p. 47).

6. The response to recent feminist biographies like Deirdre Bair's *Simone de Beauvoir: A biography* (New York: Simon & Schuster, 1990), and Blanche Wiesen Cook's *Eleanor Roosevelt, Volume One, 1884–1933* (New York: Viking, 1992) make this clear. The same feminist movement that embraces postmodern criticism treats biographies as if they existed in a special epistemological space where "Truth" still reigns. Disappointment with Beauvoir, for example, has often been voiced with a kind of shocked surprise, as if Bair had literally lifted the scales from our eyes.

7. For example, the editors of a major new anthology on feminist biography wrote in their introduction that "failing to consider [gender] distorts, if not falsifies, any account of a woman's life. This is true even when a woman is unaware of or inarticulate about the effects of gender on her life. No matter how 'free' of gender-specific conditions a woman may think she is, these conditions nonetheless affect her" (*The challenge of feminist biography: Writing the lives of modern American women,* eds. Sara Alpern, Joyce Antler, Elisabeth Israels Perry, & Ingrid Winther Scobie, Urbana: University of Illinois Press, 1992, p. 7). These assumptions about what is "really" true about women's lives continue to pervade feminist literature despite a decade of essentialist debate. I agree with Camilla Stivers that "we feminists cannot have it both ways; we cannot unmask the oppression inherent in the aim to control nature, we cannot celebrate difference, and at the same time claim that (at least eventually) we will arrive at a standpoint that trumps others because it produces 'real' knowledge while the viewpoints of others do not" (Camilla Stivers, "Reflections on the role of personal narrative in social science," *Signs,* Winter 1993, *18,* p. 424).

8. The rich literature in feminist biography includes surprisingly little about ethical issues. Although many writers mention such issues, Judith Stacey is among the few to have discussed them in detail. Her provocative and disturbing piece suggests that the intimacy of feminist ethnography may make exploitative relationships between biographers and subjects more, rather than less, likely. See Stacey, "Can there be a feminist ethnography?" *Women's Studies International Forum,* 1988, *11,* 21–27. Feminist sociologists and anthropologists seem in general to be more self-reflective than writers in other fields about the ethical ambiguities of writing lives. Among examples, see Barrie Thorne, "Political activist as participant observer: Conflicts of commitment in a study of the draft resistance movement of the 1960's," *Symbolic Interaction,* 1979, *2,* 73–88; Barrie Thorne, " 'You still takin' notes?' Fieldwork and problems of informed consent," *Social Problems,* 1980, *27,* 284–297; Arlene Kaplan Daniels, "Self-deception and self-discovery in fieldwork," *Qualitative Sociology,* 1983, *6,* 195–214; Susan Krieger, "Beyond 'subjectivity': The use of the self in social science," *Qualitative Sociology,* 1985, *8,* 309–324.

9. Janet Malcolm uses this example in *The journalist and the murderer* (New York: Knopf, 1990, p. 152).

10. John Gardner, *The art of fiction* (New York: Vintage Books, 1985, p. 97).

11. Donald P. Spence, *Narrative truth and historical truth: Meaning and interpretation in psychoanalysis* (New York: Norton, 1982, p. 175, emphasis Spence's).

12. Catherine Drinker Bowen, *The writing of biography* (Boston: The Writer, 1950, p. 21).

13. Elisabeth Young-Bruehl, "The writing of biography," in *Mind and the body politic* (New York: Routledge, 1989, pp. 125–137; quotations from pp. 125–126).

14. Leon Edel, *Writing lives* (New York: Norton, 1984, p. 20).

15. Young-Bruehl, "The writing of biography," p. 135.

16. Diane Wood Middlebrook, "Anne Sexton," typed draft (8/90) of a talk presented at Harvard University, Fall 1990.

17. Scott Vickers, untitled review of *Anne Sexton: a biography, Bloomsbury Review,* 1991 (October/November), *11,* 9; Joyce Carol Oates, "Anne Sexton: A heart laid bare," *Washington Post Book World,* 1991 (August 11), *21,* 1, 10; quotations from p. 10.

18. Alicia Ostriker, "Indecent exposure?" *Women's Review of Books,* 1991 (November), *9,* 1, 3–4; quotations from p. 3. After the biography was published, Sexton's sister and nieces published statements insisting that her childhood was more "normal" than Middlebrook made it seem. Ostriker dismissed these claims as "a sad illustration of the rhetoric of denial, which I suspect is also what lies behind the flap about the tapes" (p. 4). According to the acknowledgments in Middlebrook's book (Diane Wood Middlebrook, *Anne Sexton: A biography,* Boston: Houghton Mifflin, 1991, p. 461), Ostriker provided "repeated, extensive commentaries" on the manuscript, which may explain the partisan tone of her review.

19. Joyce Carol Oates is one of few reviewers to take note of this, which I find interesting in its own right. Having posed the question of whether Sexton would have minded being exposed in the ways Middlebrook exposes her, Oates asks, parenthetically, "Yet, who can tell? With age, Sexton might have lost her desire for self-exhibitionism" (Oates, "Anne Sexton," p. 10).

20. Martin T. Orne, M.D., Ph.D., Foreword to Middlebrook, *Anne Sexton,* p. xviii.

21. Such loyalties are equally apparent among physician-reviewers. For example, Donald Goodwin, writing in the *American Journal of Psychiatry,* exonerated Orne's release of the tapes on the twin grounds that "no one doubts that [Sexton] would have approved" and, revealingly, that "Orne didn't receive a penny in compensation" (Donald W. Goodwin, M.D., untitled review of *Anne Sexton: A biography, American Journal of Psychiatry,* 1991, *148,* 1/41–1742; quotations from p. 1742). On this view, Zweizung's actions might be seen as problematic mainly because he charged Sexton for the therapy sessions during which they had sex.

22. Among presumably feminist reviewers, Victoria Radin and Elsa Dixler are the only ones I found who raised such questions explicitly (see Victoria Radin, "Ms Dog for sale," *New Statesman and Society,* 1991 [November 15], *4,* 46–47; Elsa Dixler, untitled column, *The Nation,* 1991 [December 30], *253,* 851–852).

23. Middlebrook, *Anne Sexton,* p. xxii.

24. Ostriker, "Indecent exposure?" p. 3. Grace Schulman, "True confessions," *The Nation,* 1991 (September 23), *253,* 342–344; quotation from p. 342. Schulman also makes the odd argument that since Middlebrook used the tapes "only after years of examining letters, journals of therapy sessions and hospital records," her actions ought not to be criticized (p. 342).

25. Middlebrook, *Anne Sexton,* p. xxii.

26. This suggestion occurs in Middlebrook's 1990 talk at Harvard, but not in her book. The phrase "presumably she had forgotten [the tapes] existed," which appears on p. 7 of

the typed draft of that talk, has been omitted in the published version of that sentence, which appears on p. xxii of the preface to her book.

27. For her own account of these events and of the painful complexities of serving as her mother's literary executor, see Linda Gray Sexton, "A daughter's story: I knew her best," *New York Times Book Review,* August 18, 1991, p. 20.

28. Sidonie Smith, discussing the widespread use of personal narratives in feminist scholarship, emphasizes, as do many others, the "intersubjectivity of the biographical/ethnographical process, the mutually constitutive process of one subject writing about another subject" (Sidonie Smith, "Who's talking/Who's talking back? The subject of personal narrative," *Signs,* 1993 [Winter], *18,* p. 398). By highlighting transferential and projective aspects of this process, I want to emphasize how powerful its unconscious dynamics can be.

29. The storm of incredulity and anger that followed the publication of Bair's biography of Beauvoir illustrates what happens when a feminist biographer reveals her subject's sins. For Bair's reflections on the process, see Deirdre Bair, "Do as she said, not as she did," *New York Times,* November 18, 1990.

30. Malcolm, *Journalist and Murderer,* pp. 3, 5.

31. Malcolm, *Journalist and Murderer,* p. 162.

32. Whether it was written out of self-justification, atonement, or mere spite, *The journalist and the murderer* remains a powerful meditation on precisely those ethical quandaries I am trying to describe. If Malcolm did in fact do to Masson what she accuses McGinniss of having done to MacDonald, this only underlines her warning that knowing about the dangers of exploitation is not in itself protection against abuse.

33. Malcolm, *Journalist and Murderer,* pp. 158–159.

34. Malcolm, *Journalist and Murderer,* p. 156.

35. Malcolm, *Journalist and Murderer,* p. 161.

36. See Note 8 for some exceptions.

37. This is Malcolm's own phrase, *Journalist and Murderer,* p. 152.

38. Middlebrook, typed draft of Harvard talk, p. 28.

PART TWO

Dialogues:
Talking with Women
About Their Lives

Civil rights activists discussing plans, Albany, Georgia, August 1962. *(Photo by Danny Lyon, courtesy of Magnum Photo.)*

5

Against the Odds:
Resiliency in an Adult Survivor
of Childhood Sexual Abuse

FRANCES K. GROSSMAN & ROSLIN P. MOORE

CLINICIANS MARVEL at the resiliency of some survivors of severe childhood sexual abuse, but in fact little is known about such resiliency. In this chapter we use the seven feminist strategies outlined by Abigail Stewart (Chapter 2, this volume) to explore and illuminate four major components of resiliency as exemplified in the experience of one survivor.

In studying women's lives, Stewart urges us to look for what has been left out, to analyze our own role or position as it affects our understanding and the research process, to identify women's agency in the midst of social constraint, to use the concept of gender as an analytic tool, to explore power relationships, to identify and explore the individual's social position, and to avoid the search for a unified self or voice.

We understand resiliency as including four major capacities. First is the capacity of survivors to function well in adult life despite a history of horrendous abuse and often enormous psychological pain, both conscious and unconscious. We also use resiliency to refer to the capacity of some survivors to use the survival skills they developed in childhood to perform unusually well in at least some adult contexts. These survival skills may involve a very high threshold for pain, a capacity to remain still for very long periods of time, and a capacity to work hard and productively without feeling the need to attend to one's own needs or those of others. A third dimension of resiliency is the capacity of some individuals to transform the nature of their relationships, so that they move beyond abusive, dysfunctional ways of relating to others and become able to relate in a relatively open, trusting, and reciprocal manner.[1] Finally, for us resiliency includes the ability of survivors to make terrible childhood experiences into something that has

71

meaning not just for themselves but for others, as Elie Wiesel has done with his writing, or Käthe Kollwitz with her art. We see resiliency as not one single ability but many. As will be seen in the experience of a survivor, these capacities are contextually evoked or inhibited, range on a continuum, and wax and wane with development. Her experience has both given her strength and continued to haunt her.

We interviewed Susan[2] in the context of an ongoing research project. She was the first participant in our study. Her sister had called one of us from out of state after reading about our study of survivors. We said she would have to come to Boston to be in the study, and she said maybe her sister, who lived locally, would do it instead. She then called Susan and suggested she volunteer, which she did. We (FKG and AC) interviewed Susan in the office of one of us on five occasions, for about two hours each, and paid her twenty dollars per visit.

Due to space considerations as well as sensitivity to Susan's current life, we focus here on only one major aspect of the interviews: Susan's relationship to her parents. Throughout, we have struggled to represent faithfully Susan's various perspectives on her history and on the research project, as well as our own feelings toward and thoughts about her story as she told it to us.

Susan's Background

To briefly introduce Susan as we saw her at the beginning of the interviews, and as she undoubtedly appeared to others in her social setting, she was then a forty-six-year-old competent, humorous, busy, upper-middle-class woman. She was the mother of three teenage children whom she loved and who apparently loved her. She was married to an engineer in an essentially traditional, and clearly strained, relationship. Susan had a college degree, and at that time was employed part time in two jobs: She gave private music lessons to children and she was the master teacher on a grant she had helped obtain to teach music to children in a nearby community. She was also very active as a volunteer, particularly providing music for church activities. Her life seemed on the face of it busy and full, with the only obvious sore point her relationship with her husband.

After dealing with preliminaries such as informed consent, we suggested to Susan that we start with her family tree and asked if she had ever done a formal family tree. Susan's opening comment to us was:

> Well, actually, my daughter for her ninth grade family project did a family tree, and my, both sides of the family really are into all the way back to the Mayflower, you know, I mean, it is like it goes and it goes and it goes. And it's this huge thing, so I'm sure we're not going that far.[3]

As her comment suggests, her family can trace its roots far back into history. She is the middle of three daughters. Her father was an only child whose father was a postal worker and whose mother was a Latin scholar with a college degree. Susan said with pride that her grandmother "read books and did crossword puzzles and recited Latin until the day she died."

The women on Susan's mother's side of the family were also very interested in education. Susan's maternal grandmother, who was a teacher for forty years, and her Great-aunt Sally put their eight younger siblings through school after their father died. Great-aunt Sally was one of the first women lawyers in her state, managing to pass the bar exam without the benefit of law school. Great-aunt Sally was "quite involved with helping troubled women." Susan remembers these women well, even though they died when she was young. Sally was tall, skinny, and Victorian, in contrast to Susan's grandmother, who was large, buxom, and earthy. "I think the differences between them has a lot to do with my mother's sexual identity problems. (Giggles.) Because I think there was weird stuff that went on."

"Weird stuff" had gone on in Sally's family for at least several generations. Some of it involved a strange and problematic relationship between her grandmother and her grandmother's sister Sally. The rivalry and (probably) hatred as well as emotional attachment between them appears to have been intense. Susan said that Sally was a proper, Victorian lady, and Susan's grandmother was always trying to shock her, particularly around issues of sexuality. For example, Susan described her grandmother parading about naked at inappropriate times and places just to get a rise out of Sally. (Later, Susan's mother did this with her family, even when her children were adults and visiting with their children.)

Susan's grandmother was physically, emotionally, and sexually abusive to Susan's mother. She apparently used her daughter sexually (Susan did not know precisely what occurred), locked her in the closet for punishment, and beat her with switches. When Susan's mother wet the bed as a twelve-year-old, her mother shamed her by hanging the bedsheets out for everyone to see. (The bed-wetting itself in a girl that old is suggestive of sexual abuse.) For her own convenience, the grandmother kept Susan's mother home from school until the third grade. Susan suspected that her grandmother was jealous of Susan's mother's relationship with her father, since her mother was "very much his toy and the apple of his eye." (Although Susan did not suggest abuse by her grandfather of her mother, we worry about the meaning of being "his toy" and how that was manifest in their relationship.)

Although there are aspects of this story that we do not understand, it is clear to us that something was very amiss in this family. Further, Susan shared this view. With this family history as backdrop, we turn now to Susan's description of her parents and her relationships with them, selecting this material out of more than three hundred pages of transcripts.

We begin with Susan's mother, since she was such a central player in Susan's story. Susan remembered only fragments about her childhood with her mother. She remembered her mother caring deeply about exposing her children to educational and cultural opportunities, but rarely really listening to the children or paying attention to them. She remembered that her mother drank every day, beginning before dinner, and the more she drank, the more driven and the more outrageous she was. And she remembered abuse, as discussed below.

Susan had more extensive adult memories of her mother, who had died several years prior to the interviews. It was very important to Susan that we understand her pride in her mother's accomplishments and commitment to volunteer work for worthy causes. Susan was especially appreciative that her mother often found ways to combine these two areas of interest and produced lovely creations for such institutions as hospitals and libraries. Her mother was also very bright and knowledgeable and extended herself to bring the wider world of art and culture to her children. Finally, Susan was proud that her mother wanted to be a better parent to her own children than her parents had been to her. Susan's mother took "a lot of psychology courses" in hopes of learning how to be a better parent, and Susan honored her for that effort.

Over the course of the five interviews, we also came to learn about the negative aspects of Susan's mother's personality. In the first interview, Susan's description of these more problematic aspects of her mother was, "My mother was colorful and difficult ... and a lot of times she was outrageous." Later, when in the third interview we asked what relationship over her lifetime had been the most damaging to her, she said, "Oh, probably my mother, in a lot of ways." At different times Susan told us about mistreatment by her mother, ranging from insensitivity to physical and sexual abuse.

As an example of insensitivity, Susan described her mother coming to visit when Susan's first child was three months old. Susan had asked her mother not to give the baby water; indeed, not to give her anything, since Susan was nursing her. "And I can see her yet, she was sitting in that rocking chair, trying to give her water." The mother totally disregarded both Susan's wishes and also Susan's authority over the care of her own daughter.

Beyond indifference to others' needs, Susan's mother at times was actively cruel. Susan said, "You would be going along and all of a sudden *zappo,* you know, there was something just off the wall, and feeling that you were never really safe." The hurtful comments sometimes targeted Susan directly. Susan had an abortion when there was a possibility that a wandering IUD had caused a defect in the fetus. Although she felt it was the right thing to do under the circumstances, it caused her intense psychological pain, as well as shame and guilt. Not long after, Susan's mother introduced Susan to one of the mother's friends by saying, "And this is my daughter, this is my middle daughter, Susan, the one who had an abortion."

The aspects of her mother's behavior that Susan was most clear were abusive contained the issues of intrusiveness and preoccupation with sexuality. Susan stated explicitly, "Well, from what I know right now ... I don't think that I was sexually abused by my father, but by my mother, yes. And she sexually abused all of us. And emotionally abused all of us. And ... and I thought it was normal ... "[4] She gave more details. "There were lots of enemas, there was ... she was obsessed with washing and washcloths and washing genitals. ... She also ... didn't leave us space for privacy about for dressing or for, she wanted to see our bodies. She wanted ... to be in the bathroom when we were in the bathroom." (Laugh.)

Susan said she thought these experiences went on from very early until she was about ten. Although a recent letter from Susan's sister describes even more explicit and forceful sexual abuse by the mother as well as the father, Susan does not remember anything else happening to her.

During the interviews, Susan waxed and waned in her clarity about her mother's abusiveness. In her first summary of the mother-daughter adult relationship, Susan spoke about her need to put distance between herself and her mother and how difficult and outrageous her mother was. But then at the beginning of the second interview, she said she had been mulling over the question of how the relationship had been. This time she said, "I think, considering all that we've been through, it was amazingly good, our relationship. We wrote, we called, we were in touch." Thus, throughout the interviews, Susan struggled both to acknowledge and represent the complexity of her mother and father and their legacy to her, as well as to know and honor her own inner truth about her experiences.

Susan's Views of Her Father

Susan voiced several views of her father in the course of the interviews. First, she noted his abuse of her sister. The abuse, revealed in a letter Susan had received from her sister the year before the interviews, was mentioned several times in our meetings. Susan's predominant view of her father was offered within minutes of her naming him as a perpetrator of abuse:

> My father was the ... saint. My father was, walked on water. My father was the whole reason why we're sane. My father was Mr. Community. My father was Man of the Year. My father started the library, um, Friends of the Library. My father was the town alderman. My father, there wasn't a person he met that wasn't his friend. My father got the scholarship for the lady in the drugstore who's going back to nursing school 'cause her husband left her. Ya know, I mean he just would respond to people, and and people loved him and he was wonderful.

Susan frequently spoke about her father in glowing terms, and her conscious memories of him were mostly positive. She described him as singing in the car, going fishing with her and her sisters, being fun to be with. Susan reported that he gave her a sense that she could be anyone she wanted to be or do anything she wanted to do. She mentioned several instances of his support and understanding of her making an important difference in her life. In one such instance, knowing how distressed she was, he gave her a toy giraffe as she was returning to college depressed and suicidal, and in her view, that gift helped keep her alive. Susan told us that her father had understood how badly she felt and that she had felt greatly moved by his gesture, but it seemed to us that she got by on very little.

A third perspective on the father, added to the "abuser" and the "saint" images, was that of a passive witness who failed to protect his children from the mother's abuse, who both sided with the mother and also was verbally abused by her.

> I felt my relationship with him was good and that I could go to him … but that he was never going to protect me from her. …
>
> But where my father is in all that … totally passive, didn't stand up to her, afraid of her I think probably … afraid that she had something on him and she could use it and would. …
>
> He didn't intervene when she was really saying nasty things. And he didn't defend himself when she was saying awful things about him or making fun of him or ridiculing him or putting him down either. … We never really understood why he didn't come to … our defense, when things were clearly out of control.

Susan struggled as an adult to understand and accept what her sister revealed. When Susan learned about her father's abuse of her sister, she began having difficulties in her sexual relationship with her husband. At one point, we asked her what she had in mind when she checked off on a rating sheet that she sometimes cried after she had an orgasm.

> After … I found out about what had happened to my sister, that happened a lot. After this letter, and … the revelation … it was hard, it was so hard to imagine that my father was, did those things, and that my sister was in so much pain and had gone through all that, and that I was right there and didn't even know it, or if I knew it, denied it, or … walked away from it, or who knows. But it sort of hits me at some very visceral level.

We suspect that the information Susan got from her sister's letter stirred up some still-unconscious memories of what her father might have done to Susan as well. But although she was aware of the negative impact of her sister's revelation of abuse by the father on her own sexual relationship with her husband, by and large at the time of the interviews, Susan maintained a positive view of her father, viewing him as the one who helped her keep her sanity in the unsafe and chaotic situation created by her mother.

A Feminist Perspective

Feminists attend carefully to what is not said, including unspoken fears and feelings and also unspoken cultural rules and practices. Feminist theorists would be interested in the fact that Susan's feelings were left out of her descriptions. It appears to us that some knowledge of what happened to her was also left out. We also wonder how her freedom to think clearly about what happened to her in her history was compromised. Susan often expressed amusement at events that seemed to us quite painful. Her story is replete with instances about which we imagine most people would have strong feelings. She managed the positive feelings, but hardly ever expressed anything negative about her mother or her mother's actions. Thus Susan's feelings were left out both at the time these events occurred and later as she told us her story.

Susan was also missing many memories. For example, she remembered very little around the many enemas given to her and her sister by her mother. She wondered, as do we, where she was when her sister was being sexually abused by the father. Like many survivors, she had to leave out of her understanding of her history what she could not remember.

Susan's limited ability to think clearly about her history and her family was illustrated by the fact that she never asked where her father was when she was being abused by her mother. As we noted above, she mentioned his absence to us, but said he was afraid of her mother just as the daughters were. However, that response does not really deal with the issue: Where was he as a responsible parent, and if as seems clear, he was not there to protect and support members of his family, then why was he not held responsible for it at least in Susan's later retelling? What is striking is the extent to which Susan did not consider these questions. We wondered if Susan was following some family rule that forbade those who were abused and exploited from stating explicitly what was being done to them. As feminist theorists would note, there is a great deal left out of Susan's story.

Using Stewart's guidelines, we tried to analyze our various roles and positions as they affected our understanding and process. Susan said that it was helpful to her to tell her story again; she had told it to her therapist previously, but we gave her a chance to process it again. She also liked the idea of contributing to a book, and she said being interviewed triggered new memories. At the end of the last interview, when asked how the process had been for her, she said she was disappointed that the interviewers had not talked more: She had hoped "for there to be more of an exchange than just me talking all the time."

The experience of both interviewers was also mixed. At times we experienced her as likeable and admirable; at other times, she was frustrating to be with or listen to. It was often difficult to get her to respond to particular questions. We sometimes felt ignored and kept at a distance.

The second layer of this interactive process is how our own roles and histories affected our understanding of both the data and the process. On the one hand, we wanted to minimize the power differential and let Susan share in the control of the process, both for the sake of better data and to avoid revictimizing her. Yet when Susan did take control, for example by not answering questions we asked, we felt frustrated.

The stories about her mother, as well as about other members of her family, were often painful to listen to. The discrepancy between our empathic understanding of Susan's pain and her often amused description of events was jarring. At times, however, we did feel connected, as did others of our research group who read the transcripts, and we noted these moments seemed to occur when Susan appeared most connected to her inner feelings. It was as if Susan's own vacillating connection and disconnection from her feelings, and particularly from her pain, resulted in what we experienced as a vacillating connection and disconnection from us. Although it was at times uncomfortable to experience the feelings she evoked in us, we understood that her relative distance from her inner feelings was her way to survive, in the past as well as in the present.

No discussion of silence or power would be complete in a feminist analysis without considering the power relationships between Susan and us, the interviewers, and what effect that relationship might have had on the story Susan told us or the way she told the story. We know that inevitably we were in a position of power over her in this situation. We knew—more or less—what the research was about, we got to ask (most of) the questions. We were the experts with the societally conferred trappings of position. Susan had power in this situation, but it was much less direct. She had the power to tell or not to tell, to be more or less responsive to our questions.

Returning to Stewart's points, another layer for a feminist perspective in Susan's story derives from her understanding of gender. How did Susan view being female, how did she present the males in her story? It is hard to comment on these without also looking at another of Stewart's variables, that is, how gender affects power relationships. Gender and power are very interconnected in Susan's story.

Her mother, as far as we know, was not financially independent, nor was she raised to be emotionally independent. She had herself been abused as a child, which could have left a residue of a felt sense of powerlessness as it has in others. In Susan's story, the question of men's power is complex and variable. Even her father, "the saint," who she said saved her sanity, in Susan's view, was afraid of her mother. At the time we interviewed Susan, she was struggling to integrate the additional information that he sexually abused her sister.

The consequences of Susan's lack of understanding of gender and power are worrisome to us. At the time of the interviews, she appeared to have trouble seeing how her own relative powerlessness as a female influenced her later life. We believe she continued to be vulnerable in her relationships with men. Given the generations of women in her family that have abused their children, we worry that she might neglect or abuse her own despite her fervent efforts not to, perhaps not even seeing what she did.

Another of Stewart's points, certainly not unrelated to power, is the need to focus on women's agency, or ability to act, despite their relative powerlessness. Agency is closely related to resiliency, and we return to this issue later when we discuss Susan's resiliency.

Finally, Stewart enjoins us to avoid the search for the unified self or voice. There were many voices in Susan's story, some silent that we can only guess about, for example, the child's voice of anger and helplessness. Others were quite audible. For example, there was the dutiful daughter who looked nice, the young wife who insisted on distance from the mother, the abused-child-become-mother who worried about victimizing her own children. There was a self that believed her sister when the sister described abuse by their father, and also another side of Susan that avoided and sometimes could not hold on to that truth. Thus Susan, like most survivors (and probably like all of us), spoke in many voices, and some of the voices were opposed to one another. Our task, then, is to provide a framework for understanding Susan without denying the importance and reality of her many voices or her inner confusion and fragmentation.

The Perspective of Resiliency

Turning back to the four dimensions of resiliency in our understanding, Susan clearly was resilient in her ability to function in her life despite her history of abuse. Although much material had to be left out of this discussion of Susan's relationships with her parents, throughout the interviews we were impressed with her amazing ability to overcome certain kinds of obstacles. With regard to the second aspect of resiliency we described—the sometimes unusual abilities of survivors, such as indifference to pain or the ability to persist despite extreme fatigue—Susan showed a capacity to persist in the face of difficulty and even opposition and a capacity to do very hard work that seem to us to have derived from her history.

We want to explore the third component, the capacity to transform the quality of intimate relationships from abusive ones to positive reciprocal connections, at greater length. This aspect of resiliency seems akin to an aspect of agency, as Stewart uses the term (see Chapter 2, this volume). We see Susan as having begun this process, but with much work still to do. Using the material describing her relationship with her mother, we here trace the ways Susan dealt with and began to transform the abusive aspects of that relationship. In childhood, perhaps the major way Susan attempted to cope with the abuse that was occurring was to repress it, or failing that, to minimize it. Although her own maturation, aided by her psychotherapy, had helped her to reclaim more of her own reality, at the time of our interview she continued to struggle with how much she could afford to acknowledge her anger at her parents and her pain at their betrayal. She frequently emphasized to us the value of emphasizing the positive, which she had also taught her children to do. She told us, "I guess phrasing it in the positive sometimes comes across as being a little Pollyanna, but with all the layers of pain underneath it all, if anybody thinks it's Pollyanna, they've missed the point, you know, because there's so many layers of pain."

Yet Susan not only focused on the positive, she continued to have difficulty holding on to the painful aspects of the truth she knew about her mother. In the third interview, after approximately five hours of conversation, Susan offhandedly mentioned her mother's drinking. Her mother drank daily around dinnertime, which led to outrageous verbal attacks on everybody at dinner. Susan was aware that she had forgotten to tell us about her mother's drinking, although it was a central aspect of her family life.

When we asked Susan how upsetting these experiences with her mother had been for her, she said, "I guess after a while you sort of numb yourself to some of it." When she had been away and then would see her mother for a visit, "it would come as a surprise that she would say things or do things that just didn't fit in the way I thought mothers ought to be."

Susan was quite aware of her use of humor as a way of surviving. "I think that saves a lot of situations. ... I mean, I think that way, I was thinking about why I'm not in an insane asylum somewhere." At another point she said, "it just puts everything in perspective."

In young adulthood, according to Susan, she knew she "had to put some distance between us." In the early days of her marriage, when she and her husband were thinking of relocating, Susan was clear that an hour's car drive separation was not sufficient. "And I said it's not far enough and our marriage won't survive—it just won't work." Four hours' distance felt safer.

As we have described, there were a number of incidents in which Susan felt her mother violated her boundaries and Susan felt helpless to intervene. She mostly did not feel able to protect her own children from her mother's cruelty, although she worried a great deal about the effect on her children. When we inquired, "Did you ever consider saying that your mother could not have contact with your children?" she said no, she had not. She was still too closely caught in the family framework of how she was supposed to see the world and respond to it to even consider taking that step.

Although Susan was at times passively able to resist her mother's control and demands, the first instance in which she actually said no involved her sister's elopement and her mother's continuing complaints about this event. Susan says it was like pushing the button on a tape recorder and the complaints would all come out. "There was no interrupting the tape. You had to get the whole thing. And I turned to her at one point, sitting at the dining room table, and I said, 'Mother, I know you're disappointed. I know you're not happy about this. I don't want to hear about it anymore.' " The immediate consequence of Susan's saying no to her mother was that her mother threw a phone book at her—a Manhattan phone book. "Missed. Stormed out. (Laugh.) Slammed the door. And didn't speak to me for three months. (Giggle.) Didn't invite me for Thanksgiving. I was not invited for Thanksgiving. But it was worth it." We see this incident as representing Susan's beginning awareness that it was important to her to give voice to her own feelings and needs, important enough to risk a rift with her mother, who was a central figure of attachment for her.

As Susan grew older and clearer about her own development, even before her mother's death, she began to be able to represent her own feelings in the face of her mother's disregard. One notable occasion was a boat trip on which Susan's mother mocked Susan in front of strangers by imitating the noises she had made as a child when she practiced the violin. The situation of Susan's being embarrassed by her mother was certainly common. What was not common was Susan's response this time, which was to say, "Mother, when you say things like that, it hurts me." We see this as a big step for Susan, who had had to practice it a number of times with her therapist before being able to say it.

As regards the fourth dimension of our understanding of resiliency, or using the experience of abuse in a way that has meaning for other people, we saw Susan struggling to do this in several ways. We understand her participation in the research project as a move in that direction. She also began writing poetry, which seems to us an important effort to make use of her pain in ways that have meaning for other people.

In conclusion, we understand Susan to illustrate the four dimensions of our definition of resiliency. She had the capacity to function well—she was employed and married, with children who were doing okay in the world. She had skills probably developed as a way of surviving an abusive childhood, especially the ability to perform sustained hard work. She was beginning to learn how to transform dysfunctional ways of relating to more whole, reciprocal connections. And she was exploring ways she might be able to use her painful and difficult history in a way that would have meaning for other people in the world.

Two of us met with Susan to show her a draft of this chapter and ask for her comments. We worried what the experience would be for her, whether it would be hurtful, and how it would feel to us if she experienced it in that way. It turned out to be a powerfully affirming meeting for all of us. Although she wasn't in therapy at the time, Susan clearly had continued to grow and change, justifying our sometimes tentative belief in her resiliency. Second, she was fascinated by our description of her. She was caught most strongly by our perception that she had held us at a distance at times, that she didn't let us be close. She first said she didn't feel close to us because we didn't tell her anything about ourselves. We pointed out that we had been prepared to tell her more and reminded her that we had offered to answer questions, but she didn't ask. She responded, "Oh really! I would have loved to have known more, but I thought that as professionals, I just thought you wouldn't." (At that point, she did ask us each a personal question, which we answered.) Later she said she uses her humorous style, which we found distancing, to protect the listener. "You might be hurt by my stories, even more than I am. I can deal with this, I'm strong, but ... so I'm going to be a little bit funny and then you can sort of chuckle." We pointed out that such a maneuver might have been essential in her family, and indeed might continue be useful with some people. One consequence of her history had been to make it difficult for her to check out her current context and see if those old maneuvers were indeed still necessary. For us, the humor felt disconcerting and distancing despite what she intended.

Finally, Susan was clear that she had benefited from the experience of the study. "See, I'm learning a lot about myself through this and that's an important part of it." We also felt we had learned from the interviews with Susan, both about doing this research and about ourselves in the research context.

Acknowledgments

A number of individuals have participated in the research and writing of this chapter. The Boston University Resiliency Project is a group that has met for about three years, designing and carrying out the project of which this interview represents a part. In addition to the authors, individuals who have participated in that group are Cheryl Baresi, Ruth Bell, Antonia Bookbinder, Alexandra Cook, Kate Culhane, Karen Curto, Colleen Gregory, Judith Jordan, Selin Kepkep, Jodi Kilgannon, Judy Lam, Rhea Paniesen, Deborah Ruben, Etay Shilony, Brad Stolback, and Anne Watkins. For further information about the larger project, contact Frances K. Grossman at Boston University, Department of Psychology, 64 Cummington Street, Boston, MA 02215.

Notes

1. We are indebted to Judith Jordan for making us aware of the centrality of this dimension of resiliency in survivors.

2. Names and identifying information have been changed to protect her privacy.

3. We have selected a middle level of detail in transcription, leaving in the more striking pauses and backtracking, but not attempting to record every speech disruption.

4. It's necessary to add that members of the research group are not confident that Susan was not abused by her father.

6

A Word and a Kindness:
The Journey of a Black
Social Worker

ROSARIO CEBALLO

MARY, MY FRIEND'S GREAT-AUNT, is an elderly African-American woman I first met at a college graduation in 1986. I was taking pictures of a rally for South African divestment when Mary was pointed out to me. I was struck by the ease with which she settled in among the crowd of college students. Most of the other parents and family members of graduating students watched the event from a safe, neutral distance. But Mary joined the rally, chanting with determination and raising her fist to the air. I was immediately drawn by the spark for life I saw in her.

In the years that followed, I had several opportunities to get to know Mary better. I was delighted when she allowed me to do an oral history of her life for my graduate school class on the psychology of women. I interviewed Mary over a span of three days during winter 1992, when she was seventy-six. We talked in the living room of her home in Oxford, North Carolina, and she allowed me to tape-record most of our conversations. I have sought Mary's approval on everything I have written about her life, and she has therefore read and commented on all drafts of this chapter.

Mary was the youngest of nine children born in the Jim Crow South in 1915. She was only three years old when she experienced the traumatic loss of her mother, who died of TB. Three of Mary's older siblings also died around this time, and as a result, Mary grew up as the only female child in a family with her father and five older brothers. Mary's father, William, remained committed to raising all of his children himself with only periodic help from relatives. Although he initially hired people to look after the children, he later relied on his sons to look after Mary. The result, as Mary remembered, is that she was often left alone for much of the day. "They [her brothers] had to take care of me. But I remember that they would go off during the day and leave me in the house by myself. And they wouldn't come back until it was time for Dad to get home. Then they'd show up. I don't think I ever told on them."

Mary described her father as a quiet, undemonstrative, distant man, somewhat inept at managing the household of children he had been left with. Although he did not receive a formal grammar school education, he was taught enough in a neighbor's home to pass the entrance exam to Shaw University in Raleigh, North Carolina. After college, he "read law," apprenticing with a white lawyer for seven years. Upon passing the bar, William moved his family from Oxford to Durham, North Carolina, where Mary was born. As a young child, Mary spent several summers back in Oxford, where she stayed with relatives from both her father's and her mother's family. In 1926 when Mary was ten years old, William moved the family to Washington, D.C. Mary then lived in other people's homes or in apartments where she, her father, and an older brother shared one rented room. "You see, we lived in rooms. We never established a home or anything. We had a room in somebody's house. That was the way we grew up."

While in the eleventh grade, Mary developed rheumatic fever, and her education was consequently interrupted by a series of hospitalizations. As a complication of this early illness, Mary was afflicted by a reactive arthritis, a form of ankylosing spondylitis, in her right hip. This condition was treated surgically, but Mary has slightly dragged one foot ever since. Despite these medical difficulties, Mary graduated on schedule with her high school class in 1934. She spent the next four years caring for the house and children of her oldest brother, Bob, whose first wife had passed away. She cooked, cleaned, did the laundry, and provided child care. Mary remembers those Depression years as particularly bleak and dreary. Her experiences during those years likely influenced the steadfast determination with which she later sought her independence. At age twenty-three, Mary gathered the determination and financial resources to enroll in Howard University. By 1948, she had received a master's degree from the Smith College School for Social Work and launched a successful career in the field of social work.

Mary's life story is marked by an ongoing struggle to cope with personal misfortunes and institutionalized systems of racism and sexism. In this chapter, I will explore how Mary's sense of identity emerged from interwoven layers of membership in different social groups and incorporated her transition in social class status. I will underscore Mary's use of relationships and surrogate family systems as a source of resilience. Finally, I will outline and examine the development of Mary's awareness of systems of racial oppression, beginning with her virtual lack of contact with white people as a child, extending to her pioneering efforts as the only black social worker in all-white social service agencies, and culminating with her participation in the civil rights movement as a fifty-one-year-old, single black woman. I will also address how Mary's involvement in the struggle for civil rights influenced her reaction to the women's movement.

Identity: Race, Class, and Gender

Black feminist scholars have recently emphasized the need to explore interconnections between gender, race, and social class when investigating black women's
identities and experiences with oppression. In addressing Mary's identity, I therefore wish to heed Patricia Hill Collins's (1990) advice of not starting "with gender
and then adding in other variables such as age, sexual orientation, race, social
class, and religion, [but rather thinking] of these systems as part of an interlocking matrix of relationships" (p. 20). Indeed, as an adolescent Mary struggled with
understanding just this kind of complicated matrix in her own identity.

Mary straddled the painful and complicated boundary of simultaneously belonging to an educationally privileged group of blacks while living under conditions of economic hardship. Academic achievement was a greatly esteemed and
prominent value in Mary's family, and Mary excelled in all of her scholastic pursuits. Yet despite her father's legal career, Mary's family always lived under conditions of economic hardship. "It was a very, very peculiar kind of situation," Mary
explained. "My dad, he was a good lawyer ... but he never made money." William
never became a prominent, financially well established attorney, in part because
of his inability to participate in the social networks of the black middle class. He
was a loner who did not care for the social obligations that accompany business
life. For example, he attended church regularly, but never used the opportunities
offered by the church's social network to foster a business clientele.

The tenuous interconnections between Mary's membership in different social
groups marked several painful life experiences. For instance, Mary described the
incompatibility of her educational privilege and lower socioeconomic status
when she lived in the status-conscious black community of Washington, D.C. She
described herself as a "little ragged kid who never had any decent anything. And
here I sat in this school with these fancy D.C. folks' kids. When I had to go into
another grade, you had to say what your daddy did. And I had to put on this thing
that my daddy was a lawyer, and here I was looking like a Rag-a-muffin."

Moreover, the socially segregated climate of the black community in Washington, D.C., was not solely based on economic and occupational status. Discrimination pervaded all institutions, including the school system, where it was based on
personal attributes such as hair type and skin color. Mary recalled a particularly
illustrative school experience with great detail.

> I remember one time, I sat next to Charlotte. Her father was a doctor. She was very
> pretty, and very fair, and so on. She and I got along fine. A new teacher came and the
> first thing she did was rearrange the class and put all of the kids, the socialites, in
> front. And all of us, the rest of us had to go in the back. This is absolutely true, I am
> not lying. This was based on color and clout. Color and status. ... Yes, I was the
> blackest, and the poorest [in that class that went on to Dunbar high school].

Thus, Mary's sense of identity developed in recognition of her complex membership in different social categories of race, gender, and social class. Her sense of

herself as an adolescent incorporated the ambiguous nature of her family's social class—a father who worked as a lawyer, but maintained a working-class lifestyle, her privileged academic orientation, her experiences as the only female child in a family of men, and the "blackness" of her hair and skin color. By the same token, Mary experienced the interlocking force of several oppressive systems. She simultaneously encountered classism due to her family's limited resources, racism based on the color of her skin, and sexism due to her gender. Mary's burden in navigating race-, class-, and gender-based oppressions was not like carrying separate and distinct weights, for as Elizabeth Spelman (1988) explained, "How one form of oppression is experienced is influenced by and influences how another form is experienced" (p. 123). It becomes clear then that the form of discrimination Mary experienced in school was linked to her gender (by the feminine attributes valued in black girls) as well as her lower socioeconomic standing.

Relationships and Families

A significant source of Mary's resilient functioning lies in her ability to foster and then make use of relationships and surrogate family systems. Her father was unable to create a cohesive family unit following his wife's death, and Mary quickly learned that she would have to rely on a foundation of relationships with people outside of her immediate family to gain strength and nurturance. Mary's relational coping strategy is consistent with the psychological literature on "resilient children" who function adaptively in the face of severe and enduring strain. Stable relationships with adults buffer these children from a host of adverse life circumstances (Rutter, 1979; Werner and Smith, 1982).

Mary sought and found early positive role models among the extended family she visited in Oxford, North Carolina, during her childhood summers. For example, she frequently found a way of escaping the church revivals, attended mostly by the older people in the community, and visiting with the younger relatives, her maternal aunts. These aunts were young black teachers in their teens and early twenties who became important role models for Mary. She recalled that during her last summer in Oxford, "Sally was nineteen. That [teaching] was her first job, and I thought that was so wonderful, that she was going to be a teacher at nineteen! ... Lena, Beecher, and Sally. They were all teachers."

Further, Mary was able to use a network of relationships to facilitate her own emotional growth and introspection during a difficult time in her life. After graduating from high school, she was hospitalized again for several long periods. During these hospitalizations, she was in a body cast for several months at a time. She believes the time spent in the hospital cured her of her "dependency needs." "I knew all of the residents," she explained, "and everybody in the hospital knew me by then. I got a lot of attention, a lot of strokes. ... I think I cured my dependency problem. ... I mean I had all these needs that hadn't really been met. All the feelings I had about not being well taken care of somehow were satisfied during this period."

Although the story of Mary's unconventional route to college is poignantly heartwarming, it also illustrates how her life was powerfully shaped by the ties she established with others and how her professional beliefs incorporated an understanding of the primary role relationships may occupy in one's life.

> Let me tell you about how I happened to go to school. I came down here [Oxford, North Carolina] that summer, and Beecher [a maternal aunt] always somehow, was kind of special. I was special to her. She said to me, "We should have kept you after your mother died. If we had kept you, you would be finishing college this year." And it was true. If I'd stayed, I would have gone to college. So I went back to Washington, I told my brother, Buster, that I wanted to go to school. And he said, "okay," and he said that "it was way late, but I'll help you." And I went to Howard and applied, and they accepted me, and he paid my tuition all through. He was working at the post office. He sent me through school.

I said, "And that all came about …" and Mary finished, "because of what Beecher said. And you never know. This is one of the things in the helping profession. This is one of the things I've learned. You never know the effect you're going to have on people. You never know. Just a word, or a kindness, or something can mean a lot to a person in life. The whole pattern of my life was set from just this one comment that she made."

Mary found a significant mentor and role model at Howard University, where she majored in sociology. E. Franklin Frazier chaired the Department of Sociology at that time, and Mary, who proved herself to be conscientious and dedicated, became one of his favorite students. The importance of familial ties and relationships had a profound influence on the professional goals Mary pursued after Howard. During an earlier hospitalization, Mary became friends with Catherine, her doctor's daughter. Catherine was a young black woman who was finishing her studies at the New York School of Social Work. Mary's motivation to become a social worker evolved out of this friendship. Upon graduating from college in 1943, she enrolled in Howard's two-year certificate program in social work and did her first clinical placement in a family agency. In view of her search and desire for supportive family connections, "it seems natural in terms of working, you work in a family agency. … The first job I had was in a family agency. Basically, my whole professional experience was with families."

Mary identifies her search for close, familial relationships as a salient theme resonating throughout her life story. "Throughout all of this, lack of family, lack of stability, I gravitate to situations where I'm in a family." In 1945 there was a small group of black professionals living in Milwaukee, Wisconsin, where Mary accepted her first job. This small professional group provided a supportive network for incoming members like Mary. Mary lived with one of these professional black families for ten years until she moved to accept a prominent position in a Philadelphia agency. To this day, they remain a surrogate family for her.

This family cushioned Mary's transition in social class status. Her socioeconomic position changed greatly as she became a securely established member of the black professional class in Milwaukee. Like her father, Mary spurned a socially elite lifestyle. However, her new family modeled positive attributes among middle-class blacks that Mary could accept. "This black group that I was in was not based just on social things. It was based on professional things, civic responsibility, … That, I could accept."

Developing Racial Awareness

As Mary found ways to overcome the impediments that life placed before her, her awareness regarding systems of racial oppression developed in a remarkable fashion. Having come of age in the Jim Crow South, Mary's childhood was virtually devoid of any contact with white people. Black families who were financially more secure, like Mary's, could avoid interacting with whites to a great extent. Her parent's relatives owned their own land in the rural county surrounding Oxford, North Carolina. Because their primary source of income was farming, they did not have to work closely with white people in Oxford's city proper. The adults would take vegetables and butter to Oxford to sell to white people, but "that's the only contact they had [with them]. … They didn't work for them. They weren't maids or cooks for them." The amount of contact Mary had with white people was also influenced by her gender. For example, Mary's brother, William, Jr., was allowed to earn money by delivering newspapers to the white students at Duke University in Durham, North Carolina. In these instances, her family's financial circumstances and her gender shielded Mary from experiencing the subservient roles blacks occupied in their interactions with whites.

Not only did Mary have few physical interactions with white people, but the extent to which white people entered her daily thoughts and consciousness was negligible. I asked Mary, "What did you think about white people? What were you told about white people? How did your father feel about white people?" Mary explained, "He [her father] didn't talk about them. Certainly didn't talk about the racial part of it. You know, it was very interesting in the South. Because you just avoided everything. Your parents, they didn't tell you anything. They didn't talk about it." It was not until Mary was nine years old and spent a year in Boston living with her older brother George and his wife, Isabella, that she interacted with white children on a regular basis. In Boston she played and went to school with both black and white children.

As a child, Mary's understanding of racism did not emerge from a context of white-black relationships, but rather from experiences with the internalized racism exhibited by black people among themselves. Mary experienced discrimination in school at the hands of her black teachers who valued wealthy, well-dressed, light-skinned black children above the rest. When I asked Mary what she thought about the discrimination she had experienced at school, she replied, "We thought that the teachers were prejudiced. You just accepted it. It was just the way things are. I don't remember having really strong feelings about it one way or another. … I don't think I thought anything, except that it wasn't right. … That's just the way it was done. It wasn't anything you questioned." At this point, Mary did not have the life experiences to understand the hideous connections between society's racism and the ways in which black people came to despise their own culture. Mary resigned herself to accepting discrimination as part of the way the world worked.

Through her late twenties, Mary's awareness of racism continued to lie dormant. With a social work certificate in hand, she accepted her first job at a family agency that sought a black social worker to work with its black clientele. Mary remained the agency's only black social worker for several years. Although as a therapist, Mary saw only black clients, the clients of the white therapists were always white. Despite this practice, the social work profession in general avoided cultural issues in theoretical philosophy and clinical practice. The prevailing attitudes seemed to coalesce around a doctrine of unadulterated color blindness.

Mary learned to embrace this color-blind philosophy that asserted that race and culture do not enter into the clinical equation. At the time, she did not think that cultural factors influenced her professional work. She remembered not believing that race and culture "made any difference at all." After acquiring a master's degree in social work, Mary returned to work at the same Milwaukee agency where the policy of assigning therapists to clients of the same race had been abolished. Mary wondered how white clients would respond to working with a black therapist, but she did not discuss her concerns with anyone. "I think what happened in our day is that we didn't handle it," she explained. "It was really always covert. It was never really out in the open and on the table, unless some client came in and said, 'I will not work with a_____,' and then changes had to be made. But if it ever happened, then that was the only time it was discussed."

The denial of the presence and importance of racial issues applied not only to her views about clinical practice but also to her conceptualization of society at large.

> I think we [black women] kidded ourselves. I think we sort of bought into this total picture, treated ourselves as if we were totally like the white community, and that's absolutely not true. ... Maybe it was not until the agitation from the civil rights [movement], where we began to take a look. You really had been kidding yourself. It's different. Society is different. Blacks have had a different experience. The black experience is different. ... You really do live in a segregated society. No matter what you think, how you change your hair, where you live, how much money you make, as far as you go.

The Civil Rights Movement

Mary's participation in the civil rights movement marks a dramatic and striking departure from her earlier ideas about the role of race and culture in our society. A new and deeper awareness coupled with a national movement of protest sparked Mary's desire to resist racial oppression. Her involvement in the movement sprang from a well of rising and unsuppressible anger.

The whole anger, the whole thing just sort of caved in at me. … As far as my working relationships, they were good, and I didn't have serious problems. But suddenly, socially, the many feelings that I had harbored throughout my life about being black and how I was treated and how blacks were treated just sort of caved in on me. And I just had to get out and get involved.

The events that created a movement in Selma, Alabama, drew Mary back to the South to join the struggle for civil rights. Alabama's proportion of blacks on the voter registration rolls was one of the lowest in the nation. Student Non-Violent Coordinating Committee (SNCC) workers in Alabama made voter registration a top priority in 1963, and the Southern Christian Leadership Conference (SCLC) began a similar campaign in 1965. In Selma, Sheriff Jim Clark's repeated use of force against blacks attempting to register received national media coverage. Coverage of the obstacles faced by blacks trying to vote continued with Martin Luther King, Jr.'s arrest, a march to the courthouse by over one hundred black school teachers, and the arrest of over a thousand people, including five hundred protesting school children (Carson, 1981; Garrow, 1978; Williams, 1987).

The shooting of Jimmie Lee Jackson, a twenty-six-year-old black man, during a nighttime march stimulated renewed protest and SCLC's announcement of a fifty-mile march across the Edmund Pettus Bridge in Selma, along Route 80 to the Montgomery capitol. On Sunday, March 7, 1965, Alabama state troopers met 2000 marchers on the Edmund Pettus Bridge. Tear gas was fired onto the marchers as policemen on horseback charged into the crowds. The day was dubbed "Bloody Sunday." King announced that the march would begin again as planned two days later. Hundreds of people from all over the country went to Selma for this march (Carson, 1981; Garrow, 1978; Williams, 1987).

Following King's announcement of another march attempt, Mary spontaneously bought a plane ticket to Selma. "I really called the airport, got a reservation, and just took off without too much thought about anything. I just wanted to be on that bridge, across the bridge, that was important to me." The rage that inspired Mary to buy a plane ticket on the spur of the moment marked the beginning of her activities in the civil rights movement. Mary's heightened awareness of her anger at racial injustice released a sense of rage and urgency and a strenuous desire to change society. "I had all these feelings in me, and I never recognized them or had not permitted myself to recognize them. And suddenly I'm angry … [and have] the anger and the energy to begin to do something about it, to fight, and to declare some of it." The Justice Department strongly urged King to call off the march. But before turning the march around, King led 1500 people across the bridge to face a line of state troopers on March 9, 1965. After the "Turnaround Tuesday" march, Mary returned to work, but she was not deterred by King's decision to abort that march. (It was not until March 21, 1965, that thousands of people set out on the march that would ultimately reach the Montgomery capitol with 25,000 people as Congress debated the Voting Rights Act.)

The following summer, Mary decided to go on a trip to Jackson, Mississippi, sponsored by a group called "Wednesdays in Mississippi," a subgroup of the National Council of Negro Women established in 1964 (Fitzgerald, 1985). This group consisted of black and white women who worked closely with SNCC's freedom schools, held conferences to discuss the problems blacks were facing in Mississippi, and developed programs to address these concerns. Afterward, Mary decided to join SCLC and spend the rest of her summer vacation participating in civil rights activities in the South. "The idea was to spend the whole vacation in the South. I don't know what I thought I was doing. I guess I thought I was being helpful, but I think that basically it was just an expression of my own anger at all of it."

During her vacation, Mary worked in Jackson, Mississippi; Atlanta, Georgia; Greensboro, Eutaw, Selma, and Birmingham, Alabama. Her memories about this time eagerly rushed forward, her words spilling over each other with enthusiasm. She remembered staying in King's house and being "the only old person there. The rest of them were young people. There were kids from all over the country in this house." She was stunned and outraged by the severity of the poverty she saw among the blacks whom she encouraged to vote and attend church rallies. She also recalled several frightening encounters with state troopers in which she knew her life was in danger.

Many black women have described a process of self-affirmation as a result of their involvement in the civil rights movement. For example, Bernice Reagon explained it as having "a sense of power, in a place where you didn't feel you had any power … a sense of confronting things that terrified you … [leading to] a change in my concept of myself and how I stood" (Cluster, 1979, p. 29). Similarly, Mary's experiences in the movement gave her insight into the strength and force of her own potential and abilities as a black woman. In this context, she explained her determination in the midst of extreme danger. "At this point I was so angry that I didn't care. I was scared that I might get killed, but I was determined. … In other words, you gotta fight it. Unless you get there and fight it, you gotta be willing to die or else nothing will ever happen. That was the way I was feeling." Standing for a principle that she believed in completely and resolutely and accepting the consequences of her actions yielded a powerfully self-affirming and liberating force on Mary's sense of identity.

Mary's desire and expectations for social change were also fulfilled during this time. "This was change," she explained. "This was definitely change. When blacks were staying in the [white] motel in Jackson, Mississippi, and when blacks were registered, and when I was standing on the sidelines seeing voters register in a small, rural community of Alabama, that was change!" Mary's sense of herself and of society was transformed by the movement's quest to end the legacy of slavery, segregation, and other racial injustices. She is immensely proud of having played an active role at a time and a place where history was made.

Mary's emerging awareness of her anger and her participation in the struggle for civil rights may appear somewhat sudden, but they are understandable if viewed in the larger context of the time. Mary had previously accepted society's systems of institutionalized racism because there were no practical alternatives, not because she found these systems and their values to be morally justifiable. The civil rights movement opened a door for the possibility of concrete change. It provided an alternative, a vehicle for channeling the accumulation of lifelong anger and the hope that change could happen. Belief in the possibility of change tipped the odds in favor of participation and action. Moreover, the impetus to act was reinforced by the belief that implementing change could not be left up to the federal courts. Black people had to assert control over their own destiny and unequivocally demand their basic human rights. The key issue then, as Mary sees it, is captured in a phrase from a song that she often heard during the movement: "The only thing that we did wrong was to let this go on so long."

It seems surprising that Mary felt her activities in the civil rights movement did not affect her professional work in a family agency. She identified her involvement in the movement as being of an extremely personal nature that did not permeate other areas of her life and career. "It was really personal. It didn't have to do with my working experience." When she returned to Philadelphia, it was "business as usual." Nothing had changed "in terms of my job and profession." She did not even share her experiences with co-workers. Stewart and Healy (1989) posited that the impact of historical events on women's individual development is dependent upon a woman's age and life stage. Perhaps Mary's experiences in the civil rights movement were not immediately integrated into her professional work because they occurred when Mary was an older adult with firmly established life patterns and commitments.

Feminism and the Women's Movement

I wondered if Mary's heightened awareness of racial oppression influenced her reaction to the women's movement. In contrast to her involvement with the civil rights movement, Mary's sense of connection to the women's movement is very faint. She acknowledged the similarities between the women's movement and the goals of blacks during the civil rights movement, but personally her heart was only drawn to one of these agendas. Her identification with the struggle of black people runs deeper than her association with the experiences of women as a whole.

Feminist scholars have offered a multitude of theories to explain black women's limited involvement in the women's movement. Hooks (1981) argued that as a result of their participation in the civil rights movement, black women came to value "race as the only relevant label of identification" (p. 1). She went on to explain, "When the women's movement raised the issue of sexist oppression, we argued that sexism was insignificant in light of the harsher, more brutal reality of racism. We were afraid to acknowledge that sexism could be just as oppressive as racism. We clung to the hope that liberation from racial oppression would be all that was necessary for us to be free" (p. 1). Historical accounts have also documented that black female leaders of the civil rights movement were generally united in their belief that sexism was of secondary importance to the discrimination and oppression faced by blacks (Giddings, 1984; Standley, 1990).

Indeed, black women had many reasons to be suspicious of the women's movement, which quickly concentrated on the concerns of white, middle-class women. However, as Giddings (1984) remarked, "Not only were the problems of the White suburban housewife (who may have had black domestic help) irrelevant to black women, they were also alien to them" (p. 299). This situation was aggravated by the fact that white women continued to compare their status within society to that of blacks. In addition, black women in the civil rights movement did not experience the same degree and form of sexism that white women did. Black women were not, for example, entirely shut out of leadership circles, as the experiences of women like Diane Nash, Ruby Doris [Smith] Robinson, and Ella Baker attest (Giddings, 1984). Black women were also suspicious of the women's movement because its rise coincided with the decline of the civil rights movement, and black women were keenly aware of the fact that it was not only white men but also white women who perpetuate racism (Giddings, 1984; Fitzgerald, 1985). Several explanations may therefore account for the tenuousness of Mary's connections to the women's movement.

Although it is true that Mary's sense of connection to the women's movement remains weak, her endorsement of feminism is steadfast. To claim that black women felt no ties to women's rights and other issues raised in the women's movement is far too simplistic, especially following their experiences in the civil rights movement. Black women were consistently in the forefront of the civil rights struggle; they carried the momentum and provided the stamina for the movement's progress. Black women did not "reject feminism itself but only the bourgeois white feminism that was at the heart of the women's movement" (Fitzgerald, 1985, p. 5) at that time. Mary showed no hesitancy in identifying herself as a feminist. "I consider myself a feminist because I believe in women's rights, but it isn't the feminism that I think whites are talking about, because my stronger feelings are about the racial thing."

To a great extent, many areas of Mary's life are characterized by feminist goals and values. As a young woman, Mary was guided by a burning desire to establish her independence and acquire a professional career. In her master's thesis at Smith, she directly addressed gender issues in professional relationships. She studied the working relationship between psychiatrists (the majority of whom were male) and the predominantly female social workers who made up an enormously undervalued segment of hospitals' mental health teams. Mary never acquired the traditional female roles of wife and mother. Moreover, she never felt an imperative to be married. "I never had the feeling that I had to be married. My feeling is that it would have to be somebody that I would want." She firmly declared a lack of regret about her life decisions and identified ways in which feminism has shaped her thinking. For example, she explained that "the new feminism has absolved me from much anxiety about the single state."

Conclusion

Mary's life is marked by her strong-willed determination to overcome the personal and societal obstacles that fall along her path. The obstacles have been numerous and significant: the early death of her mother, her family's limited financial resources, discrimination in the Jim Crow South, the absence of family unity, and a series of health problems and hospitalizations. Mary did not simply persevere and cope with these obstacles, she resisted their limitations and excelled beyond the boundaries they imposed on her. She attained exceptional academic, professional, and personal success. However, black female experiences should not, as hooks (1981) cautions, be romanticized into the stereotypical image of the "strong" black woman. Strength alone does not allow us to circumvent the forces of systemic oppression, but Mary and other women like her have given me courage and inspiration for continued struggle. As a woman of color who was raised in a working-class, immigrant family and as someone starting a career in psychology, I am strongly drawn to Mary and the ways in which she has lived her life despite the many obstacles in her path.

Academics in many fields, including psychology, have traditionally framed the study of black families on a deficit model. The use of white, middle-class families as a standard and basis for comparison draws out and highlights areas of deficiency and neglect among blacks in the United States. Mary is not privileged by her race, gender, or original social class position. She is neither white nor middle class, and she was not raised within the bonds of a cohesive nuclear family. Yet it would be a grave mistake to characterize Mary's life as deficient when her life and accomplishments are in fact remarkable in their richness. Approaching Mary's life with a focus on strengths and resiliency offers one road toward understanding how people located in the margins of society struggle with, resist, and in many ways, surmount oppression.

Appreciating the complexity and significance of intersecting social locations in Mary's life experiences also requires a sufficiently broad feminist perspective. A focus relying solely on gender as an analytical technique would conceal rather than illuminate our understanding. For instance, Mary did not resonate to the feminism she felt white women were addressing in the 1960s. She instead sought a balance between her feminist allegiance and those loyalties based on race and culture. To have narrowly zoomed in on a single historical moment in Mary's life would have provided a static picture. Instead, I have tried to document how the degree and nature of her feminist and racial awareness varied and changed throughout her life course as they do for all of us.

References

Carson, C. (1981). *In struggle: SNCC and the black awakening of the 1960s*. Cambridge, MA: Harvard University Press.

Cluster, D. (1979). *They should have served that cup of coffee*. Boston: South End Press.

Collins, P. H. (1990). Women's studies: Reform or transformation? *Sojourner: The Women's Forum, 10,* 18–20.

Fitzgerald, T. A. (1985). *The national council of Negro women and the feminist movement 1935–1975.* Washington, DC: Georgetown University Press.

Garrow, D. J. (1978). *Protest at Selma: Martin Luther King, Jr., and the voting rights act of 1965.* New Haven: Yale University Press.

Giddings, P. (1984). *When and where I enter: The impact of black women on race and sex in America.* New York: Bantam Books.

hooks, b. (1981). *Ain't I a woman: Black women and feminism.* Boston: South End Press.

Rutter, M. (1979). Protective factors in children's responses to stress and disadvantage. In M. W. Kent & J. E. Rolf (Eds.), *Primary prevention of psychopathology: Vol. 3.* Social competence in children (pp. 49–74). Hanover, NH: University Press of New England.

Spelman, E. V. (1988). *Inessential woman: Problems of exclusion in feminist thought.* Boston: Beacon Press.

Standley, A. (1990). Women in the civil rights movement: Trailblazers and torchbearers, 1941–1965. In V. L. Crawford, J. A. Rouse, & M. Walker (Eds.), *Black Women in United States History* (pp. 1–11). New York: Carlson.

Stewart, A. J., & Healy, J. M. (1989). Linking individual development and social changes. *American Psychologist, 44,* 30–42.

Werner, E. E., & Smith, R. S. (1982). *Vulnerable but invincible: A study of resilient children.* New York: McGraw-Hill.

Williams, J. (1987). *Eyes on the prize: America's civil rights years 1954–1965.* New York: Penguin Books.

7

Speaking Against the Silence: One Maya Woman's Exile and Return

M. BRINTON LYKES

Esta postal me recuerda gran parte de mi vida y quiero compartir esos recuerdos contigo, asi como he compartido los momentos dificiles. Muchos abrazos "fuertes."

This postcard reminds me of much of my life and I want to share those memories with you in the same way that I have shared the difficult moments. Many "warm" hugs.

I BEGIN WITH a recent communication from Maria Izabel to show you that the woman whose story I share in these pages is not only an informant, the subject of a research project, but a colleague and friend. Maria Izabel and I met in 1984 when she was approximately 18 years old and living in Mexico. Since that time, nearly ten years ago, I have experienced some of the multiple meanings of speaking, silence, exile, and return through work with Maria Izabel and other Guatemalans. Through this work I sought to extend my earlier work with Guatemalan women refugees (see, e.g., Lykes, 1989) and to explore the impact of return on one refugee woman's self-understanding and praxis. Maria Izabel was willing to be interviewed, partly in response to my interests, partly as she herself would say in our interview, to share what she described as an "alternative image" of the Maya[1] with the audiences to whom I would direct this work.

The story[2] presented here was thus co-constructed within the context of a ten-year friendship between two women with distinct life experiences who are separated by age and social class background. We are from differing ethnic/racial and national groups and from different regions of the world. Our shared commitment to the Guatemalan people's struggle for self-determination was the context for our initial contact and remains central to our continuing friendship. The latter, developed through shared praxis, has been further nurtured by personal caring.

Our interview thus grows out of many years of diverse experiences and provides an example of the construction of knowledge in a context of "passionate scholarship" (see Du Bois, 1983; Lykes, 1989). This text contributes to the growing tradition of women's narratives (see, e.g., Personal Narratives Group, 1989). I will write elsewhere about the important methodological considerations raised in this work.

Maria Izabel is the name selected by my informant for purposes of this project.[3] She is a Maya, born in a rural community in the Highlands of Guatemala. She now lives in her native Guatemala, where despite an ostensible "return to civilian rule and democracy" in January 1986, the military continues to wage the now more than thirty-three-year-old war against insurgent forces (Jonas, 1991; Kinzer and Schlesinger, 1983; McClintock, 1985). The insurgents' major objective has been to achieve a more equitable distribution of resources for the majority of Guatemalans, nearly 80 percent of whom live in extreme poverty (UNICEF, 1992). Human rights organizations have documented some of the effects of war and state-sponsored terror in Guatemala (see, e.g., America's Watch Report, 1989, 1990; Amnesty International, 1987; Jay, 1993). I have written elsewhere of its social, psychological, and cultural consequences (see Melville & Lykes, 1992; Lykes, in press).

The multiple truths of Maria Izabel's story reveal the particularity of one life while contributing to our understanding of a larger reality. She creates a multilayered text through her account of particular experiences of exile and return, of deeply felt often contradictory emotional responses, and of subsequent efforts to make meaning of her life in a context of continuing war. Maria Izabel brings to life the impersonal and seemingly affectively hollow testimonies of hundreds of thousands of Mayas who survive continuing repression. Her text "makes flesh" the suffering and survival of countless Guatemalans. Through her expressed emotions we feel the horror we seek to forget—that many did not survive (see, e.g., Langer, 1991). Despair contests hope. Material conditions of atrocity and loss are reframed and silence disrupted by voice.

My commitment to accompany Maya women and children's struggles (see Lykes, in press) and my interests in woman's development and alternative notions of the self frame this particular version of Maria Izabel's story. The text we jointly developed reflects a particular form of theorizing about human personhood, stretching toward a notion of self that posits praxis as central to identity (see below). Our reflections on selected moments in one woman's development in a context of ongoing war and terror contribute to ways of thinking about self, survival, and subjectivity.

The Roots of Change

Maria Izabel describes her childhood in terms that were not normative for Maya girls of her generation. In contrast to many of her peers, she attended school and in that context began to learn Spanish.

MI: There [in my village] girls learn to weave when they are seven or eight years old ... [but] in addition to this we went to school. ... [It] was more or less in the 1970s, [that] my father sent us to school. But ... the people criticized us, saying that ... it was only a waste of time [and] that what we ought to be doing was learning to make tortillas, learning to mash the nixtamal[4] finely, to weave well, in order to marry ...

MBL: ... How is it that [your father] had ideas that were more open towards women?

MI: First, ... we did not have brothers, we were only women. ...[Also,] he learned to read and write alone. He spoke Spanish very well; but it was entirely through his own effort. For these reasons, and even more because we were all women, he said: "You have to be more, you cannot stay here in the community, you have to achieve other things than we have been able to achieve." So I think that he motivated us with these ideas because it was he who obliged us to wear shoes, he obliged us to speak Spanish. ... So it was with lots of effort that we learned to manage for ourselves [in Spanish] ... [but my mother] can't manage in Spanish. She doesn't read or write. ... In my mother's family no one knew how to read or write.

The military intruded upon this family and community in the early 1980s. Maria Izabel was away from home at the time, but heard details from her sisters. Having already killed a leader of Catholic Action[5] and threatened her father, the military returned, tortured him until he lost consciousness, stole everything of value, and burned what remained. The family fled, spending the next ten years among the Communities of Populations in Resistance (CPR) in the Highlands of Guatemala.[6] It is a story of flight, establishing new roots, building community, and fleeing again, often under the threat of helicopter bombing and invading troops. The military frequently burned crops to prevent their harvest. Women ceased to wear their traditional handwoven skirts and blouses, their *traje,* since the clothes on their backs had worn thin and there were no threads for weaving (see AVANCSO, 1992; Falla, 1992; Guatemala Health Rights Support Project, 1992).

While her family resisted repression within Guatemala's boundaries, Maria Izabel went into exile. Although she has spoken in other contexts of the particular events that precipitated her exile, she recounts here both the process by which she decided to engage in a particular form of resistance that necessitated exile and her feelings about her people and about a particular friendship:

MI: We were various young people, cousins [and] neighbors. We saw so much injustice so we said that this could not continue, that we had to do something. They had killed several [of our] relatives, and they had killed our first cousins. And this gave us more rage because we reasoned that if they would kill those who weren't doing anything, who only wanted the good of the community—it was then that I decided. I decided more because I had a cousin with whom I had a very close relationship. We got along very well and we studied together and everything. We loved each other lots, and he said: "Well, I am going to organize;

Guatemalan Maya refugees with military guard. *(Photo by Derrill Bazzy.)*

what happens, happens." But, when the situation was very difficult they killed him.[7]

So I said, I am not going to stay the way I am. If they are killing others and they killed this cousin, my duty is greater now. So it was that I said, come what may, I am going to do what is necessary. We said—either we remain with our arms crossed and they kill us at any moment because that's the way it was— ... or you do something. So I said: "Better that they capture me really doing something ..." So it was then that I decided ... I also knew that my family was not there. I knew what had happened so I said that if all of that had happened to them and if people continued to suffer in this way, we needed to denounce it. ... Our action had international repercussions so we had to leave [Guatemala]. We had ... to continue denouncing what was happening in the countryside [of Guatemala], in the Highlands: the bombings, the burning of forests, the rape of women and all that was happening at this time [1980–1982]. So we left there and gave many press conferences, interviews, and tours in the United States, in Europe, and in South America. ... these were huge changes for me.

MBL: Do you remember how you felt?

MI: You know, when we left there, I didn't even know what a press conference was, nor a talk, nor what any of it was; I didn't know anything. I only knew that I had to do something.

Maria Izabel described the enormity of the changes in her life—to leave a rural community where she barely spoke Spanish, to leave her country, to leave the life she had known. Journalists asked her many questions—about the history of her country, the invasion of U.S. troops in 1954, the rights of indigenous peoples, the experiences of women. She reported that as a sixteen-year-old who had never left rural Guatemala she "knew very little." She described her growing awareness of the isolation of rural Maya life: "Only if one reads newspapers or listens to the news does one know something of the richness of [other peoples]." She suggests that this growing knowledge led her to ask questions about herself, her people, and the ways in which they live.

Exile: Multiple Experiences Inside/Out

I had known Maria Izabel in Mexico and wanted to know more about how she thought about her experiences there now that she had returned to Guatemala. Most of the psychological literature about refugees focuses on the experiences of exile. I hoped to deepen my understanding of this experience by exploring how one woman, my friend, had withstood/managed/coped with these experiences of loss both in exile and upon return. She began by sharing some details of her experiences in Mexico:

> I got together with another group that was thinking of organizing a different sort of project. This project had to be administered by indigenous people themselves. We said that it was time that we take into our own hands various responsibilities. ... It had always been others who ... directed the project, and we did the work.
>
> I thought that this would be better than it was before. ... Mostly it was selling [Maya] crafts, principally to survive in Mexico. We also began to discuss political issues and proposals for solving a number of problems that we had encountered and criticized in our previous work. It was thus that we began to participate in various forums and in exhibits sharing our Maya culture, explaining the significance of *traje*, photography exhibits, and talks. We began to edit pamphlets on Maya history, ... it was a way of showing that we are really capable of doing our own projects and of educating another sector that was not manipulated by an ideology that has been used since the Spanish came. This ideology has been managed by "superiors" while those who were in these lands were "inferiors."
>
> It was then, I believe, that we also began to talk about women's rights. It was the first experience of writing, from outside the country, where the process of women's coming to consciousness through participation in various different struggles was described. It was a very interesting experience. I also was able to participate in one of the Latin American feminist international congresses. These were experiences that helped me to argue that as women we also have our own rights. We had shown this also within our Maya community in terms of the human rights we have. But, within these same rights, women have their own rights.

It was in Mexico that Maria Izabel also had the opportunity to participate in a mental health workshop that was being organized among refugee women. In our conversation about this experience she shared her emotions, her feelings of loss, and some of the multiple meanings of exile.

> **MI:** The methods used here were new for me, the group techniques that they used, the ways of participating, the themes that were presented. At times we thought they were not important.

MBL: For example?

MI: The fact of having lost our families, for example. What help can one give to a person who has lost her family, who has lost her home, who has lost her country and is an orphan outside her country? I think that the women who participated were helped a lot emotionally and we were helped in the sense that we were refugees, with problems, but also with a life to lead. We had to confront this. We shouldn't frustrate ourselves but, on the contrary, look for better solutions for these problems. It was [thus] that I accepted that I was a refugee.

MBL: And before you didn't?

MI: At the beginning, no, because I had one foot here [in Guatemala] and the other foot in Mexico. So anything I did, I felt badly. For example, I said to myself that I was going to buy a pair of shoes but I always tried to buy the simplest of shoes, because I said that it was a lot of money to waste on shoes while my family was starving or my people had nothing to wear. I denied myself many things. ...

The workshop helped first and foremost because it offered a group experience in which women could talk about how they felt, what they thought, what their problems were. Some problems they reframed through the group process and sometimes solved.

> For example, in the case of the cousin that I was telling you was killed, I suffered a lot and cried lots about this, until recently. ... In the mental health workshop we made diagrams of our genealogy. Thus we began to see from whence came our grandfathers, our grandmothers, and our brothers. We began to see how everything that we had [in Guatemala] had crumbled, to see the deaths that we had experienced, the separation, all of this. We saw that in this moment we were reliving all of this and as much as we might have wanted we had not been able to let it go. [But] we were now letting go of some of it, and we began to feel a little calmer.
>
> I began to see life from another perspective and this helped me to say, well if I am a refugee, then I am a refugee. But I am going to prepare myself for when I return and then I will be able to bring things to the people who have not had this opportunity. I will be able to help because I will understand their necessities. ... All these Saturdays helped us to know ourselves. ... I think it helped me to know myself, who I was and, in some way, to know to what I was going to commit myself. That is, am I just going to live a personal life or will I do something?

I wondered how she felt during these years in Mexico. I experienced a solitariness or sense of loneliness in her words, and so I asked:

MBL: Did you feel alone in Mexico?

MI: Yes, incredibly. First, with the people with whom I [fled Guatemala], we had not known each other. It cost me to adapt to them. ... At one point I met a woman who had been [in Mexico] a while. I felt that she was like my family. I always went to her house and we ate together. ... I think that at a given moment I substituted my family, because that's the way it was. One had to make friendships with people even if they were unknowns. ... I lived alone one year. But there was a time when I had established myself a bit emotionally and then three friends I had got married ... and I was left alone [again] ... and many times I felt very alone, especially the weekend. ...

Here [in Guatemala] I had not cried. … But in those days [in Mexico] I cried lots, I [wanted] to know what [my family was] doing, to know that they were alive, I didn't know anything. Sometimes one year, two years, passed, without any news of them. When I once again had news of them I was calmer.

MBL: What was the most difficult thing for you in Mexico?

MI: To be alone there. I tell you I had friends but I felt alone, I missed something, perhaps the ambience of my country, the ambience of my family or the stability. I think I got over lots of this, because there were many things that I had there [in Mexico]—many friendships, movies, theater, supermarkets, parks, swimming pools everywhere, but there was always something missing—and that always came to mind. So at times I think that perhaps I was filling myself with activities in order not to feel the loneliness. … And the holidays were horrible for me. I wished that there were never holidays. … All of this came together and was in- supportable at some point … I felt that I just couldn't stand to be away any longer. It was then that I decided to come here [to Guatemala].

Maria Izabel went on to describe a difficult decision in her life concerning a boyfriend that she had when she was fifteen and living in Guatemala. He showed up in Mexico, and after seven or eight years of separation they discovered that they still felt deeply for each other. However, he could not remain in Mexico and Maria Izabel was not able to return to Guatemala at the time of their reencounter. His proposal of marriage and offer to arrange her papers if she would follow him provoked in her a new level of decisionmaking about her own life plan. He was returning to the Communities of Populations in Resistance and she had envi- sioned her commitment in other terms. Despite their love for each other she felt that she could not abandon her plans, her life project, to follow him. She de- scribed the difficulty in choosing not to follow him and the consequent stress. She reports having been deeply hurt and losing a lot of weight. On the other hand she said, "But it also helped me lots to gain more self-confidence." She described con- fiding in the mental health group, sharing the pain of choosing against one she loved: "It hurt lots because I loved him but I loved myself more and how much this hurt me. I described how contradictory life is, that I love him and he loves me, we have known each other for years, we get along well, we understand each other but we can't—I stayed here, better not to go with him."

Exile meant being alone—living outside her community of origin, without news of her family. The loss gave way to an emptiness that Maria Izabel struggled to negate by refusing to admit her status as a refugee and by denying her feelings of loss through multiple activities and casual friends. Yet exile was also the context of political and personal growth for Maria Izabel. She codeveloped a new organi- zation with Maya leadership and developed her consciousness of women's rights. Although the mental health workshop could not dissolve the loneliness, it pro- vided a context for self-exploration and a space of contention that enabled her to manage and use her feelings and to develop her identity as an exile. Recognition of herself as a refugee entailed recognition of multiple losses—the death of her cousin; the flight from her village; the absence of news from her family; the loss of her language, her dress, her country—and an encounter with loneliness. Her interpretation of her decision not to join her childhood partner suggests her growing encounter with herself-in-transition and echoes her father's earlier admonition, "We had to prepare ourselves to give more."

Constructing Selfhood Through Return

I was drawn to the language Maria Izabel used to describe her loving of/choosing of self over another and asked her whether or not such a choice had been conceivable prior to her time in Mexico. She explained that working among other women outside of her community of origin had been a necessary condition, enabling her to know herself in such a way that she later would "choose herself." She went on to describe the process of valorization not only of her psychological self but also of her body and of the functions of parts of herself that contributed to the whole of who she is.

It was in this context that I asked her to tell me who she was, how she would describe herself as an indigenous woman. She acknowledged again that before her time in Mexico she "had no idea who she was," as no one had ever asked her. But now,

> I definitely defined myself as myself and I said that I am who I am. First, after analyzing my family origins, why I have the ideas I have, I said: the first thing is what I inherited from my father who sowed these ideals and these values, and from my mother, who criticized me a lot, but who finally accepted me for who I am. Who I am comes from the simplicity that my mother taught us, because she did not know how to read or write. So I think that I have at least a little of her. I learned other values from other people, who if they had lived would have been important people and would have contributed lots. So, if I live, if I have the opportunity to be, I define myself as giving all that I can give, all that is within my possibilities and capacities and to continue forward! This is how I have defined myself up to now. I think that among the new plans that I have now, I think that among my strongest aspirations is to complete university study and I hope I will achieve it.

Talk of herself and of the future led her to reconsider her return to Guatemala from Mexico. She shared a more detailed description of the return, of crossing the border alone on foot, of her fear once she found herself on Guatemalan soil. Her first words were to a friend who welcomed her and from whom she borrowed her *traje*. She had worn pants for years in Mexico, but the moment she entered Guatemala she describes a desire to reappropriate her dress.

> **MI:** She lent me her skirt, her blouse and I put on the *traje*. The following day I walked around in my *traje*, but I did not say much as my Mexican accent was so clear, and I was always afraid that people would know that I was not from here and had just arrived. I felt as if everyone knew my entire story. I felt nostalgic for Mexico. I asked myself if it was the right thing to come back and I felt that I was not going to find myself here. I felt that … I was living another contradiction. I was here and I wanted to go back there again. …

I began to know more people and little by little I adapted. At the beginning it was costly. ... Everything is very contradictory. Having been outside [Guatemala], you hear that the situation is too difficult and that you cannot live here. And since you bring all this fear back with you, you fear that it will be here ... that there will be military commissioners everywhere and that you can't move around without them seeing you. So I was very afraid of all this, but little by little I adapted. ... I grew accustomed as well to hearing news every day of murders. Every day there are murders, who knows how many. I was very frightened. Later, it's also ugly because one becomes accustomed to all of this.

MBL: Incredible! no?

MI: Yes and before I was horrified when I heard about a murder, but now, no.

MBL: And what do you think of this?

MI: Well, it's worrisome, because if I am like this how much more so the people who have never been aware that it was bad; the majority of people don't see it.

The Scars of Repression: Reconstructing Family Relations

Maria Izabel's return to Guatemala coincided with her family's decision to leave the Communities of Populations in Resistance and return to their village of origin. When she returned to Guatemala she initiated contact with them.

I contacted my uncle and went [to my village] with him. I was really quite impressed because I was very young when I left there but despite that there are things that one does not forget, as if they were engraved, and one never forgets them. Then we met my family: my mother came, my father, and two of my sisters. ... Everything was different, eleven years later, they had grown and my father was much thinner, my mother also was older and my sisters had grown. We just looked at each other as if something—that these eleven years that separated us—much had happened, and all we did was look at each other and, then, ... they told me about their lives and said that the most valuable thing was that I was here. They did not want to tell me about my other sister. They didn't want to tell me anything about her.

Maria Izabel learned for the first time that a sister who had joined the guerrilla had been wounded while fighting in a remote part of the country. Lacking adequate medical care, she died. Her mother was most deeply hurt by the impossibility of burying her daughter due to the distance that separated them.

Maria Izabel's descriptions of her family reflect the complexity of reconnecting and her emotional responses to these frequently contradictory experiences.

I always try to help them. ... the major part of my salary I send to them, even though they say that I should not be worried about them because they have a house there, and land and fruit trees, but I send it to them because ... how do I say it? For so many years I did not help them, I believe that I have an even greater obligation to catch up on all those years.

Yes, they are my family. But there is also something cold, it's not them. Sometimes I still don't understand things well because I give them all that I have and I feel good doing it but when I am with them it's like we are strangers—there is still a distance. Yes, my mother treats me well and all but it's like I said, those eleven years are hard to reestablish and I see the way [my parents] interact with my sisters and it's different.

Maria Izabel described her relationships with her extended family, reporting that she and her younger male cousins get along well. They frequently refer to her as "a very unusual cousin," words that communicate trust and confidence to her.

> Including, they say: "You are strict, but you are correct." One of them told me: "I think I have more trust in you than in my own parents." ... I tell them it is good to study to improve ourselves, to show as Mayas that we are capable, that we are intelligent. But then they say to me: "Where can I study, with what resources, how does one do this?" And I say to myself, yes, I can help one or two but not the rest. And the other young people in the community ask me to find them work, [or] scholarships because they are anxious. Where am I going to get these resources? It is really something that is truly beyond our means.

I remember well her asking me for help in finding scholarships for her nieces and nephews and for the additional children that had been adopted into her sisters' families while they were "on the run." I tried without success to find resources among several religious organizations that I am familiar with in Guatemala. I felt the same frustration bordering on despair that she described during our interview—one can tell them to go to school, to improve their own conditions, but with what resources? Yes, one can help one or two, but fifteen or twenty, or five hundred or 5000? Not able to stand the resonance of her sense of powerlessness with my own, I retreated to a topic that had surfaced earlier and that I hoped would be less painful, gender.

> **MBL:** Do you feel that the relations with your male cousins are different from those with your female cousins?
> **MI:** You know, my male cousins look for me. My female cousins love me a lot because among the people who have left, when the women return ... they don't want to speak [their Maya language], they don't use their traditional dress. They are different because they are alienated. Clearly that's the way that most of our people think: to reject our ways is the most positive thing, and to imitate others' cultures is the way to improve oneself.
> But I don't believe this. I wear traditional sandals and speak [our language] with everyone, and greet the older men and women [with respect]. ...
> So, they see me as someone special, different, and, as I was telling you, they also love me. I argue when I have to but not with all of the people, and not for just any reason. ...
> On the one hand, I think that we are integrating well. But, on the other hand, there are the people who lost family members, my aunts, [for example], many of whose sons were kidnapped or killed. They see us as guilty of all of this. So they don't come over much, only their husbands. [One aunt] speaks to me because I speak to her but she does not visit me, nor come close. What I see in her is that she in some way resents me, and my other aunt, too. They killed six of her eight sons. ... She was cheery and was the first to see me when I returned. She was

happy but then among the things she said to me was: "How good that you are here, how good that you are alive, but what about my sons? Why do I have to pay so much? In some way you are guilty."

MBL: And what did you feel?

MI: I felt badly, badly because they are the people with whom one shared an understanding, the people one knew well. The closest ones are no longer close.

Also sometimes I feel a little guilty. That is to say, they killed them and I am still here, so how much must I do? Or why, if they could have contributed so much, are they not still among us? What do I know? There are a mountain of things that come to mind. But that's the way it is. It's as if, to live something that one believes, perhaps in a determined moment, will turn into a scar. But it's as if one is scratching the wound and sees the sore, and sees that this has not been resolved. There is a scar that still hasn't healed. To speak with my aunts, they still haven't recovered from this suffering of having lost their husbands, their sons. So it's to live a reality that weighs on one, that hurts, and to see the suffering in them, the pain that they carry in them. Whatever else, one carries this problem. … It's something that is not going to heal. … But I tell you, my aunts, my sister, really, it's as if my presence helps them a little but one comes back from there with these problems that torment one.

Maria Izabel described life in the 1990s in the village where she was born, where her family now lives.

It's a zone totally under the control of the army. … The army is there, the guerrilla is there. … It's a vicious circle. One leaves, the other arrives, as if they were playing cat and mouse. But the saddest thing is [knowing] who is really involved. In the guerrilla, the Maya are the troops; and in the army, the Maya are the troops. And who suffers? We do. So it is not anything that is spread out, it's something that only we are pursuing, paying for all of this. …

The [people] prefer to be quiet about all of this, or not to focus on it … it is that terror, that fear, that insecurity. [But] as I was saying, one goes and everything is calm, everyone is working.

Maria Izabel's reference to her male cousins led me to frame a question seeking to understand whether or not gender played a critical role in extended family relations among youth in Maria Izabel's community. Her response is a deeply textured description of the gendered nature of suffering and loss among the Maya. The husbands and sons are, most typically, dead or disappeared; their widows, left with psychological and relational wounds that refuse to heal, are grateful to welcome home a relative formerly believed to be dead, yet resentful, angry, and accusatory. They demand some explanation or justification from the survivor, hoping to ease the pain of their losses. The women accept her because she has not rejected their language and dress; yet they resent her because she has survived.

Maria Izabel feels both the intense closeness that family brings and the duties and obligation inherent in those relationships. Yet family has changed: former relations of warmth are now cold. The sisters who accompanied her parents into internal exile are treated differently. The sister who joined the guerrilla is dead. Maria Izabel always tries to help her family yet she never has enough to meet their articulated and implicit needs. The contradictions implicit in descriptions of earlier experiences are in bold relief here. The contradictory experiences generate contradictory feelings. Things are calm, apparently people are not suffering; the army and guerrilla are ever present, and people live in silence and terror.

We continued our discussion of the contemporary reality of Guatemala. Maria Izabel spoke of the repercussions of silenced rage, unhealed losses, and continuing terror among Maya more generally. Speaking more personally, she described difficulties encountered in trying to develop a project with Maya women and the challenges of being a single woman within Maya communities. Despite the difficulties of living without a partner she insisted that now that she "had defined herself" she would not risk that self-definition for a relationship.

> Since birth I have had this sense that I have something to give. Doing what I do, I feel good. To think of myself as a housewife with children, without being able to go out, without participating in activities, without preparing myself, without aspirations! If I matured this way, I could not imagine myself! I would not be me if I was this way. I would stop being me. ... If I had really not had the opportunity to leave [Guatemala], I think that my life might have taken a very different turn. I would have married and been more normal. I would have had children by now, who knows! I can't imagine my life. ...
>
> As long as I feel good doing all [that I do], I will keep doing it. ... I think that sometimes people criticize me because I demand too much of myself, and they say, really you don't ever rest, nor do you enjoy things; but I tell them that I feel good doing these things. To the contrary, I enjoy studying, preparing myself more, and so it is a way of life to which one accustoms oneself. ... If at some point I need to dedicate myself more to myself or to other questions, then I will do it.

I wanted to better understand the self-definition that emerged in Maria Izabel's discussion of the Maya today. I asked her what she meant when she spoke of the Maya, that is, how she would define what being Maya meant. She recounted the many terms imposed by the Spanish—Indians [*indios*], natives, primitives, natural, indigenous ("when they sought to soften the situation a little"), and most recently, ethnic groups. Maria Izabel sees this most recent label—one that includes the twenty-two groups of Maya but not the mixed-race Ladinos,[8] who are, the Maya insist, the "national culture"—as intended to maintain divisions among the other groups, until with time the Maya assimilate to the national culture. As Maya, Maria Izabel rejects all of these labels and asserts Maya collective identity as a people [*el pueblo Maya*] who, as such, demand respect:

> **MI:** We have different languages, different words, different linguistic communities, [for example,] the K'iche' linguistic community, the Poqomam linguistic community ... that form part of the Maya community. So we define ourselves and there are other groups that are not Maya, such as the Garifunas, the Xinka, of whom there are very few, and the Ladinos. There are four groups in the country, therefore, four communities, four cultures [see, e.g., C. Smith, 1991; Warren, 1992, for further discussion].

MBL: And what does it mean to belong to the Maya community?

MI: It is to say that I identify myself with this community, that I recognize myself as Maya inasmuch as I am part of the community. There can be different reasons for this. I could say that it is because my father is Maya, and also my mother, I was born in a Maya community, I have Maya family names, I use my Maya *traje*, I speak my Maya language, so I define myself as Maya. Others could say, ... I was born in this country and my mother was Ladina but she also had Maya blood, and she was mestizo because of the violations against women in this country but she also had Maya blood. It depends on whether one wants to define oneself this way.

MBL: Is it a subjective definition then?

MI: Yes, but it is also practical and real because if one only says, I am indigenous, and one's activities are otherwise, and one does not make an effort to learn one's language, to get closer to one's people—no it's not just a subjective thing. ... If one is not doing these things one's definition is very empty; it has to do with one's practice.

Imagining/Imaging the Self

Maria Izabel's story shuttles between her experiences in exile, framed by her family's internal exile, and her return to Guatemala. This text represents a series of stops and starts in continuing processes of war, repression, survival, and resistance. The language used in describing her early experiences in Guatemala is permeated by a sense of material constraint—war, hunger, death. Similar images pervade her description of the family and community of origin she encounters upon return—scars that don't heal, desires for self-advancement that can't be realized. This is perhaps most graphically revealed in the words she chose to describe the military and guerrilla presence in her community of origin—a vicious circle, a cat-and-mouse game where the losers on both sides are the Maya.

In contrast, the images conjured by her talk about her life in Mexico are more elastic. A language of choice, of decisions needing to be made, is evident in her discourse. There are many stories and stories within stories—details about her decision to leave the group of peasants with whom she worked in Guatemala and with whom she fled her country; her decision to begin working with women and with children in Mexico in a Maya-run organization; and perhaps most significant, her decision to return to Guatemala.

The continuities and discontinuities within her text reveal a subject embedded in changing family and community systems who is both transforming these systems and transformed by them. As Maria Izabel herself said, identity is both subjective and "practiced." Who she is as Maya woman is defined by her family of origin, her language, her decision to wear her *traje*, her attachment to her community and to the land. Yet she determines herself through her concern for her people and her praxis in and among them. She has been chosen, yet, she chooses.

Her description of her experiences of exile, her gradual development of a firm identification of herself-as-refugee, reveals her incorporation of a transitional identity. As painful and somehow "foreign" as the process seemed to her, she became a refugee for a particular historical moment and that identity marked her for the future. Thus she experiences and constructs her return to Guatemala through herself-as-refugee, that is, through her experiences of living in exile. The nostalgia for Mexico she experienced upon return to Guatemala was "another contradiction. I was here and I wanted to go back there again." Yet it is precisely her capacity to feel and to think about herself-out-of-context that enables her to become "myself the refugee." She thereby repositioned herself as she began a process of self-discovery and reintegration, or as she said, "adaptation" to the Guatemala-of-return.

Maria Izabel describes multiple contradictory feelings and experiences in her account of exile and return. She positions herself within these contradictions, living into and through them, by situating herself outside of her community of origin, of, but not among, her people. Upon her return to Guatemala she is both inside and outside of the terror of contemporary Guatemala. She sees the daily horror and reflects upon her responses, her acting "as if" within the terror. She is within the fragments that are her family ("they love me" because I don't "reject our ways"), her community, and her people—despite the scars that never fully heal. The blame of others, her own feelings of guilt and torment, and the ongoing war and repression serve to keep the wounds raw. Yet she is, in some small way, beyond the horror as she reflects upon its effects and the effects of taking it for granted.

Maria Izabel's words, the text of her life, re-present the "normal abnormality" of state-sponsored terror and war described by social psychologists (e.g., Martín-Baró, 1988, 1990), anthropologists (Taussig, 1986/1987, 1989), and philosophers (Scarry, 1985). Her story suggests that contrary to much of the psychological literature, surviving war is neither primarily about posttraumatic stress disorder (see, e.g., Eth and Pynoos, 1985; Herman, 1992; Terr, 1991) nor about resiliency (see, e.g., Luthar and Zigler, 1991; Werner and R. S. Smith, 1982). It is, rather, about the multiple daily experiences of "living a life" under "traumatogenic structures" (Martín-Baró, 1990, p. 4). Maria Izabel's embodied text, her lived *testimonio,* reveals multiple moments in her development of her sense of self as Maya woman. As Sampson (1985) suggested, "Personhood does not derive its order from being a thoroughly integrated singular thing but rather from its being a continually evolving process" (p. 1206).

For Maria Izabel, exile proved opportunity—but only after she was able to live into the losses that were re-presented by being a stranger in a strange land. The experience of self-as-refugee enabled Maria Izabel to fully plan for her return. She commented on this experience and its reverberations in her emotional life.

> If you had asked me all of these questions while I was living in Mexico, it's possible that I would have cried, who knows how many times, because there are questions

that, as I was saying, are like wounds that one scratches again and that hurt. Outside [Guatemala] one becomes more sensitive. But here, facing the reality, one must become hardened or one dies of sadness or anguish or fear, whatever it might be, if one cannot resist. I think that it is one of the values of the Guatemalan people that they have known how to resist so much. I have always said that although we have wounds in our hearts, we only think of things in a cold manner, knowing that anything can happen, that I can turn on the radio and hear that someone was killed, that an accident occurred, or who knows! So these things are such that one becomes more serene. ... Now I feel serene but worried ... worried that one has to accustom oneself to talk about these things as if they were normal.

Maria Izabel realized one of her objectives for our conversation through sharing some of the experiences through which she has come to be who she is today and her responses to them. She agreed to our interview in hopes that those who hear her story hear more than a story of terror and oppression: "The most valuable part of this [the interview] is that we really began to reflect upon many situations ... so that the community where these messages go ... won't only see wounds or suffering—but that they also see human beings."

Acknowledgments

This work, completed in 1993, is dedicated to the thousands of women and children in Guatemala's thirty-three-year war—the survivors, the massacred, the disappeared, those killed in political and economic violence, the exiled, and the returnees. The author thanks Abigail J. Stewart, Carol E. Franz, Deborah Tolman, Marcelo Velázquez, and two anonymous reviewers for comments on earlier drafts. Earlier versions of this chapter were presented at the Faculty of Psychology, University of Buenos Aires, Argentina, and at the American Psychological Association Annual Convention, Toronto, Canada, in July and August 1993, respectively.

Notes

1. The term *Maya* refers historically to the indigenous populations of what is today southern Mexico, Belize, and Guatemala and parts of Honduras and El Salvador. In this chapter, the term refers to the more than 56 percent of the Guatemalan population that is indigenous and is principally concentrated in the Northwestern part of the country, including the departments of Sololá, Totonicapán, Quiché, Chimaltenango, Quetzaltenango, Huehuetenango, and the Verapaces. Their numbers within these departments oscillate between 40 and 95 percent of the total population (see, e.g., COCADI, 1989; Cojtí Cuxil, 1991).

2. The eight-hour interview that constitutes the more formal basis of this work was conducted by the author in Spanish, tape-recorded, and later transcribed by Amelia Mallona, a Nicaraguan doctoral student at Boston College. Although neither Maria Izabel nor the author are native Spanish speakers, it is the language in which we communicate. All translations from Spanish to English were done by the author. The lack of literary polish reflects my desire to remain faithful to the structure and style of the original Spanish interview.

3. Due to the ongoing war and state-sponsored terror in Guatemala, Maria Izabel chose a pseudonym for this work and chose not to reveal selected details about her life.

4. Nixtamal is a corn-based mixture from which tortillas are made.

5. Catholic Action represents one of the Catholic church's first efforts to engage with rural peasant organizations from the base of their needs. One project in Guatemala included the training of local catechists who then educated the population. This movement was later influenced by liberation theology (see Frank and Wheaton, 1984; Warren, 1978/1989).

6. The Communities of Populations in Resistance (CPR) represent three major groupings of internal refugees who neither fled their country nor were captured by the military and housed within model villages subsequent to the military's destruction of more than four hundred rural villages in 1980–1982. They have remained internal exiles ever since. In fall 1990 CPR issued a statement demanding recognition of civilian status both by the Guatemalan government and by international organizations. The Guatemalan government, military, and press frequently accuse them of association with the Unidad Revolucionaria Nacional Guatemalteca (URNG), the guerrilla forces within Guatemala.

7. During the worst of the counterinsurgency war against the Guatemalan civilian populations, approximately one million people were displaced. The numbers of dead have been estimated between 40,000 and 100,000. Most were civilians engaged in community projects for self-determination (see Carmack, 1988).

8. The terms *Ladino/Ladina* and *mestizo* are used interchangeably to refer to persons of mixed Spanish-indigenous parentage. The term *Ladino/a* is also used today in Guatemala to refer to anyone who is not Maya.

References

America's Watch Report. (May 1989). *Persecuting Human Rights Monitors: The CERJ in Guatemala*. New York: America's Watch Committee.

————. (March 1990). *Messengers of Death: Human Rights in Guatemala, November 1988–February 1990*. New York: America's Watch Committee.

Amnesty International. (1987). *Guatemala: The Human Rights Record*. London: Amnesty International Publications.

AVANCSO (Asociación Para el Avance de las Ciencias Sociales en Guatemala). (1992). *Donde Esta el Futuro: Procesos de Reintegración en Comunidaded de Retornados* [Where Is the Future: Reintegration Processes Among Returning Communities]. Cuadernos de Investigación, Guatemala, 8.

Carmack, R. M. (Ed.). (1988). *Harvest of Violence: The Maya Indians and the Guatemalan Crisis*. Norman & London: University of Oklahoma Press.

COCADI. (1989). *Cultura Maya y Políticas de Desarrollo* [Maya Culture and the Politics of Development]. Chimaltenango, Guatemala: Ediciones COCADI.

Cojtí Cuxil, D. (1991). *La Configuración del Pensamiento Político del Pueblo Maya* [The Forms of Political Thought Among the Maya People]. Quetzaltenango, Guatemala: Talleres de "El Estudiante."

Du Bois, B. (1983). Passionate Scholarship: Notes on Value, Knowing and Method in Feminist Social Science. In G. Bowles & R. D. Klein (Eds.), *Theories of Women's Studies* (pp. 105–116). London: Routledge & Kegan Paul.

Eth, S., & Pynoos, P. (1985). *Post-Traumatic Stress Disorder in Children*. Washington, DC: American Psychiatric Press.

Falla, R. (1992). *Masacres de la Selva: Ixcan, Guatemala (1975–1982)* [Massacres in the Jungle]. Guatemala: Editorial Universitaria de Guatemala.

Frank, L., & Wheaton, P. (1984). *Indian Guatemala: Path to Liberation: The Role of Christians in the Indian Process.* Washington, DC: EPICA Task Force.

Guatemala Health Rights Support Project. (July 1992). *Communities of Populations in Resistance.* Available from Guatemala Partners, 945 G Street, NW, Washington, DC 20001.

Herman, J. (1992). *Trauma and Recovery.* New York: Basic Books.

Jay, A. (1993). *Persecution by Proxy: The Civil Patrols in Guatemala.* New York: Robert F. Kennedy Memorial Center for Human Rights.

Jonas, S. (1991). *The Battle for Guatemala: Rebels, Death Squads, and U.S. Power.* Boulder: Westview Press.

Kinzer, S., & Schlesinger, S. (1983). *Bitter Fruit.* New York: Doubleday.

Langer, L. L. (1991). *Holocaust Testimonies: The Ruins of Memory.* New Haven: Yale University Press.

Luthar, S. S., & Zigler, E. (1991). Vulnerability and Competence: A Review of Research on Resilience in Childhood. *American Journal of Orthopsychiatry, 61*(1), 6–22.

Lykes, M. B. (1989). Dialogue with Guatemalan Indian Women: Critical Perspectives on Constructing Collaborative Research. In R. K. Unger (Ed.), *Representations: Social Constructions of Gender* (pp. 167–185). Amityville, NY: Baywood.

_____. (1994). Terror, Silencing and Children: International Multidisciplinary Collaboration with Guatemalan Maya Communities. *Social Science and Medicine, 34,* 543–552.

Martín-Baró, I. (1988). La Violencia Política y la Guerra como Causa del Trauma Psicosocial en El Salvador [Political Violence and War as Causes of Psychosocial Trauma in El Salvador]. *Revista de Psicologia de El Salvador, 28,* 123–141.

_____. (August 1990). *War and the Psychosocial Trauma of Salvadoran Children.* Paper presented by Adrianne Aron at the Annual Meeting of the American Psychological Association, Boston.

McClintock, M. (1985). *The American Connection: State Terror and Popular Resistance in Guatemala* (Vol. 2). London: Zed Books.

Melville, M. B., & Lykes, M. B. (1992). Guatemalan Indian Children and the Sociocultural Effects of Government-Sponsored Terrorism. *Social Science and Medicine, 34*(5), 533–548.

Personal Narratives Group. (Ed.). (1989). *Interpreting Women's Lives: Feminist Theory and Personal Narratives.* Bloomington & Indianapolis: Indiana University Press.

Sampson, E. E. (1985). The Decentralization of Identity: Toward a Revised Concept of Personal and Social Order. *American Psychologist, 40*(11), 1203–1211.

Scarry, E. (1985). *The Making and Unmaking of the World.* Oxford, UK: Oxford University Press.

Smith, C. (1991). Maya Nationalism. *Report on the Americas, 25*(3), 29–33.

Taussig, M. (1986/1987). *Shamanism, Colonialism, and the Wild Man: A Study in Terror and Healing.* Chicago: University of Chicago Press.

_____. (1989). Terror as Usual: Walter Benjamin's Theory of History as a State of Siege. *Sociological Text,* Fall/Winter, 3–20.

Terr, L. C. (1991). Childhood Traumas: An Outline and Overview. *American Journal of Psychiatry, 148*(1), 10–20.

UNICEF (United Nations Children's Fund). (1992). *The State of the World's Children.* New York: Oxford University Press.

Warren, K. (1989). *The Symbolism of Subordination: Indian Identity in a Guatemalan Town.* Austin: University of Texas Press. (Original work published 1978)

———. (1992). Transforming Memories and Histories: The Meanings of Ethnic Resurgence for Mayan Indians. In A. Stepan (Ed.), *Americas: New Interpretive Essays* (pp. 189–219). New York: Oxford University Press.

Werner, E. E., & Smith, R. S. (1982). *Vulnerable but Invincible: A Study of Resilient Children.* New York: McGraw-Hill.

8

Coping with Internment:
A Nisei Woman's Perspective

DONNA K. NAGATA

"WHAT WAS IT LIKE BEING IN JAIL?" ask Sachi Kaneshiro's grandchildren. The jail they speak of is not the kind of penitentiary most of us would envision, nor is their grandmother a hardened criminal. In fact, Sachi was never even tried for committing a crime. Her grandchildren are referring to her years of internment during World War II. Soon after Japan bombed Pearl Harbor in December 1941, Sachi and more than 110,000 other Japanese Americans were ordered by the U.S. government to abruptly leave their homes along the West Coast and parts of Arizona and move to internment camps in desolate areas of the country's interior. Citizenship and constitutional rights did not matter. More than two-thirds of those imprisoned were U.S. citizens like Sachi, born in this country. All that mattered was ethnic heritage. Anyone of Japanese extraction living near the Pacific Ocean was considered a potential spy, capable of disloyalty. The uprooted internees spent up to four years of their life in what the government called "relocation camps" surrounded by barbed wire and armed guards.

Many recent scholars consider the term "relocation camp" a euphemism: The internment camps actually fit the definition of a concentration camp (Daniels, 1986). Thorough examinations of historical records show that the mass removal represented a "grave injustice" and that Japanese Americans suffered a gross violation of their civil rights (Commission on Wartime Relocation and Internment of Civilians [CWRIC], 1982). Equally evident today is the fact that the internment affected Japanese Americans in deep, psychological ways that extend far beyond legal or political analyses (Mass, 1986; Morishima, 1973). Several writers have described the experience of "camp," as it is referred to by many Japanese Americans (e.g., Okada, 1981; Sone, 1991; Tateishi, 1984; Uchida, 1982). These accounts chronicle a range of circumstances and reactions surrounding the internment.

In this chapter, I do not cover the historical facts surrounding the internment, but strongly encourage the reader to refer to other sources for this information (e.g., CWRIC, 1982; Daniels, 1981; Weglyn, 1976). Instead, I highlight the internment experience of one woman, Sachi Kaneshiro. Sachi is a U.S.-born, second-generation (Nisei) Japanese American woman. Her story is one of struggle, survival, and coping in the face of extreme disruption and uncertainty. The information presented is based upon my in-depth interviews with Sachi in 1992 as well as her autobiographical writings (Kaneshiro, 1988, 1992). I chose to interview Sachi for this chapter because through her writing she had given much thought to her life around the years of internment.

There are aspects of Sachi's story that mirror the experiences of many others who were in camps. However, Japanese Americans varied in their internment circumstances (Williams and Coleman, 1992), and it is important to recognize the uniqueness of Sachi's life. As a young adult, she was affected differently than Nisei who were young children in camp. In addition, although most families remained intact during the internment, Sachi's family was separated in three directions.

Pearl Harbor and Internment

The experience of internment is integrally linked to the experience of being Japanese American. The "Japanese" side of Sachi's identity stemmed from the fact that her parents emigrated from Japan. Her father left Okinawa, Japan, traveling first to Mexico, and then, in 1904, to California. He worked hard as a truck farmer raising and selling vegetables and berries for the produce market and at a roadside stand. As an Issei, or first-generation Japanese, he was denied the right to own land, so he leased a ten-acre farm in Covina, in Southern California. Sachi's mother, who also came from Okinawa, was twenty years younger than her husband and arrived in 1918 through an arranged marriage. Both the wide age discrepancy and the arranged marriage were common for Issei women at that time (Nakano, 1990). And like other Issei women living in rural areas, Sachi's mother helped run the farm, in addition to caring for the children and maintaining the home.

Sachi was the oldest of six children in the family, with three sisters and two brothers. She recalls her upbringing as reflecting the "typical upbringing" of most Nisei in rural Southern California. Although one of the few Japanese Americans in a high school with an enrollment of some seven hundred students, she distinguished herself by becoming the president of the Girls' League, the highest office a female student could attain. Sachi was well aware of the racial boundaries that separated her from her Caucasian American peers. Her presidency of the Girls' League, she noted, came from being an honor student, her extracurricular activities, and through a popular vote. Yet, although the Caucasian American students acknowledged her diligence, they rarely reached out to the Japanese Americans socially. "We were different," she recalled, "and seen in that light."

Her parents could not afford to pay for her higher education, but Sachi's achievements won her scholarships. She attended the University of California at Los Angeles. At that time, college attendance was unusual for a Nisei woman. Less than 7 percent of Nisei females in 1940 had completed one to three years of college in California (Thomas, 1952, as cited in Nakano, 1990). Sachi, however, was ambitious and completed a bachelor's degree in international relations. She originally planned to work in the foreign service or as a foreign correspondent, a goal that she now considers unrealistic.

> From the standpoint of the relations between Japan and the United States at that time, how could I possibly get anything in that field? My dream, and this again was very naive, was to become a foreign correspondent. Instead, my mentors in high school, a couple of high school teachers who took an interest in me, wanted me to get into the diplomatic field. So I went along with what they wanted because they really pushed me along the way ... . In those days there were very few Japanese from the country area who went to college at all and I guess these teachers always perceived Japanese Americans as kind of "buffers" or "catalysts" to better relations between the two countries.

Sachi was unable to locate a position in her field after graduation and attributed this to both the negative economic conditions at the time and to her being Japanese American. Instead, she registered with the National Youth Administration and took a job with the California Department of Employment. In November 1941, at the age of twenty-one, she became a junior interviewer, screening potential job applicants in downtown Los Angeles.

Then Japan attacked Pearl Harbor. Sachi clearly recalled that day:

> It was Sunday and it was nice and quiet and I turned on my radio. It was very strange, a lot of static on the radio. I thought something was wrong with my radio and I was switching from station to station.
>
> My feelings were mainly of disbelief and confusion. Because I was an international relations major and had some background in our relations with Japan previous to the bombing ... it was like knowing that a hurricane is headed your way but hoping with all your heart that it will veer to the north or the south of you or disintegrate before it hits. Like a nightmare. I kept thinking, "I've got to wake up from this!" I remember that so clearly. The way I've recorded it in my book is:
>
> "The same garbled reports pierced the air, disturbing the morning calm. Just as my mind began piecing together the fragments, the newscaster confirmed my worst apprehensions. Japanese planes had bombed Pearl Harbor. War was imminent. I could not believe it. I felt a sudden chill, then nausea. ... Vague fears crowded my consciousness. When I learned where Pearl Harbor was, I wondered if California would be the next target. I wondered what would happen to Japanese Americans and our parents. There was sure to be an impact on us."

Sachi had been taught, and believed, that as an American, her rights were inalienable. Yet, the aftermath of Pearl Harbor soon disproved that belief. Fifteen hundred Issei men were arrested the night of the attack (Daniels, 1988). Their families often had no idea where they had been taken. Community members heard that people were being victimized. Japanese Americans were being run off the streets and many feared that anyone found to have links with Japan would be punished. Sachi's father, like many other Issei, burned all of the family's Japanese books, scrolls, kimonos, and many heirlooms. Sachi's reaction to this loss at that time surprises her now. "You know," she said, "I wasn't sad about the incineration. ... I thought, 'Well good. I got rid of my heritage.' I felt that my heritage had dogged me all my life."

But the painful reality of her situation could not be denied. Returning home from work one day, she found the house in chaos; drawers were turned upside down, and books scattered about. The sheriff's department had searched the home, violating the privacy of her family, and confiscated all cameras and radios. Sachi's books and papers were examined. She even found old letters she had received from a Caucasian American friend scrutinized, with sections underlined in red. "I began to feel like a criminal about that time. ... I felt like I must be doing something wrong or something is wrong that I'm being investigated. Without having committed a crime, I began to feel like I was on trial."

Sachi was soon put into a back office at her work and no longer permitted to interview applicants. According to her supervisor, she was "too visible." Then in February 1942, President Roosevelt signed Executive Order 9066. The order officially authorized the removal of Japanese Americans from the West Coast. By the beginning of April, the mass evacuation began. Because the permanent camps were not yet completed, some 92,000 people were moved first to temporary assembly centers (CWRIC, 1982). Most assembly centers were located at fairgrounds or racetracks; living quarters consisted of whitewashed animal stalls or exhibition halls where hundreds at a time were housed. The average stay before moving to the permanent camps was three months (CWRIC, 1982).

It was during this time that Sachi was transferred to the Wartime Civilian Control Administration (WCCA) in Los Angeles. The WCCA was an agency designed to provide information regarding evacuation to those who were about to be removed. Since the government restricted the travel of all Japanese Americans to within a five-mile radius of their home, one of Sachi's duties included the processing of permits for those who wished to travel outside that boundary. She remembers the absurdity of the whole situation: In some cases, individuals had to drive twenty miles to her office to apply for a permit to travel outside the five-mile restricted zone!

Japanese cultural values strongly influenced her response during this difficult and uncertain time. "You felt like you were being shunted from one place to another. But the cultural values of resignation and obedience to authority were so ingrained in me that I just did what I was told."

Anxieties surrounding an uncertain future also bred suspicion and distrust within the Japanese American community. Some saw Sachi's job as "working for the government." They felt she would be accorded special privileges, that she would be spared the internment. Nothing could have been further from the truth.

Japanese Americans at the Turlock, California, Assembly Center, May 2, 1942. *(Photo by Dorothea Lange, courtesy the National Archive.)*

In fact, Sachi, unlike most Japanese Americans, actually volunteered to relocate. She had heard through her work that conditions within the temporary holding centers were dehumanizing. Volunteers were needed to help establish the more permanent camps. Part of her felt relief by volunteering: She could escape the tense environment of her community. But, more important, she hoped that by volunteering, she could go ahead of her family and help prepare a place for them in camp. Although two of her sisters had already gone to live in New York with an uncle to avoid internment, Sachi still worried about her other younger siblings and her parents. She was led to believe that the government would keep families together and planned on her family rejoining her soon afterward.

While employed with the WCCA, Sachi met Maki, a woman who was to make a deep and lasting impact on her life. Maki was a social worker and community leader from San Francisco who directed the Japanese American YWCA in Los Angeles. As Sachi noted, "One of the few positive experiences of internment was getting to know her. She was so remarkable ... a great organizer and administrator, and also a very compassionate person. ... She had a way of making everyone feel very important."

Maki led Sachi and a group of young single women from Hawaii to help establish an internment camp in Poston, Arizona. (The Nisei from Hawaii had been staying at the YMCA attending trade schools when they became stranded on the mainland after Pearl Harbor.) Joined by other women and men, the volunteers boarded a bus to an unknown destination. The army ordered them to keep the shades drawn, making it impossible to determine the direction of travel. None of the volunteers knew what lay ahead or how long they would be separated from their home. They ended up in the Arizona desert.

Camp life brought numerous hardships. The heat was relentless, with temperatures frequently over 120 degrees. Without refrigeration the first week, many internees contracted dysentery. Dust and sand were everywhere, along with rattlesnakes and scorpions. In addition to the loss of freedom, there was a loss of privacy. The communal facilities meant that everyone now toileted, showered, and ate together. There were lines for everything. "That became the only thing you had to look forward to, your meals. So you started lining up early. ... After a while you became numb to the deprivation and didn't think too much about it."

Fear added to the uncertainty, Sachi recalled. "One of the sentries killed a man who was trying to climb over the fence and the rumor spread like wildfire, like all rumors do in a place like that, that we were all going to be gunned down and shot."

Threat of violence within the camps also came from fellow Japanese Americans as hostilities grew between factions of internees. Individuals were singled out as "informers" and beaten. Maki, Sachi's closest friend and adviser, angered a group of men who opposed her endorsement of the government's attempt to recruit Nisei from the camps into the armed forces. Worried that agitators would enter their barracks and beat them, as had happened to others, Maki, Sachi, and their roommates slept with football helmets on and baseball bats by their beds for several nights. Fortunately, the attack never materialized.

Sachi began to "settle into" her surroundings, working as an assistant to the Poston administrator in the employment office of the camp. Her $19 per month salary was the highest pay an internee could make. Wages for Caucasian Americans were much higher. Whereas a Nisei doctor earned $19 per month, a Caucasian American librarian in camp earned $167 a month (CWRIC, 1982).

Sachi had planned to establish a place for her family at Poston, but heard nothing from them for more than two months. Finally, a letter came from her mother from Heart Mountain, Wyoming, saying that the family had been moved to a camp there. Sachi immediately applied to transfer from Poston to Heart Mountain, but seven more months passed before she was permitted to do so. When the time came, she felt excited at the prospect of reuniting with her family. Yet, there was apprehension as well. Sachi described her feelings as she left Poston:

> It [camp] became such a safe place. As I said before, we had become kind of numb and just the idea of going outside and knowing of a hostile world out there was very scary. I remember going from Arizona straight up to Wyoming not even leaving my seat except to go to the lavatory and just getting something to eat, avoiding eye contact with people. I felt they could see I had been in a prison. You know, I can imagine how ex-prisoners feel because of that experience. You just visualize your prison num-

ber stamped across your chest. ... I remember these things very clearly. ... The war was still on, of course, and there were men in uniform. I thought they really had license to attack me. So I just stayed in my little corner and tried to make myself as invisible as I could. ... It is a frightening experience when you've been confined, to go out where you don't know who's going to do what to you.

Although Sachi arrived safely and joined her parents, brothers, and one sister, conditions at the Heart Mountain camp were as harsh as those she had left. In her manuscript, she refers to it as "another Poston," only covered with snow instead of sand. Sachi recalled feeling somewhat surprised by this: She had fantasized that somehow a place called "Heart Mountain" would be different.

The reunion itself raised mixed emotions. Sachi was happy to see her family, but immediately noticed how much her father had aged during the months of separation. In ten months his hair went from black to white. Once physically fit from farm labor, his body had become fleshy. His personality changed drastically as well. Before camp, Sachi described her father as "a forceful person, demanding and authoritative." The man she met at Heart Mountain was completely different:

My father had withdrawn and was very dejected. ... [He] faded more and more into the background until he became a shadowy figure there. ... It had a lot to do with the fact that he was no longer the provider. Japanese, in general, have a thing about being on welfare and the government was now the provider. There was nothing he could do to change that. He felt powerless and became very depressed. ... I believe many of the fathers changed in the same way. They lost their status and identity in the family unit.

Seeing her sister Dorothy at Heart Mountain was also emotional. Before volunteering to leave for Poston, Sachi felt sure Dorothy would not be interned. As a toddler, Dorothy was accidentally hit by their father with his car and suffered pelvic and hip injuries. A Swedish American couple, the Lanphears, frequented the family's roadside stand and noticed that Dorothy could not walk. They offered to take her into their home and pay for whatever operations and therapy she needed to recover. Dorothy ended up living with the Lanphears for nine years. At the time of the internment, Dorothy was in a cast from the waist down, recovering from hip surgery. As Sachi later wrote, "Surely there would be extenuating circumstances that would apply to a disabled girl requiring medical supervision. What possible threat did she pose to national security?" (Kaneshiro, 1992 p. E4). Anna Lanphear fought to keep the government from evacuating Dorothy, and when Sachi's family was moved to the temporary assembly center at the Pomona Fairgrounds, Dorothy remained in a hospital for physical therapy. The military agreed that Dorothy would not be interned if she was unable to walk when the family moved to a permanent camp. However, on the day of the family's departure, Dorothy arrived by ambulance at the fairgrounds with crutches and was interned along with everyone else.

Whereas Sachi's father seemed to fade away during internment, her mother blossomed, finding a new freedom in camp. As for many other Issei women, camp life freed her from many domestic chores (Matsumoto, 1988). She joined clubs, took classes, and did needlework for the first time. The contrasts between Sachi's mother and father at Heart Mountain were striking.

Sachi remained another four months at Heart Mountain. By then, the government began allowing young Nisei to leave the camps if they located a sponsor in the East or Midwest who would provide them with employment or if they volunteered for military service. Sachi's uncle in New York had already employed two of her sisters when the war began and was now able to sponsor Sachi as well. In 1943, she left Heart Mountain to work at his shop with him. Another year passed before she saw her parents and siblings who remained in camp.

After Internment

Sachi went to Hawaii in 1946, married, and started a family. She and her family then spent a brief time in New York before moving to California in 1952. Following the birth of two more children, Sachi started a career in social work in 1958. Postcamp life seemed to move increasingly toward stability. However, Sachi lost her oldest son in a tragic car accident in 1969. Two years later, she moved again to Hawaii where she remained for thirteen years. Life in Hawaii brought additional challenges, including the ending of her marriage. However, living where Japanese Americans and other Asian Americans were so numerous had a positive impact on Sachi's self-esteem. There was great comfort in being able to blend in, to go to a sports stadium and find that nearly everyone around her had black hair, too. In 1984, she retired and moved back to California where she has lived since.

Coping with the Impact of Internment

From an outside perspective, it is impossible to fully understand the effects of internment. Before camp, Sachi led a sheltered life. Her basic needs were always met. Internment represented her first experience of deprivation. Sachi learned to take things "one step at a time" and "grin and bear it." From her reflections upon her reactions at that time, it is clear that the camp experience had pervasive impacts.

> I'm sure the whole experience made me lose self-esteem. ... I became an ex-prisoner or an ex-criminal. It created a lot of self-doubt ... feeling unworthy, feeling like we deserved what we got ... feeling very timid about going into places where you may not be welcome. To this day, I kind of have my radar out thinking, "Is somebody not going to like me." I tend to play it pretty safe. I'm not proud of it but I try to avoid confrontation, being uncomfortable, or feeling unwelcome.

The experience also created skepticism and cynicism. "Many of us felt betrayed," she explained. "For the longest time I didn't even vote. I guess I didn't feel American anymore. I didn't feel that I had rights. Why should I vote?"

How does one cope with the psychological aftermath of such an experience? In Sachi's case, several factors influenced her coping reactions. For Sachi, as for many other Nisei, repression and denial became adaptive responses in the years following the camps (Mass, 1986). She describes her feelings as having been stored away in her "denial file" for decades: "For the longest time I wouldn't allow myself to think about it, but like a hangnail that hurts when brushing against something, the pain would resurface with some reminder. It was always there, and as long as nobody mentioned something that happened in camp you didn't think about it. But, when you were forced to think about it everything kind of rushed back." Conversations about camp with other Nisei remained superficial, allowing Sachi and other Japanese Americans to avoid the topic. When Nisei did discuss the internment, they talked only about the funny things that happened, never the painful memories. When non-Japanese Americans asked Sachi directly about her experiences, she answered as briefly as possible, maintaining a distance from her feelings.

Although both culture and gender have shaped her coping style and worldview, Sachi felt that culture took precedence over gender in many ways. *Gaman*, a Japanese term that refers to stoic patience and the suppression of emotion (Kitano, 1976), was most influential. As Sachi explained, "*Gaman* means to endure adversity. ... My father used to say in response to the slightest pain, 'You have to endure.' I'm quite sure it helped me cope. It wasn't a conscious thing and it's only in retrospect that I've come to realize that I learned to *gaman* in camp."

A second Japanese term, *on*, which refers to a sense of fatalism, also helped Sachi to cope. Although she acknowledged that such resignation may have prevented her and other Japanese Americans from asserting themselves in the face of injustice, it also helped provide a frame of mind for adjusting to the trauma of relocation and incarceration. "The practice of *on*, and [the saying] *Shikataganai*, being resigned to whatever the situation is. That helped. In a way it wasn't helpful because you never became assertive, but it made it OK for you when you resigned yourself to it. You think, 'Well, that's the way it is and there's nothing I can do about it.' In a way, it helped." Finally, the group orientation within the Japanese American community encouraged conformity and a "going along to get along" mentality (Nakano, 1990). This, in combination with *gaman* and *on*, shaped the responses of internees like Sachi.

Sachi's reactions of avoidance, resignation, and endurance persisted for decades. She did not talk freely about camp, even when her oldest son confronted her about it. These coping responses provided a means of managing her emotions, but did not resolve the feelings of stigma or vulnerability created by the internment. Sachi did not feel they directly raised her self-esteem. Close friends, together with living in Hawaii's Asian American environment, played a greater role in increasing her confidence. In retrospect, however, she noted that her coping experiences have increased her sense of resiliency.

> I'm a survivor. I learned to cope and just as I learned that there was life after internment, I knew there was life after the death of my child, after divorce, or any kind of loss. It helped me in my coping with adversity. ... I remember each time thinking,

"This too will pass" because I had gotten through the internment experience and I never fell apart. I remained strong for the rest of the family and I think this was because I learned to gaman.

When asked to consider if and how gender had influenced her experiences, Sachi paused to think, and then stated that she had not previously considered gender as a specific factor. However, she indicated that she has been more liberal than conservative on women's issues and wondered whether this might be due to the fact that Japanese Americans have been such "underdogs." Perhaps there was an indirect link between her experiences as an oppressed Japanese American and her sympathy toward the women's movement.

In reviewing her life during the war years, it also seemed to her that women (in particular, her mother and Maki) were the most influential figures. Sachi's years with Maki shaped her decision to follow the same career path and become a social worker. Observing the changes in her mother in camp also affected her image of Japanese American women. Although Sachi grew up viewing her mother as a submissive woman who catered to her domineering husband, Sachi saw her mother become assertive and independent during the internment. Sachi recalled: "She [Sachi's mother] was calling the shots and telling my father what to do, which she never would have done before. I was real proud of her. It was a change that served her well the rest of her life." Both Maki and Sachi's mother, then, served as important role models of strength and showed Sachi how Japanese American women could cope assertively.

Writing has provided a powerful means of coping as well. Upon retiring from social work, in 1985 Sachi joined a creative writing class. She had long been interested in writing, but had no intentions of writing about her internment experience. However, members of her writing class were very interested in her story and urged her to write about it. Sachi's volunteer work at that time with relatives of terminally ill patients also influenced her decision to record her experiences. As a volunteer, Sachi encouraged surviving relatives to keep a journal to help cope with their feelings. She recalled, "That got me interested. I thought, 'Well, maybe if I write about it it'll go away.'" Sachi proceeded to write an entire book, entitled *No Bitter Tears,* about her experiences and found this to be extremely therapeutic. "It was a real cleansing," she noted. "Initially I felt reluctant going back and looking at what had happened but the more I wrote about my experience the less painful it became."

External events have also aided in the coping process. The successful passage of the Civil Liberties Act in 1988 played an important role. The act included an official acknowledgment of wrongdoing and apology from the U.S. government and authorized the redress payment of $20,000 to each surviving internee. For Sachi, the most important consequence of the redress effort was not the money, but rather seeing widespread media coverage on the internment. "I think it really did help. I used to think, we went through all this and nobody knew about it and it's going to happen again. But I just feel now that there's too much documentation to allow it to happen again. I'm not sure but I would hope so."

Sachi's life story and responses to the multiple challenges of racism and the effects of internment powerfully demonstrate the long-term effects of trauma and injustice. The betrayal and unjustified suspicion of disloyalty by her own government left her, like many other Japanese Americans, feeling ashamed and unworthy (Mass, 1986)—in her own words, like an "ex-convict." The effects lasted for years. Yet, Sachi's life also teaches us about resilience and strength in the face of adversity. Early on she strove to excel academically in a social climate that excluded Japanese Americans and women. Much of her coping in response to the internment reflects internalized strengths fostered by her Japanese cultural heritage. These include *gaman, on,* and a focus on the importance of family. Her decision to leave home and volunteer to settle the camp at Poston also shows us a nonpassive proactive response to the stressors she faced. Sachi took on the role of a pioneer, leading the way for her family. Her ability to write about the camp experience some fifty years later reflects additional strength and courage as she has moved her feelings and perceptions out of the "denial file" and shared them in a public record. In the process, Sachi has had to revisit many painful memories.

We can learn much about Sachi's life through her sharing. Her story gives us invaluable insights into the internment and its consequences. As a third-generation Japanese American (Sansei), I feel an especially strong connection to the internment: Both of my parents were interned. I am grateful that Sachi would speak with me so openly about her experiences. At the same time, I feel like an intruder when I ask about the camps, asking her to again reach in and remember the past. My own research confirms that many Sansei feel a similar ambivalence when it comes to discussing the camps with those who were interned (Nagata, 1989, 1993). They wish to know about the event, but worry about reraising painful memories. Sansei such as myself have also felt significantly less racism and discrimination than the Nisei. It seems presumptuous to research and "analyze" Sachi's life when I cannot truly understand the depth of her experience. And writing *about* Sachi in the third person creates an impersonal, distanced tone when describing events that are clearly personal and emotional.

There is also, however, a dilemma in viewing the internment at a personal rather than a political level. A case study approach to examining the effects of internment provides rich data not obtainable through large-scale group methods. At the same time, "psychologizing" about Sachi's life and focusing on her individual coping reactions fails to capture the broader sociopolitical issues that are so crucially linked to the internment.

Finally, I am aware that this chapter reflects my perspective, my analysis, in describing Sachi's life. I have shared all drafts of this chapter with Sachi in an effort to ensure its accuracy. Nonetheless, my words shaped the representation of her story. Sachi would, I think, be reluctant to refer to herself as a pioneer or a courageous individual. Yet, in my mind, these descriptions are entirely fitting for her.

References

Commission on Wartime Relocation and Internment of Civilians. (1982). *Personal justice denied.* Washington, DC: U.S. Government Printing Office.

Daniels, R. (1981). *Concentration camps, North America: Japanese in the United States and Canada during World War II.* Melbourne, FL: Krieger.

_____. (1986). The conference keynote address: Relocation, redress, and the report: A historical appraisal. In R. Daniels, S. C. Taylor, & H.H.L. Kitano (Eds.), *Japanese Americans: From relocation to redress* (pp. 3–9). Salt Lake City: University of Utah Press.

_____. (1988). *Asian America: Chinese and Japanese in the United States since 1850.* Seattle: University of Washington Press.

Kaneshiro, S. (1988). *No bitter tears.* Unpublished manuscript.

_____. (May 1992). Brought together for the sake of a little girl. *Los Angeles Times,* pp. E1, E4.

Kitano, H.H.L. (1976). *Japanese Americans: The evolution of a subculture.* Englewood Cliffs, NJ: Prentice-Hall.

Mass, A. I. (1986). Psychological effects of the camps on the Japanese Americans. In R. Daniels, S. C. Taylor, & H.H.L. Kitano (Eds.), *Japanese Americans: From relocation to redress* (pp. 159–162). Salt Lake City: University of Utah Press.

Matsumoto, V. (1988). Nisei women and resettlement during World War II. In Asian Women United (Eds.), *Making waves: An anthology of writings by and about Asian American women* (pp. 115–126). Boston: Beacon.

Morishima, J. K. (1973). The evacuation: Impact on the family. In S. Sue & N. N. Wagner (Eds.), *Asian Americans: Psychological perspectives* (pp. 13–19). Palo Alto, CA: Science and Behavior Books.

Nagata, D. K. (1989). Long-term effects of the Japanese American internment camps: Impact upon the children of internees. *Journal of the Asian American Psychological Association, 13,* 48–55.

_____. (1993). *Legacy of injustice: Exploring the cross-generational impact of the Japanese American internment.* New York: Plenum.

Nakano, M. (1990). *Japanese American women: Three generations, 1890–1990.* Berkeley: Mina Press.

Okada, J. (1981). *No-no boy.* Seattle: University of Washington Press.

Sone, M. (1991). *Nisei daughter.* Seattle: University of Washington Press.

Tateishi, J. (1984). *And justice for all: An oral history of the Japanese American detention camps.* New York: Random House.

Thomas, D. S. (1952). *The salvage.* Berkeley: University of California Press.

Uchida, Y. (1982). *Desert exile: The uprooting of a Japanese American family.* Seattle: University of Washington Press.

Weglyn, M. (1976). *Years of infamy: The untold story of America's concentration camps.* New York: William Morrow.

Williams, J. E., & Coleman, A. M. (1992). *Lest we forget: The Japanese and America's wartime mistake.* East Rockaway, NY: Cummings & Hathaway.

9

"I Didn't Want a Life Like That": Constructing a Life Between Cultures

AMY SCHULZ

A lot of times I felt I should have been a man. It's been hard to be a woman in a time of transition, when we're going through a lot of changes culturally. You try to respond to those changes, then are told it's not proper to act this way.

(Anne, age 32)

ANNE WAS BORN in the late 1950s and has lived most of her life in the Navajo Nation in the southwestern United States, where her family has lived for generations. Her story here is filtered through the eyes of a fourth-generation Swedish- and German-American: I was also born in the 1950s; I live in the midwestern United States where my great-grandparents settled in the late 1800s. Anne and I first met on one of my early visits to the Navajo Nation when we were introduced by a mutual friend who knew that we had similar work histories and interests. Later, when I returned to conduct doctoral research that explored identity and social change through the life stories of Navajo women, Anne agreed to work with me as a participant in the study. The intensity of Anne's story, and her power as a storyteller, led me to contact her when the opportunity arose to contribute to this volume. After some thought Anne agreed to the chapter, but she preferred not to be identified by name in order to protect her own privacy and that of her family—"Anne" is a pseudonym. We worked together to construct the framework for the chapter, and Anne read and commented on earlier drafts. Much of the story is told in her voice; mine is present in the analytical, interpretive, and summary aspects of the text.

Navajo and other North American Indians have experienced direct and often coercive pressure to replace traditional cultural systems with those of European-Americans. During the late 1800s and much of the first half of the 1900s, the U.S. Indian education system explicitly promoted the replacement of Indian cultures with European-American language and values. Concurrent with the attempts of the schools to "civilize" Indian children through education were the efforts of missionaries to convert American Indians from their own religious beliefs to Christianity. More recently, such direct assimilation policies have been replaced with the language of tribal self-determination and control over the content and process of the education of Indian children. However, continued erosion of tribal economic systems and lifestyles undermines the cultural forms based in these systems and contributes to the challenge of maintaining tribal language and culture. The complexities of assimilation and resistance as they play out in one individual life are explored through Anne's story.

This analysis speaks to the ongoing dialogue within the social sciences regarding the balance between structure and agency—or sociocultural rules and personal autonomy—in shaping human action and social change. Bourdieu (1977) emphasized the role of structure as a determinant of action, whereas more recent work has emphasized human autonomy as a force shaping action within structural parameters. William Sewell, Jr. (1989), proposed that culture may be understood as a system of rules and resources that shape but do not determine human action and ultimately reproduce or transform existing structures. Similarly, the sociologist Ann Swidler (1986) conceptualized culture as a "toolbox" from which individuals draw as they manage their lives, again emphasizing individual autonomy within the parameters of a cultural framework. Tools may take the form of rules or schemata that suggest appropriate action or interaction. These rules may be found in underlying assumptions that guide behavior without conscious articulation and may appear in religious ceremonies, as recurrent themes in stories and legends, or in the "taken-for-granted" activities of everyday life.

A central theme within Navajo spiritual and cultural practices is the idea of harmony or balance within the individual and between the individual and the systems within which she exists. In times of rapid transition this balance may be disrupted, and human actions (such as Navajo ceremonies) become necessary to restore harmony. As Anne told her story she described three major challenges or disruptions that occurred in her life: an arranged marriage that challenged her relationship with her maternal clan relatives; a breach of trust that challenged her relationship with her husband; and a difficult period with her son that challenged her personal resources but ultimately strengthened her sense of connection to family and tribe. Her description of these challenges and her strategic use of resources from both Navajo and Anglo cultures as she responded to them illuminates intentional, motivated action as an aspect of cultural re-creation and transformation.

This chapter begins with a description of Anne's childhood and the early events that influenced her evolving identity, followed by sections based on each of the three challenges she described. Anne's choice of strategies to respond to these life events is explored in the context of competing pressures and the resources and options available to respond to these pressures. Throughout her story, Anne describes her struggle to balance independence and interdependence, autonomy and cultural expectations, and to create her own identity in a time of cultural change. Reflecting on the challenges she faced and her determination not to allow her life course to be molded by others, she said simply: "I didn't want a life like that."

The Evolution of Identity:
Early Childhood

Anne's parents separated shortly after her birth and she lived with her mother and older sister for most of her early childhood. Her early school experience was similar to that of other Navajo children living on the reservation in the 1950s and 1960s: Most attended reservation boarding schools during their elementary years and moved to nonreservation boarding schools for junior and senior high school. U.S. Indian education at the time explicitly promoted preparation for employment in urban communities as part of federal efforts to terminate tribal rights.[1] The English language was promoted and Navajo language and practices were discouraged:

> We went to school at a BIA [Bureau of Indian Affairs] boarding school. I remember we hated to go. My mom would come and pick us up and we'd go home for the weekend, and then she'd bring us back on Sunday and we'd be there for two or three weeks until she'd come again. I just hated to go back. I remember they never wanted us to talk in our native language, and when we did they'd wash our mouths out with soap. It was the only school around for miles, and it was only elementary school. When I finished the grades there I would have had to go to a boarding school off the reservation, and the closest one was in New Mexico.

When Anne was about eight years old her mother remarried. Anne became very close to her stepfather, usually referring to him as her father, and his traditional knowledge and training were an important influence throughout her life. Anne's biological father was not an active presence in her life and does not appear in this chapter; throughout, "father" and "stepfather" refer to this stepfather. When Anne was eight years old, her mother and stepfather agreed to send her to live with a Mormon foster family off the reservation, in part because of the educational opportunities they believed this would offer.[2]

> So I went to live with a family in Arizona—not very far from here, but it seems like a long ways. I had a hard time getting used to it. They had two kids, a boy and a girl. Their daughter was about the same age as I am, just a few months older. And then the boy was a few years younger. They were just super, and they accepted me right off and really made me feel right at home. For the next four years I would come back [to the

Navajo Nation] during the summers for about four weeks and then go back again
and spend the rest of the year with them.

During the time she lived with this family, Anne was immersed in the Mormon
religion.

> When I went and stayed with them for four years, every Sunday we went to church,
> and we had Sunday school on Sundays also, and then we had little things in between.
> Like Wednesday, I think it was, we'd have classes at the church and it seems like a lot
> of it just revolved around the church. Most of the family activities anyway. And then
> whenever we did go on vacation, we'd go to places like Salt Lake City and look at the
> Temple and … everything had to do with the church, their religion. So the more and
> more I stayed there, the more and more I believed it. … And after four years they
> wanted to adopt me, and I wanted to go live with them too. It was like my own life
> over there, and over here it was just like—four weeks out of the year and I didn't re-
> ally know anybody anymore. I didn't know my cousins. A lot of my aunts had gone
> off and had their own families and had children that I didn't know. So I was like a
> stranger in my own family.

Anne's mother objected strongly to the adoption, and insisted that Anne come
back to live on the reservation. At the age of twelve, Anne returned to attend one
of the first schools on the reservation to teach Navajo language and culture in addition to English, math, and science. After living away from the Navajo Nation for
four years and attending an English-speaking day school, the adjustment to
boarding school and the use of Navajo language was not easy:

> And then I found out that they required a Navajo language and culture class in order
> to graduate from the school. And I thought—my God—I felt like such an outsider
> going there, because I didn't talk fluent Navajo. I certainly couldn't read it, I certainly
> couldn't write it. It was just a big burden on me it seems the first three or four years
> that I went there. Finally during my junior year I told myself "You've got to get this.
> This is your language, this is your culture." So I read all the books that I could find on
> culture that had come out of Rough Rock, and Rock Point, and NCC [Navajo Com-
> munity College].[3] I got to the point where I knew my culture really good, the history.
> And my stepdad, during this whole time, whenever I got a chance to go home and he
> was there, I used to ask him a lot of questions like "What can you tell me about the
> Long Walk period, or how we came into the Fourth World?"[4] And he would tell me.
> A lot of the cultural stuff I had to try and relearn when I came back to the reservation.
> The language—not so much talking it, but reading and writing it—was difficult for
> me. And that was one of the requirements to graduate and I had such a hard time.
> But I did it.

As Anne described this accomplishment, her Navajo identity—"This is your
language, this is your culture"—was key. Despite the time that she had lived away
from the Navajo Nation and her brief period of conversion to the Mormon faith,
she retained a sense of herself as Navajo and worked to regain her Navajo spiritual
and cultural understandings through cultural studies at school and conversations
with her stepfather. However, her acceptance of these traditions was not passive or

unreflective; throughout her story she described struggling to define the meaning of her identity as a Navajo woman on her own terms.

Challenge I: Arranged Marriage, Resources, and Resistance

Through the early 1900s it remained fairly common for Navajo parents to arrange the marriage of their daughters and sons. An older Navajo woman I interviewed described parental rights to arrange marriages during her youth in the 1930s, saying: "If you ran off and married someone, they said 'you stole yourself from your parents.'" Although such marriages were less common in the 1970s, when Anne was in her mid-teens her mother and maternal grandmother arranged her marriage to a man twenty years her senior.

The summer before I started my Junior year of high school, a family came by with my grandma. I thought, "These are people I haven't seen—it must be important." So my younger sister and I went after the sheep and stayed out there. My older sister came and found us and she said "Mom wants to talk to you." By the time I got back my grandma and my mom were standing out in front under one of the trees, so I walked up to them and asked what they wanted and they said "This family came up here looking for a wife for their son." And right then I started crying, I said "No, not me. I'm not ready." And I cried and cried. I stood there crying, and then finally one of the ladies inside came out and she talked to me and told me about her son and I was just really bitter. I didn't say anything—I didn't say hello, I didn't say goodbye. I just didn't say anything, I didn't even look at her. And then my mom says "Well, she's gonna be a Junior this coming year, so why don't we wait until a week after her graduation, her high school graduation, and then we'll go ahead and have the wedding." So they arranged everything. They arranged everything and I just cried the whole time. My dad wasn't there.[5] My mom said yes on her own. A lot of times when my mom and my dad disagreed about things as far as my older sister and myself were concerned my mom would always say "Well, they're not yours so you have nothing to say over them—they're mine." So, I don't know, it seems when I look back on it now my dad probably felt like his hands were tied. During those years he always said "I'm gonna adopt you—I'm gonna give you my name." But it never got to that point—he was never around here to where like he could ... where he had time to do that. I remember though, my mom didn't tell him when he came back. On Sunday when he was leaving I said, "Well, what did you tell dad?" She said, "Well, dad doesn't have any business knowing, he's not your dad." So that was that.

Anne's sense of powerlessness was compounded by her isolation from her stepfather, who she saw as her only ally within the family. She turned next to other potential resources—her friends and teachers at school.

I had a boyfriend that went to school at_____ all of his life. He read Navajo fluently, he spoke it fluently, he just knew Navajo language, history, and culture inside and out. I was impressed with him. We had talked about getting married, but we both said after college and if we're still interested, and after that even. Throughout the years, we just got closer and closer. When I went back during my Junior year, around Christmas time, I told him. I said, "You know, my mom and my grandma have this plan for me—I'm going to be married a week after my graduation." Most of the time I just cried every time I thought about it, because I really couldn't do anything. If I was to run away from home it seemed like there was really no place for me to run where she wouldn't find me. I was terrified about running away. … When we got back from vacation my boyfriend said "Well, I don't want you to marry this guy and I know you don't want to, and we did talk about getting married after high school, but why not before?"

To this point, Anne had considered just two options—to go along with the arranged marriage or to run away. The first would have maintained important connections with family and clan, but at the expense of her autonomy. The second would have maintained her autonomy, but separated her from family and community. Her boyfriend's suggestion offered a third alternative through which she could both avoid the arranged marriage and maintain ties within the Navajo community through her husband's family, although risking her relationship with her maternal clan.[6]

However, this option was not problem free. Anne believed that her mother would not agree to the marriage because she was bound by her agreement with the other family. In addition, Anne was concerned about the close kin relationship between her family and her boyfriend's.

> I remember asking one of my aunts about his clan, if he was related to us, and then I asked my culture teacher "Is this clan related to my clan?" I found out that sure enough, our clans were really close. We just went round and round and round and round. All these things they tell you—if you marry into your own clan you come out with kids that are retarded or something missing or something like that—it just sticks in your mind.

Anne and her boyfriend ultimately decided to go ahead with their plan to marry despite their close clan relation. Believing that her mother would not permit the marriage, they devised a plan that bypassed her authority. "So finally, we decided that the only way my mom would let us get married to each other was if we had a baby. So that's when we got pregnant. I was a Junior in high school and I was able to hide it throughout the summer, up to Christmas I was able to hide it. I was due in January."

Anne concealed her pregnancy from her parents as long as she could. In contrast with her childhood experience with BIA boarding schools, the community school became an important resource and source of support. The boarding school enabled her to hide the pregnancy from her parents and provided access to a sympathetic teacher who offered both material and emotional support.

> The only person that knew I was pregnant was my Home Ec teacher. Because I would ask her "How do you alter?" and she would show me how to alter clothes and that's when I learned. I altered my own clothes. And then when I had my baby, I put them back to the regular size. I talked to her about the pregnancy, but I didn't tell her why.

She just said she knew I'd tell her when I was ready. But she said "We're gonna have to tell your mother sooner or later." I kept telling her "Please don't tell her," because I knew my mom would be furious.

In December, her ninth month of pregnancy, Anne returned home for the winter semester break.

During Christmas my father had taken vacation for two weeks. He said "You look really thin up here [gestured to face] but I can tell you're putting on weight here—are you gonna have a baby?" This was my father asking me and I couldn't lie to him. I said "Yes, I am." He said, "Well, do we know the father?" And I said, "No, I don't think so but he's willing to come up here and meet you." He took out his truck keys and said "Go get him—we'll spend Christmas together."

As Anne had anticipated, her mother was furious when she learned of Anne's pregnancy—an anger that would shape their relationship for years to come. Her stepfather was supportive, however, and immediately accepted her boyfriend into the family. A week after Christmas Anne's family held a traditional Navajo wedding ceremony, and the next day a ceremony within the Native American Church (NAC), in which her father-in-law was a roadman, or spiritual leader.[7]

I'll never forget that day. I was gonna have a baby the next week and you have to sit up all night. ... In the morning in the Native American Church is the time they tell about what the ceremony is all about ... where it came from, how he got it, and how they were able to perform the ceremony. Before midnight is when you as a couple tell the people that came what your intentions are, what your plans are, what your goals are, and then during the night they pray for you. And then in the morning, tell the visions they saw and how we should go about this and that.[8]

During the ceremony, Anne's new in-laws told of the visions they had for the young couple, which included advice about where and how they should live:

My in-laws said that we had to make a house and it's gonna have to be where my husband is from. I didn't agree. My house is where my mother is living or close to her.[9] It was always pounded into my head that you never go to live with the man's family. You never move all your belongings over there. He comes over to your side of the family. So even if I wanted to, inside there was still this teaching that I had all my life. Everybody that I can remember—I have seven aunts, my grandfather, my grandmother—all the years I was growing up they all said "You make your life, build a house for your family where you're from—not the man's residence." So, even if I wanted to there was always something in the back of my mind that said no.

And then, the other thing they tell you a lot about in the ceremony is "This is how you should live your life. ... This is the path that you should take." I told them at that time that I probably won't make you happy as in-laws. ... I told them that even as new in-laws, I didn't appreciate being told how I should live my life. ... [My father-in-law] told me one of the things I should be thinking about was not necessarily to go on to college or school but stay at home and make a home for my kids. And that I shouldn't be taking any kind of birth control, contraception, nothing. And that just blew me away. I wasn't going to have him tell me how many kids I'm gonna have. I said that's my decision, so what I choose to do with my body and what I choose to put into my body is my decision. It just went on and on with us, going back and forth, and my husband kept nudging me, telling me [to stop]. ... He knew how I was. Finally we came to an agreement where my father-in-law says to make your own choices.

Later in the ceremony, Anne received unexpected support from her mother, despite the tension between them:

I think I felt closest to my mother toward morning when she told everybody that I was right in a way. Because I had been off the reservation for four years and when I came back I had my own set of ideas, my own way of thinking and it didn't matter what anybody said, I'd go by what I thought was right. My mom said, "She's different in that way"—and that makes me proud of her because none of us as ladies, I don't think, were like that. Not very many ladies would do that. See, ladies are forbidden to speak unless they're asked a question in a [NAC] meeting.

Anne's resistance to these efforts to shape her future may have been grounded in her experience living off the reservation as her mother suggested. The exposure to different family and social patterns through her time off the reservation, as well as her years at boarding school, certainly influenced Anne's sense of options and alternatives when confronted with the pressure to accept an arranged marriage or the advice of her in-laws. Her willingness to confront her in-laws directly, despite her husband's discomfort, may also have been influenced by a growing sense of personal power derived through her successful use of available resources to resist the arranged marriage. Having "stolen herself" from her parents by marrying a partner of her choice, she had also claimed herself[10] and was unwilling to relinquish her new power by moving in with her new husband's family. Through this process, Anne had renegotiated the terms of her relationship with her family, moving from dependence to a more autonomous position.

There were, however, long-lasting repercussions. Fifteen years later, Anne reflected: "My mom and I had a lot of conflict. ... She wanted different things for me and I wanted different things for me. Throughout the years I think she learned to accept ... or not really accept but ... I don't know, maybe sometime she'll grow out of her anger. Just the way I went about growing up I guess."

Challenge II: Marital Conflict, Personal Power, and Social Resources

Anne's second challenge came in the form of a crisis in her marriage. Following the birth of her son and her graduation from high school, she stayed home while her husband worked to support the family. Soon after the birth of their second child, a daughter, Anne discovered that her husband's nights out with his friends involved alcohol and other women. Her response was swift, angry, and decisive:

When I found out what he was doing I hauled all his stuff back up to his mom and told them I won't be treated that way. I don't want a life like that. His mom kept telling me that these are some of the things that a man goes through. And I said well, I'm not gonna go through it with him. My daughter was about three months—I remember she was still in a cradleboard. We were separated for about six months and during that time he kept coming around, saying he'll never do it again. I said—I don't care. You can do it all you want—I just want out of the marriage. I said it evidently didn't mean the same thing to you as it did to me. And then his parents came over several times. They would talk to my mom, they would talk to my dad. My mom would talk to me, my dad would talk to me. I told them, I don't want to have anything to do with him. He's the one that made the decision that he needed somebody else—let him have somebody else, but I'm not gonna be there.

Anne's anger became a catalyst for personal and interpersonal change. She rejected the efforts of her husband, his parents, and her own parents to change her mind and began instead to work toward personal and financial independence.

And then I started checking into the schools. I checked into NCC [Navajo Community College] and enrolled myself for the next year and then I took a job with _____: I was a group home parent. That way I was able to hold down a permanent job and still go to school during the day. Before that I hadn't worked at all. It was kind of fun. The kids would take my mind off everything. They gave me an apartment to stay at here in town. Gosh, my paycheck was something like $199 a month and they took out about $98 for rent. So I only had like a hundred dollars once they took out the rent. To me that was a lot of money. I went to school up there at NCC during the day, took both kids with me, put them in day care up there.

The path to independence was not a smooth one, as Anne juggled the responsibilities of caring for her young son and infant daughter with work and school. In addition to the challenge of managing these multiple tasks, her stepfather became terminally ill.

At about that time my father was diagnosed as having cancer. We went back and forth a lot to [the town where the hospital was]. Sometimes there was nobody to take him, so I would miss my class and take him up and bring him back home. I went through one semester doing all that.

During that time my husband kept coming by and saying he wouldn't ever do it again. His mother kept coming by and saying well, how you gonna raise your kids, you can't do it alone. I said "I am doing it alone. I'm going to." So I was just stubborn! Well, I didn't like the way I was treated back then. I just told myself, you can do it without him. ... I filed for divorce and then I had to wait three months to go to court. During that time my husband got a letter saying that I had filed for divorce and he came over crying and said "how could you?" And I said "how could you?" He said he was just being pressured a lot by his friends and that's the only reason he did it. Because when we met, he never drank or anything. I told him how I felt about what he did, and that I didn't want a life like that—I wanted something different. And if that meant that he was going to be out of the picture then that's what it meant, because I wasn't going to live like that.

Once again her husband's family intervened, arranging a NAC meeting for the couple. Initially Anne refused to attend, but eventually she agreed, feeling that it was important to defend herself against the accusations that would be made. Her parents could not attend due to her father's illness, so one of her sisters came to offer support. Anne's suspicions were confirmed:

> Throughout the meeting, sure enough, they said I wasn't acting appropriately and that's why my husband started drinking, that's why he started running around with other ladies. And that got me so angry. What was I doing besides staying home and taking care of the kids, doing his laundry, making sure he had something to eat when he got home, making sure he had clean clothes to wear. I said, "I just became a mother to him—so you are right, I wasn't being a wife, I was being his mother. I'm through baby-sitting. I don't want to be raising a twenty-year-old guy. I have enough problems taking care of my two kids and myself."
>
> Throughout the whole meeting they tried to make me feel like I was at fault, that I was the one that was making him do all those things. I said the only way I could make him do what he was doing was to hold a gun to his head. I wasn't doing anything like that. Finally my husband said something—he said it was all his fault—"There's no sense blaming her."

Anne's determined position and her husband's eventual acknowledgment of his own responsibility led to a shift in the meeting:

> So after that they talked to me and finally they said, "Well, why don't you stand up here. We're gonna bless you and then you can go on with whatever you want to do in your life, and that way we will have separated the two of you. As far as your mind is concerned, it won't be anything that's holding you back in the future—just thinking about what could have been."
>
> That sounded good to me. So I stood up there and before I know it my husband was standing by me. My father-in-law had us hold hands and then he started praying over us. About five minutes into what he was doing I felt that love coming back for my husband. I thought, I really don't want to separate, but I also don't want to be living like this in the future. I thought about my kids and, just a lot of things went through my mind. Then I looked at my husband and he looked at me and I could hear him thinking that he wasn't ever going to do it again. I tried to look away from him and just stare into the fire. My father-in-law was saying a prayer all this time. I thought, he's not trying to separate us. He's actually bringing us back together.
>
> The way he's doing it was to make us remember how we felt about each other when we first met. That's when I believed in what my father-in-law could do [as a spiritual leader]. Being as stubborn as I am it took me a while to come around. We got back together about two months later—my daughter was almost a year old and my son was a little over two, so they don't remember that part in their lives. Which I think is good. They don't ever remember their father doing anything like that.

As in the first challenge, the balance between independence and interdependence was transformed through this episode. The breach of trust in her relationship with her husband became a catalyst for Anne to decrease her economic dependence through education and employment. Anne's clear personal boundaries and her refusal to accept responsibility for her husband's actions, even in the face of intense social pressure, laid groundwork for renegotiating the terms of the relationship.

Challenge III: Spirituality, Harmony, and Balance

Eight months after our initial conversations, when Anne and I met to develop the outline for this chapter, her first words were "A lot has happened since we talked in the fall," and she proceeded to describe her most recent challenge. Several months before, her son, then fifteen, began to have difficulty in school, and Anne and her husband tried to talk with him. Initially he refused to talk to them, claiming both that nothing was wrong and that he could handle anything that happened. However, continuing problems led to an emotional family meeting.

> I told him I don't want to hear that you don't know or that nothing's wrong. Something is bothering you. And I want to know now or I'm going to take you to the mental health people and have them talk to you. I just want you to talk to somebody.
>
> At that moment he just broke down and cried. I felt guilty, because I thought I was being too harsh. And my husband was just sitting there surprised. ... Finally [my son] says "I just can't take it anymore." I said "What is it?" He says "My friends talk about being with their grandparents ... especially [his best friend]. He says, you should have seen my grandfather. We had so much fun, we did this, we did that." He said "I can't take it anymore that I don't have that person there to do things for me, that I can do things with."[11] Then we let him talk and my husband and I kept looking at each other [thinking] he's too young, he shouldn't remember his grandfather. Maybe just what he looked like or something, not much more than that. I was thinking that.

Anne and her husband did their best to support and comfort their son, assuring him of their love and concern and encouraging him to seek out other family members to fill the role of his grandfather. Her son remained troubled, however, and on a visit a few weeks later, Anne's mother noted her grandson's behavior and questioned Anne. Upon hearing of the events of the past several months, her mother made immediate arrangements for a traditional Navajo ceremony. "The medicine man did a prayer for him, kind of like a person in between to talk to my father for my son. A lot of the prayers were in the old Navajo language, where I kind of had to do some translating for my son."

During the first part of the ceremony Anne's son, who had been raised primarily in the Native American Church and had never before been the subject of a traditional ceremony, remained somewhat skeptical and aloof.

> But as the prayers went on, you could tell that it was working. When the medicine man said "Comfort your grandson right now, he's in trouble ... comfort him right now as you did when you were here," that's when I felt really that he was in the room. That's when my son started crying. My oldest daughter too, she started crying. ... I

just felt my dad there, and I thought "I can take on anything, I have the strength." At that point I realized the ceremony was helping my son—he just let everything out.

During the ceremony, family members were invited to speak to the spirit of Anne's stepfather and to tell of their hopes and prayers for her son.

I said a prayer, and I said a prayer to my dad. I told him things like "Don't let him feel this way, let him feel like you are here with him, that he can talk to you freely, or either me or his grandmother. Don't let him feel all alone, that he can't get any help from anybody." My mother said basically the same thing—"Please help him, help him deal with some of his problems that he's facing." Even my mom's new husband said a prayer, like "You're gone, I'm here. Let me take over for you. Let me do the things you wanted to do, that you never did. Let me have that relationship with your grandkids."

The ceremony began a process of healing for Anne's son and for the family as a whole. Whereas in the first two challenges Anne's experience with religion was as a medium through which others attempted to exert control over her, in this case it became an important resource for her and her family. The ceremony provided an opportunity for public display of support and caring and moved the family toward a restoration of harmony and balance. The deep connection Anne felt with her stepfather during the ceremony strengthened her own spirituality. She and her mother have since begun to resolve their long-standing conflict. "I guess for a long time, ever since my mom wanted to marry me off to a man that I didn't know, our relationship just kind of drifted apart. And we never really got back together—somehow it just got further and further. And when my son was going through that and I needed help, she was there. It seemed like our relationship now is where it should be as mother and daughter. I feel closer to her than I have in years."

Conclusion

Throughout Anne's life she found strength in her Navajo identity and in Navajo cultural resources, renegotiating or rejecting those rules she found too constraining or personally damaging. Her social position as a Navajo woman in the United States in the latter half of the 1900s set the stage for the challenges she faced: Few women younger than Anne will ever face an arranged marriage, but few of her elders whose marriage was arranged had access to the resources Anne drew on as she resisted the marriage. So too with the conflict within her marriage—the availability of jobs and educational opportunities on the reservation enabled her to resist family pressure to remain in the marriage and to demand changes in the terms of the relationship. And finally, when her son encountered a difficult period, Anne and her family were able to draw upon traditional spiritual practices as a source of strength. The challenges Anne encountered highlight tensions that arise at the interface of Navajo and European-American cultures: The strategies she enacted in response drew upon the cultural frameworks and material resources available from both social groups to create a life that she *did* want. Her life story, with its particular configuration of motivations, challenges, and resources, provides insight into the role of individual agency in weaving the complex patterns of social and cultural change.

Acknowledgments

I am grateful for the thorough and thoughtful comments of Diana DeVries, Carol Franz, Dorothy Henderson, James House, JoEllen Shively, and Abigail Stewart on earlier drafts of this chapter. I am also deeply indebted to the women who taught me through their words and through the stories of their lives of the conflicts and courage involved in living every day between cultures. And most of all, I am indebted to "Anne."

Notes

1. For discussions of Indian education policy and its relationship to termination of tribal rights during the 1950s and 1960s see Szasz (1974) or Senese (1991).

2. The Church of Jesus Christ of the Latter Day Saints (the Mormon church, or LDS) actively recruited children from Navajo families, placing them with Mormon foster families off the reservation as part of the church's efforts to convert the Navajo to the Mormon religion.

3. Rough Rock and Rock Point were two of the first schools in the Navajo Nation at which the Navajo took advantage of changes in federal legislation that allowed Indian communities to develop and manage their own school systems. These schools are well known for their innovations in bilingual and bicultural education beginning in the 1960s and continuing to the present day. Navajo Community College is a tribally run and supported college with branches throughout the Navajo Nation.

4. The Long Walk refers to the surrender of the Navajo to Kit Carson and his army in 1864 and the three hundred–mile walk to internment at Fort Sumner in New Mexico. Elderly, ill, or pregnant Navajo who were unable to keep up were shot by the military as they fell behind. During the four years they remained in New Mexico, many more died as a result of inadequate diet and subsequent disease. Finally in 1868, a treaty was signed that allowed the Navajo to return to their homeland. The Fourth World refers to the Navajo creation story, in which the ancestors of the Navajo traveled from the First World through successive worlds until they emerged on the earth's surface in the Fourth World (in some versions, the Fifth World). For a more complete description of the Long Walk period, see Locke (1989). A brief version of the Navajo creation story is found in Newcomb (1967); for a more detailed account, see Zolbrod (1984).

5. Throughout her childhood, Anne's stepfather worked on the railroads in California, as few opportunities for steady wage work were available on the reservation. He returned home on weekends and holidays.

6. The maternal clan has particular significance in Navajo culture. Clan lineage is traced through the mother's family, with children born "into" the mother's clan and born "for" the father's clan. "Stealing herself" from her maternal relatives, who had acted within their traditional rights in arranging her marriage, would show disrespect within a family system that placed great emphasis on respect for, and obedience to, elders.

7. The Native American Church (NAC) is a pan-Indian religion in which many Navajo participate, either exclusively or in combination with traditional Navajo practices.

8. During the all-night NAC meetings participants seek visions to provide spiritual guidance for the subjects of the ceremony—in this case Anne and her new husband.

9. Traditionally, most Navajo daughters and their husbands settle near the mother's home on land to which the maternal clan claims rights. This arrangement reinforces the resources available to women, as they have rights to the house and the land; the man contributes his labor and sometimes a wage income to the extended family. An arrangement among some Navajo is for the couple to set up housekeeping in the man's mother's camp. Increasingly, in part to be close to wage work, couples make living arrangements independent of either family.

10. My thanks to Diana DeVries for pointing out that "stealing yourself" from those who were previously perceived to have legitimate power over you is also an act of "claiming yourself" through recognition of your own power.

11. Anne's stepfather died from cancer when her son was about six years old.

References

Bourdieu, P. (1977). *Outline of a Theory of Practice.* Cambridge, UK: Cambridge University Press.

Locke, R. F. (1989). *The Book of the Navajo* (4th ed.). Los Angeles: Mankind Publishing.

Newcomb, F. J. (1967). *Navajo Folk Tales.* Albuquerque: University of New Mexico Press.

Senese, G. B. (1991). *Self Determination and the Social Education of Native Americans.* New York: Praeger.

Sewell, W., Jr. (1989). *Toward a Theory of Structure: Duality, Agency, and Transformation* (CSST Working Paper #29). Ann Arbor: University of Michigan.

Swidler, A. (1986). Culture in Action: Symbols and Strategies. *American Sociological Review, 51,* 273–286.

Szasz, M. (1974). *Education and the American Indian: On the Road to Self Determination, 1928–1973.* Albuquerque: University of New Mexico Press.

Zolbrod, P. G. (1984). *Dine bahane': The Navajo Creation Story.* Albuquerque: University of New Mexico Press.

PART THREE

Overcoming Distance in Studying Women's Lives

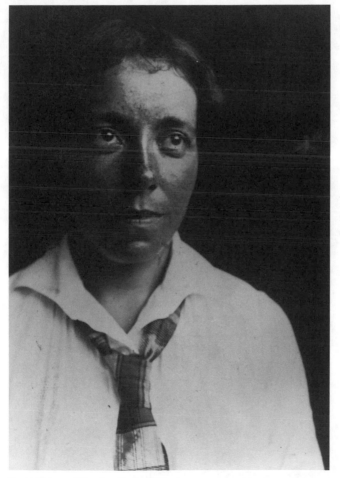

Karen Horney. *(Courtesy Susan Quinn.)*

10

Who's That Girl?
A Case Study of Madonna

LYNNE LAYTON

IN A TOUCHING MOMENT in her documentary *Truth or Dare* (Keshishian, 1991), Madonna, who rarely shows any hesitation, stammers as she admits to her female dancers/singers that sometimes she feels insecure about her abilities:

> I'm in my dressing room sometimes and I think to myself, who do I think I am? Like trying to pull this off. You know. And I sometimes, I'm very much, but I can only al-low myself to think it once in a while because if I do I'm I'm I'm gone. And that is, I think of you guys and thinking, sitting in your dressing room going, you know, who this bitch think she is? ... But I know that I'm not the best singer and I know I'm not the best dancer but but but [the women are interrupting here] I'm not interested in that. I'm interested in pushing people's buttons and being provocative and being po-litical.

And provocative and political she is. Part of what makes Madonna so controver-sial—hated and loved, defamed as a talentless manipulator and hailed not only as an artistic genius but also as a postmodern feminist—is her repeated insistence that she controls her life, her work, and her image. I contribute to this myth by letting Madonna control the title of this chapter, for "Who's That Girl?" was the title both of the 1987 film in which she starred, and in the usual Madonna public-ity tie-in, the 1987 concert tour that preceded and promoted the film. I chose this title not to add to the myth, which I intend rather to challenge, but to suggest that in Madonna's life and work we see crystallized some of the tensions in the ways we currently think about identity (see Dyer, 1991). For another marker of Madonna as a subject of controversy is her capacity continuously to reinvent herself and thus to question the notion that identity is a stable and enduring construct. On the question of identity, then, Madonna's two projects, the assertion of individual control and the deconstruction of that same secular humanist notion of a con-trolled, rational, ego-centered self, are contradictory. Yet it is this very contradiction that accounts for Madonna's enormous popularity, a popularity that crosses lines of gender, race, class, and perhaps most curious, education. For Madonna has become not only the darling of young girls of all classes, of lesbians, of black and white gay males, but also an icon for academic feminists immersed in postmodern theory.

In writing this chapter, I join the legions of journalists and academics who have been writing about Madonna since 1985 and who have succeeded perhaps less in capturing Madonna's identity than in creating a Rorschach design that reveals something about our own identities (two recent anthologies on Madonna are Schwichtenberg, 1993, and Sexton, 1993). I have written about Madonna before, and I feel that I must introduce this chapter with a description of what it is like to write about her. As several journalists have commented, once you write about Madonna, you yourself begin to partake of her fame. The day after a newspaper article I wrote about her appeared, people called asking me to go on television and radio, to be in a documentary. This resulted in some subtle shifts in my own identity—for example, getting in touch with an exhibitionist strain that had barely been tapped in teaching and presenting at conferences. My fifteen minutes of fame also caused a marked change in how I viewed Madonna: She became a piece of property, *my property*, and where I had previously felt amused and bemused by how many people were writing about her and the claims they were making for her, I now felt more critical and territorial (a loss of pleasure for me). Perhaps more unfortunate, I became less able to be critical of her. I watched *Who's That Girl?* (Foley, 1987), which the critics hated, and wondered if I liked it only because I had become attached to Madonna, or on the other hand, if critics panned it because so many of them hate Madonna. I of course cannot answer this question, but I present it as a caveat: What follows is not "objective." A strength of this lack of objectivity is that by writing and reading about Madonna, I have grown more empathic toward her. But because Madonna is an icon and I have something to gain from being connected to her, in this chapter I largely refrain from definitive evaluations and focus instead on what I think she is doing with identity and how what is written about her expresses an identity crisis in contemporary culture.

I begin with some biographical material relevant to an understanding of Madonna's work and her image. I call it "material" rather than "fact," because a very important part of Madonna's work is her image, which includes what she chooses to present to us about her life. Although Madonna clearly has a lot of control over her image and may indeed wish to convince us that behind every one of her masks lies only another mask, I do not agree with those who say that all we know of Madonna is what she chooses to reveal. This is, I think, a trivial claim, for in some sense, all we ever see of people is what they show us. Yet, people are not transparent to themselves, and so they always reveal more than they think they reveal— and Madonna is no exception. Thus, we are dealing here with various and contradictory but also informative levels of Madonna's life: those parts of her work and her image that she consciously fashions and those that lie outside her conscious control.

Madonna was born Madonna Louise Veronica Ciccone on August 16, 1958, in Bay City, Michigan, the first daughter of Silvio and Madonna Louise Fortin Ciccone of Pontiac, Michigan. She says that her name in part determined her sense that she was destined for something special: "I sometimes think I was born to live up to my name. How could I be anything else but what I am having been named Madonna? I would either have ended up a nun or this" (quoted in Hirschberg, 1991, p. 160; see Walkerdine, 1986, for a discussion of how the names and nicknames others give us become constitutive of our identity).

Madonna has two older brothers, Anthony and Martin, two younger sisters, Paula and Melanie (about whom one hears very little), and a younger brother, Christopher, who works as her artistic director. In interviews, Madonna repeatedly talks about the death of her mother from cancer (when Madonna was five) as the pivotal event of her psychic life: "I knew I could be either sad and weak and not in control or I could just take control and say it's going to get better" (quoted in Skow, 1985, p. 77). As we shall see, the concept of control structures not only Madonna's autobiographical narrative but the narratives of her biographers as well.

Madonna has also many times said that her insatiable craving for love and approval is a result of her mother's death and her guilt at the thought that she may have played some part in it (she often repeats an anecdote about forcing her mother to play with her when her mother was already quite ill): "[When she died, I] said, 'Okay, I don't have a mother to love me; I'm going to make the world love me'" (quoted in King, 1991, p. 246). Part of Madonna's mania for control, then, arises from loss, and her wish to have the largest possible audience love her is a wish to negate that loss.

Madonna has acknowledged an early envy of male privilege and identification with masculinity, which she attributes both to seeing her brothers' real privilege and to not having a mother:

> I know if I'd had a mother I would be very different. It gave me a lot of what are traditionally looked upon as masculine traits in terms of my ambitiousness and my aggressiveness. Mothers, I think, teach you manners and gentleness and a certain kind of, what's the word? I don't want to say subservience, but a patience, which I've never had. Then, when my mother died, all of a sudden I was going to become the best singer, the best dancer, the most famous person in the world, everybody was going to love me. I've been to analysis and I understand that about myself. (quoted in Deevoy, 1991, p. 20)

The second blow to Madonna's sense of being loved was the remarriage of her father to one of the family's housekeepers, Joan Gustafson (who had two children of her own), when Madonna was about eight: "It was then that I said, okay, I don't need anybody. ... No one's going to break my heart again. I'm not going to need anybody. I can stand on my own and be my own person and not belong to anyone" (quoted in Andersen, 1991, p. 27). When Madonna announces she needs no one, she distances herself not only from her view of femininity but from that of feminist psychology as well, which defines connection as the core of female selfhood (see, for example, Chodorow, 1978; also Miller, Jordan, Kaplan, Stiver, and Surrey, 1991). Yet, *Truth or Dare,* the interviews she gave to promote the film, and several of the songs in her 1989 album *Like a Prayer* center on longings for family connections and particularly on her image of herself as maternal.

In interviews, Madonna and her friends and family members frequently cite her lifelong need to be the center of attention and early scapegoating by siblings angry at how she forced attention onto herself. Madonna claims her stepmother made her feel like Cinderella in requiring her, as eldest daughter, to take care of her younger siblings; on at least one occasion, her stepmother smacked her in the face hard enough to cause a nosebleed. Her disciplinarian Catholic father impressed her with the sense that leisure opens the door to the devil; along with making up for loss, Madonna cites her father's philosophy as a source of her workaholism. As for early training in gender identity, she reports that her grandmother and the Catholic church made her believe that women are either virgins or whores.

Madonna's own legend has it that she felt ugly and not special until at age fourteen she met her dance teacher, Christopher Flynn. Not only did he tell her she was beautiful and make her feel "fabulous," but he introduced her to the gay discos of Detroit, to life on the margins, and to fun. Her subsequent devotion in her life and work to people on the margins—young girls, blacks, Hispanics, gays—attests not only to her connection to Flynn but to her own lifelong feelings of somehow being different and unloved.

Madonna attended the University of Michigan for a while on a dance scholarship and there met Stephen Bray, her future songwriting partner. She left the university to pursue a dance career in New York. Next came a few years of living in poverty (punctuated by a brief period of luxury in Paris under the tutelage of two French producers who wanted to make her into their version of a star; it was not Madonna's version, so she left). There are those who from her first public appearances in discos could not stand Madonna (for example, Michael Musto [1990] of the *Village Voice,* who with foot in mouth recalls in a 1990 documentary his early premonition that Madonna wouldn't go anywhere because she was such an egocentric bitch). But most of the people who have been part of her success machine from the beginning remain in awe of her drive and her charisma.

Her first album came out in 1983 (*Madonna*), and when videos later appeared to promote it, sales soared and eventually reached nine million. Six of the songs on her first album became Top 10 dance hits. Everyone agrees that Madonna and MTV, which began broadcasting in 1981, are a match made in heaven. Music video is Madonna's medium. In September 1984, her second album (*Like a Virgin*) was released and sold eleven million copies. Already enormously popular with gay and black disco audiences and with young girls, Madonna got the attention of the white adult audience when she costarred with Rosanna Arquette as Susan in

Susan Seidelman's 1985 film, *Desperately Seeking Susan*. The Virgin Tour (later to be a video) promoted this film, and Madonna's song in the film, "Get into the Groove," promoted both album and tour. This familiar pattern of "intertextual" promotion peaked in 1990, when Madonna's Blonde Ambition Tour promoted her 1989 *Like a Prayer* album (already promoted not only by MTV but by the canceled Pepsi commercial version of the title song, which although shown only a few times, netted Madonna $5 million and a lot of publicity). Simultaneously, the tour promoted Warren Beatty's film, *Dick Tracy*, in which she plays Breathless Mahoney. *Dick Tracy* in turn promoted *I'm Breathless*, Madonna's 1990 album of songs inspired by the movie.

If that wasn't enough Madonna for one season, she also appeared on the cover of almost every major magazine in spring and summer 1990, with interviews promoting her entire oeuvre and high fashion photographs by the likes of Helmut Newton that were yet another showcase for her talent of self-reinvention. And then of course the Blonde Ambition Tour became the basis of her 1991 documentary, *Truth or Dare: On the Road, Behind the Scenes, and in Bed with Madonna* (Keshishian, 1991). This kind of career control left the staff of *Forbes* magazine "breathless" as they vainly sought an interview for the October 1990 issue, which featured Madonna on the cover and a story titled: "A Brain for Sin and a Bod for Business" (Schifrin, 1990).

I have left out a few Broadway plays, the scandal attending the unauthorized publication of nude pictures taken in Madonna's early years in New York when she made money by posing for artists, the movie flops, and of course, her highly publicized marriage to Sean Penn in 1985 and equally publicized divorce in 1989. What I do not want to leave out is what people wrote about her during these years, and I begin with two of the three unauthorized biographies that appeared in 1991 (Norman King's *Madonna: The Book*; Christopher Andersen's *Madonna Unauthorized*; the third, David James's *Madonna*, is really little more than a photohistory with a bit of laudatory biographical filler).

Although these biographies tell us very little about Madonna beyond a chronology of events in her career, they tell us a lot about what pop biographers think people want to know and how these biographers conceptualize lives (Andersen and King seem much more concerned with getting a book out quickly than with checking even such rudimentary information as how many brothers and sisters Madonna has). Andersen's book is, I think, typical. It is held together by the thin red thread of Madonna's relationship with Sean Penn. The book begins with the marriage and ends with the question of what she saw in him. In between are two contradictory narratives: In one, Madonna goes from rags to riches almost overnight and with no work; in the other, Madonna goes from rags to riches because of her devotion to work and her extraordinary discipline.

David Lusted (1991) described this contradiction as lying at the heart of the U.S. myth of individualism. I agree, with one amendment. The no-work side of the myth has a slightly different twist when male critics apply it to Madonna. In a male artist's story, biographers attribute meteoric rises to genius. Madonna's biographers, on the other hand, attribute her rise to the many important men she slept with, the many men and women she seduced and abandoned; in short, she is famous because she is a bitch and a slut. The no-work narrative is thus nasty gossip, the discipline narrative a boring chronology of career events. The only genius Madonna is granted is a genius for making money. Although the tone of the second narrative is awestruck, the tone of the first is damning and the overriding effect of the whole is negative. King, for example, ends with a chapter titled "High Priestess of Hype"; Andersen's last paragraph cites the same material with which I opened this chapter, but in taking it out of context, he reveals his disdain:

> Today, however, she is very much alive and millions pray at the altar of Madonna, Our Lady of Perpetual Promotion. She is ubiquitous, part of the furniture of our lives. More than merely reflecting her times, Madonna is a virtual fun-house hall of mirrors, casting back distorted and fragmented images that both dazzle and disturb. In her film *Truth or Dare,* she says, "I know I'm not the best singer. I know I'm not the best dancer. But I'm not interested in that. I'm interested in pushing people's buttons."
>   Believe it. (p. 334)

Andersen alters Madonna's comment in a way that makes her appear superficial; what she actually said is, "I'm interested in pushing people's buttons and being provocative and being political."

Elsewhere I have argued that the anger with which male critics dismiss Madonna reveals more than merely worry about a lowering of artistic or moral standards. The anger always seems to refer back to how much money Madonna makes, to how much power she has (Layton, 1990, 1993). Power is central to these biographers, and their narratives, like Madonna's autobiographical one, celebrate the individual in control of her destiny. On the surface, nothing could be further from this reverence for control and power than what postmodern feminist critics have to say about Madonna and identity. And when you contrast male anger toward Madonna with the celebratory tone of postmodern feminist critics, you get some idea of the role gender plays in critical responses to Madonna.

As a postmodernist, Madonna is both celebrated and reviled, a paradox that reflects the two different meanings of postmodern that currently circulate in the culture. One sense of postmodern refers to the project that critiques notions of universal truth, inevitable progress, male domination, innate heterosexuality; in short, a project that reveals the social construction of reality and the varied interests that are served by particular constructions. This critique attacks the binary oppositions at the basis of Western logic and deconstructs the most oppressive of them, such as male/female, nature/culture, good/evil, heterosexual/homosexual; in doing so, it reveals the implicit hierarchy in each and who tends to benefit from maintaining that hierarchy.

Another sense of postmodern refers to imposture, posing, inauthenticity, pastiche. Although the two senses are related in that a pose often reveals the constructedness of what one has taken to be the original (see, for example, Cindy

Sherman's art), the two camps that use postmodern in this sense are not really adherents of the project described above. One camp is represented by cultural conservatives who despise what they see as the mocking inauthenticity of the postmodern; these are people who still believe in the nonconstructed original—for example, that heterosexuality is normal and homosexuality unnatural. A second camp does not seem to believe in anything; this camp fetishizes the pose and thereby loses the sense of postmodernism as critique. For them, nothing is serious, everything is play (for further elaboration of these differences in the context of psychology, see Kvale, 1992; in the context of feminist debates, see Flax, 1990, and Nicholson, 1990). Madonna is adored by those who engage in postmodern critique, reviled by the cultural conservatives, and fetishized by devotees of the pose (see Schwichtenberg, 1993).

Major targets of postmodernism as critique are "commonsense" notions of identity. Lacan's work, for example, is an attack on ego psychological "fantasies" about the integrity of the ego. For Lacan, the ego is a fictive entity, an entity that fantasizes itself whole and solid, that tries to claim for itself a fixed identity, but that really knows itself to be fluid and fragmented. Lacan restored to prominence the Freud who discovered the innate bisexuality and polymorphous perversity of children, the Freud for whom the Oedipus complex violently forces social constructions of masculinity and femininity onto children. Although children are socialized to adopt their culture's version of gender identity (as well as other aspects of identity), Lacan (1983) emphasized that repressed versions remain in the unconscious and constantly destabilize the ego's wish to keep these lost possibilities at bay.

Enter Madonna, darling of Lacanian and other postmodern feminists. Madonna's continuous self-reinvention, her adoption of a variety of characters and voices, her gender-bending crotch-grabbing, cross-dressing, bisexual enjoyment of the most polymorphous of perversities upsets those who feel that authenticity and family values are slipping away even as she delights those who feel that authenticity and family values have always been code words used by one group to oppress another. An example of Madonna as deconstructionist: In her *Like a Virgin* video, Madonna sets one narrative, in which she is a bride in white, against a second, in which she sexily writhes in her trademark Boy Toy Belt with midriff revealed and multicrucifixed top. As critics such as John Fiske (1989) and E. Ann Kaplan (1989) point out, Madonna here takes familiar signifiers, such as the crucifix, and wrenches them from their familiar context (the purity of the church), placing them instead in juxtaposition to things that signify the cultural opposite (sexiness). In this way, Madonna takes the lesson of her grandmother that women are either virgins or whores and rewrites it so that women can be both sexy and virginal, good and bad; the culturally approved version of femininity is not allowed to exhaust the possibilities in Madonna's universe. Indeed, she makes us question what is so good about good and what is so bad about bad (Layton, 1993). And that is why young girls love Madonna; as Judith Williamson (1985) wrote, "she retains all the bravado and exhibitionism that most girls start off with, or feel

inside, until the onset of 'womanhood' knocks it out of them" (p. 47), that is, until the culture codes these feelings "bad."

Perhaps the most provocative claim for Madonna's postmodernism comes
from Susan McClary (1990), a musicologist. McClary not only pointed out how
Madonna's video narratives upset a Western narrative musical tradition in which
sexually provocative females must die at the end of the story (e.g., *Salome*,
Carmen) but also claimed that the musical structure of some of Madonna's songs
performs a Lacanian destabilization of identity and of the male/female hierarchy.
In McClary's view, Madonna's "Like a Prayer" and "Live to Tell," for example, begin like most musical narratives with a dominant chord (read male) answered by
a nondominant (read "Other," female) that sets the narrative conflict in motion.
Rather than resolve back to the dominant at the end like in most musical narratives, Madonna's songs end by alternating between the two, refusing to resolve in
favor of the male, refusing to vanquish the voice of the female.

The controversies surrounding Madonna thus reflect the tensions of a culture
in which some cling for dear life to a notion of stable identity and others do what
they can to destabilize the notion because they are convinced that it has been used
to define as deviant anything that is not white, middle class, and male. The voices
of disapproving critics betray this tension: There is Tom Ward (1985), who referred in the *Village Voice* to Madonna's multiple identities as a "multiple hedging
of bets" against what will sell best (p. 55). Jon Pareles (1990), in an otherwise positive assessment in the *New York Times* of Madonna's "evolving persona," wrote:
"The only constant is the diligent effort that goes into every new guise, which
made her the perfect pinup in the careerist 1980's" (p. C-11). Michael David (1989)
argued in *Manhattan, Inc.* that postmodern pastiche (the ironic putting together
of incongruous existing elements) creates nothing new and has no passion and
concluded "She's the ultimate postmodern pop star: her creation is herself, not
her music" (p. 98). And Jay Cocks (1990) in *Time*: "The deliberate artfulness of
her various personas stresses artificiality above all. The common coolness of each
role she plays keeps everything at a safe distance, stylizing all the sensuality out of
passion until only the appearance remains" (p. 75).

Noteworthy is a tendency among male critics to deny that Madonna is sexy, to
assert that her sexuality is about power and not about passion. Apparently, for
these critics, power is not sexy when wielded by a woman. Writing in the *New Republic*, Luc Sante (1990) epitomized this tendency: "Between the teasing simula-
tion of carnality and the real passion for efficiency lies Madonna's bona fide erotic
territory. ... All the sexual imagery in the show, behind its rococo and vaudeville
trappings, was single-mindedly fixated on power and its representations" (p. 27).
This response shows better than any the gender gap in the Madonna polls, for her
female fans love her precisely because she is both sexy and powerful and thus
makes them feel sexy and powerful.

Lest one think all Madonna's critics are male, I cite Ellen Goodman (1990), who
in her response in the *Boston Globe* to Madonna's *Justify My Love* video (1990),

represents a liberal and humanist conception of identity, one in which stability and consistency are paramount virtues:

> But what bothers me is a belief that she offers the wrong answers to the questions, or the crisis, of identity. Especially female identity.
>
> If the work of growing up is finding a center, integrating the parts, Madonna spotlights the fragments and calls them a whole. If the business of adulthood is finding yourself, she creates as many selves as there are rooms in her video hotel. If we must evolve as grown-ups, she switches instead, like a quick-change artist between acts. And if there is a search among Americans for authenticity, Madonna offers costumes and calls them the real thing. ... The star of this show makes little attempt to reconcile the contradictions of her life and psyche. She insists instead that all the fragments of a self be accepted. (p. 13)

What critics and fans elucidate in these critical fragments is a controversy about the very nature of contemporary identity, and in this fan-critic's opinion, both sides have appeal—intellectual as well as popular. For I believe that Madonna is popular because she represents to fans both sides of the identity debate, reflecting our own uncertainties about identity. On the one hand, she is the fragmented daughter of a dysfunctional family, who publicly exposes her pain, propounds her own version of family values, and is as much caught up as the rest of us in the kind of self-doubt that drives one to lose weight, change costume, and go shopping. On the other hand, she is a liberated, highly successful postmodern artist, who in performance transcends her pain by playfully and politically arranging and rearranging the fragments. By deliberately making her life a part of her work, Madonna presents us with both a public and a private persona. From a psychological perspective, these two personae often contradict one another.

Madonna as artist, playing her multiple roles in multiple relational contexts, well exemplifies the psychologist Robert May's (1986) object relational view that at our healthiest we carry within us "a fund of ... contradictory images and fantastic aspirations" on which our "capacity for change and development depends" (p. 188). Following Lacan, May asserted that there is no such thing as unity when it comes to identity; she who clings to a fixed notion of feminine identity, for example, is both resistant and impoverished. In the course of development, we internalize relational patterns in which we play all kinds of roles vis-à-vis important others, for example, tomboy to aggressive father, little mommy to big mommy, femme fatale to heroic mother and father, and so on. As May wrote, "These disparate identifications, these various and shifting images of self and other, this chaotic and contradictory jumble of wishes and worries, *this* is in fact our characterological treasury" (p. 188). Madonna's own words about her project, spoken as she looked up at a gigantic image of herself on the set of the Who's That Girl Tour, echo those of May:

> "Oh God, what have I done? What have I created? Is that me, or is this me, this small person standing down here on stage? That's why I call the tour 'Who's That Girl': because I play a lot of characters, and every time I do a video or a song, people go 'Oh,

that's what she's like.' And I'm not like any of them. I'm all of them. I'm none of them. You know what I mean?" (quoted in Gilmore, 1987, p. 88)

This is the Madonna of those who celebrate fragmentation. But there is as well the Madonna who wants to show us ever more of her off-stage self, the Madonna who needs to test our love for her by showing us and hoping we will accept her "bad" side. This is the driven, often bitchy Madonna of *Truth or Dare,* and this Madonna is perhaps better described by such diverse commentators on identity disturbance as Otto Kernberg (1976) and Heinz Kohut (on narcissistic and borderline personalities, 1971), John Bradshaw (on the dysfunctional family, 1988), Christopher Lasch (*The Culture of Narcissism,* 1979) than by May. For this is the totally scheduled, not the playful Madonna, the Madonna who has dyed her hair so many times that her hairdresser warns her it will fall out (Sessums, 1990), the Madonna who works out for two hours per day and who points to a picture of a woman squeezing her stomach and says: "That's like me. ... Always looking for fat" (quoted in Hirschberg, 1991, p. 200), the Madonna who can be abusive to those around her. This Madonna conceives all relationships in terms of power and hierarchy, and although she claims loudly in video and interview that she is always in control and thus on top of any conceivable hierarchy, our look into her private life shows that sometimes she is on top and other times she is in despair at the bottom. This is the Madonna whose concept of religion can be entirely self-serving, as when she prays before each concert that her show will be better than ever. This Madonna injects a dose of sadomasochism into most of her songs and videos (lately, the dosage is increasing), and this Madonna, contrary to her self-perception, is not exactly what most of us would call maternal. This is the Madonna whose dream of being loved has clearly *not* yet come true, despite her own mythmaking. And this Madonna is decidedly *not* in control. Indeed, this second Madonna exemplifies a kind of fragmentation that most psychologists would not want to celebrate, the kind shown by those who have difficulty constituting a self, whose internal world is harsh and split from early traumas or losses. In this painful state of fragmentation, control and power are highly desired but only fleetingly experienced or deployed in abusive ways.

Each of these two Madonnas has popular appeal, exemplified here by the views of two fans. My hairdresser, who is incredibly thin, tells me that she preferred the pre-aerobics Madonna because she acted as if she loved her body, which at the time did not fit cultural stereotypes of thinness (Madonna's lawyer's daughter apparently felt the same way. He told Madonna, "You've lost weight, my daughter's going to be so upset. You finally gave girls who are voluptuous a new lease on life, don't get any skinnier, okay?" (Chase, 1987, p. 193). I remember feeling similarly when I saw her in *Desperately Seeking Susan,* my first encounter with her. I thought that it was amazing that this woman who was not gorgeous and did not have a great body could strut around as if she was God's gift to the world. Indeed, several critics have suggested that it is the very way Madonna treats her ordinariness as special that accounts for her popularity. This Madonna is so self-assured that she can try out various roles and challenge fixed identities that have constricted women (and men) for centuries. This Madonna is as comfortable in a men's business suit (especially when pink lingerie peeks through) as in the buff. And this Madonna is inspirational mother to those who cannot quite break out of the constricting roles culture prescribes for them.

When I last rented *Truth or Dare,* the salesclerk told me that she loves Madonna and has written at least fifty papers on her since fourth grade. I asked her why she loves her, and she responded that it was because Madonna's mother died when she was so young and she was raised by her father. She then told me her favorite video is *Oh, Father* (1989), which depicts the life of a girl whose mother dies and whose father (and later, lover) is abusive. In the song, Madonna attributes her low self-esteem to the father, repeating the refrain, "I never felt so good about myself." At the song's end, the grown Madonna merges in shadow with her child self, walks away from the abuser, and sings the refrain in such a way as to suggest that she never felt so good about herself as she does now. This video and song, haunting and beautiful, could easily be the theme for Bradshaw's treatises on healing the child within.

Another song about abusive relationships, "Till Death Do Us Part" (1989), ends less happily with the female stuck in an emotionally abusive dyad. I believe that Madonna has only increased her popularity by turning to confessional songwriting, and particularly by making it her project, evident in *Truth or Dare,* to blur the lines between her private and her public life. The public craves the regulating ideal of a person who has it all (together) as much as it craves a star who struggles with her fragments like an ordinary person.

I have said that this second Madonna is decidedly not in control. To conclude this chapter, I would like to challenge the myth of the individual in Madonna's own style, which primarily revolves around her notion of control. In 1985, Dave Marsh, an astute music critic, noted that whereas Madonna seems to think that she is the product only of shrewd individual calculation, she is actually the product of a particular historical moment. The song "Material Girl" was a hit at the time he wrote, and he found the intersection of Madonna and history in the way she honestly speaks the materialism of the 1980s, proclaiming a girl's right and wish to own things as well as a woman's sexual desire in a puritanical but sex-filled era. The feminist movement and the sexual revolution of the 1960s created the conditions that allowed Madonna to share her enjoyment of an assertive sexuality with a large population of girl fans.

Many have spoken of Madonna's capacity to set trends in fashion. But when you read Madonna's self-reinventions against the backdrop of Susan Faludi's *Backlash* (1991), what emerges is that Madonna, like you and me, is just as much at the mercy of trends as she is the setter of trends: Madonna's switch from lace underwear to high glamour between 1985 and 1987 fits right in to Faludi's description of the manipulations of the fashion industry. And the authors of *The Famine Within* (Gilday, 1990) would find Madonna emblematic of a time in which women who experience increasing success and opportunities for greater autonomy find themselves increasingly obsessed with physical fitness and hatred of body fat.

Madonna's move to make her life her work can be seen as a postmodern refusal to maintain a rigid line between the self as artist and as woman, or it may be seen as part of the same confessional trend that has secured the popularity of Oprah Winfrey and Sally Jessy Raphael.

And Madonna is also the unlikely spokesperson for a particular version of family values, hot topic of the present moment. In "Papa Don't Preach" (1986), she asks her father to understand that she intends to marry the boy he thinks is not good enough for her, and she intends to keep the baby she is pregnant with. This song angered liberals, who saw it as encouraging teenage pregnancy. *Truth or Dare,* which opened in May 1991, is also structured by Madonna's yearnings to be a mother. In many interviews she has spoken of having somehow unconsciously chosen a tour entourage of emotional cripples toward whom she felt maternal. Madonna does not seem at all aware of the idiosyncratic nature of her concept of the maternal. As portrayed in the film, her maternalism is oddly deficient of love. Although Madonna's mothering at moments keeps the children from hurting each other, it is mostly marked by teasing and humiliation, sexual play with the children in and out of bed, buying the children goods at Chanel to make up for their deprived childhood, and making them stars.

Madonna's relationship to her father is also central to the film, particularly her craving for his approval. Here, again, Madonna's rebellious assertion of autonomy is conditioned by her longing for love. Both her provocations and the way she performs them are products of her agency and of her place in a relational dynamic over which she does not have total control.

Truth or Dare ends the way the Blonde Ambition show ends, with Madonna's tribute to family values, "Keep It Together." The song proclaims: "When I look back on all the misery/And all the heartache that they brought to me/I wouldn't change it for another chance/'Cause blood is thicker than any other circumstance." The song is performed in the manner and costume of *A Clockwork Orange,* with more than a hint of mutual family torment. Here, as in her double attitude to materialism, what marks Madonna is not that she is in control, but that she is honest about the pros and cons of family and obviously echoes the experience of many in our culture.

What is most ironic, as Daniel Harris (1992) pointed out, is that the very Lacanian, Foucauldian, and Baudrillardian academics who laud Madonna for challenging the fantasy of wholeness claimed by the rational, ego-centered bourgeois individual have made of her an auteur, sole generator of her image, songs, videos, shows. These alleged postmodernists have thus contributed at least as much as Madonna's biographers to her self-generated myth that she as individual is in control. For example, McClary wrote as though Madonna is solely responsible for creating her music, which is not the case even for the two songs McClary analyzed. Nor do her lyrics, which Madonna does write, unequivocally exemplify postmodern positions on identity. In analyzing "Like a Prayer," for example (co-written by Patrick Leonard), how could McClary miss the fact that the lyrics show longings for origin, for merger, and as always, are marked by a mood of dominance and submission?

In a culture distinguished by black-and-white thinking, one rarely finds Madonna critics who can live with shades of gray. I will not speculate on why many of her academic critics have chosen to look only at her triumphs and not at her pain, but pain and contradiction are clearly present, and Madonna herself seems unafraid to reveal them, although she may not be aware of how much she reveals. And revealing her pain has made her all the more popular ("Lucky me," she might say).

Thus it is that Madonna's two projects are contradictory and irreconcilable yet highly representative of contradictions with which most of us daily contend. In trying both to destabilize fixed identities *and* speak for the discrete, autonomous self of Enlightenment ideology, Madonna mirrors the identity dilemmas of our culture. Madonna herself tells us that the need to maintain the fantasy of control comes from unresolved pain, the kind of pain that marks most of us on both an individual and a cultural level. It is thus not the postmodern ideal self that masks unhealthy fragments but the bourgeois individual, who puts up a front of unity while desperately trying to control an identity-disordered, fragmented self. Madonna both mocks the bourgeois individual and incarnates her. And so, I answer the question "Who's that girl?" with the suggestion that Madonna is the likely icon of a cultural moment in which progressive social movements (such as feminism, gay liberation, and civil rights) coexist with abusive families, violence, and the loss of community accompanied by compensatory rampant materialism—a moment with tensions that make us all wonder who we are.

References

Andersen, C. (1991). *Madonna unauthorized.* New York: Simon & Schuster.

Bradshaw, J. (1988). *Bradshaw on: The family. A revolutionary way of self-discovery.* Deerfield Beach, FL: Health Communications.

Chase, C. (July 1987). The material girl and how she grew. *Cosmopolitan,* pp. 130ff.

Chodorow, N. (1978). *The reproduction of mothering.* Berkeley: University of California.

Cocks, J. (December 17, 1990). Madonna draws a line. *Time,* pp. 74–75.

David, M. (August 1989). Postmodern girl. *Manhattan, Inc.,* pp. 98–99.

Deevoy, A. (June 13, 1991). If you're going to reveal yourself, reveal yourself! *Us,* pp. 18ff.

Dyer, R. (1991). Charisma. In C. Gledhill (Ed.), *Stardom: Industry of desire* (pp. 57–59). London & New York: Routledge.

Faludi, S. (1991). *Backlash.* New York: Crown.

Fiske, J. (1989). Madonna. In *Reading the popular* (pp. 95–113). Boston: Unwin Hyman.

Flax, J. (1990). *Thinking fragments: Psychoanalysis, feminism, and postmodernism in the contemporary west.* Berkeley: University of California Press.

Foley, J. (Director). (1987). *Who's that girl?* [Film]. Warner.

Gilday, K. (Director). (1990). *The famine within* [Film]. Panorama Entertainment.

Gilmore, M. (September 10, 1987). The Madonna mystique. *Rolling Stone,* pp. 37ff.

Goodman, E. (December 6, 1990). Another image in the Madonna rolodex. *The Boston Globe*, p. 13.

Harris, D. (June 8, 1992). Make my rainy day. *The Nation*, pp. 790–793.

Hirschberg, L. (April 1991). The misfit. *Vanity Fair*, pp. 160ff.

James, D. (1991). *Madonna*. Lincolnwood, IL: Publications International.

Kaplan, E. A. (1989). *Rocking around the clock: Music television, postmodernism, and counterculture*. New York: Routledge.

Kernberg, O. (1976). *Borderline conditions and pathological narcissism*. New York: Aronson.

Keshishian, A. (Director). (1991). *Truth or dare: On the road, behind the scenes, and in bed with Madonna* [Video]. Live Home.

King, N. (1991). *Madonna: The book*. New York: William Morrow.

Kohut, H. (1971). *The analysis of the self*. New York: International Universities Press.

Kvale, S. (Ed.). (1992). *Psychology and postmodernism*. London: Sage.

Lacan, J. (1983). *Feminine sexuality*. New York: Norton.

Lasch, C. (1979). *The culture of narcissism*. New York: Norton.

Layton, L. (December 16, 1990). What's behind the Madonna bashing? *The Boston Globe*, p. A15.

———. (1993). Like a virgin: Madonna's version of the feminine. In A. Sexton (Ed.), *Desperately seeking Madonna* (pp. 170–194). New York: Dell.

Lusted, D. (1991). The glut of the personality. In C. Gledhill (Ed.), *Stardom: Industry of desire* (pp. 251–258). London & New York: Routledge.

Marsh, D. (1985). Girls can't do what the guys do: Madonna's physical attraction. In D. Marsh (Ed.), *The first rock & roll confidential report* (pp. 159–167). New York: Pantheon.

May, R. (1986). Concerning a psychoanalytic view of maleness. *Psychoanalytic Review*, 73(4), 175–193.

McClary, S. (1990). Living to tell: Madonna's resurrection of the fleshly. *Genders, 7*, 1–21.

Miller, J. B., Jordan, J., Kaplan, A., Stiver, I., & Surrey, J. (1991). *Women's growth in connection*. New York: Guilford.

Musto, M. (1990). [Interview]. In N. Haggar (Director). *Madonna: Behind the American dream*. BBC Omnibus Series (first broadcast in Great Britain, December 7, 1990).

Nicholson, L. J. (Ed.). (1990). *Feminism/postmodernism*. New York & London: Routledge.

Pareles, J. (June 11, 1990). On the edge of the permissible: Madonna's evolving persona. *New York Times*, pp. C11–C12.

Sante, L. (August 1990). Unlike a virgin. *New Republic*, pp. 25–29.

Schifrin, M. (October 1, 1990). A brain for sin and a bod for business. *Forbes*, pp. 162–166.

Schwichtenberg, K. (Ed.). (1993). *The Madonna connection*. Boulder: Westview.

Sessums, K. (April 1990). White heat. *Vanity Fair*, pp. 142ff.

Sexton, A. (Ed.). (1993). *Desperately seeking Madonna*. New York: Dell.

Skow, J. (May 27, 1985). Madonna rocks the land. *Time*, p. 77.

Walkerdine, V. (1986). Video replay: Families, films, and fantasy. In V. Burgin, J. Donald, & C. Kaplan (Eds.), *Formations of fantasy* (pp. 167–199). London: Methuen.

Ward, T. (January 8, 1985). Opaque object of desire. *Village Voice*, p. 55.

Williamson, J. (October 1985). The making of a material girl. *New Socialist*, pp. 46–47.

11

Image, Theme, and Character in the Life Story of Karen Horney

DAN P. MCADAMS

KAREN HORNEY (1888–1952) was a pioneer in the psychoanalytic movement who became internationally famous for her eloquent and revolutionary writings about neurosis and the human mind. An early disciple of Freud, Horney broke away from the psychoanalytic establishment in her midlife years and articulated a new theory of human behavior that emphasized social relationships and interpersonal conflicts in human lives. She was a therapist and training analyst, and she taught classes for clinicians on theory and technique. A mother of three daughters, Horney was especially sensitive to how radically the life experiences of women differ from those of men. She was an engaging writer who made difficult psychological concepts come alive for professionals and for the nonprofessionals who read her many popular books. Because her ideas did not fit well into the patriarchal orthodoxy of U.S. psychoanalysis in the early 1940s, Horney was expelled from the New York Psychoanalytic Society, after which she established a rival group of her own. In the two years before her death, she became interested in Zen Buddhism and hoped to incorporate ideas from Eastern philosophies into her evolving theory of human personality.

In the Foreword in Susan Quinn's (1988) illuminating biography of Karen Horney, Leon Edel suggests that Horney's life, like that of most adults, lacks coherence until the biographer comes along to give it pattern and form:

> As with history itself, human lives tend to be dispersed and fragmented, sunk often in the world's turbulence—anxieties, disasters, triumphs. It is only when a biographer—who is a specialized kind of historian—has gathered the fragments, read the yellowing letters and crumbling diaries, searched in the dusty archives, learned more than any subject ever can remember about himself or herself, that a figure of the past emerges in a mosaic totality, with a significance for posterity that it never possessed in its own time. (p. 7)

I believe Edel is only half right. Karen Horney's life may indeed be "dispersed and fragmented," "sunk" deeply "in the world's turbulence." And Horney's biographers may be obliged to gather together the fragments to create a synthetic whole, a coherent and purposeful pattern or script with significance for posterity that the life itself may not have possessed during its own tenure on earth. But it is not only biographers, I contend, who perform this task. And it is not only some other's life—Karen Horney's or Henry James's or Richard Nixon's—that is subjected to this kind of synthetic activity. Rather, I submit, as self-conscious and more or less introspective adults living in contemporary Western society, almost all of us engage in a narrative ordering, a "mythological rearranging" of selves in time (Bruner, 1990; Cohler, 1982; Hankiss, 1981; Hermans, Kempen, and van Loon, 1992; Howard, 1991; Sarbin, 1986). And we all do this for *our own* life, as well as for the lives of others. We are not content as adults to construe lives as dispersed and fragmented, especially when the life is our own. We search for coherence, meaning, and purpose in the dusty archives of our own remembrances of things past and in our anticipations for the days to come. And we find coherence by consciously and unconsciously constructing for ourselves and for others a self-defining *life story* (McAdams, 1985, 1990, 1993).

My task in this chapter is to discern the integrative life story that Karen Horney constructed to provide her own life with unity, purpose, and coherence. In my reading of Quinn's (1988) biography, Horney's (1980) adolescent diaries, and Horney's theoretical writings on human personality (e.g., Horney, 1937, 1939, 1945, 1950), I am listening for the narrative that Horney may have fashioned as an adult to make sense of her own reconstructed past, perceived present, and anticipated future—an evolving and dynamic narrative of the self that could sustain and affirm Horney's efforts to express again and again, as the title of Quinn's biography puts it, "a mind of her own." In listening for Horney's own self-defining story, I do not wish to assimilate Horney's life to some preconceived pattern or theory. I do not seek to confirm, support, or reject a particular hypothesis about Horney or about the lives of women working in the first half of this century as colleagues, followers, or critics of Freud. Rather I focus on Horney's story so that I may pass on a very brief and abstracted version of what I think that I hear, a version that may find parallels in the lives and life stories of some contemporary women (or men) whose struggles, triumphs, and disappointments are reminiscent of Horney's. It is a version that highlights three different but interrelated features of any life story—the story's imagery, themes, and characters.

Imagery of Movement and Light

She was born Karen Danielson, the second child and only daughter of a ship captain and his wife, who lived just outside Hamburg, Germany. From an early age, Karen surpassed her older brother in schoolwork and was prized as an intelligent and energetic girl. Growing up in Hamburg, she witnessed a good deal of the social ferment in the 1890s, including a strong movement in support of women's rights. In the nascent women's movement, she may have found support for some of the highly unconventional goals she formulated for herself as an adolescent. She sketched out elaborate plans for studying at the Gymnasium and ultimately becoming a doctor.

Karen was a passionate and fiercely independent teenager. Rejecting the strict Christianity of her parents, she favored "the riotous sensuous exuberance" of the Greeks in their Dionysian festivals, as she described it in her adolescent diaries (Horney, 1980, p. 63). "Passion," she declared, "is always convincing." Karen's emerging views about sexuality and women's place in the world were way ahead of her time, much closer to those of our current age than of the Victorian era in which she grew up. Women should be able to achieve all of the professional goals that men achieve, she believed. Women should engage their worlds in an openly sensual manner, unashamed of their sexuality. Karen's idealistic and romantic engagement of her world is evident in this passionate section written for her diary at age seventeen, a passage laden with *images* of *movement* and *light*:

Everything in me is storming and surging and pressing for light that will resolve the confusion. I seem to myself like a skipper who leaps from his safe ship into the sea, who clings to a timber and lets himself be driven by the sea's tumult, now here, now there. He doesn't know where he is going.

> *Homeless am I*
> *With no sheltering abode I rove about.*
> *Safe and quiet*
> *I lived in the old masonry*
> *stronghold that thousand of years*
> *had built for me.*
> *It was gloomy and close—*
> *I longed for freedom.*
> *A little light only, a little life.*
> *Quietly, driven by an inner urge,*
> *I began to dig.*
> *Bloody my nails, weary my hands.*
> *Mockery from others and bitter scorn*
> *the end reward for the endless toiling.*
> *The stone came loose—*
> *one more powerful grip and*
> *it fell at my feet.*
> *A ray of light pressed through the opening*
> *greeting me kindly,*
> *inviting and warming,*
> *waked a shiver of delight in my breast.*
> *But hardly had I drawn into myself*
> *this first shimmer*
> *when the rotting masonry broke to pieces*

and buried me in its fall.
Long I lay
thinking nothing
feeling nothing.
Then my strength stirred, so freshly drunk-in
and I lifted the fragments with muscular arm.
All aglow with strength,
bloom of the storm,
delight flowing through me
I looked out far and wide.
I saw the world,
I breathed life.
The brightness of light
almost blinded me—
yet soon I was used to its brilliance.
I looked about.
The view was almost too wide,
my sight could roam to unlimited distances.
Oppressive almost
the New, the Beautiful invaded me.
At that an all-powerful longing seized me,
almost bursting my breast,
and it drove me forth to wander
in order to see, to enjoy
and to know the All.
And I wandered—
restlessly driven
I rove about,
released from the dungeon
I joyfully sing in jubilant tones
the old song of life,
to freedom, to light.
Only an anxious question often hems me in:
toward what goal am I striving?
A gentle longing, a mild lament:
When at last will you come to rest?
And I think I understand the answer
in the murmuring of the woods:
"Rest is only behind the prison walls,
life, however, does not know it."
Watchful searching
with no cowardly complaints,
restlessly striving
with no weary despair:

> *that is life—*
> *dare to endure it.* (1980, pp. 55–57)

What Erik Erikson (1963) described as a person's *ego identity* may be conceived as an integrative life story that binds together a person's reconstructed past, perceived present, and anticipated future (Grotevant, 1992; McAdams, 1985, 1990, 1993; Rosenwald and Ochberg, 1993). Beginning in late adolescence, the person adopts a historical perspective on the self in order to arrive at a narrative understanding of who she was, is, and will be in the future (Hankiss, 1981). The life story that Karen began formulating in late adolescence and young adulthood may have drawn liberally upon the imagery of movement and light, along with a number of images reflecting her relationships with her father and other childhood themes—ships, seas, storms, and so on. Karen's adolescent diaries and the letters she wrote in her early twenties to her future husband, Oskar Hornvieh, are filled with the imagery of movement and light. In love for all of two days with Ernst Schorschi—a young man with "sunny sparkle" in his eyes—she found herself "chasing after happiness in every form" (Horney, 1980, p. 83). Months later as she came to reflect on Ernst's rejection of her, she wrote that her "blood flowed sluggishly after the great loss, but it is already beginning to pulse more rapidly" (p. 79). The Swedish writer Ellen Key—an early heroine for young Karen—"lit the sacred flame of enthusiasm for me." She was "the lustrous star toward which my soul directed its way," the one name that, above all, "shines brightly" above me (p. 92). With a new lover later in medical school, "we naturally romped around like two dogs" (p. 167). In contrast, her husband-to-be seemed to move more slowly and clumsily, as if movement did not come naturally to him, but rather he inclined "to splash through life in heavy rubber boots" (p. 166).

Quinn (1988) reported that in later life Karen Horney claimed that she traveled to South America as a nine-year-old girl on one of her father's steamships. The biographer doubted the validity of the story. Still, we see Horney employing the imagery of movement, epitomized in travel and adventure. The same biographer reported that Karen's best-loved resource for her frequent flights of childhood fantasy were the stories of Karl Friedrich May. Karen's hero in these was the fictional American Indian named Winnetou. Winnetou is "a noble savage, capable of swimming faster, creeping through woods more softly, and covering his tracks more deftly than any other mortal" (Quinn, 1988, p. 38).

For Horney, rapid movement signified youth, vigor, passion, being in the flow of life, taking life on with no doubts and no fears. When things go badly, life bogs down, one feels sluggish, movement seems unnatural, as if one were wearing Oskar's heavy boots. Pregnant with her first daughter in 1911, Karen repeatedly complained of feeling languid, sluggish, unable to move. "I do so desperately want to be active," she wrote in a letter to her analyst. One must always be active, stay on one's toes, keep moving if one is to find happiness and fulfillment. And if one must indeed rest on occasion, then it is best to rest *in the sunlight.* After two days of hiking through the deep snow, Karen and friends took a break: "At noon we lay in the sun and ate our provisions. Yesterday our resting place was a little pine wood, snow all around on a slope—in it a little round clearing in full sun, moss-covered with a few great stones; and my only wish was to lie there for my whole life, staying in the sun" (Horney, 1980, p. 192).

For Horney, sunshine, light, flame, star, brightness, sparkling—all these had wonderfully positive connotations, like fast movement. Light seemed to symbolize truth, understanding, clarity—a familiar linkage for all of us, to be sure, as we often speak of some thing being "illuminating" or of occasionally experiencing "enlightenment." But from her adolescent years onward, Horney seemed to have a special fascination with these images. More than most of us, she invested strong emotion in images of light and movement, driving her to employ them often and effectively to convey what she was thinking and feeling. Hers is a life story colored by the rich imagery of movement and light. The themes, plot, and characters of the story must accommodate this basic fact of imagery. The story must be one in which movement and light may operate freely and effectively as evocative and meaningful images.

Thematic Lines: Control, Surrender, and Resignation

When one moves from imagery to *theme,* one moves to a more complex dimension of narrative. Theme refers to the goal-directed action in story, to what characters in the story are trying to do, what desired end states they pursue, and what obstacles stand in their way (McAdams, 1993). It is at the level of theme that we begin to see conflict and tension in a story, as when a character repeatedly tries to attain some goal and is frustrated, or when conflicting goals or discordant allegiances arise with conflicts of interest, motive, and value. Theme implies a temporal dimension in narrative, whereas image does not. An image is like a snapshot or a single, synchronic chord in music. It exists in the moment. Theme, by contrast, is like a segment of action in a movie, or a melody, structured diachronically in time, across moments.

Theme and imagery inform each other; theme may develop out of imagery, and imagery may be modified to accommodate theme. A life story centered on the individual's striving to become a powerful force in the world (theme: the striving for power) may draw upon imagery of battles, athletics, speed and racing, discovery and adventure, mystery and intrigue, and so on. The discrete words, symbols, images, metaphors, and pictures we create in life may partly reflect what we recurrently strive for, what we want in life. And what we often want is some variation on the two central thematic clusterings in life stories—agency (power, control, separation, individuation) and communion (love, intimacy, merger, togetherness) (Bakan, 1966; McAdams, 1985).

The thematic lines of Karen Horney's evolving personal myth began to show themselves clearly in her early adult years. After completing her studies at the Gymnasium, she enrolled as a medical student at the University of Freiburg, one of only a handful of women in medical studies at the time. In 1909, she married Oskar, and they moved to Berlin where he began a successful business and she continued her studies in psychiatry. Freud was beginning to enjoy a wide audience in Europe and the United States, and Karen became enamored with psychoanalytic theory. She found Freud's ideas about neuroses, the unconscious, and childhood sexuality to be the most exciting concepts she had ever encountered. They became integral parts of her therapeutic orientation and of her overall ideological setting in life. For a time she was in therapy with the famous psychoanalyst Karl Abraham. In 1915, she completed her psychiatric training. She began to treat patients and to write papers in psychoanalysis.

At the same time, Karen and Oskar were struggling to raise a family. In 1911, her first daughter, Brigitte, was born. Two more daughters, Marianne and Renate, followed shortly thereafter, during the frightening years of World War I. After the war, Oskar's business began to fail, and the marriage took a turn for the worse. Apparently, both Karen and Oskar had numerous sexual affairs during this period, and finally the marriage ended in 1926. It is about this time that Horney began to separate herself as well from the mainstream of the psychoanalytic movement. Between 1922 and 1935, she wrote a series of fourteen papers on the psychology of women, culminating in a total rejection of Freud's ideas on femininity and the female Oedipus complex. In 1932, she moved to the United States, and by 1940 she had established herself as a powerful and independent voice in the world of psychoanalysis.

Already as a young woman, Karen was strongly motivated by both agentic and communal needs. She wanted power and love, and she wanted them fast. As she anticipated adult life in the realms of work and home, she struggled over just what kinds of fast movements to make. In Karen's life story, there appear to be two very different kinds of movements she could make, and each is tied to a corresponding motivational theme. The first is the agentic and self-expansive move toward independent *control*. As a brilliant student and accomplished doctor, Karen could express the controlling power of her rational mind. To do so, however, she needed to free herself from feminine sensuality. At age twenty she wrote: "To be free of sensuality means great power in a woman. Only in this way will she be independent of a man. Otherwise she will always long for him, and in the exaggerated yearning of her senses she will be able to drown out all feeling of her own value. She becomes the bitch, who begs even if she is beaten—a strumpet" (Horney, 1980, p. 104).

From the standpoint of Karen Horney's life story, a woman may control the world and the self through reason and intellect. As a young woman, Karen feared that her impulses would get out of control—that love would destroy her freedom. To enhance control, she watched herself carefully. She cultivated what she called "an unremitting, ever more refined self-observation that never leaves me, even in any sort of intoxication" (p. 166). Yet, she also longed desperately to escape from this controlling state, to free herself *to* the "brutal naturalism" (her words) of im-

pulse. A woman is inexorably drawn to sensuality. She could not help herself,
Horney believed. She would surrender to passion time and time again.

Thus, *surrender* is the second kind of movement in Horney's self-defining story.
Despite Horney's belief that women should unashamedly assert their own sexuality, she appeared to thematize warm and sensual interpersonal relations in terms
of one partner surrendering either to the other or to her or his own desires. Thus,
surrender is indicative of a communal need to merge with others in self-effacing
and passionate bonds. According to Quinn (1988), Horney "wanted to experience
abandon, to be tossed about in the stormy seas of passion, under the sure lead of a
man who would be skillful enough to awaken her" (p. 84). Surrender may lead to
a certain kind of freedom, too, and this brings joy and excitement. Surrender was
Horney's characteristic communal mode of eroticism and intimacy. It was the
way for Horney to connect with others on what she called "a more elemental
level." In her psychoanalysis, Abraham called this Horney's "inclination to passivity," and he identified it as the governing force in her love life. She surrendered
again and again through a remarkable lifelong series of sexual and emotional involvements. One might also suggest that surrender was the mode of her early love
affair with psychoanalysis, to which she surrendered at first in a totally uncritical
way. In Horney's self-defining life story, surrender means moving quickly again,
lest the "ever-refined" function of "self-observation" catch up and reason, once
again, take the reins. Horney seemed to believe that she could not live happily
without her impulsive surrenders. As with the agentic desire for control, she had
to be quick with them. She must run swiftly, swim fast, cover her tracks. Like
Winnetou.

Lurking beyond agentic control and communal surrender is a third thematic
domain in the life story of Karen Horney. I will call it *resignation*. Resignation is
what happened when Horney *could not move*. During the most difficult periods
in her life—when she felt trapped at home after the birth of her first daughter,
when she felt abandoned and cut off upon her emigration to the United States,
when she was rejected by the New York Psychoanalytic Society—Horney sank
into deep depression, became listless, and seemed to succumb helplessly to what
she called in her theoretical writings "basic anxiety." These were periods in which
agency and communion, power and love, control and surrender no longer seemed
to provide thematic coherence for her life. Fortunately these periods were relatively infrequent and short lived. For most of her life, Horney remained on the
move.

In 1945 Horney published *Our Inner Conflicts,* in which she outlined three
strategies for coping with neurotic conflicts. She called them "moving against,"
"moving toward," and "moving away from" others. In moving against, the person
"glorifies and cultivates in him- or herself everything that leads to mastery of
others" (Horney, 1950, p. 214). In moving toward, the person seeks approval, acceptance, and friendship with others, but at the expense of "anything that con-
notes ambition, vindictiveness, triumph, seeking his [or her] own advantage"
(Horney, 1950, p. 216). In moving away from others, the person withdraws from

all interpersonal engagements and seeks to live in a self-sufficient and unassailable world. Each of the three neurotic strategies is designed to minimize conflict in dealing with people. In their milder forms, each of the three may be an adaptive strategy for healthy living. But in the case of neurosis, basic anxiety and hostility force the individual to use the styles in an inflexible and debilitating manner. Horney (1945) wrote:

> As we have seen, each of the basic attitudes toward others has its positive value. In moving toward people the person tries to create for himself a friendly relation to his world. In moving against people he equips himself for survival in a competitive society. In moving away from people he hopes to attain a certain integrity and serenity. As a matter of fact, all three attitudes are not only desirable but necessary to our development as human beings. It is only when they appear and operate in a neurotic framework that they become compulsive, rigid, indiscriminate, and mutually exclusive. (p. 89)

Horney's three strategies for coping with interpersonal conflict—moving toward, moving against, and moving away from people—bear striking resemblance to what I have identified as the life story themes of control, surrender, and resignation, respectively. It would appear that the broad theory of personality Horney ultimately formulated in her midlife years bears the strong stamp of a life story that she seems to have been constructing from adolescence onward. The three motivational themes in her own identity appear to have been transformed into more general categories for explaining the behavior and experience of others. This is not to suggest that Horney's theory is merely a projection of her own identity. As Horney's writings convincingly show, her many ideas about normal and neurotic personality functioning have their origins in her clinical case examples as well as in her reading of and exposure to a plethora of sources about human lives. But theories, like lives, are overdetermined, and it would seem that Horney's own life and the life story she may have constructed to make sense of her life were important sources for her theorizing, as well.

Changing Characters Over Time

Horney was extremely proud of all three of her daughters. Brigitte grew up to be a glamorous movie actress in Germany during the years of the Third Reich. Marianne became a psychiatrist. Renate raised a family. In her later years, Horney told a friend that she had wanted as a child to be either an actress, a doctor, or a mother. Now, "you see I'm already living on through my children" (Quinn, 1988, p. 418). But it would also appear to be true that Karen Horney managed to live out each of these roles as well, through the *characters* she formulated in narrative. During her twenties and thirties, Karen Horney struggled to realize her needs for control and surrender in the realms of work and family. As she made provisional commitments and consolidated social roles, she began to formulate the central characters in her life story. By the time she reached midlife, there would appear to be three characters on the scene—the actress, the doctor, and the mother.

A number of contemporary theories of identity and the self suggest that adults define themselves by fashioning multiple "characters" or "subselves" to capture the many different social and psychological roles that modern adults enact. For example, Markus and Nurius (1986) argued that each adult organizes information about herself or himself in terms of a family of "possible selves," each representing what the person may wish to become or fear becoming. Hermans et al. (1992) described the adult self as a "polyphonic novel," with different "voices" emerging to express different parts of the self. Well-functioning people do not have "multiple personalities," but different personified parts of the self coexist and interact over time, producing what Hermans calls a "dialogical self." In my own life story model of adult identity, I conceive of the different characters in a person's life story as personified idealizations of the self. Each character, or "imago," integrates a subset of the person's behaviors, values, choices, and social roles into a particular personified schema of the self—a little "me" within, who functions as a main character in my life story. In keeping with the current emphasis on multiplicity in selves, research suggests that more than one prominent imago, or main character, may be identified in most adult life stories.

In Karen Horney's case, there would appear to be some evidence for three main characters, each of which was an internalized version of one of her daughters. Thus, actress, doctor, and mother may be viewed as three idealized personifications in Horney's own life story. Not only do they correspond to the social identities assumed by her three daughters, but they also appear to capture significant aspects of Karen's own multifaceted identity. This is not to suggest that the life story origins of Horney's dominant imagoes were her children. She did not come to see herself in these terms because her children grew up to assume these roles. Nor is it to suggest that Horney worked to guide her children into social roles consistent with her own strivings and desires. Instead, I am suggesting that Karen Horney developed, believed in, and lived according to a particular narrative whose protagonists were actresses, doctors, and mothers. From childhood on, the roles of actress, doctor, and mother were especially appealing to her. As she moved through adolescence and adulthood, these roles were psychologically magnified (Tomkins, 1987) and enriched to become especially salient characters in her self-defining life story. In the story, the three characters express themselves, furthermore, through the themes of control, surrender, and resignation and via the imagery of movement and light.

The actress is the least well developed, the most primitive, and her roots are in Karen's childhood dreams to be a star on stage. The actress is a personification of Karen's restless and flamboyant nature, a childlike incarnation of spontaneous movement and fast escape from reality and reasonableness. In Horney's private mythology of the self, the actress was the woman who can surrender to the momentary role. No long-term commitments are necessary. The actress moves from one role to another, throwing herself into each performance. She acts with great passion for the moment, for passion is always convincing. But next month, she may be playing a different role, with a different leading man. In her last writings, Horney (1950) noted a neurotic tendency to split off parts of experience from the real self. The actress seems to be split off, in a sense. She does not appear to have *the* star role in the story that Horney created to provide her life with unity and purpose. Manifest more in lifelong impulsivity in romantic relationships, the actress is an unintegrated imago in Karen Horney's identity. In other words, the actress is in the story, but her episodes are split off from the main plot line, like little asides that run parallel to the story's main action.

By the time Karen Horney was in her thirties, the imagoes of the doctor and the mother were well integrated into her life story. As a professional psychiatrist, Horney healed broken lives and psychic wounds. Even before she broke with Freud, she was an effective therapist who treated many of her clients in her own home, with well-paid nannies helping her care for the children. In adolescence, she had planned to be a doctor, and as a young adult she accomplished those plans. She juggled the roles of doctor and mother about as well as any woman could do it in the 1920s. Her role as mother generalized beyond the home, as well. Karen Horney "was like a mother to me," remarked a young companion who accompanied her to Japan (Quinn, 1988, p. 406). "She was 100% maternal type," remarked Dr. Leon Saul, who enjoyed an affectionate relationship with Horney during her first few years in the United States (Quinn, 1988, p. 172). Horney was a mother figure in psychoanalysis in the 1920s and 1930s. One of the few women of prominence in the movement, she nurtured and promoted the development of many young analysts in Chicago and New York.

But perhaps the most profound and intriguing way in which Karen Horney's life story provides us with an idealized personification of the mother is that *by becoming a mother Horney helped move mother to the center of psychoanalytic thinking*. In thematic terms, by *surrendering* to the social demand to become a mother, Karen Horney was ultimately able to change, that is *control*, psychoanalytic thinking. For Horney, therefore, the communal imago of the caregiving mother proves to be extraordinarily agentic as well! According to Freud, childbirth was a woman's symbolic substitute and partial compensation for the lack of a penis. Horney's first creative breaks from the psychoanalytic establishment involved her thoroughgoing critique of the Freudian view of motherhood, a critique that grew directly out of her experience as a mother. Quinn (1988) noted:

> There is a wonderful irony here. Like most women pioneering in a male world, Karen Horney had devoted a great deal of energy trying to be one of the boys. And she *had* felt trapped, in the beginning, by the undeniably feminine position in which pregnancy placed her. And yet, as a result of the experience of birth, she felt compelled, for the first time in her professional life, to take an independent position. It was because the experience differed so strikingly from analytic theories that she was forced to propose an alternative theory. Birth was too remarkable to be only a substitute or a sublimation. In the end, because she was a truth seeker, she couldn't deny her femi-

ninity. And it was her femininity that led her to her first original, and important, conclusion. (p. 172)

Horney's first original and important conclusions appeared in her ground-breaking essay, "The Flight from Motherhood." Written when she was forty-one, the essay marks Horney's move into midlife and heralds her emergence as a creative psychoanalytic theorist. At this time, we see her moving beyond the conventional universals of Freudian orthodoxy to a more nuanced and particularized theory of human behavior, illustrating a movement toward the contextualized kind of thinking that is often associated with midlife (Labouvie-Vief, DeVoe, and Bulka, 1989; Rybash, Hoyer, and Roodin, 1985).

The essay also symbolizes an evolution in Horney's life story *through an integration of opposites.* In her midlife years, the opposing imagoes of the doctor and the mother *merged* to form a larger and more generative character that for Horney's life story I would call "the teacher/visionary." This most integrative and influential imago is an adult incarnation of a prescient statement that Karen made in one of her earliest diary entries. "School is the only true thing, after all," she confided on January 3, 1901, at the age of fifteen (Horney, 1980, p. 22). Quinn (1988) noted, "Horney's most important contribution to the history of psychoanalysis grew out of her teaching role" (p. 200). Her gifts in this regard were legendary, including a down-to-earth and empathic style of presentation that made her students feel that she was speaking and listening especially to them. Listeners came away from lectures given by leading male analysts feeling that they had encountered a brilliant mind or a dazzling argument. But as Quinn (1988) put it, "they came away from Horney's lectures feeling they had encountered themselves" (p. 300).

As she moved through her midlife years, Karen Horney seemed to refine her identity to capture in narrative the ever-widening influence she had on the world around her. As the opposing imagoes of "the doctor" and "the mother" came together in midlife to form "the teacher," Horney shifted her energies away from direct caregiving and healing to the formulation of new ideas that she could pass down to her students and the readers of her many influential books. Through teaching, she created a legacy of scholarship and practice that survives with great vigor even today. Movement and light remained her strongest images as she moved deftly and creatively in her midlife years to enlighten others with the insights she had gained. Control, surrender, and resignation remained the central themes in her life story, the first signifying agency ("moving against"), the second signifying communion ("moving toward"), and the third suggesting the dreaded failure to experience either agency or communion ("moving away"). As she moved through midlife, these images and themes were reworked in light of the emergence of new characters, who are amalgamations of the old. Some conflicts were resolved but others remained problematic. Although the story seemed to evolve smoothly to accommodate the heroic teacher/visionary, the actress remained split off from the plot.

There may be an inherent developmental logic in narrative that ideally moves the developing woman or man to formulate more and more adequate stories about the self over time. The psychological criteria of identity maturity therefore may be viewed in inherently literary terms. The especially adequate (mature, good) life story is coherent, credible, open to new possibilities, richly differentiated, reconciling of opposites, and integrated in a generative manner within the context of the best and most vitalizing cultural myths of the day (McAdams, 1993). In the case of Karen Horney, the emergence of the teacher/visionary in her life story marked a significant step toward wholeness, integration, and generativity. It signaled a growing ability to synthesize contrasting parts of the self. In that the teacher seeks to leave a legacy of the self for the next generation, furthermore, this midlife character in Horney's myth signals her growing apprehension of a sense of ending and of the new beginnings that may carry on in her children, her students, and her readers. Although the disconnectedness associated with the actress imago seemed to remain an identity problem to the end, Karen Horney left us with an inspiring life story of triumph and integration, a narrative that her readers and followers can bring into their own life as fresh and invigorating raw material for the stories of the self that all of us continue to create, to tell, and to live.

Conclusion

Existentialist writers emphasize that persons are "thrown" into the world at a particular time and place, endowed with certain blessings and curses that come with the territory of historical time, geographical place, social structure, family origin, biological gender, social class, and even temperamental constitution. There is no getting around the "thrownness," the arbitrary luck of the draw. Yet, modern adults are still challenged to make meaning of their life. As Baumeister (1986) and others have observed, for at least two hundred years, middle-class Westerners have been psychosocially concerned with creating meaningful personal identities for themselves, as a result of a broad spectrum of historical forces that have conspired to focus our attention on the individual self, on creating selves that are unique, coherent, purposeful, and meaningfully organized over time and across situations, selves that likewise are well integrated into a social nexus, niche, or community. I have suggested that to arrive at an identity that provided her life with unity and purpose, Karen Horney fashioned a life story couched in the imagery of movement and light; organized by the themes of control, surrender, and resignation; and animated by the characters of the actress, the doctor, and the mother. It was a complex and multifaceted story that reflected how Horney struggled to find meaning within the world into which she was thrown.

In sketching the outlines of what I believe Horney's story to be, I have not focused on the factors that might have been instrumental in making her story what it was. I have not examined *why* she created the story she created or *how* the story reflects the forces and factors in her environment (and within herself) that make up the thrownness of her life. Such an ambitious effort is beyond the scope of a chapter like this. Yet in a book about women's lives, it is surely worthwhile to remind ourselves of the obvious: Karen Horney's life story, whatever else it might have been, is and was a gendered construction, the reflection of one woman's efforts to find meaning and purpose in a world wherein the opportunities for identity expression appear to have been much more plentiful and flexible for (middle-class) men than for women.

Heilbrun (1988) wrote that women's lives traditionally remain "untold" because they cannot be assimilated to the conventional narrative forms prized by Western patriarchal societies. For example, women's lives do not traditionally fit the "quest" story type—the exciting narrative of self-discovery and conquests traditionally animated by "the hero" (e.g., Campbell, 1949). But what about heroines? Modern lives may not need to be heroic, but heroines, like Karen Horney, may provide narrative forms and possibilities that can be appropriated by those women (and men) who look beyond conventional sex roles and gender stereotypes to find inspiration for the making of their own identities. Indeed, from a very early age, Horney saw herself as transcending the roles her society seemed to offer her. In a sense, she pushed her thrownness to the limits, challenging the constraints that would probably have stifled most young women of similar talent and ambition during her day. In 1904 at age nineteen, Karen Danielson, set forth her two "moral laws" for the future:

> 1. *Thou shalt not lie.*
> *And*
> 2. *Thou shalt free thyself from convention.*

Acknowledgments

This chapter is based on an address given for the conference "The Study of Individual Lives" at the Henry A. Murray Research Center, Radcliffe College, May 11 and 12, 1990. Significant portions of the chapter also appear in Chapter 9 of D. P. McAdams (1993), *The Stories We Live By: Personal Myths and the Making of the Self* (New York: William Morrow). Preparation of the manuscript was greatly aided by a grant from The Spencer Foundation. Address correspondence to Dan P. McAdams, Program in Human Development and Social Policy, Northwestern University, 2003 Sheridan Road, Evanston, Illinois 60208.

References

Bakan, D. (1966). *The duality of human existence: Isolation and communion in Western man.* Boston: Beacon.

Baumeister, R. F. (1986). *Identity: Cultural change and the struggle for self.* New York: Oxford University Press.

Bruner, J. (1990). *Acts of meaning.* Cambridge, MA: Harvard University Press.

Campbell, J. (1949). *The hero with a thousand faces.* New York: Bollingen.

Cohler, B. J. (1982). Personal narrative and the life course. In P. Baltes & O. G. Brim (Eds.), *Life-span development and behavior* (Vol. 4, pp. 205–241). New York: Academic Press.

Edel, L. (1988). Foreword. In S. Quinn, *A mind of her own: The life of Karen Horney*. Reading, MA: Addison-Wesley.

Erikson, E. H. (1963). *Childhood and society* (2d ed.). New York: Norton.

Grotevant, H. D. (1992). *The integrative nature of identity: Bringing the soloists to sing in the choir*. Paper presented at the Wellington Adolescent Identity Conference, Victoria University of Wellington, New Zealand.

Hankiss, A. (1981). On the mythological rearranging of one's life story. In D. Bertaux (Ed.), *Biography and society: The life history approach in the social sciences* (pp. 203–209). Beverly Hills, CA: Sage.

Heilbrun, C. G. (1988). *Writing a woman's life*. New York: Norton.

Hermans, H.J.M., Kempen, H.J.G., & van Loon, R.J.P. (1992). The dialogical self: Beyond individualism and rationalism. *American Psychologist, 47,* 23–33.

Horney, K. (1937). *The neurotic personality of our time*. New York: Norton.

———. (1939). *New ways in psychoanalysis*. New York: Norton.

———. (1945). *Our inner conflicts*. New York: Norton.

———. (1950). *Neurosis and human growth*. New York: Norton.

———. (1980). *The adolescent diaries of Karen Horney*. New York: Basic Books. Copyright © 1980 by Basic Books, Inc. Excerpt from pages 55–57 reprinted by permission of Basic Books, a division of HarperCollins Publishers Inc.

Howard, G. S. (1991). Culture tales: A narrative approach to thinking, cross-cultural psychology, and psychotherapy. *American Psychologist, 46,* 187–197.

Labouvie-Vief, G., DeVoe, M., & Bulka, D. (1989). Speaking about feelings: Conceptions of emotion across the life span. *Psychology and Aging, 4,* 425–437.

Markus, H., & Nurius, P. (1986). Possible selves. *American Psychologist, 41,* 954–969.

McAdams, D. P. (1985). *Power, intimacy, and the life story: Personological inquiries into identity*. New York: Guilford.

———. (1990). Unity and purpose in human lives: The emergence of identity as a life story. In A. I. Rabin, R. A. Zucker, R. A. Emmons, & S. Frank (Eds.), *Studying persons and lives* (pp. 148–200). New York: Springer.

———. (1993). *The stories we live by: Personal myths and the making of the self*. New York: William Morrow.

Quinn, S. (1988). *A mind of her own: The life of Karen Horney*. Reading, MA: Addison-Wesley.

Rosenwald, G., & Ochberg, R. L. (1993). (Eds.). *Storied lives*. New Haven: Yale University Press.

Rybash, J. M., Hoyer, W. J., & Roodin, P. A. (1985). *Adult cognition and aging: Developmental changes in processing, knowing, and thinking*. New York: Pergamon.

Sarbin, T. (1986). The narrative as a root metaphor for psychology. In T. Sarbin (Ed.), *Narrative psychology: The storied nature of human conduct* (pp. 3–21). New York: Praeger.

Tomkins, S. S. (1987). Script theory. In J. Aronoff, A. I. Rabin, & R. A. Zucker (Eds.), *The emergence of personality* (pp. 147–216). New York: Springer.

12

The Complexities of a Young Adult Woman's Relational World: Challenges, Demands, and Benefits

ELIZABETH L. PAUL

THROUGHOUT THE LIFE COURSE, individuals are involved in numerous interpersonal relationships, often taking part in several close relationships at any given time. Such networks of relationships pose a multiplicity of challenges and demands and offer a variety of potential benefits. Psychological research has explored the dynamics of specific types of relationships (e.g., friendships, family relationships). However, the ways in which relationships impact on each other and how individuals manage the demands of several concurrent close relationships have yet to be considered. In the present case study, I explore the ways in which the various close relationships of a young adult woman both challenged her with pressing relational demands and collectively provided her with a variety of relational functions and a context in which to further develop her identity.

Young adulthood is a critical time for learning to manage multiple relationships and to satisfy one's need for intimacy in a complex interpersonal context. This period is quite distinct from other times in the life course, particularly the years preceding the advent of adulthood. The familial context is the primary relational arena for children, but they soon build friendships and other connections in school and community contexts. Caretakers are primarily responsible for the management of the various relationships in which children are involved, aiming to preserve some "family time" while also allowing children time to socialize with peers. As adolescents begin to individuate from family and assume greater autonomy, they assume more responsibility for managing their network of close relationships. Friends begin to fulfill more and more of adolescents' interpersonal needs, complementing those functions served by parents. During adolescence, conflict is often experienced between friends and family as the two primary sources of support and other relational functions. The conflict is often experienced as an "either/or" proposition: I can be close *either* to my family *or* to my friends.

Yet it is in young adulthood that the challenge of managing various close relationships becomes most pressing. In addition to meeting the pressures of establishing a "life of one's own," young adults are faced with negotiating various relational demands and their own interpersonal needs. This relational challenge becomes compounded with the addition of a variety of roles assumed by many individuals during young adulthood. Some young adults become co-workers, spouses, and parents all in a brief period. Most young adults also build a network of friendships and maintain family ties. Moreover, some young adults assume caretaking responsibilities for ailing parents or other relatives. Besides creating additional demands, however, the expansion of one's network also provides increased potential for support and a variety of positive relationship functions. Thus, the young adult's challenge is to manage various close relationships, realizing the positive interpersonal gains and keeping the potential draining effects in check.

Patricia ("Pat") Frazer Lamb's young adulthood showcases the ways in which multiple close relationships can complement and compete with one another. Pat was a young adult during the 1950s, when the cultural expectation, for women in particular, was to assume the primary roles of spouse and parent in early young adulthood. Responsibility for meeting the demands of both familial roles rested primarily on women. Women were not encouraged to assume a career role and if they did so, little if any support was provided for balancing the additional responsibilities. The women of "the silent generation" thought about challenging the conventions, but in these years just prior to the women's movement, received little support for asserting themselves. Pat suggests that one of the reasons she married a British doctor was to catch a glimpse of the intellectual life she so desired. Describing herself and her close friend Joyce Hohlwein she explained,

> We wanted to travel, to see the world, to expand our horizons, to share in the great feast of the intellect for which university seemed to be preparing us. But we were obedient daughters of our time, destined and eager for marriage and motherhood. Both of us resolved the conflict between these personal ambitions and the social commitment to marry by choosing husbands who would shape the travels, the glamorous careers, the horizons, the life styles for their wives. (Lamb and Hohlwein, 1983, pp. xvi–xvii)

Pat grew up in Los Angeles in a working-class family she describes as "articulate, amusing, fun-loving, supportive, strongly imbued with a deep sense of family loyalty" (Lamb and Hohlwein, 1983, p. xv) and in which women formed the strong and stable core. Yet she recalls of her childhood that "education, at least beyond high school, was not considered possible or even particularly desirable, since where could it lead, what difference could it make, in a world ruled by the rich and the powerful?" In retrospect, Pat "sees her teenage self as wanting desperately to educate herself out of her background, however caring, and to move into a totally different world" (Lamb and Hohlwein, 1983, pp. xv–xvi).

Pat pursued a college education at the University of Utah, where she met Joyce Hohlwein, a classmate who would become a lifelong friend. Pat married after her first year of college; however, the marriage only lasted a few months. During her second year of college, a family death necessitated a return home so that she could help her mother. The following summer, her mother helped Pat go to Europe where Pat met and married a young British medical student, Philip.[1]

For eleven years after marrying, the entirety of Pat's young adulthood, Pat and Philip traveled internationally, including nine years living in Tanganyika. Pat described a sometimes active social life and mentioned a variety of acquaintances who moved through their life while they were abroad. Yet she frequently lamented the lack of any "local" close relationships beyond those with her spouse and children. Indeed, she often felt quite stifled and isolated by the expectations of subservience and silence in women in East Africa, echoing (perhaps even more strictly) U.S. gender expectations. During this time, however, she kept in regular contact with Joyce and with her mother, Georgia Kerr Lucas, through correspondence.

Thus, the primary relationships during Pat's young adulthood were with her husband, Philip; her friend Joyce; her mother; and her children. A direct comparison of the functions served by Pat's relationships with her mother and Joyce can be made by comparing the available correspondence from Pat to both women.[2] This correspondence is particularly rich and enables a detailed account of the role of each woman in Pat's young adult years. The role of Pat's husband and children, though less rich in description, was gleaned from her comments in correspondence to Joyce and her mother.

Pat drew important benefits from each of her close relationships. Her relationship with her mother seemed to serve as a secure base for her. She frequently wrote to her mother (often more frequently than she wrote to Joyce) and gave very detailed accounts of her day-to-day experiences, thoughts, and feelings. Though Pat wrote less often to Joyce, her letters to her friend were more often emotional and introspective, delving into complex ideological issues, mostly about marriage, motherhood, and life as a young woman in the 1950s. Early on, Pat expressed contentment and closeness in her marriage to Philip, feeling a union unmatched (at least in kind, if not in strength) by her other close relationships. Her children brought her a sense of the wonder and magic in life.

But her close relationships challenged Pat as well. Her interdependence with her mother, though a strong attachment, was trying to her at times, especially given her inability to spend time with her mother. Pat felt this most keenly when she or her mother experienced an important life event (e.g., the birth of Pat's children, upward and downward turns of her mother's new job or romance). The two were vigilant in keeping up their correspondence, but written communication was not enough during trying times.

Though Pat also longed for Joyce's company, the primary challenge in their re-lationship was more ideological. Though Pat and Joyce had shared very similar life experiences in young adulthood, they pursued different pathways in life. Both had decided feminist leanings and were unconventional in many of their views for the time, but each managed these nontraditional views differently in meeting the demands of young adulthood: Joyce struggled to balance intellectual pursuits with family demands; Pat squelched her intellectual interests and focused instead on being a devoted wife and mother.

Though Pat expressed contentment in the early years of her marriage, she fre-quently lamented the lack of communication or a sharing of emotions with her husband. She often confided to her mother and Joyce things she felt she could not share with Philip. She expressed excitement at being involved in aspects of her husband's professional life, though it was not the intellectual activity she would have chosen for herself. Over time, her assertions of contentment faded as she be-came leery of the changes her marriage was undergoing. (In fact, her marriage to Philip ended in divorce several years later.) Finally, though Pat enjoyed mother-hood and felt very attached to her children, she also yearned for intellectual activ-ity and independence from her children.

Several themes emerge from a consideration of the ways in which Pat's close re-lationships intertwined to both benefit and challenge her. Each of these themes will be considered in turn.

Absence Makes the Heart Grow Fonder

Pat visited her mother and Joyce only once during her years of international travel. Thus, the "work" of each relationship was carried out primarily through correspondence. Typically, the correspondence was regular and frequent, espe-cially with her mother, and rich in personal detail. However, the role of distance and the absence of face-to-face contact and "dailiness" in these close relationships is an important backdrop for a consideration of the functions each relationship served.

Pat provided her mother with very detailed accounts of her day-to-day activi-ties, and she did not seem hesitant to share the intricacies of her thoughts and feelings with her mother. But occasional incongruities between Pat's letters to her mother and to Joyce suggest that Pat scaled back the descriptions of some of her more turbulent experiences, possibly to protect her mother. For example, during Pat's pregnancy with her second son, she told her mother she weighed more than she told Joyce she weighed, and in fact she seems to have bordered on being un-derweight.

The effects of distance seemed to be greater for Pat's relationship with Joyce than with her mother, perhaps due to the greater identity exploration and defini-tion that took place in her relationship with Joyce. The potential for more closely monitoring and controlling one's self-presentation to others is certainly greater in correspondence. Pat once remarked to Joyce about the distorting effect of dis-

tance on relationships (specifically regarding her early relationship with her husband): "*How* a long correspondence without a previous long, stable and thorough
knowledge of the other can—well, not exactly mislead one—but put garlic in the
dressing perhaps, or substitute quite ridiculous (on better acquaintance) orchids
for perfectly adequate and really quite stimulating daisies!" (May 28, 1957).

Indeed, Pat's theory about her early relationship with Philip could be applied to
her relationship with Joyce as well. Pat and Joyce developed their friendship during their short time together at the University of Utah. Though they felt a close
connection during this time, largely based on their apparent similarities, it is de-
batable that their brief time together engendered a "stable and thorough knowledge" of one another before they were launched into the separate lives that would
take both of them to the far reaches of the globe. They had to rely on correspondence to fill in gaps in their knowledge of one another—a formidable challenge
given that both women's identities were quite fluid and as yet not fully defined. As
will be discussed later in this chapter, both women relied heavily on this correspondence for much of their self-exploration and identity definition work.

In fact, Lamb and Hohlwein's (1983) description of their reunion after seven
years apart suggests that their previous correspondence had painted not altogether recognizable pictures of the paths each had taken. Each woman was surprised by what she saw in the other during their reunion—new identities that
were not as evident in the correspondence. Such discoveries, though not revealed
to each other at first, provided fodder for lively debates and discussions in the future correspondence as Pat and Joyce further defined their identities and life
goals.

The fact that two of Pat's closest intimates were spatially far away allowed for a
different management of the relationships from what would have been possible
had the women been nearer. Two close relationships can sometimes "compete"
with one another at times of need. For example, if both Joyce and Pat's mother
were having trying times, Pat would need to make choices regarding the expenditure of resources to each—both in actual time spent with each and the dedication
of emotional resources. With the exchange of support between Pat and her intimates taking place predominantly through correspondence, Pat had more control
over her expenditure of resources.

Pat exercised fluidity in the balance of give and take characteristic of each relationship, withdrawing energy from one and investing it in another when war-
ranted. For example, when Joyce wrote emotional letters soliciting Pat's support
and comfort, Pat would write an unusually lengthy and thoughtful response to
Joyce, then increase the frequency of her letter writing to her mother. Moreover,
some of the requests for advice and philosophical meanderings usually directed to
Joyce would be shifted to her mother for a brief time.

Such balancing of relational demands also applied to her other close relationships—namely with her husband and her children. Pat more frequently corresponded with Joyce during the more troubling times of her marriage. And it is
questionable whether Pat would have been able to maintain such close extramari-

tal ties in person, given the seemingly tight bounds imposed on Pat by her marriage.

Thus, distance appears to have affected both the course of her relationships as well as the functions the relationships served for Pat, especially her friendship with Joyce. Had the two women been in close geographic proximity to one another, the relationship may have developed very differently or not at all. Nonetheless, this long-distance relationship, as well as her bond with her mother, constituted much of the relational base of Pat's young adulthood.

Emotional Connection

Clearly, the most emotionally rich relationships in which Pat was involved during young adulthood were with her mother and Joyce. Through their correspondence, Joyce and Pat's mother provided Pat with companionship and closeness unmatched by persons in her physical environs, including Philip. In fact, Pat's sharing of her feelings and insights about her life experiences with her mother and Joyce seemed to fill a void in her marriage. Prior to the birth of Pat's first child (who was stillborn), Pat wrote to Joyce of Philip, "He's done his best for me, which is all I can ask. He loves me, takes good care of me, is very sympathetic, and is as thrilled and excited over Baby as I am. But I *still* miss and want my Mother and a friend like you. So damn it, WRITE to me! It helps" (September 26, 1954).

Though Pat maintained that she was comfortable with Philip during the early years of the marriage, she lamented that "I only wish he would talk more to me, open up and share the things of the heart" (October 27, 1955). Pat frequently confided feelings to Joyce that she felt she could not share with Philip. For instance, several months after Pat's first child, Trevor, was stillborn, she confided to Joyce: "I haven't thought about it now for months and months, but it's so hard to believe that Trevor would have been a year old six weeks ago. I'll admit to a few tears in private every now and then, though I haven't said anything to Philip" (November 15, 1955).

Later she remarked to Joyce more pointedly, "God knows, I could use some real human exchange. Our silences (P[hilip]'s and mine) are deafening and soul-destroying, for me. I feel desperately unloved and hence unloving" (May 19, 1958).

Even during the times when Pat expressed comfort and happiness in her marriage, she cautioned that marriage cannot be all things to a person. She wrote to Joyce, "it certainly is not everything in life to me, because it (meaning Philip, our social pattern together, I guess) cannot cover every bit of every complexity of my ego, my life, my personality" (November 30, 1953). In correspondence to Joyce, Pat often pondered the complementarity of her friendship and marriage:

> I am so glad we were both born of the same sex. I can feel lifelong gratitude for a lasting understanding and the deepest sort of friendship between two women. ... I love you very dearly, in short, and treasure your respect and love as I do hardly anybody's. ... A different part of the same subject—I really feel that a man and woman can reach an empathy that is impossible between two of the same sex. ... That is, lovers find something that friends don't ... *but,* friends reach a state of mutual behavior on the

same levels with the same motivations and deep sympathies of such intensity that is impossible between lovers. Thus the advantages of a great love plus a great friendship. (November 30, 1953)

Another indication of the emotional connection between Pat and the two important women in her life were her frequent expressions of longing and loneliness at their separation. While traveling in France, England, and Africa, she expressed her loneliness both to her mother and to Joyce, longing for their companionship. She often wrote of her longing for her mother: "I get so homesick and lonesome for you every time I think about it … never before have I realized how much my family means to me. … Especially at this time now, I'd give anything to have you near me and to feel the warmth and coziness and security of all of you" (August 24, 1954). And to Joyce she often wrote such statements as: "You're my one friend, whom I really miss" (May 6, 1954).

Pat's emotional connection with her mother seemed more secure than her growing relationship with Joyce, helping Pat feel more grounded when she was away from home. At one point when her mother had not written to Pat in some time Pat wrote to her, "I'm beginning to feel like a complete expatriate man without a country" (May 10, 1956). But her reliance on her mother for "grounding" also seemed metaphorical for her efforts to maintain continuity between the child self she had been and the adult self she was becoming. In other words, as Pat worked on establishing a new identity, she liked to feel grounded in her earlier self, which was represented by her connection with her mother.

Self-Exploration

Pat worked on self-exploration in both relationships, exploring her identity as spouse, parent, daughter, friend, and most important, woman. Pat worked especially hard during her young adulthood at defining herself in her new roles as mother and spouse, while also struggling to hold on to her "intellectual self," which so often felt incompatible with her new roles. The East African society in which she found herself for many of her years abroad failed to support her intellectual interests. She exclaimed to Joyce at an early point in her East African experience:

> Something is going on in our social life that I'm uncomfortable about, and can't quite come to terms with. You know how political and in the thick of things I've always been (and loved to be), and how I love to talk about politics and the world situation till the wee hours. And I'm not exactly illiterate. … And here I am, finding that I'm expected to keep my mouth shut and listen sweetly to the men, along with all the other stupid uneducated wives. Philip gets quite cross with me when I forget myself and break in with my two cents' worth, so I'm learning painfully to keep quiet. (August 15, 1955)

Lacking support from her husband or from society, Pat frequently relied on social comparison, especially with Joyce but also with her mother during this time as she tried to better understand the new experiences she was having. She would weave in and out of emphasizing similarities between them and recognizing differences.

Pat frequently referred to the mutuality, or *simpatico,* she felt was uniquely characteristic of her friendship with Joyce. In fact, such a shared sense of identity was characteristic of their relationship in the beginning stages: "We discovered immediate rapport, through music, ... books, movies, a similar sense of humor and, most of all, a nebulous desire to achieve goals we shared but could not articulate very clearly" (Lamb and Hohlwein, 1983, p. xvi).

This feeling of shared experience and identity was undoubtedly heightened as Pat and Joyce began to share the experience of several life events as their lives took seemingly parallel paths during their twenties. Most notably they shared the births of their first children (nearly a year after the stillbirth of Pat's first child, Trevor). Shortly after the births of their sons, Pat wrote to Joyce: "Enough ravings about the joys of motherhood. You too, I know, are filled with it all, and I long to hear from you, to share this with you. How I should love to in more than letters" (February 10, 1956). She later continued, "I would so like to see you and your baby, to talk with you about how motherhood suits us both, all the things I don't seem to even want, let alone be able, to share with anyone else about life at this stage" (April 5, 1956).

Pat also worked with Joyce to sculpt her identity as a mother so that it was consonant both with the mother she wanted, and indeed was expected, to be and the mother her personal philosophy and identity *could* be. She wrote to Joyce on one occasion,

> I feel terribly fierce and protective when something startles him and he puckers his lower lip, quietly gulps and sobs and turns his head into my shoulder or the pillow. I love him so very much, but am I horrible and unmaternal when I whisper quietly to you alone that he is not my whole life? I know I'll be a good mother, perhaps the better for wanting him to develop and stand on his own feet, and not wanting to clutch him to my breast always. Have you felt anything conscious of this sort? Do all mothers feel it and are just ashamed to admit it, or am I unnatural and different? (April 10, 1956).

Pat often pondered her future, feeling at age twenty-six that her life was reaching an uncomfortable plateau. She was interested in more actively exercising her intellect, yet voiced ambivalence about doing so given "societal discomfort" over mixing work with motherhood, particularly pronounced in East African bourgeois society. She frequently discussed both with Joyce and with her working-class mother (who always had financial responsibilities for her family) ways in which work or intellectual activity could be balanced with motherhood. In fact, Pat's relationship with her mother seemed to grow during Pat's young adulthood, especially during Pat's early motherhood as she thought of her mother's trying young adult years: "I don't know how you stood it when you were so alone, carrying me" (August 24, 1954).

In forming her new identity as mother and considering the ways in which her intellectual interests could be integrated with that role, it appears that Pat tried to transcend her working-class background and experience motherhood in a more bourgeois lifestyle. In her frequent comparisons of her lifestyle with Joyce's, she often drew attention to the differences in their upbringing. Pat grew up in a working-class family; Joyce was raised in a more privileged middle-class family. In some ways, it seems that Pat and Joyce traded places socioeconomically in their young adult years. Though Pat was enjoying a more privileged lifestyle, Joyce was struggling to make ends meet as she had not had to before.

This incongruity between Pat's and Joyce's lifestyles paralleled their different responses to the challenge of combining motherhood and intellectual activity. With a more privileged lifestyle, Pat experienced greater social pressure to "do the right thing," which at that time was to be a good wife and mother. Thus, she tried to squelch her intellectual interests and focus on her family. In contrast, Joyce gained higher education in English and pursued a teaching career while also nurturing her family. Though Pat and Joyce at first avoided calling attention to this contrast in their roles as wife and mother, their different choices gained increased attention in their correspondence as time grew on. Perhaps the increased salience of this topic paralleled Pat's feelings of ambivalence about her choice, which can be detected in her lamentations about her unmet intellectual needs, her repeated "sermons" to Joyce about the wisdom of her choice, and her rare admissions of envy over Joyce's life choices.

Pat frequently relied on Joyce as a sounding board for her feelings of "intellectual disintegration." After she married Philip she wrote to Joyce of her lapsing intellectual and political activities. She and Joyce would encourage each other to write and frequently sent each other books to read and discuss. After becoming a mother, Pat wrote to Joyce, "I vegetate quite happily most of the time, but get all fired up about it every now and again, and worry that my mind will disintegrate entirely one of these days if I don't do *something* about it!" (September 18, 1956). As she sometimes contemplated how to integrate some intellectual activity into her life as wife and mother, she observed, "My baby is so very much in my life, I can lavish all the affection and love and care on him that I have in me. But I have to admit there are still some chinks and holes through which a cold wind comes blowing unbidden sometimes" (July 15, 1956).

Yet Pat also tried to hold fast to her choice to focus on motherhood and expressed concern about Joyce's decision to also pursue intellectual goals: "I think I'm living up to do what Philip has a right to expect of me, and I am determined to continue to do so. ... It's more important than writing, or anything else. I hardly ever any more wonder what it would have been like to have been an opera singer or a foreign correspondent or the first woman on an Everest expedition." (February 20, 1957). Pat later wrote to Joyce:

> I have always felt so sorry for you because you have missed these years with Reinhard [Joyce's first child], and the totality of homemaking all by yourself ..., because I do

think that the latter is important to the development of a woman, as such. And as for the former, although it is irksome, and the lack of money a problem ..., the ordered simplicity (to a husband's eye), the graciousness that can only come to a home through the efforts of a wife who is nothing else first, at least in those first years when homemaking begins, and especially when the children arrive, from their birth until they are well established in school, can be begun and maintained only by a woman who does not work. (November 28, 1960)

Later Pat began to admit her envy of Joyce's life choices: "And in a tiny whisper, I admit to being envious of your working" (December 15, 1960). These admissions became more desperate as time went on and Pat's marriage to Philip was failing:

Oh, Joyce, what hope is there for us? I still cling to a forlorn hope of creativeness of some sort, self-expression. But very forlorn, and not much hope. I am a lousy wife, at least with Philip, and I'm fairly sure I would be with anyone else too. Oh, I do all the necessities reasonably well and fully, to compensate for the lack of any real emotional basis on my side. I feel (but this I *cannot* fully admit to—it's a sometimes thing) a moderate (could it be?) failure as a mother. And for heaven's sake, what *else* have I been doing the last eight years? You at least have been teaching and have been a real success at that. I have nothing to claim. (March 14, 1962)

It appears from Pat's correspondence with Joyce that in the later years of Pat's marriage to Philip their friendship was instrumental in encouraging Pat to consider other life options, including intellectual activities of her own:

I'm starting to keep a sort of journal, ideas, jottings and quotations book which I am beginning to think is indispensable equipment for anyone who wants to write anything, particularly if the mind is as disordered, discipline as hopeless, and memory as faulty as mine. Besides, it's good practice, like scales. If it hadn't been for our correspondence these last arid years, I should be so rusty altogether, I shouldn't even be able to write a paragraph without danger of imminent mental collapse. (December 5, 1958)

Pat's mother seems also to have served as an important role model for the unleashing of Pat's buried intellectual aspirations. Pat sometimes reflected on her mother's life and the importance of having individual interests and activities in older adulthood. Pat's recognition of the value of such activity was also reflected in the support she gave when her mother accepted a new job.

Another way in which Pat relied on her close relationships as a context for self-exploration was in trying to find a way to be comfortable in her new role as wife. Pat and Joyce frequently compared the changes in their respective new marriages, wondering if either of the marriages would live up to the hopes with which they entered the relationships. Pat often ruminated over the experiences she and Joyce were having, using their experiences as fodder for intense self-exploration. Often Pat would respond to Joyce's pleas for understanding and support by recounting her own experiences. She once answered: "Where shall I begin? ... How to tell you how my heart aches for you in the loneliest, awfulest, of worlds? Perhaps, because everyone analyzes everyone else from one's own inner being, you, being an impingement upon *my* consciousness, can only be seen by me through the light of my own experience. Perhaps, then, I'll tell you a little of myself" (March 5, 1956). She went on to offer a rich account of her own experiences accompanied by many insights and reassurances of understanding and empathy.

Pat also self-reflected while extending support to her mother as her mother experienced various life events in her older age. For example, just when her mother was contemplating remarriage, Pat was beginning to question the future of her own marriage. In support of her mother, she remarked, "I think it would be wonderful for you to be happily married again, but I do hope he's good enough for you, and of your mental and spiritual class" (February 7, 1956).

Defining a Relational Self

Pat and Joyce worked at developing their *individual* identities within the context of their relationship, but they were also learning how to be intimately connected with another individual. They were each developing a "relational template" that could be applied to their other close relationships. Such relational self-definition work was not as characteristic of Pat's relationship with her mother. This is evidenced in part by the more frequent first-person "relational talk" characteristic of Pat's correspondence with Joyce. Pat and Joyce often wrote about their relationship with one another, commenting on the reasons each was important to the other and reflecting on the process of the development of their friendship. In contrast, beyond expressing general appreciation to her mother, Pat rarely discussed specifics about the importance of their relationship in her life or commented on the patterns of their exchange.

Perhaps the greater emphasis on relational definition in Pat's relationship with Joyce was simply due to the need in young adulthood to take what one has learned about relationships within one's family and early friendships and apply it to adult peer relationships. However, this greater frequency of relational talk may also be due to the fact that their friendship was still growing when Pat and Joyce parted ways; much of the groundwork of their relationship had to be developed in correspondence. In fact, when they agreed to write to "keep in touch" after college, it appears that neither envisioned the intimate connection that would be formed. Thus, more frequent declarations of closeness and commitment were a necessity for nurturing the developing closeness. In contrast, Pat's connection with her mother was secure and stable, making constant reminders of their dedication to one another less necessary. Instead, what little relational discussion there was in Pat's correspondence with her mother was more often third-party observation. For example, Pat frequently recounted observations of others' relationships (usually distant acquaintances) and sometimes commented on her sister's romantic involvements.

Another way in which Pat worked with Joyce to define her relational self was through frequent discussions of her relationship with Philip. In contrast, comments to her mother about her relationship with Philip were more guarded and less frequent. For instance, in the later years of Pat's marriage, Pat was struggling to find a way to engage in a meaningful relationship with her husband without the marriage engulfing her individuality. She wrote to Joyce, "For the first time since our marriage, five and a half years now, I am the one who is beginning to draw back a little, to reveal less, to give a little less of my soul, my personality, my ideas, my comments. And perhaps it's a good thing" (December, 5 1958). And later, after an initial separation from Philip in which Pat first entertained divorcing Philip, she exclaimed: "The frightfulness and fear of these last months have taught me one thing anyway, to keep withdrawn and at a distance from others the things most precious to my inner harmony, not to *attempt* to share the basically unshareable, but to force myself to turn inward for communion and a sense of the justification of my own substantive values" (September 22, 1959). Pat also frequently responded to Joyce's pleas for advice about her own marriage.

Thus, in the context of her close relationships, Pat was struggling to develop a set of relational skills that might in turn enrich all of her close relationships, including the more tenuous relationship with her spouse.

Conclusion

This case study raises many important issues for further research on the ways in which individuals balance several close relationships that can both tax and enhance their psychological well-being.

Pat's relationship experiences demonstrate that a single relationship rarely satisfies all of an individual's relational needs. It is more likely that a constellation of relationships meets these needs. At any given time, each of Pat's close relationships provided some functions in common, but more often each close relationship served a unique purpose. Even those functions that were provided by more than one relationship were experienced differently depending on the specific relationship context. For example, the "flavor" of emotional connection often differed from relationship to relationship, including experiences of emotional security, emotional exchange, and emotional support. This makes for a complex web of unique connections to be managed.

Moreover, it appears that the needs each relationship meets are fluid over time, signaling the importance of a longitudinal perspective in understanding the psychosocial functions of close relationships. At one moment, one's relationship with a close friend might meet needs for emotional support, and at another time, it might be one's relationship with mother that serves this function. What is the process whereby the source of such support is determined from one time of need to the next?

Pat's strategies for managing her various relationships included shifting portions of her emotional investment from one relationship to another, sometimes "replenishing" her supply in one relationship only to "expend" it in another relationship. Surely, such management strategies might have been facilitated by the physical distance between Pat and the others. Although it may have been frustrating for Pat to be apart from these intimates during both troubling and happy times, the distance also enabled her to orchestrate the flow of her energies more autonomously. Further exploration is needed of the additional management strategies that might be employed given closer physical proximity in a relationship.

Another salient issue in Pat's young adulthood is the intricate intertwining of self- and relational development as she struggled to define the different dimensions of her newly emerging adult self in the context of various close relationships. Each relationship seemed to contribute to her self-development in a unique way, challenging Pat to integrate and synthesize the different messages into a cohesive self. In fact, at times, others' expectations (including various societal expectations) for Pat's self-definitional work contrasted and competed with one another.

Pat explored many aspects of her identity in the context of her close relationships, including her "relational identity." During her young adult years, she struggled with developing a satisfying way of relating with others while also upholding her personal needs, values, and interests. Pat sometimes used her contrasting relationship experiences to "try out" interaction patterns in one relationship that were more characteristic of another close relationship. Such relational identity definition work in young adulthood is in need of exploration in psychological theory and research.

Clearly, Patricia Frazer Lamb's young adulthood showcases the ways in which multiple close relationships can both challenge and benefit us and how they can both complement and compete with one another. Pat's young adult years were somewhat unusual in that she was isolated from her closest companions (her mother and Joyce) as she moved with her husband. Yet her avid letter writing during this time allows us a rare in-depth view of the complexity and richness of her relational world. Indeed, case studies are a productive approach for exploring such uncharted territory and suggesting future directions for theory and research.

Notes

1. Pseudonyms as assigned by Lamb and Hohlwein (1983) have been used throughout this chapter.

2. Correspondence from Patricia Frazer Lamb to Joyce Hohlwein (copyright 1983 Patricia Frazer Lamb and Joyce Hohlwein) and Georgia Kerr Lucas (Lamb's mother) was used by permission of Lamb and Hohlwein and was obtained from the Schlesinger Library of Radcliffe College.

References

Lamb, P. F., & Hohlwein, K. J. (1983). *Touchstones: Letters between two women: 1953–1964.* New York: Harper & Row. Republished in paperback, 1986, Boston: G. K. Hall.

13

Traumatic Historical Events and Adolescent Psychosocial Development: Letters from V.

OLIVA M. ESPIN

IN THIS CHAPTER, I present and analyze the experience of a Latin American adolescent, who was separated from her parents because of her country's political circumstances. The study is based on the data provided by seventy-one letters written by this young woman, here called V. These letters span the period of nine years, in which V. was between the ages of thirteen and twenty-two covering not only her adolescence, but also the most traumatic period in her life. At age thirteen, V. was abruptly separated from her parents when they were imprisoned as political dissidents. A year later, while both her parents were still in prison, they decided to send their children to another country. There she was cared for by a family who had volunteered to be her guardians. Thus, to the trauma created by political events and her parents' imprisonment, the traumas of uprooting, migration, and adaptation to foster parents were added. After nearly a decade of separation, when she next saw her parents, V. was married and expecting her first child. Her primary outlet for the pain, grief, frustration, and uncertainty of those years was writing letters to one of her former teachers who had also emigrated. This teacher was herself a young twenty-two-year-old woman at the time this correspondence started.

A previous study of these letters (Espin, Stewart, and Gomez, 1990) focused on the applicability of Erikson's (1963, 1968) general model of psychosocial development to this adolescent's development. That study employed a coding system for analyzing personal documents based on Erikson's stages of psychosocial development devised by Stewart, Franz, and Layton (1988). A time-series analysis of the data provided by the coded letters showed that "despite the severity of her losses and her uprooting at the beginning of adolescence, V. seems to have experienced

Erikson's hypothesized normal course of psychosocial development" (Espin et al., 1990, p. 358) while simultaneously some unique features, such as "unexpectedly high levels of preoccupation with intimacy and even with generativity" (p. 358) were present.

In that study, we concluded that "in future work it will be important to identify the personal and circumstantial factors that facilitate maintenance of normal personality development in the face of traumatic loss" (Espin et al., 1990, p. 362). This chapter is an attempt at identifying those factors, using a qualitative approach to the data and thus allowing V.'s words to present the reader with her process as she described it. My analysis focuses on themes of coping and resilience in addition to references to Erikson's theory.

Reading these letters we witness the writer's development process as she experienced it. Her description of and reflections about her life experiences provide firsthand understanding of the impact of historical/political events on her life.

As Allport (1942) argued, "In the analysis of letters, the psychological and historical methods fuse" (p. 109). Reading these letters, it is difficult to disentangle the effects of historical/political events on V.'s life course from her individual psychological development. Indeed, it is impossible to understand individual psychological development without considering the specific historical circumstances in which that individual is immersed. It is also problematic to determine the interplay between the two because it is difficult to "specify the process by which historical events are manifested in the life course, [although it is evident that] psychological questions are posed by knowledge of the particular historical situation and its life course effects" (Elder, 1981, p. 97). That is why research on individuals who have experienced traumatic historic/political events

> can yield knowledge unlikely to be gained from more traditional samples—knowledge about psychosocial development under conditions of concentrated and chronic adversity, knowledge about the factors that influence whether adversity will or will not be overcome, and finally, knowledge that is not only important for developmental theory but essential for the formulation of social policy. (Jessor, 1993, p. 119)

V.'s individual experience, then, is invaluable. Although it cannot help us disentangle the effect of historical/political events on all individuals, it does provide a concrete case through which to describe the lived experience of one adolescent.

V.'s adult psychological makeup most probably would not have been the same without the attendant cultural/political/historical events that framed her life. As a thirteen-year-old, before the events that transformed the course of her life, V. was bright, vivacious, and slightly shy. Through her childhood and early adolescence she appeared to be reasonably well adjusted, did well in school, and was well liked by her peers. Most probably, her ability to withstand the traumatic events of her life was related to her previous adjustment and maturity. As an adult V. has had a productive, apparently healthy life. She has been successful in both her personal and professional life. Yet the question remains: How did historical conditions interact with her biography to create her individual psychology? Moreover, is there any "biography" outside of historical events for V. or anyone else? Most people are not aware that they are immersed in a particular historical context. For most of us it is only when that context becomes traumatic or in other ways "unusual" that we start questioning its psychological effects (Espin, 1992). In this chapter, I probe the interplay between history and psychology by focusing on the experience of one individual.

The Impact of History

From V.'s letters we know that during her adolescence, when the upheaval was most intense, she was acutely aware of her historical circumstances. Her letters include regular reference to the effects of political/historical events on her everyday life and on her relationships with people. She writes frequently of the fear and anxiety created by those events, both directly and through veiled and "encoded" allusions that she trusts her correspondent to interpret. From her first letters, references to the relationship between events in her life and political upheaval are constant. As she presents, describes, and interprets those events, she reveals her unique mixture of unusual maturity and childish expression. Simultaneously, she exposes her internal anguish and concern for the well-being of the adults no longer able to provide her with protection because of their own helplessness.

In her first letter, written before her emigration, she tells her correspondent: "I would love to be with you, but I would not judge myself to be a good person if I left my parents now when they need me the most. Also I have been very agitated these days because my grandfather was taken to a farm for vacation. It was short, but I was terrified as hell" (July 15, 1961). This story about a "farm" her grandfather is "taken to for vacation" is in fact a veiled description of his recent brief arrest and unexpected release. It terrifies her because with her parents already in prison, she fears for her fate if her grandparents are also imprisoned for an extended period of time.

The depth of her terror and the intensity of her anxiety come through in words that seem unlike a thirteen-year-old's: "We are OK, but my parents are still in the hospital and I am really desperate and cannot take it anymore. Only belief in God sustains me" (October 6, 1961). This time "hospital" represents the prison. In this letter, as in many others, God is seen as the only source of consolation, strength, and meaning to mitigate the traumatic experience. The situation was indeed terrifying for a thirteen-year-old living in a context where rumors were the only source of information: "I went to see my father on Wednesday. But I am very nervous because under each section of [the small island where the men's prison is located] they have placed 25,000 pounds of dynamite. So there are 100,000 pounds under the place. You can imagine what it is for, so that makes me very nervous" (June 11, 1961).

In the first letter she writes after leaving her country she explicitly articulates her fears and the events' impact on her life. In this letter, the psychological transformation that resulted from her early losses begins to manifest:

I have decided to leave my country and come to this country only because my parents were desperate for me to do so. However, it makes me feel like a coward. I feel bad not being able to do anything. My hands are tied, although I would be willing to give my life for my country and for God. That is why I feel desperate not being able to do anything about the horrible political regime in our country. I have wanted to say this to you for a long time, but I could not do it while I was there: I could have endangered my parents. ... I know you understand that I am serious about these words that I need so much to say to someone. I know you know that I am only a child in body, but in the last few months there has been a radical change in me. It is not my choice, but I am not the same as I was: I have been forced to become a grown woman at fourteen. (August 24, 1962)

Indeed, her letters reveal unusual maturity for her age. She perceives that the traumatic events have pushed her development beyond what was expected at her age for other adolescents of her culture and social class. This letter, perhaps more than any other, illustrates her uncanny ability to analyze her experience. It also presents with clarity one of the themes that reappear constantly in the letters: The wishes of others and the will of God are at the center of her life decisions and inform the acceptance of her fate.

During nine years of letter writing, V. never met her correspondent face-to-face. Their eventual meeting was cathartic for V. As is common for trauma victims, reviewing the experiences after several years fostered a sense of integration and healing of the painful memories (e.g., Herman, 1992). The encounter with her correspondent facilitated this process and fostered a sense of reconciliation with the past. This process may or may not have happened without this visit, but if nothing else, the visit and long hours of conversation after so many years of letter writing facilitated the opportunity for the reviewing and integration of the painful events.

Immediately after their first visit, V. reflected on the impact of these historical/political events on her life course. "I believe that today I have hated [all those events and the political leaders who have created them] the most. It is terrible to have to live away from someone who can understand us just because events beyond our control have determined our fate and where we are to live" (February 13, 1970). She differentiated between positive and negative results of her experiences, however. Not everything in the forced migration and loss of country was destructive to her:

I guess that I can also thank [the political leaders I hate] for good things in my life and even my happiness. If I had met my husband in our country, he probably would have never talked to me. Not only because I had more money than him but also because I would not have lowered my social status for his sake. In fact, thanks to these horrible events I have learned that money is not worth much and neither are social position and family name. As you can see, I seem to owe [those political leaders] more than one thing in spite of everything else. (March 4, 1970)

Yet her pain cannot be forgotten that easily. As often happens with grief, any event may trigger it again. Years after her emigration and a few months after the visit of her correspondent, V. wrote: "I am watching a film that takes place in our country about forty years ago. I am seeing familiar views of that all too familiar land. It seems impossible that such simple things after so many years can move us so much. It is as if I had left only yesterday. The pain and the memories are there all over again" (May 8, 1970).

V.'s Psychosocial Development

Many theories have been proposed for the study of adolescent psychosocial development. Of these, Erikson's (1963, 1968) is probably the best known and provided a valuable theoretical frame for an earlier study (Espin et al., 1990) of these letters: "Overall the pattern of V.'s [development] suggests broad support for Erikson's theory that identity preoccupations are the focus of psychosocial development for adolescents, and that as they are resolved, and a secure identity established, they gradually give way to increasing intimacy concerns" (p. 358). However, in V.'s case, "it is interesting that the developmental trends are much stronger for intimacy and generativity than for identity" (p. 358). Yet overall, "despite the severity of her losses and her uprooting at the beginning of adolescence, V. ... seems to have experienced Erikson's hypothesized normal course of psychosocial development in terms of both individuation (identity) and connection with others (intimacy and generativity)" (p. 358).

Themes of *identity* appear consistently in V.'s letters. She expresses these concerns in several ways. As with other adolescents, career concerns emerge as an expression of her search for identity:

> You may think that I change my mind easily because in a recent letter I told you that I wanted to study Psychology. But it is my worst subject this year, so I have realized that God does not want me there and I have decided for journalism. ... Something in writing has a powerful attraction for me. I think writing about things that are important is something that fulfills me. (March 25, 1965)

Her career concerns intermingle with considerations about how best to be of service to God and others: "Let's see if I can find in a newspaper the most effective place to work for Christ. ... To help others see the injustice in which some people live is also something that does not let me remain silent. And I think a newspaper is the best means to help others see things" (March 25, 1965).

She also expressed concerns about her identity through statements about herself, often portrayed in a negative light. References to her personal deficiencies serve as running commentary throughout the letters: "I am so stupid! The truth is that I deserve everything that is happening to me" (February 5, 1963); "I am intolerable, nothing comes out right because of my own fault. I am boring, silly, and stupid and you must be tired of this ridiculous friend" (June 10, 1966). Only once in a while does a positive comment slip through, and not without being immediately followed by some of the usual negative comments about herself: "At this point I am beginning to believe (please don't think I am vain) that I am pretty, even though I continue to be shy and easily embarrassed" (December 5, 1965).

It is possible that some of this self-criticism may have been a normal part of adolescent identity testing, an initially awkward and exaggerated effort at gaining a sense of perspective on aspects of her own character. At the same time, V.'s comments appear to have been part of a maneuver to achieve mastery over a chaotic, painful, and confusing situation by attributing all difficulties to personal deficiencies that could be more or less easily overcome. As conflicts and difficulties arose, it was easier for V. to blame herself and her deficiencies than to blame others or confront the reality that she was immersed in a situation completely beyond her control.

In spite of these negative self-appraisals, she was sensitive to nuances of feelings, to her own internal states, and to others. Statements about who she is and who she is in relation to others appear more frequently in the letters than any other theme, revealing her overriding adolescent concern with identity, and to a lesser degree, intimacy. At times her "self-analysis" helps her avoid acknowledging further losses. For example, when her correspondent leaves the country, she wrote: "You know I am stupid ... like when I didn't want to go to the airport to say good-by to you, just because I was embarrassed. I don't know how to express my feelings, I never do" (July 7, 1961).

Oftentimes, her "self-analysis" comforts her in the face of loss, as when she left her country: "I am perfectly ok and I haven't even cried. I don't even know myself; I am surprised because I have never been strong. ... I feel completely mature and I am not just saying this to say something. ... I have had to become a grown woman at 14" (August 25, 1962).

V.'s concerns with *intimacy* are expressed in her letters in reference to boyfriends, classmates, and other friends. Her first mention of a boyfriend has a young adolescent's characteristic naïveté: "What's happening is that I am in love even if I am too young for that. But I guess this is something that cannot be avoided or resisted" (January 5, 1963). Three years later, in letters where she mentions her future husband, she shows increased maturity in her understanding of the meaning of love and commitment. She has become a young woman making significant life decisions on the basis of relationships: "I have made the decision to get married a few months after I finish high school. He is good and intelligent. But I am scared. I am scared of confronting life, but this is the decision. I already bought the graduation shoes that will be my wedding shoes too" (June 10, 1966).

Throughout the letters, V. expresses intimacy concerns vividly in the context of her relationship with her correspondent. Their friendship, through correspondence, provides a very important source of strength and emotional support for V.: "If you only knew how much I would like to be with you, because I love you and miss you more than you can believe. I never really considered you as a teacher but as a friend even if I never said it because I was embarrassed to say so" (July 15, 1961).

Generativity issues are also present in her early letters as she reveals her concern for her parents. Later, this theme reemerges when she talks about her children. Through their years of correspondence, she also expresses care for her correspondent and for others mentioned in the letters: "You are living alone in that place and that makes me upset. It is not fair that you have to be alone. I would give anything to be there with you for a while. I don't know if I am conceited but I think that you would be happy to have me bugging you for a couple of months" (February 26, 1965).

Throughout the letters V.'s constant concern for others and her minimizing of her own feelings fits a very typical "female pattern." Miller (1986) and Gilligan (1982) among others described this pattern. They identified it as one of women's strengths, but clearly this pattern also has significant drawbacks for women (e.g., Kaschak, 1992).

Coping with Loss

For persons like V. in traumatic or catastrophic social situations, a variety of protective mechanisms prevent the individual from realizing the gravity of the occasion (Allport, 1942; Rodriguez-Nogues, 1983). They may show little or no reaction for weeks, even years (Herman, 1992; Parkes, 1972; Rodriguez-Nogues, 1983), if the bereavement occurs at a time when they are confronted with important tasks. The same pattern is present when there is a need for maintaining the morale of others.

Research suggests this can be a positive form of adjustment to a traumatic situation. Rodriguez-Nogues (1983) studied Cuban girls who emigrated to the United States as unaccompanied minors. She found they usually denied their actual losses and concomitant psychological pain at the time of the events. This tended to create a delayed grief reaction and posttraumatic effects, but also facilitated their functioning at the time of the events. Similarly, as events transformed the course of V.'s life, she suffered a few minor psychosomatic reactions. Yet, on the whole she seems to have coped with the situation without further complications.

Clearly, V. experienced an acute sense of loss in early adolescence when her parents were imprisoned and she left them and her country. When confronted with loss, children, adolescents, or adults may progress though psychosocial stages by developing new bonds to special individuals. This is one of the most effective strategies for coping with the loss of significant relationships and familiar places and the threats to identity imposed by migration (Espin, 1987). V.'s early capacity for intimacy served her well. It provided her with skills to establish new bonds. Demonstrably, her relationship with her teacher/correspondent/long-term friend flourished. This bond is particularly noteworthy because maintaining friendship through letters is not a highly valued skill in the modern world. The relationship V. established with the nuns and classmates at school also contributed to her emotional survival. It is interesting to note that with the exception of her future husband, it appears that all her significant relationships were with women.

Loss and grief affect one's image of oneself (Parkes, 1972) as V.'s letters well illustrate. Yet, her attribution of all negative events to herself, despite the pain and self-negation involved, paradoxically also provided her with a sense of control over the situation. Attributing negative events to herself was preferable to a total sense of helplessness in the face of uncontrollable events. Thus in the letters she actively denies her suffering or copes with her losses by attributing her painful feelings and experiences to personal deficiencies or to the privilege of having been especially chosen by God. She never faults the reality of the situation or others' wrongdoing.

Her interactions with her foster mother vividly illustrate how she coped with the loss of her mother:

> I am really intolerable today and I am about to cry because something simple happened. I asked my "aunt" to fix some clothes for me because they were hand outs from others and very old fashioned and she told me I was too proud. I might be wrong to take her rejection too much at heart but you know I am too sensitive and easily hurt. Please don't feel sorry for me. What happens is that I am only 15 years old and even if my situation is not so bad, sometimes I explode. (January 18, 1963)

A few months later she wrote in a similar vein:

> I don't talk about feeling bad because everything is only in my nervous system. Besides, I am embarrassed to ask them for help. For example, last night I was throwing up in the bathroom, my "aunt" came to the door and when she found out that it was me and not her daughter, she just left. I felt bad. It is horrible to miss your mother's love. But, on the other hand, perhaps my aunt did not think it was important. And you know that I am extremely sentimental and extremely proud. Don't think that it is I am depressed, it is just how I am. (May 3, 1965)

Significantly, V.'s pejorative self-descriptions and negative self-evaluations contradict her actual accomplishments and positive relationships with others. For example, her school grades are always high, her classmates elect her "queen" of the class, the nuns in her school are fond of her and treat her with great kindness, and she has several boyfriends through adolescence. She also belongs to a theater group and is accepted and loved by friends. Other positive events occur in her life. However, she consistently uses negative self-statements, apparently to deny the intensity of her pain and her losses. Alternatively, her denial of her true feelings may fuel her negative self-perception. Even when she is unable to deny the felt impact of her experiences she still tries to explain those feelings away: "I don't know what is happening to me but I feel empty regardless of what I do. I know that I have a normal life, but I am just tired of this" (August 9, 1966).

V. has yet another positive interpretation for her pain. She identifies it as God's will, even God's special choosing of her. Her intense belief in God is the only relief from a pain that cannot be explained in everyday terms by an adolescent. Her spirituality seems to afford her another nurturing and wise "parent" in God, through whom she feels "chosen" and uniquely loved. "I know that God doesn't want me to be a coward, but I have terrible moments and today is one of them" (March 29, 1964). Many months later she reasons similarly: "These problems are killing me but without problems I would not consider myself happy, because if God is sending me this it must be because he trusts that I am going to respond in a good way" (November 19, 1965).

Yet another way she expresses her difficulties is through recounting some of her peers' experiences. She refers to a girl mentioned by her correspondent whose mother has recently died. Her empathy is all the more striking as she does not know this girl: "You don't know how much she must be suffering even though she may not have told you" (May 3, 1965). Likely, V. is talking about herself and letting her correspondent know that she has not fully revealed the hardest parts of her experience.

In another instance, V. refers to a friend who may marry to escape a painful home situation. V. insists that she will never fall into this trap, no matter how difficult her own situation with her foster parents might become. She describes in great detail what this girl's feelings and doubts must be and expounds on why it is wrong for this girl to marry despite the chance of resolution for immediate tensions. In fact, V.'s long description of this girl's situation is a clear description of her own temptation to marry her boyfriend too soon in order to escape her foster home.

The Resolution Phase

Despite rationalizations to the contrary, V. married a few months after finishing high school. Although this early marriage may have foreclosed some possibilities, it certainly was an adaptive solution to her problems at that time. Indeed, it allowed her to start a new life with someone who loved her after all those years of feeling unloved and barely tolerated by her foster parents. Almost a year later, when she was ready to give birth to her first child, her parents were released from prison and joined her in exile.

As previously mentioned, her correspondent visited her for the first time several years later. This two-week visit served to reaffirm their long-distance friendship and to reintegrate V.'s memories of her traumatic adolescent years. At the same time, the separation that followed this visit prompted an intense reactivation of V.'s feelings of loss.

Upon their reunion, V. experienced a clear and direct acknowledgment of what the initial separation had meant for her. She realized the significance the correspondence had in sustaining her through her adolescence and traumatic losses and separation from her parents. In other words, it became evident that the validation of her pain provided by this friendship had been an essential and sustaining factor during V.'s adolescence:

One of the most disconcerting effects of your visit is that I have realized how influential you have been in my life without even knowing it. I realize now that I started changing my ways of being with people the moment you started to be concerned about my things. I think that has been decisive in my life. Do you realize what that means? I have reached the conclusion that a lot of what is good in me I owe to you. (February 21, 1970)

Clearly, writing these letters and receiving support and comfort through them was a saving grace in V.'s development. Yet her own capacity for deep interaction at a very early age made this relationship possible, for just as clearly, the sustaining power of this relationship cannot only be attributed to the efforts of her correspondent.

Implications of This Case Study

The established theories of psychological development presume an environment characterized by political stability, in which "environment" is equated with parental behavior. These theories do not take into consideration the eventuality of disruptive sociohistorical events and their impact on "normal" development. Obviously, dealing with the common tasks of psychological development while dealing with traumatic sociopolitical events complicates these tasks for children and adolescents. As Erikson (1964) argued, "The danger of any period of large-scale uprooting and transmigration is that exterior crises will, in too many individuals and generations, upset the hierarchy of developmental crises and their built-in correctives; and [make the developing individual] lose those roots that must be planted firmly in meaningful life cycles" (p. 96).

Violent or abrupt political events produce traumatic experiences that psychologically affect the lives of children and adolescents who undergo them. Ironically, the focus on the physical safety of both children and adults may divert attention from considerations about their psychological well-being. Usually, psychological services or research studies tailored to these populations focus on victims or survivors who manifest serious emotional maladjustment. Survivors who are reasonably well adjusted, like those who remain relatively psychologically unscathed, seldom attract the attention of psychologists and are frequently left to their own devices.

The friendship between V. and her correspondent may have buffered the impact of her losses and may have protected V. from the additional trauma that could have been created by surrounding her experience with silence. The historical events relevant to V.'s life took place years ago, but similar events are still happening all over the world. The notion that friendship with a trusted adult can be valuable in enhancing psychological survival has implications for the lives of children and adolescents whose development is severely challenged by the sociopolitical world they inhabit.

*   *   *

This chapter has presented the case of one individual who found her own path through a series of traumatic events precipitated by historical/political conditions. In constructing that path, her correspondence with a woman a few years older, a former teacher turned lifelong friend, acted as an anchoring force. This ongoing conversation, together with V.'s previous psychological health and spiritual groundedness, provided her with the strength to cope with the traumatic events of her adolescence.

It is apparent that for V., as for other individuals under her circumstances, the encounter between individual and society involved a transformation in subjectivity. Her understanding of who she is has been forever marked by those traumatic events. However, it is almost impossible to disentangle what the pure effect of those events may have been. The person that could have been without those events never came to be. Paradoxically, because we are dealing with the absence of any evident pathology or posttraumatic stress disorder, it is hard to determine what the consequences of the traumatic events were for V. But we do know that "the self is the sum of an individual's changing internal conversations, the forecastings, the recollections and the wishes, the voices that make up our intrapsychic life" (Gagnon, 1992, p. 239) and "self-understanding is always shaped by culture. The tales we tell each other about who we are and might yet become are individual variations on the narrative templates our culture deems intelligible" (Ochberg, 1992, p. 214) and on the limitations that historical events force upon us. V.'s narrative of the events of her life as transmitted through her adolescent letters is but one individual's conversation with herself through her conversation with a trusted friend. Because she was a gifted and unusually mature adolescent, she was able to make sense of her experiences in her own way and avail herself of the friendship and support provided by this correspondence.

V.'s normal life and adjustment in adulthood conceal a difficult route and reveal her strength. Other less fortunate children and adolescents subjected to similar traumatic events may respond differently or resort to other strategies to cope with trauma. But although only a single individual's story, V.'s story as presented through her correspondence is a tribute to human strength and resilience.

References

Allport, G. (1942). *The use of personal documents in psychological science.* New York: Social Science Research Council.

Elder, G. H. (1981). History and the life course. In D. Bertaux (Ed.), *Biography and the life course: The life history approach in the social sciences* (pp. 77–115). Beverly Hills, CA: Sage.

Erikson, E. H. (1963). *Childhood and society.* New York: Norton.

———. (1964). *Insight and responsibility.* New York: Norton.

———. (1968). *Identity, youth, and crisis.* New York: Norton.

Espin, O. M. (1987). Psychological impact of migration on Latinas: Implications for psychotherapeutic practice. *Psychology of Women Quarterly, 11,* 489–503.

_____. (1992). Roots uprooted: The psychological impact of historical/political disloca-
tion. In E. Cole, O. M. Espin, & E. Rothblum (Eds.), *Refugee women and their mental
health: Shattered societies, shattered lives* (pp. 9–20). New York: Haworth.

Espin, O. M., Stewart, A. J., & Gomez, C. (1990). Letters from V: Adolescent personality development in socio-historical context. *Journal of Personality, 58,* 347–364.

Gagnon, J. H. (1992). The self, its voices, and their discord. In C. Ellis & M. Flagerty (Eds.),
Investigating subjectivity: Research on lived experience (pp. 221–243). Newbury Park, CA:
Sage.

Gilligan, C. (1982). *In a different voice.* Cambridge, MA: Harvard University Press.

Herman, J. (1992). *Trauma and recovery.* New York: Basic Books.

Jessor, R. (1993). Successful adolescent development among youth in high-risk settings.
American Psychologist, 48, 117–126.

Kaschak, E. (1992). *Engendered lives: A new psychology of women's experience.* New York: Basic Books.

Miller, J. B. (1986). *Toward a new psychology of women* (2d. ed.). Boston: Beacon.

Ochberg, R. L. (1992). Social insight and psychological liberation. In G. Rosenwald & R.
Ochberg (Eds.), *Storied lives: The cultural politics of self-understanding* (pp. 214–230).
New Haven: Yale University Press.

Parkes, C. M. (1972). *Bereavement: Studies of grief in adult life.* New York: International
University Press.

Rodriguez-Nogues, L. (1983). Psychological effects of premature separation from parents
in Cuban refugee girls: A retrospective study. (Doctoral dissertation, Boston University,
1983). *Dissertation Abstracts International, 44,* 1619 B.

Stewart, A.J., Franz, C., & Layton, L. (1988). The changing self: Using personal documents
to study lives. *Journal of Personality, 56,* 41–74.

PART FOUR

One Life Among Many:
Cases Drawn from
Group Studies

Civil rights march on Washington, D.C., 1963. *(Courtesy Radcliffe College Archives.)*

14

Medicine Is My Lust:
The Story of a
Woman Physician

LILLIAN K. CARTWRIGHT

Piece I: Collaging Female Identity

I have been studying a cohort of fifty-eight women physicians for twenty years (Cartwright, 1990). These women entered medical school in the mid-1960s, before the women's movement radically influenced occupational and social roles. The subject of this narrative, Natalie Hanrahan,[1] was a medical student at a time when less than 8 percent of the medical degrees were awarded to women. In 1989–1990, about 35 percent of the graduates of U.S. medical schools were women, and the following year almost 40 percent of the first-year students were female. Times have changed and medicine can no longer be called a male-dominated profession, although power positions are still occupied by men and encounters with gender discrimination are reported frequently (Cartwright, 1987b).

Among my concerns in studying this group of women over time has been an interest in identifying the configurational aspects of their lives—what I now call role collage (earlier referred to as role montage, Cartwright, 1987a). I chose collage as a metaphor for describing the lives of the doctors for several reasons. First, on the level of face validity, there is a similarity between collage as a postmodern, late-twentieth-century art form that affords the opportunity to assimilate and portray disjunctions of form, conjunctions of content, and disruptions of context (Hoffman, 1989) and the existential experience of many professional women. This experience includes fragmentation, discontinuous careers, juggling responsibilities, and confusion caused by value conflicts originating in multiple roles and incongruous self and object role relationships (Bateson, 1990; Ducker, 1980; Helson, Mitchell, and Moane, 1984; Sandler and Rosenblatt, 1962).

Second, just as the feminist reevaluation of women's lives has led to a new look at these lives, collage is now viewed more seriously as an art form. In its inception, collage was seen as a fairly trivial form of representation, connected with Picasso's and Braque's 1907–1914 experiments in protest of realistic or photographic illusionism. With the passing of time, collage became less of a medium and more a way of portraying reality appearing to be in dissolution, multiple in forms, and pluralistic and interchangeable in respect to future directions.

Third, as the principles of the collage/montage revolution began to permeate painting, photography, literature, and criticism, the creative potential of collage was addressed by many artists. Walter Benjamin, Bertolt Brecht, Sergei Eisenstein, and more recently John Cage are just a few leading avant-garde critics, playwrights, filmmakers, and musicians who used collage. Ulmer (1983) stated: "By most accounts, collage is the single most revolutionary formal innovation in artistic representation to occur in our century." Collage, as an invention, changes our view of reality and the nature of relationships.

Last, collage has deep roots in the crafts of women—needlework, lapwork, quilts, valentines, and a wealth of decorative functional objects made from scraps that can be seen as quests for beauty within the confines of duty and relationships. Schapiro (1989) and her collective of women artists coined the word "Femmage" to describe this women's culture, the "low-art," utilitarian objects that are not highly regarded or taken seriously by the "high-art," almost always male, hierarchical establishment. From these multiple views, it feels appropriate to bring the collage concept into the study of women's lives, particularly the lives of women with a talent for disregarding conventional signposts.

Piece II: Collages of Women Physicians

Although clearly there are an infinite number of potential collages reflecting the nuances of women's lives, I described three typical patterns when the physicians in my study were in their early thirties: First, I identified "The Superwoman," who is characterized by very high intimacy and achievement needs. She aims to have a family and a very active full-time career. She juggles, orchestrates, and drives herself through multiple roles, all of which she gives top priority. Her aim is to do all things well.

The second collage, "The Career of Limited Ambition," places home and family first and career second. Often this woman works part time; she may expect to become more involved in her career once her children have grown. Parenthetically, this pattern turned out to be the case for only one woman when I reinterviewed the participants in 1990 when they were in their mid-forties. The third collage, "Medicine Is My Lust," depicts a woman who puts medicine first and decides not to raise a family for a variety of reasons. This woman may be in a relationship, but gives it a clear secondary status.

The story of Natalie Hanrahan is a story of a woman whose life conforms to the third collage, "Medicine Is My Lust," and she has maintained this pattern over time. Now in her mid-forties, she has achieved a very high degree of professional prominence and recognition in this country and abroad. She has published widely and is among the distinguished academicians in the country. She is a scholar and a great teacher, a rare combination. On the surface, hers seems like a simple collage, focused, intense, clearly differentiated. Yet its surface belies its underpainting. The *pentimenti*, or shadows, of her parents' and grandparents' lives come through and have shaped her pattern. The trained eye sees disruptions of context (geographic moves, ruptures in family ties, mental breakdown) and conjunctions of content (aristocratic lineage and heroic work; mysticism and sustained hope; family pride and independence; theater and education).

Piece III: Historic Counterpoint

Historically, it is interesting that Natalie's collage was considerably more common among the pioneer women doctors in the middle nineteenth and early twentieth century than it is today. Elizabeth Blackwell, in 1848 the first woman to graduate from a U.S. medical school, lived out this lifestyle. Blackwell's autobiography (1895) resonates with aspects of Natalie's subtexts. As you read Natalie's story, remember Elizabeth's comments on her lifetime of effort as well as her idealistic and heroic voice, which echoes her father's. He was an abolitionist who grew sugar beets as a protest to the sugar cane industry that relied on slave labor. "It is well worth the efforts of a lifetime to have attained the knowledge which justifies an attack on the root of all evil—viz. the deadly atheism which asserts that because forms of evil have always existed in society, therefore they must always exist; and the attainment of a high ideal is a hopeless chimera" (p. 253).

And consider her comments about marriage and work in lieu of an intimate partner: "I felt more determined than ever to become a physician and thus place a strong barrier between me and all ordinary marriage" (p. 28); "I cannot sympathize fully with an anti-man movement. I have had too much kindness, aid, and just recognition from men. … The great object of education has nothing to do with woman's rights or man's rights, but with the development of the human soul and body" (p. 178).

Piece IV: The Story

And now the story of Natalie, who always knew she wanted to be a physician: "There is no time when it was not my first choice." The narrative focuses on her early years and explores the family background events that informed her occupational choice. I do not speculate on unconscious motives and dynamics in this narrative and choose to let the story speak for itself. It was written when Natalie had completed her residency and held her first academic post in a training hospital in Chicago's inner city. She was working over ninety hours a week, and it would be fair to say medicine was not only her lust, but her life.

Tall and statuesque, her manner and articulate speech suggest a Shakespearean player, aware of the subtleties of timing, the color of language, and the pleasures of dramatic delivery. There is a faint theatrical quality about Natalie that evokes romantic nineteenth-century images of heroes and heroines, high deeds, and good purposes. Natalie is not a cynic or nihilist. When asked about the most important objectives of her life, she states seriously and with a touch of humor:

> All I want to do is to resurrect heroism. A hero was a person who went out and did it better than it was ever done before. I don't like monuments to mediocrity. I like people with heroic visions who try their damnedest—too many of us fail through lack of aspiration. I remember a Talmudic story where the old man told his son who was going to battle: "You may not win the battle my son, but let your body be found near the wall."

In her position as assistant director of the department of internal medicine, Natalie takes multiple roles. She serves as the chief administrator when the head of the department is away, and independently, she is a member of several standing hospital committees: medical audit, medical education, and residency review. She is skeptical of committee roles, seeing the committees as designed to perpetuate themselves yet "making you feel you've done something and are victorious."

The problem of taking care of patients as well as possible within the context of a teaching hospital represents her basic integrative task. When the needs of patients come in conflict with the needs of house staff, she plays evaluator and arbitrator. She has studied the problems of the house staff in depth, and she assumes a didactic role with residents as well as functioning as a confidant and counselor.

Natalie prefers roles connected with patient care, and she serves as the attending physician on the general medical ward. She enjoys seeing the patients presented and hearing the stories of their illness. She presents three grand rounds a year and finds this great fun—"It's vaudeville." She is fond of the formality of the didactic lecture and the general enthusiasm she can produce among the students at such times. Teaching is exciting because "There is a lot of theater in it—I'm not a grammarian of education—I don't care about the system of education, but I am a teacher." Her relationships with students, house staff, patients, and peers are rewarding to her. The patients at the county hospital are poor and many are members of minority groups. Alcoholism, drug addiction, and traumatic accidents are among the pathology seen daily—"What could be more real than Cook County Emergency?" she asks.

She says because she is a woman, she is not seen as an authoritarian figure. Patients and students are more at ease with her. She takes an ingenuous, open approach with patients and she reflects, smiling: "I get more historical data from a patient because I'm genetically not as important as a man." The intellectual, problem-solving aspect of medical diagnosis is "great fun." How she elicits the information is "feminine."

Natalie gives to the medical care system the warmth and love another woman might give her family. She replaces the handshake with a generous and strong hug. Her office has a comfortable couch with many pillows and pictures of relatives, colleagues, and friends casually arranged on the walls. When asked how she feels about not having a family of her own—not having children and a husband—she states: "My lusts lie elsewhere, I've never felt lonely, never bereft. To create a human being is a very big responsibility and I can't see combining that with medicine. I never set having children as a goal for myself to seek—it would be like cutting myself in two. I always felt I was better off on one track."

Piece V: Things Are Not Always as Simple as You Think

Is one world, one world? Only to the uninitiated, the casual onlooker. This collage's apparent seamlessness hides complexities of choice and no choice: sublimation of passion, avoidance of dissolution, and compromises and solutions that keep significant internalized objects intact and in dialogue. The grand nature of this collage, its energy and altruism, mirrors an idealized bygone aristocracy of the spirit and mind.

Piece VI: Return to Story

Natalie's family background is unusual in the sample of female physicians that I have studied. Her ethnic and religious heritage is also statistically uncommon—Russian Orthodox on the maternal side and Irish Catholic on her father's side. She attributes her love of language, high purpose, and cosmic drama to this ethnic amalgam.

Her mother's family descended from the Russian aristocracy. With the Bolshevik Revolution at the turn of the century, they emigrated to Shanghai, where her grandfather worked in diplomatic services. Her mother, Irene, she describes as a typical "Barishna"—a young gentlewoman who lived in a nineteenth-century world of romantic illusion. She knew a little French, a little opera, a smattering of the arts, but had no practical career. Irene had an abundant supply of dreams and fantasies, which she projected upon her intended migration to the United States. Here, she would surely find her true fortune. Her glorious dream was to live in Boston, the mecca of U.S. culture; to meet and marry a tall and handsome Irishman; and to have two brilliant, beautiful, and successful children. She actualized this dream, although other things also happened to her, events not anticipated.

Irene left her parents and came to the United States in the late 1930s, a time of economic revival in this country. She settled in Boston and met Michael Hanrahan, handsome, tall, and Irish. His work in public relations put his natural linguistic and persuasive talents to good use. Natalie describes her father as "bardic—he could weave music out of language, he had a talent for demagoguery and through his charismatic qualities he could generate deep feelings in others—he could utterly charm you." Despite his laugh, his good eyes, his good hair, his good hands, and his good sense of humor, Michael Hanrahan had serious problems. He was an alcoholic.

It took a while for Irene to realize that her husband could not drink like her father, like a Russian gentleman. She did not know what an alcoholic was. After six years of marriage and two children, when she began to perceive the full extent of Michael's problems, she decided to divorce him. Natalie was then two and Patrick almost four.

Piece VII: Collaging Mother

How could Irene, a foreigner, with no visible means of support, divorce her husband when many women live their lifetime with an alcoholic husband, even women with professions and occupations that secure economic independence? The answer resides in understanding Irene's collage: She was a mystical young woman who on a daily level felt in touch with cosmic forces and with God. She also believed life should be lived on a grand scale. Her collage encompassed roles of dreamer, zealot, reformer, aristocrat, and prodigal daughter. She could play the parts separately and smoothly. But when tensions and stresses increased, the parts clashed in an aberrant and disruptive manner. In divorcing Michael, she simply hoped to change him—to reform him. And she did just that. After their divorce, he stopped drinking and even became a leader in establishing centers for treating alcoholics in other countries. Natalie remembers attending such meetings with her father and hearing him talk about poetry, cures, and philosophy.

Irene and Michael maintained a friendly relationship during the years of their divorce, and neither remarried. Natalie perceived them as loving and respecting each other. She also perceived both parents as very interested in her brother and herself, despite the fact that they lived in separate households and sometimes in different cities. How unusual this kind of arrangement is, is difficult to gauge quantitatively, but from the perspective of my research and clinical experience, I believe it is rare.

Piece VIII: The Grandfather's Court

Following the divorce, Irene's father and mother reentered her life. The influence of her grandparents on Natalie's upbringing was substantial and formative. Her grandfather, an imposing figure, became her second father. He was "old Russia," a member of the Imperial Guard trained in the Prussian military tradition. Ideologically, he was allied with conservatism and sought to maintain form and the status quo. But he was also a man with a grand appetite for life. He would take the whole family—his wife, his daughter, his grandchildren—in his big car on an expedition to the library. There, they would marvel at the books and the knowledge that was theirs for the asking and they would take dozens of books back with them. These were unplanned excursions and could happen whenever the urge stirred him. His opinions and his feelings were strong and vocal and often in conflict with U.S. sentiment. He saw "good" in Hitler and McCarthy, casting them in the roles of preservers of law and order. His experiences with the Russian Revolution made him no liberal, and he disputed the U.S. view of historical events.

The grandparents' home eventually became Natalie's and Patrick's home. Irene tried for three years to make it on her own by working as an interpreter. She placed the children in a day nursery, but this was an unsatisfactory solution. She decided it was in the children's best interests to move in with her parents, who had by then migrated to the United States.

Living in the grandparents' home was like living in an independent duchy in the middle of a large foreign country. Russian was spoken. The talents developed, the traits admired, and the values were Russian. The food, the friends, and all the rest that makes up the fabric of daily life reflected the Russian ethos. In this home, there was a sense of pride in being different from the great majority of Americans.

The effects of this kind of nonnormative experience on a young girl could be potentially disastrous, but weren't for Natalie. She, like many others in the sample, perceived her family milieu as different but superior; thus her capacity for individualism and independence was strengthened and she became more or less immune to subsequent conventional pressures and slights. Because her immersion in the Russian ethos followed a three-year period of disruption of family, the new home metaphorically was paradise regained.

Although a safe haven for Natalie, going back to her parents' home and reestablishing her dependency on them was conflictual for Irene because she and her mother were still locked in an ongoing personal struggle. The grandmother, playing the role of Russian matriarch from whom all decisions and decrees concerning children and home emanate, disagreed with her daughter's child-rearing practices. Natalie believes that her mother's difficulties in separating from her grandmother made Irene determined that her children be independent, self-assertive, and strong. In looking backward, Natalie notes ruefully: "She did her job too well."

Although mother and grandmother were battling on many levels, they agreed that Natalie and Patrick were "marvelous" children. They were bright and attractive and should do whatever they chose—the world was open to them and no occupation or career would be beyond their abilities.

Natalie decided at age six that she would be a physician. It was a toss-up for a few months while she thought the work of an entomologist might be more challenging, but physicianhood won, and the victory was never again in doubt. Choosing a healing profession after three years of ruptured family life demonstrates Natalie's recuperative capacity.

From her grandfather, she learned more than free choice; she learned that "style"—the manner of execution of choice—was likewise very important. "From him I learned grace, everyone loved him without envy. He did what he wanted without pretense but always with an air of confidence." Ambition alone was not admired. Rather the appropriate quest was to do something as well as you could without vanity, without trying to prove your superiority over another human be-

ing. Competitiveness and self-absorption, two qualities often linked to achievement motivations in U.S. culture, were counter to high achievements in her
grandfather's mind, and he said: "You should live life as if everyone were looking
at you and taking example from you."

Piece IX: Growing Up

During her early grammar school years, Natalie did well academically, but was
not challenged by school. She was athletic and liked playing baseball, basketball,
tennis, and hockey as well as following the tastes of a good Russian granddaughter
in her pursuit of ballet, piano lessons, French lessons, and cooking.

In the sixth grade something changed—perhaps because of puberty—in the
intensity of her studies; school became increasingly stimulating. She enjoyed
scholarship for its own sake. This pursuit of learning continued through her junior high and high school years. She felt "happy as a lark" during these years. New
vistas were opening to her and life felt full.

Her social development followed a different path from that of her peers. Although she had many friends, she did not date much and found she had little desire to do so. She, the daughter of two very tall parents, inherited their height and
was always many inches taller than the boys her age. Because within her Russian
home it was good to be big, she was regarded by her family as attractive and
worthwhile. She was not especially concerned with her lack of conformity to U.S.
dating norms. She said: "It was in the natural course of events that I was the way I
was; I was not afflicted by concern for my physical being one way or another."

Piece X: Grandfather Dies

Of significant consequence to her early adolescence was the death of her grandfather, leaving the financial affairs of the family to her grandmother. Although her
grandmother believed herself an expert on most aspects of life, she fell short on
business management, and her daughter shared her fiscal deficiency. Within a
couple of years, what had been a relatively prosperous way of life was transformed
into a penurious one. The problems of managing on a small budget grew, forcing
Natalie to work evenings and weekends as a cashier in a movie house. By sixteen,
she was completely self-supporting as well as contributing to her grandmother's
and mother's support. At the same time, she managed to keep up a very high level
of academic performance and obtained a scholarship enabling her to pursue her
professional aspirations. Her very intense commitment to work and her ability to
work long hours began early not of economic necessity alone but also because, as
she puts it: "Work was fun, you met interesting people and you had funds."

Natalie assumed more responsibility for her mother and grandmother than
Patrick did. Patrick was clear that he wanted to exit the Russian ethos and be independent of his early upbringing. To Natalie he always seemed to be in a separate
world—more American than her world. "It seemed that he got away with an aw-

ful lot." Even though Patrick disavowed the Russian lifestyle, seeing it as eccentric, he met the family criteria for success—he was scholarly, intrigued with history, had experience in the military, and found his life's work in international affairs.

When Natalie entered college at eighteen with a Regent's Scholarship, there was no doubt in her mind that she would become a physician. Yet unlike many pre-medical students, she took courses in humanities—baroque art, Russian literature, Philosophy, and English. She had a nineteenth-century concept of the physician as a scholar and learned human being. For the first six months, she lived in a dormitory. But she felt out of place there: "There were no grown-ups, it was more trouble than it was worth with panty raids and curfews." She soon found a little summer cottage with a bed and hot plate where she lived for one hundred dollars a month and was free at last, free to stay up all night and study if she so chose.

She was valedictorian at her graduation, and although she was not a social person, she was liked and respected by her classmates. Her real friends were the teachers, but she also had a wide circle of "acquaintances." In remembering that period, she laughs at a private joke—"I am so stocked full of acquaintances that someone will have to die before I can meet you."

At the time of her interview for medical school, she describes herself as extremely naive. She had no doubts at all that she would be accepted; it never occurred to her there could be any question about her admission. "I thought they just wanted me to come." When the interviewer, as was the custom in those days, asked her "What would you do if you fell in love?" she answered "I'd marry him; I'd handle it if it came up."

Piece XI: Mother Falls Apart

The first year in medical school was traumatic and depressing because Natalie's mother became emotionally ill and was hospitalized. Michael Hanrahan had died the preceding year and Natalie and Patrick were no longer at home. Irene's romantic nature could not sustain her through these losses. The intruding, merciless recognition that she was no longer young and beautiful and her choices were limited came upon her and her collage fragmented.

Although Natalie was academically successful that year, she was very unhappy: "I felt betrayed by the cosmos. It was difficult to love my mother the way she was; she had changed so, she felt like a stranger." Natalie viewed the psychiatric resident who was treating her mother as insensitive, perhaps because of his insecurity. He would say very little or nothing at all to her when she called. That year was another year of "the malevolent cosmos" again disrupting life. She became stronger in what was becoming her way—through compassionate work.

The next year things were better. Her mother improved and went back to work, and Natalie was now taking clinical courses that involved direct patient contact. Her mother's illness increased her awareness of patients' needs and the needs of the patient's family. Before, medicine had been a highly cerebral activity; now people became vastly more important. The laying on of hands and touching people took on new significance, and Natalie was determined to build her competencies and her capacity to be trusted. In her junior year of medical school, she decided to enter internal medicine because it was "more fun" than her other clerkships. Although she liked surgery, the direct patient contact made internal medicine her first choice. The remaining years in medical school were stimulating.

In looking back over her life and selecting the most influential family experience, Natalie notes she was always given a sense of her potential and the need to take pride in whatever she did. She projects a sense of honor about high-quality work: "The intrinsic nobility of man ought to rule. One should be kind, just, and honest even if it is to one's detriment." Her grandfather is still with her.

Piece XII: The Bigger Picture: Lust Lost

A study such as this allows us to make fine-grained comparisons among women who are similar in intellect, interests, and cohort exposure to social and political events. We can contrast the shape of lives over time and begin to question the precursors and antecedent events of life patterns as well as the stability of these patterns. Of eighteen women who evinced the "Medicine Is My Lust" pattern at age thirty-three, only six, including Natalie, have adhered to this pattern. Of these six women, all but two decided before the age of ten to become a physician. They, like Natalie, made their vocational commitment at a very young age, suggesting strong early motivational roots to the decision. Four of the six are now involved in a relationship, heterosexual or gay, that supports and complements their careers. None of the six have children.

Of the twelve remaining women, by their late thirties, ten had shifted to the Superwoman configuration, "late bloomers" who began juggling career with family life. Another exited medicine and developed a career in an ancillary health profession and the last, because of ill health, adopted a "Career of Limited Ambition."

Piece XIII: Postscript from a Feminist Perspective

In Chapter 2 of this volume, Stewart advises researchers who study women's lives from a feminist perspective to ask how the life reverberates with the researcher's in order to illuminate our biases. She also recommends inspecting the historical framework and social structural characteristics that shape women's opportunities, relationships, activities, and ideology. She warns us not to simplify the life at the cost of complexity and dissonance.

With specific reference to the last guideline, I can ask if I am not painting too simple a picture of Natalie's life. It appears to be a monolithic identity. I answer,

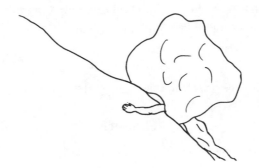

Drawing of Sisyphus by "Natalie Hanrahan."
(Courtesy Lillian K. Cartwright.)

simple on the surface, but not in etiology. The idea that Natalie may be influenced by her mother's failed Superwoman integration is our starting point. The lesson she learned from her mother's casualty status appears to be that it is impossible to combine marriage, child-rearing, and career without breaking down oneself or making it particularly hard on one's children. This appears plausible, but it needs checking out, and our sample allows us this opportunity for sleuthing.

I have a long-standing interest in early adversity, especially emotional malad-justment in the mother and its effect on female development, since I had a mother who had a major depression when I was seventeen. This event moved me from a career in art to one in clinical psychology because I wanted to understand what happened to my mother—in feminist language, what made her mad. In my sample, five women besides Natalie had mothers who suffered from severe emotional problems, including one mother who suicided. None replicated Natalie's pattern over time. Three started out with her pattern, but moved into the Superwoman configuration when they married relatively late and had children. Two of this group became psychiatrists. As I began to look at the six cases more closely, I realized that Natalie had already been in medical school when her mother became ill, and in fact, her decision to be a doctor was made by the age of six. How to put these facts together?

For all but Natalie, the mother's emotional breakdown preceded the choice of medicine as a career. In fact, for these women and for me, the mother's emotional problems were the primary motive for a career in a helping profession. In Natalie's case, the breakdown of the nuclear family was the probable motivational event. At the same time, her mother's disturbance may have colored the way she chose to practice medicine with a decidedly clinical bent—a feeling approach.

A last thought, a last image for the collage: A thread of a great, lost battle runs discontinuously through the collage and through Natalie's language as she reminisces. At our last meeting, in 1990, she, like all the subjects, was asked to draw a picture, perhaps a collage, that might in some way portray her life. She smiled and opened her file and gave me a picture—Sisyphus pushing a rock up the hill. I thought then of the Talmudic story she told me many years ago. I thought of the Russian Revolution. I smiled back.

Notes

1. Pseudonyms have been used throughout this chapter.

References

Bateson, M. C. (1990). *Composing a life.* New York: Plume.

Blackwell, E. (1895). *Pioneer work in opening the medical profession to women.* London: Longmans, Green.

Cartwright, L. K. (1990). *Women physicians at the peak of their career.* Report to Robert Wood Johnson Foundation, Princeton.

_____. (1987a). Role montage: Life patterns of professional women. *Journal of American Medical Women's Association, 42,* 142–148.

_____. (1987b). Stress and women physicians: New directions in research. In R. Payne & J. Firth (Eds.), *Stress in the health professions* (pp. 71–85). London: Wiley.

Ducker, D. G. (1980). The effect of two sources of role strain on women physicians. *Sex Roles, 6,* 549–559.

Helson, R., Mitchell, V., & Moane, G. (1984). Personality and patterns of adherence and nonadherence to the social clock. *Journal of Personality and Social Psychology, 46,* 1079–1096.

Hoffman, K. (1989). *Collage: Critical views.* Ann Arbor, MI: U.M.H. Research Press.

Sandler, J., & Rosenblatt, B. (1962). The concept of the representational world. *The Psychoanalytic Study of the Child, 17,* 128–145.

Schapiro, M. (1989). Femmage. In K. Hoffman (Ed.), *Collage: Critical views* (pp. 295–315). Ann Arbor, MI: U.M.H. Research Press.

Ulmer, G. (1983). The object of post-criticism. In H. Foster (Ed.), *The anti-aesthetic: Essays on post-modern culture* (pp. 83–110). Port Townsend, WA: Bay Press.

15

Reconstituting the Self: The Role of History, Personality, and Loss in One Woman's Life

CAROL E. FRANZ

LYDIA[1] WAS PART of a study of middle-aged white adults who had reached the age of eighteen in 1964: the first wave of the post–World War II baby boom. In contrast to the relatively prosperous and quiet early life years for these white, middle-class children, the years of their late adolescence and early adulthood were marked by great civil and political upheaval: the civil rights movement, the assassinations of John F. Kennedy, Robert Kennedy, Martin Luther King, Jr., and Malcolm X; summers of urban riots; war in Vietnam; protests over that war; and the fledgling years of the revitalized women's movement.

Standing at her door before our interview, I knew little about Lydia as an individual: simply that she was one of the few people in the sample who had been socially/politically active both during the 1960s and at the time of the follow-up when she was forty-one. Up to this point she had only been studied as part of the larger sample, but as an extension of the larger project on midlife development, I approached Lydia to explore the connections among early life experiences, 1960s activism, and long-term lifestyle expressions. I was fascinated by members of her age group—just a few years older than I am: Slightly older schoolmates whose life paths I saw disrupted by the events of the 1960s, they represented my first inkling that what happened outside of our private worlds could influence our lives. As long as I could remember I had been watching them, first as an adolescent looking for beacons to navigate what seemed to be a world in which rules no longer applied, later as a researcher.

My meeting with Lydia had two purposes—to learn more about her experiences during and since the 1960s, and to use this information to compare an individual (an idiographic approach) with the group (a nomothetic approach). Traditionally, the nomothetic approach has played a dominant role in personality research. A major criticism of the approach, though, is that it tends to obscure the complex processes, growth, and change that can only be distinguished in an individual life (Allport, 1942; Noam, 1988; Runyan, 1982; Stewart, Franz, and Layton, 1988; White, 1966). Because of the richness of the information on Lydia, gathered over many years of her life, and her willingness to be interviewed at both ages thirty-one and forty-three, I was able to examine her life from several perspectives: various points of view (her own, her mother's, and mine), the narrow focus of her 1960s involvement, and the contrast between the group and the individual data.

Several hours of mostly painful conversation were punctuated by throaty laughter as Lydia told me about her life. Although I had come to find out how the 1960s influenced her, I heard more about the harsh blows of her adult life: blows that were in sharp contrast with the ease of her childhood. That her story of choices and coping in her adult years was permeated with references to being a "sixties person" fascinated me and remained an important piece—though no longer the whole—of this individual study.

Lydia as Part of a Group Portrait of Sixties-Involved People

People in the larger sample who had actively been involved in social movements of the 1960s—for instance, participated in demonstrations or sit-ins, persistently wrote letters to political figures, worked for activist organizations or liberal political candidates, or attempted to live alternative lifestyles (e.g., living in a commune, becoming drug involved)—were considered to be "sixties involved" (nearly 35 percent of the group at age thirty-one). Lydia's activities during the 1960s placed her in the sixties-involved group. Reflecting on her late adolescence and college years, Lydia—at thirty-one—told of her past activities: "I got into a volunteer position with a learning center (working with underprivileged inner-city children). ... Politics were always big with me, I always worked for whoever the liberal candidate was." Lydia was involved in civil rights issues beginning in high school.

In keeping with other research on sixties activists, sixties-involved women in this sample were more likely to come from middle-class backgrounds and have better educated parents than nonparticipants (Franz and McClelland, in press). More children of Jewish backgrounds and fewer from Catholic backgrounds became activists. Statistical analyses indicated that mothers of these sixties-involved children asked in 1951 (Sears, Maccoby, and Levin, 1957) how they reared their five-year-old daughters were more likely than other mothers to think of their daughters as "wonderful" rather than burdensome, were less strict about house and behavioral rules, and were more permissive about the child's expression of sexual impulses (nudity, masturbation).[2] Other researchers have found retrospectively that parents of sixties activists were more politically and socially active than other parents (Block, Haan, and Smith, 1968; M. M. Braungart and R. G. Braungart, 1990; Flacks, 1967; McAdam 1989, 1992). Although such information had not been asked explicitly in the 1951 mother interview and was not represented by the nomothetic data, I turned to Lydia's mother's 1951 interview to learn more about Lydia's childhood.

Lydia's Childhood: Lydia's Mother Speaks for Herself

Lydia, five years old in 1951, was the second of two girls in her family and also had two younger brothers. The family was Jewish and categorized as middle class. Esther[3] (Lydia's mother), Lydia's father, and her grandmother were all extremely active in community affairs. Lydia's father owned his own small business; when Lydia was older he also served as a town alderman. Lydia's relationship with her father was very warm: "Lydia loves him and he loves her, that's just the way it is. ... She's his 'special child' and she adores him." The family stayed close to the children's grandparents, who were more religious than Lydia's parents.

Along with her liberal child-rearing views, Esther was unusual for her cohort in that she had been educated at an elite women's college, then worked full time as a professional writer until her first child was born and part time until Lydia arrived. Esther spoke with ambivalence about not working: Home felt like "a prison." Longing for an income of her own and the satisfaction of writing again, she also felt guilty about leaving the children. Her conflicts regarding work were not hidden from the family.

Child-centered, permissive parenting was immediately evident in Esther's interview. When asked what she enjoyed in Lydia, Esther replied: "Oh, she's fun. She is very bright, and very flirtatious and very affectionate. She is very practical. She can figure out things I can't figure out and she is the kind of girl anybody would be thrilled to have. ... She is a genius for getting along with neighborhood children." Obedience wasn't a high priority: "I don't see the point in it. ... If they did something dangerous we'd clamp down right away. ... I think you should save your strictness for the times that are important" (e.g., physical safety and eating candy). Most of the rules reflected concern with safety and appropriate limits; probed by the researcher for other family rules, Esther answered "we just don't have that kind of rules, we just treat things as they come along. It all seems to turn out all right. ... I'd rather everybody be happy."

Although the interview focused on child-rearing tactics, Lydia's own personality shone through. Her mother told the story of a typical incident: "I finally found her in [the middle of town] sitting on the curbstone in front of the candy store eating sugar things with one of her girl friends, and I asked her how she got the candy when they didn't have any money, and they said they didn't have any money, but they just went in and asked for samples." Lydia's wandering and self-assertion sometimes frightened Esther, but Lydia was seldom punished. At five, then, Lydia appeared to be very agentic. She was also quite sociable, playing vigorously with a large group of neighborhood friends after school. Esther portrayed her as a peacemaker among her friends: She "doesn't need to fight, because she knows how to get along without it. … She's a diplomat, she could be head of the State Department."

Esther expressed some confusion and concern over what she called Lydia's occasional periods of exhaustion—times when Lydia would lie listlessly around the house and complain about being too tired to do anything. She attributed these bouts alternatively to the death of the grandfather a couple of years prior to the interview, the recent birth of Lydia's little brother, or the boredom of a bright child being home. Health problems had been ruled out by the doctor. These contrasting pictures of Lydia as highly social yet autonomous, diplomatic but strong-willed, energetic and happy but depressed reemerge in her interviews at ages thirty-one and forty-three.

Esther's values and personality came through in the interview as well. In one incident, Lydia had referred to an African-American cleaning woman as a "needle face"—a term she learned from a friend. "That night," her mother recalled, "I talked to her about calling colored people needle faces. I was angry, and I said 'You know there are Chinese children and colored children and white children, all different kinds of children, and they're all nice.' I try to tell her what she's done is wrong and that she has hurt someone else." The strength of Esther's angry response to this incident contrasted sharply with her laissez-faire attitudes toward nudity, masturbation, house rules, and obedience in general. These attitudes were also reflected in the way she wanted Lydia to turn out when she grew up: "I don't want her to grow up to be the kind of a girl who is only interested in where her next mink coat is coming from, and she might be that way, if she were encouraged. I want her to feel that she is in a world where there is work to be done and it is up to her to do it." In a visit with Esther in 1992 to talk about this chapter, I became even more aware of some of the roots of Lydia's sixties-involvement. During her long career, Esther had been a prolific and outspoken writer on human rights issues and oppression: Local civil rights and antiwar groups organized in her backyard. Tributes to Esther's work on behalf of liberal causes hung on the walls of her house.

Thus the narrow nomothetic approach of examining child-rearing but not individual child or family characteristics obscured the possible contribution of Lydia's and Esther's personalities to Lydia's later activism. Lydia's openness to experimentation with new ideas and roles such as those of the social movements of the 1960s had multiple roots: her personality, the responsiveness of her family system to her individuality, the social responsibility taught in the home, and her parents' admiration and permissiveness.

Lydia Grows Up

For the years between ages five and thirty-one little information on Lydia was available. Testing in third grade indicated that her IQ was among the top 10 percent in the sample; her third-grade teacher wrote: "Mature and stable and well-liked by her class mates. Conscientious and industrious. ... Appears to be a happy and well-rounded child." In her high school year book she seems bright, active, and creative: Membership in the National Honor Society and the Greater Boston Youth Symphony Orchestra were among her other activities and interests. The next contact with Lydia was an interview with data collection at age thirty-one in 1978. At this time, Lydia brought the interviewer up to date on her life from high school on.

Young Adulthood:
Lydia Speaks for Herself

Lydia struggled personally, but not academically, in the elite college she attended during the mid-1960s: "I felt alien and hostile to the whole philosophy of life. Everybody was looking for the exotic in life. I rebelled and wanted to look for the regular" (e.g., working with disadvantaged children in the inner city). She changed her major from archaeology to education: "My thesis got me disgusted with it [archaeology], it was a good thesis and all, but got me disgusted." She elaborated on her motives for changing her major: "I wanted to do something more with people. ... Education and teaching were the alternative to more academic archaeology ... to get away from the analytic college environment."

At age thirty-one, reminiscing about college, Lydia saw her father and sister as crucial in providing support: "I've always had a big need for support. Without my family I probably would have gone into drugs." At the same time, she found the parental relationships "oppressive." Everything in her family was done by "approval or disapproval, I had no limits as a child," Lydia recalled bitterly. "I was never spanked, never sent to my room, in the end that's more oppressive. I had to go to [an elite college] to please father. Pleasing was the only right way, not by rules and make your own choices."

Two events highlighted Lydia's struggle for autonomy at a time in college when she also wanted (and struggled against her need for) support from her family:

> After freshman year in college I had a camp counselling job. The camp was like a prison; it was 24 hours a day, 2 days off all summer. I called home and said I wanted to quit. My mother always pushed responsibility too far. She said that 'I would not quit.' I came home at the end of the summer totally withdrawn. ...
>
> My second year in college I got plastic surgery. My father pressured me into it. I didn't do it because I thought it was a good thing. I got very depressed by that, I was confused by college. [The surgery] turned out okay, but I didn't want to do it.

Lydia contrasted the pressure from her parents to comply with their wishes with her own decision to quit her job in an inner-city public school: "It was my own conscious decision. The job was so bad that I was miserable to be with. I was being responsible. ... I don't feel as if you should finish something that is not helpful to you."

Lydia's attempt to find the regular wasn't as easy as she anticipated. For reasons she didn't elaborate, her brief experience in the inner-city school had been terrible. She quit after a month—describing the situation tersely as "ridiculous ... got depressed about it." Through these years, Lydia's activism continued to be oriented toward civil rights and Zionism rather than the more popular antiwar activities on campus. Perhaps because of her political socialization during childhood and adolescence, the growing liberal sentiments on campus were nothing new to Lydia and seemed far from real-life concerns and action.

In the two years following college, Lydia completed her master's degree in education and married an Israeli professional man who worked at a local university. Her next teaching job was in a blue-collar town; she liked the sense of possibilities for the children she was teaching and "the close-knit community aspect of [the town], the kids were working class. It's a small community, people are devoted to each other." Lydia's flute playing and artistic bent continued during these years. Her home was decorated with her artwork, and she and her first husband participated in community chamber music groups.

After two tubal pregnancies followed by a hysterectomy, at age twenty-seven Lydia and her husband decided to adopt a child. Six months following the adoption of an infant boy—"D."—her husband died instantaneously, at work, from a brain hemorrhage. At the time, Lydia was on leave from her teaching job. In shock, she moved back to her parents' home; she needed their help with her son and wanted to live in a Jewish community. At thirty-one—three years following her husband's death—she described herself as "apolitical ... personal tragedies have turned me off from politics. It doesn't seem to matter. My husband was apolitical, I'm apolitical except for my interest in Israel." Basically, she claimed, since her husband died, "my life is totally disconnected from my life before. When I moved in with my parents, I regressed to an 8 year old. ... It exaggerated how passive I felt, I felt like god was punishing me. ... My grief came out in anger at my parents."

Reconstituting the Self

Lydia struggled to provide security for her young son and stability for herself. Although life insurance and social security helped out, Lydia returned to work when D. was one and a half. She found herself in a quandary:

> I wouldn't get along psychologically if I were alone and not working. ... I don't make much money after paying the sitter and social security. My mother felt 'martyred' by not working, I feel 'martyred' by working. ... They say it's 'the quality of time not the quantity.' I think that's a lot of bullshit. Time I spend with D. is half good and half bad. So, when I work there is less good time with him.

D. was not an easy baby, but at this point she assumed that had to do with his father's death—or her inadequacies as a mother. Lydia taught fifth grade in a day school associated with the conservative temple, her first foray into Jewish education. After two years living with her parents, at thirty, Lydia moved to a nearby apartment.

At thirty-one, Lydia reflected on the three years since her husband's death and what had pulled her through: "Part of the academic pushing from my parents was learning to be extremely responsible. This is good. It's why I can hold a job, get my lesson plans done, etc. It's how I got through 'hard times,' in that sense it's good." Work had a double edge to it, though; it interfered with Lydia's care of D. at the same time it held her together. There was ambivalence, too, in her relationship with her parents. On the one hand, with them she regressed, was angry, and felt the pressure of their approval and disapproval of her handling of her husband's death. "My mother went on and on about being a career woman; 'one did not stop working because of a mere child,'" Lydia reminisced resentfully. "I loved not working the year I was on leave with D., I would have enjoyed not working a few more years." On the other hand, she needed her parents' psychological support.

Lydia found a new source of strength during these three years: "Religion is the biggest organizational group in my life right now. ... That's the other reason why I'm sane after all the things I've been through." Joining the conservative temple brought together two threads in Lydia's life—her grandparents' and her husband's valuing of religion: "I shared this feeling about religion with my husband; it can give a sense of stability to my son and I." Belonging to the conservative temple consolidated her commitment to Zionist causes (a concern she and her husband had shared) at the same time that it gave her a sense of belonging, community, and security: "I feel like I'm working month to month and day to day on a sense of security." At thirty-one, Lydia's sixties activism clearly took backstage to the events of her early adulthood.

I caught up with Lydia twelve years later when I interviewed her at age forty-three. What had happened, I wondered? How had she coped? Had she sold out from her sixties activism? She filled in details of the years between interviews. Soon after the age thirty-one interview, Lydia and D. packed their bags and moved to Israel so Lydia could work in Israel and study Hebrew for a year. This trip was "the most significant event for the best" in her life: "The best, I think for me, was going to Israel, because it was when I asserted my independence, even though I came back. It proved something to me that was really important." In the five years after her husband's death, Lydia had been concerned about D.'s rate of emotional and learning-skills development. During the time in Israel, it became clear that D.'s "problems," were serious, chronic physiologically based difficulties. As if this weren't enough, D. had an accident that left one leg badly broken. People "came out of the woodwork" to help; both the community and a "kosher boyfriend" became important sources of support and belonging. She told me, contemplatively: "I feel like D. has had a terrible life in many ways. But he's also had all these people who come forward to help take care of him and they always seem to come out of the blue. Sometimes I think it's God."

In spite of the complexities of working, going to school, and caring for her son, this time Lydia chose to stay where she was instead of going home. The one year in Israel turned into two years. These two years consolidated Lydia's commitments to independence from her family, to living in a supportive community, and to Jewish education. It confirmed for her that she could take care of herself and her son—and that in times of trouble, people would help. Before she discovered that communities and religion could provide emotional support, Lydia felt constrained by what she experienced as her parents' approval or disapproval: When so dependent on her parents, how could she both make her own choices and feel supported?

On her return from Israel, Lydia focused on finding meaningful work (that did not conflict with taking care of her son) and a community in which to live. Seeking a town that would serve as a supportive community and not suffocate her individuality, she moved to one that had a large blue-collar population, an artists' community, and a small Jewish community—hearkening back to her early preferences for what she called "real people."

Lydia's return from Israel signified new steps forward, but she still felt overshadowed by her first husband's sudden death. At forty-three, Lydia still highlighted his death as the most insurmountable event in her life—because, she said, of the shock of it, its impact on her finances, life choices, and her and her son's personality. Following her husband's death, Lydia felt entirely unprepared to cope with the demands of adult life. By comparison, her childhood had been exceptionally easy; overwhelmed in adulthood, she felt she had no strengths on which to draw—life was a struggle just to survive.

Middle Adult Years: After Israel

By this point in the interview I felt some relief—Lydia had struggled through her husband's death, but she seemed well on her way to living the kind of life that was meaningful to her. She laughed—a "there's more" type of laugh—then sadly shook her head. Two years after she returned from Israel, her family had what she phrased as "a really terrible summer." Although her father had been dying for a long time and had already lived far longer than expected, that summer he died. Her father had also been like a father to D. As if this loss wasn't enough, the same summer, D.'s reading tutor was murdered. Lydia commented bitterly: "It was not what my son needed at the time in his life, she had been a very special person for him." Later that summer D. was molested by a local person. Once again support seemed to come "out of the woodwork": "We've been very lucky because by that time we had a lot of support—we had good friends and—it is a close community." This time a neighbor sought out D., offering the adolescent boy friendship and a job. But once again, life seemed like a daily struggle to maintain a sense of balance.

As D. grew up, Lydia became painfully aware of the weaknesses in the educational system for special needs children. After battling with public and private schools, including the town school board, to get her son "a decent education," she ran for town offices. In addition, she started writing a newsletter for the local Jewish community, became secretary for an organization for children with special needs, and worked for the social action committee for the local temple. "Special needs here are like garbage pails," she said angrily in a tone of voice that reminded me of her mother's: "They would take this class and they would give it a sadistic teacher. D. would get beaten. That's what got me into politics; I ran for school committee because the situation was so bad and nobody listened." In order to get her son into the local vocational school, Lydia became the area representative and agitated to get him enrolled. During that time—just turning forty—she was employed at a local community college, free-lanced for local newspapers, and taught Hebrew at the local temple, choosing to piece an income together by working part time in order to spend more time with D.

When I talked with Lydia at age forty-three, she had become principal of the local Hebrew school, finally making use of those "diplomatic" skills of which her mother spoke when Lydia was five. Work in the Hebrew school met complex needs, providing important feelings of belonging to the Jewish community, allowing expression of her activism and ideals, and integrating pieces of her past at the same time that it sustained her sense of competence and autonomy. Her job choice also reflected her tendency, evident in college, to blend work, activism, and values in a practical way.

When I asked her what strengths had brought her through these difficult adult years, Lydia's reply was initially vague, then pained about the blows of her adult life. "I do at this point come to expect the worst. ... I'm terribly paranoid about disasters happening. ... I'm a truly religious person, I feel that probably the thing other than my father and his very caring parenting that has gotten me through all the troubles in my life has been my religion. ... I'm proud of my writing, I get satisfaction out of my work too." Lydia felt she was finally beginning to find herself again:

> My life has been better ... actually my personal life is good and in terms of my competence I have become a writer as well as a teacher. I just discovered I could write—it just happened—it was like something dropped from the sky. What I discovered about writing, which I still treasure about it, it was a way of taking the fact that my life had been shitty and turning it into an advantage because I have lots of material. I try to take all the bizarre experiences I have had and turn them into writing of one kind or another.

Although writing had been a piece of her life since early childhood (she told me she "learned to write at her mother's knee"), she had just started reclaiming this part of herself.

Near the end of the interview, Lydia told me that she just recently remarried—to an artist/carpenter she described as a "sixties person." The story of that relationship was pretty much absent from the interview; given all we had talked about, I felt uncomfortable asking more questions and she volunteered little information. I found it interesting that in spite of this new relationship, Lydia's thoughts were so much tied to the past. I asked her to think about the future. Her major hope for the future was that her son could lead an independent life, and perhaps, some day marry: "People have questioned whether he can live independently. But I believe he can. I try to keep in mind that my father really believed in D.; I try to think that if I keep believing in him he's going to make it."

With D. nearing the end of high school, Lydia dared to think more about her own future; up until that time all her plans and dreams had been short term and focused on her son's needs. She contrasted two different paths her life might take. Her most serious plans involved becoming a rabbi, and her thoughts about rabbinical school were clearly self-integrating:

> I feel as if my work has gone in the direction of Jewish education, as principal I feel like I do all the work rabbis do without the pay. When I was growing up, being a rabbi was not an option for women. It was something I might have considered when I finished college. ... I feel as if I could do it now, I've had all the training and background. ... I've worked for all these rabbis—male rabbis—and I get really frustrated; I know I'd be a better rabbi than they are. ... Religion has been very meaningful to me, so I think it would be a good thing to do if I could ever afford to do it.

In a recent phone call with Lydia to talk about this chapter, she told me that she had just been accepted at rabbinical school. Reading the chapter, she added, made her realize that her first husband's death no longer dominated her life the way it had earlier.

Was Lydia Influenced by the Sixties?

The original reason for contacting Lydia had been to explore with her ways in which the 1960s affected her life. Although Lydia had experienced her husband's death as the most important event of her adult life, she also identified herself as a sixties person. Because her husband's death had in fact dominated the interviews, I went back through everything I knew about Lydia—transcripts of the age thirty-one and age forty-three interviews—to look explicitly for those places in which she talked about the 1960s. In both interviews, Lydia saw numerous specific life choices as based on her identification with her 1960s cohort: her determination to teach disadvantaged kids and live in blue-collar towns, her search for a community (rather than remarriage) that would provide emotional support for herself and D. and allow her autonomy, her decision to move to Israel, and her motto that "one must make one's own choices."

Lydia's views on raising her son reflected a sixties ethos: "Children are like little flowers, learning is like eating, it doesn't help to worry about it, children naturally want to learn." Rebellion in children "is a sign of strength and ego. It's important, it's not a bad thing to rebel." Finally, Lydia described her second husband in terms of the sixties: "He's Italian, a nonprofessional, an artist. This is a community where a relationship like ours is not considered weird, we have a lot of friends and he's a sixties person. I think that's crucial in our relationship." She went on with a chuckle, "I always tell people that I'm sure that if I ever did become a rabbi, I'd like to be a rabbi in a gay synagogue in Arizona. … So it probably wouldn't matter that my husband is Catholic—that's part of being a sixties person."

At each transition or decision point, endorsement of sixties values made Lydia's choice of less conventional paths seem more possible. In Lydia's difficult situation, her nontraditional choices to move to Israel, to seek support through community, to remain single, to raise her son alone, and to seek work and a lifestyle that were personally meaningful and integrative may have been fostered by her identification with the sixties.[4] An examination of Lydia through the focused question about "the influence of the sixties" adds a new level of understanding of her life, the values that guided her adult decisions, and a sense of greater inner continuity in the midst of her experiences of discontinuity. Given other aspects of Lydia's childhood, personality, and life, though, the idea that the sixties played a causal role in her adult life is far too simplistic.

Lydia in the Context of the Group: A Nomothetic Approach

How did Lydia compare with the rest of the women in this sixties-involved sample? Lydia's individual data from numerous questionnaires can be placed in the context of comparisons between sixties-involved women and those women in the sample who were the same age, lived in the same town, and experienced the same historical and social events, but did not get involved in social or political activism. In general, by age thirty-one, sixties-involved women were more educated, worked at higher occupational levels,[5] were less likely to be married, and had fewer children than other women in their cohort. They viewed authorities as having little importance in their lives; they didn't think it was important to teach their children the value of respect for authority. Teaching children to fulfill themselves and to understand and serve others was regarded as having greater merit. Sixties-involved women rated as least important traditional lifestyles and values such as happiness and family security. They attributed to themselves more power motivation—that is, such personality characteristics as assertiveness, dominance, and argumentativeness. They were more positive about people in general in their lives, more likely to donate money to social causes, more cooperative, and higher in principled morality (Rest, 1976) than women not involved in sixties activities.

In spite of the turmoil in her life after college, Lydia's values and self-presentation were well represented by these facts. From an idiographic perspective, Lydia's life could be seen as challenging the validity of the group results—wasn't she single because her husband died? Didn't she only have one child because of her hysterectomy? Wasn't she working only because she had to support herself? What role did being identified as part of a sixties-involved cohort play in her adult life? The interviews with Lydia revealed that she had alternatives following the death of her husband; she persistently made unconventional choices. She chose not to remarry until she was ready and decided against adopting additional children; she preferred to further her education in Israel; she decided to live in a supportive community. But what would Lydia's life have been like if her first husband had not died? Would she have been more conventional in spite of her identification with the sixties?

Conclusion

For a partial answer to the question "What if?" Lydia's childhood experiences, personality, and life interviews become important sources of information. Throughout her life, Lydia attempted to balance the somewhat contradictory needs of seeking autonomy and social support. Her motto that "one must make one's own choices" sometimes meant separation from people she needed. Some of the people willing to give her support demanded that she "please them" rather than herself. When she was thirty-one, these conflicts seemed paralyzing; by midlife, Lydia found multiple solutions. To what extent did social changes of the 1960s, especially for a woman who endorsed them, offer Lydia a broader range of life options from which to choose?

In spite of the fact that Lydia perceived great discontinuity in her life, surprising continuities from her past materialize in the story of her life—religion, familial support, activism, writing learned at her mother's knee, diplomacy. Both her autonomy, so in evidence in childhood and adulthood, and her sense of responsibility were empowering. Her choice of supportive communities met her needs for getting social support without the depression and sense of oppression that came from some individual relationships. Lydia's solutions to the problems posed by her unexpectedly difficult adult life emerge as creative constructions in which she utilized a plethora of internal and external resources.

The different approaches to studying Lydia's life—through her own and her mother's interviews, through the group data, and through focusing specifically on the influence of the 1960s—provided congruent but somewhat different information concerning her personality and the precursors to and consequences of her sixties involvement. Lydia's questionnaire data corresponded well to the personality characteristics, values, and life outcomes of the group of sixties-involved women in this and other samples. Through the nomothetic approach we gain a sense of her as part of a cohort that became engaged with a particular social/historical experience. Similarly, her childhood data closely paralleled the background characteristics of many of the other sixties-involved women. The nomothetic data seems to be pat and empty, however; we are left with little sense of how or why it is valid.

Through exploration of her mother's interview we see Lydia as a resourceful, sociable child who was allowed to stretch limits and taught about social responsibility. We also see her struggle and withdraw under the stresses of losing a grandfather and gaining a baby brother. There is little sense, though, that these child-centered, permissive parents would later be experienced by Lydia as oppressive.

Using the approach of examining the data with a focused question in mind—that is, how the 1960s affected her—it was evident that Lydia identified with her cohort in ways that were congruent with and extended the meaning of the nomothetic data. Until I tried to listen with an unfocused openness to Lydia's story, however, the ways in which the focused question I had imposed on the data sometimes distorted and sometimes clearly reflected Lydia's experiences of her self were not evident. The 1960s were the lens through which I wanted to see her life, not her way. By listening to Lydia's story in an unfocused way, her individuality and a sense of the processes of her life as lived in a particular historical and developmental context were far more evident.

An alternative way of thinking about the use of different sources of information and different analytic approaches is to recognize that the approaches are not mutually exclusive. Each approach rendered an appropriate picture of Lydia; depending on the goal of the researcher, any or all of the approaches may be adequate. Just as researchers with dissimilar interests might write different but valid stories about a person's life, the choice of approach also changes the story told. What is important is to recognize what is changed in the picture because of the perspective chosen.

Robert White (1966) recommended that the study of individual lives be undertaken out of a sense of social responsibility. In an age in which people feel hopeless and helpless, he argued, the study of the individual life allows the natural growth and the activity of the person back into the story, which then can become a source of optimism and empowerment. Lydia's resourcefulness and resilience in the midst of a difficult life only became apparent when she was put back into the story.

Acknowledgments

I am very grateful for the comments of Tracy Eells, Janet Landman, David McClelland, Joan Ostrove, Abigail Stewart, and John Strauss in the preparation of this chapter. Most of all, I am indebted to the willing participation of Lydia and Esther.

Notes

1. The name Lydia is a pseudonym.
2. The data are controlled for social class, since higher SES parents were more permissive than other parents.
3. Esther is a pseudonym. Information has been modified to protect the confidentiality of the family.
4. Other longitudinal studies corroborate these findings in other women activists' lives. Women activists during the 1960s tended to come into movements with greater experience than the men; they also remained activists longer as adults (McAdam, 1992). Interview data suggest that the combination of the social movements with the growth of the feminist movement provided strength and an identity for these women, who as adults remained

connected and lived out adult lives consistent with the social/political causes for which they fought (M. M. Braungart and R. G. Braungart, 1990; McAdam, 1992).

5. These data are reported on in full in Franz and McClelland (in press), "The life course of women and men active in social protests of the 1960s: A longitudinal study." Women from middle-class families were likely to get more education and to be more sixties involved; even so, the sixties women were more highly educated than other middle-class women. All results at age thirty-one and forty-one are reported with the effect of education partialed out.

References

Allport, G. W. (1942). *The use of personal documents in psychological science.* New York: Social Science Research Council.

Block, J. H., Haan, N., & Smith, M. B. (1968). Activism and apathy in contemporary adolescents. In J. F. Adams (Ed.), *Understanding adolescence: Current developments in adolescent psychology* (pp. 198–231). Boston: Allyn & Bacon.

Braungart, M. M., & Braungart, R. G. (1990). The life course of left-wing and right-wing youth activist leaders from the 1960s. *Political Psychology, 11,* 243–282.

Flacks, R. (1967). The liberated generation: An exploration of the roots of student protest. *Journal of Social Issues, 23,* 52–75.

Franz, C. E., & McClelland, D. C. (in press). The life course of women and men active in social protests of the 1960s: A longitudinal study. *Journal of Personality and Social Psychology.*

McAdam, D. (1989). The biographical consequences of activism. *American Sociological Review, 54,* 744–760.

—————. (1992). Gender as a mediator of the activist experience: The case of Freedom Summer. *American Journal of Sociology, 97,* 1211–1240.

Noam, G. G. (1988). The self, adult development, and the theory of biography and transformation. In D. K. Lapsley & F. C. Power (Eds.), *Self, ego, and identity: Integrative approaches* (pp. 3–29). New York: Springer-Verlag.

Rest, J. R. (1976). New approaches in the assessment of moral judgment. In T. Lickona (Ed.), *Moral development and behavior: Theory, research, and social issues* (pp. 198–218). New York: Holt, Rinehart & Winston.

Runyan, W. M. (1982). *Life histories and psychobiography: Explorations in theory and method.* New York: Oxford University Press.

Sears, R. R., Maccoby, E. E., & Levin, H. (1957). *Patterns of child rearing.* Evanston, IL: Row, Peterson.

Stewart, A. J., Franz, C. E., & Layton, L. (1988). The changing self: Using personal documents to study lives. *Journal of Personality, 56,* 41–74.

White, R. W. (1966). *Lives in progress.* New York: Holt, Rinehart & Winston.

16

My Dirty Little Secret:
Women as Clandestine Intellectuals

CAROL TOMLINSON-KEASEY

WOMEN CONSTITUTE OVER HALF of the population, yet their lives as individuals have often been conducted in the shadows of their more prominent social roles as wives and mothers. Only recently have psychologists focused the light of their investigative powers on women's individual hopes, goals, desires, and fears (Giele, 1982; Gilligan, 1982; Grossman and Chester, 1990; Gustafson and Magnusson, 1991). Their work has brought into sharp relief the realization that women's lives may not follow the same developmental patterns as men's lives.

Earlier theories developed by Erikson (1950), Vaillant (1977), and Levinson (1978) all offered accounts of adult development (see Tomlinson-Keasey, in press). Erikson's theory, pathbreaking though it was, served more as a sketch of adult lives, briefly outlining the challenges adults face and their resolutions of those challenges. As a description of women's lives, its details were meager. Vaillant and Levinson presented longitudinal accounts of men's development, focusing heavily on the occupational forces that directed men's lives, but both recognized the inadequacy of their theories as descriptions of women's lives.

More recent writings concerning adult women suggest that intimacy is as central to women's lives as achievement is to men's lives (Gilligan, 1982). When women describe themselves, they often portray a relationship, depicting their identity in the connection of their role as mother, lover, wife. Rather than achievement, they discuss the care they give to relationships. Gilligan's (1982) small sample of successful women seldom mentioned their academic and professional distinctions. On the contrary, they often regarded their professional activities as jeopardizing their sense of themselves. In contrast, men's descriptions of themselves often radiated from a hub of individual achievement, great ideas, and distinctive activities. These differences occurred despite the fact that both the men and women were in the same college class and were similarly situated as to occupational goals and marital status. The women's portraits seem much softer, less clear, and their identity becomes fused with intimacy. The women tend to depict themselves by their connection with other people (Gilligan, 1982).

David McClelland at Harvard has spent his career examining achievement motivation and power among men and women. He concluded (a) that women are more concerned than men with both sides of an interdependent relationship; (b) women are interested in people, whereas men are interested in things; (c) men are analytic and manipulative, whereas women are more interested in the complex, the open, the less defined (McClelland, 1975, pp. 86–88). His studies, like Gilligan's vignettes, suggest that women's lives often are driven by forces that men do not find as compelling. A drive for intimacy appears and reappears in women's TAT stories, looking much like the drive for achievement that fills men's interviews.

Eccles (1985) tackled the difficult issue of gender differences in achievement. She suggested that the individual's expectations for success and the importance attached to various career options influence women's choices. Women, she noted, often have perfectly sound reasons for selecting a particular course of action. The point to be drawn from Eccles's remarks is that women, for whatever reason, march to a different drummer, one seemingly less captivated by career success.

Eli Ginzberg was jolted into an awareness of gender differences in adult development when he contacted men and women who had excelled as graduate students at Columbia between 1944 and 1951. The questionnaire he drafted was duly returned by both sexes, but the women objected strenuously to the omission of salient aspects of their lives. After redrafting his questionnaire, Ginzberg reported the different paths that women took in their adult lives (Ginzberg, 1966; Ginzberg and Yohalem, 1966).

These snapshots of some of the major longitudinal studies of adult development remind us forcefully that descriptions and predictions of male achievements, personality, and intellectual interests cannot be applied indiscriminately to women. To alter male models to fit women or to discover alternative life paths that women follow, detailed, long-term studies of women's lives must be undertaken (Heilbrun, 1988). Only in such descriptions, in which women are encouraged to give voice to the salient aspects of their lives, will the patterns of women's lives emerge.

Given the differences in the life paths of men and women, it is easy to echo the following sentiments of Gilligan: "Among the most pressing items on the agenda for research on adult development are studies that would delineate *in women's own terms* the experience of their adult life. … As we have listened for centuries to the voices of men and the theories of development that their experience informs, so we have begun more recently to notice not only the silence of women but the difficulty in hearing what they say when they speak" (Gilligan, 1982, p. 112).

In the present chapter, as in this volume generally, Gilligan's charge is taken seriously. Through case studies, we can listen as women explain the forces that shape their lives. Nora Sol's[1] life, which is detailed in the present chapter, is sprinkled liberally with relationships, with vague career aspirations, and with choice points to analyze. In addition, as a subject in the Terman Genetic Studies of Genius, Nora was identified as a gifted child. Her life story holds particular interest because it allows us to see how one woman attempted to balance her substantial intellectual gifts with the many role demands made on women.

Nora Sol

Lewis Terman first came to know Nora in 1922 as an eleven-year-old who was identified as a gifted subject for his study. From that point until his death in 1956, Terman followed Nora and over 1,500 other gifted boys and girls as they traversed adolescence, left their families, and established their own homes. Terman maintained contact with his subjects as adults through twelve questionnaires between 1936 and 1992. In addition, the study files contain holiday greetings, personal letters, and occasionally, notes from subjects' visits to Stanford. Terman maintained an active interest in each subject's life, offering encouragement and advice on particular problems when it was solicited. Nora's file was selected for this chapter initially because it was one of the most complete. In addition, the standard questionnaires were supplemented by long letters from both Nora and her father describing the various twists and turns in Nora's life.

Nora describes her intellect as her "dirty little secret," a secret layered in veils of different opaque qualities. She says, as if admitting to some major character flaw, "I am an intellectual." For eighty years, she has muted and buffered her intellect in ways to fit society's constraints as interpreted to her through her family of origin, her extended family, and her three husbands. Despite the opaque veils that screen her intellect from public view, she nurtured an active, private, dedicated intellectual life. As we watch her life unfold, we need to ask how she came upon this strategy of hiding her intellect when necessary, yet letting it peek through the veils periodically, in safe and accepted situations.

Family of Origin

Nora's family of origin was a swirling maelstrom of friction, chaos, hostility, and lack of nurturance. Her father, an autocratic taskmaster, listed his occupation as adventurer, explorer, and writer. Her mother was diagnosed as paranoid schizophrenic soon after her parents' marriage. By the time Nora, the oldest child, was four, her mother moved to a state hospital. During the family's occasional visits, Nora's mother often did not recognize her and occasionally denied that Nora was her daughter. Once, after visiting her mother and being rejected in the most palpable ways, Nora retired to her room and cried for three days. Recounting this period many years later, she said, "I was nine and the reality of my situation struck home for the first time. I would never have a mother, I had never had a mother that I knew and the tragedy and permanence of that situation drove me to my bedroom in tears." Nora's tears were linked to the profound understanding that reality is slippery, that her mother lived in a world of illusion and delusion and wasn't aware of it, and that both she and her mother experienced a cruel reality.

Nora's relationship with her father was a constant battle. She says from her vantage point as an octogenarian, "I was a bad girl until I was fifteen." Although her father's disciplinary measures seldom included any corporal punishment, Nora lived with a variety of strictures, both moral and real, that reinforced her notion that she could do nothing right. She remembers a favorite housekeeper saying "Why don't you learn to manage your father?" She admits that such management was "not in my repertoire, it wasn't in my nature. My nature was to go head to head against him."

Nora's father detailed their stormy relationship in the questionnaires he returned to the Terman study. He described Nora as "willful, headstrong, a lawyer, a liar," commenting that her moral instruction had been constant and that he had disciplined Nora frequently: "She is a problem, morally—on the verge of being sent to a convent. … We, two educated, thoughtful, painstaking adults, are in despair. … She lies, steals, and bears false witness, is slovenly, lazy, unclean, yet vain. In the category of her sins, few could truthfully be omitted, she having, it seems, about all the vices and few or none of the virtues appertaining to civilized life." His threat to send Nora to a convent was realized in 1924, when Nora was twelve. After two years at convents, her father described her behavior as much improved: "The periods of calm have lengthened. In these intermissions, she shows distinctly human traits. In especial, she seems to have developed a conscience. … She's a very good girl, patient with her brothers and even with her father; conscientious, rather honorable, even sweet, and damnably pretty."

Nora viewed these years in the convent in very different terms. They offered her peace, a seclusion, a sanctuary from the craziness of her family of origin. The life was structured, the demands were reasonable and easy to fulfill, she was no longer a "bad girl." She was accepted for who she was and she was able to satisfy some of her intellectual needs. Although her description of these two years was beatific, twelve-year-olds who are sent to convents must feel some rejection. Nora acknowledged that of course she had felt rejected, "but at home I had already been rejected. My actions, my person were always rejected. At the convent, I was accepted."

Nora's relationships with her two brothers, from whom she might have received some nurturance, were rocky and tenuous. The family's financial situation precluded any privileges, or much in the way of material possessions. Rather than binding the children together, the deprivation they experienced prompted them to fight over every detail of existence. The relationships with her brothers did not improve after these difficult childhood years. Her brothers snitched on Nora when she read a forbidden book. They chronicled every misadventure to her stern father, who responded with harsh punishments.

Nora's father offered only negative comments about her superior intelligence, a tested IQ of 150. When asked about indications of intelligence, he commented that she used her intelligence for excuses, alibis, and scheming to outwit and avoid the consequences of her misdeeds. In a long letter to Terman, he glorified a son's intellectual capabilities and minimized Nora's. It is noteworthy that the boy was not a subject in Terman's study.

By fifteen, Nora had skipped two grades, had read widely, wrote well, and was an important writer for the school paper. At every phase of her life, Nora describes reading voraciously, but as a child, she often had to conceal her reading material. "I had my history book and I would conceal an acceptable writer like Dickens in the history book, but inside of that I had something by Jim Tulley. At home, there were layers of concealment, always."

One of Nora's first chances to follow her intellectual bent went awry during her senior year in high school. The family's financial situation worsened and the parade of housekeepers who had raised Nora stopped. Nora was given the primary responsibility for managing the home, a responsibility that she admits she performed perfunctorily. She says she always got into trouble because she would be reading instead of doing her chores. In the inner life she fashioned for herself, Nora read two to three books a week. As she says, "My problems paled in comparison to poor Eliza's in *Uncle Tom's Cabin*." A conference with Nora's teachers indicated that Nora was in line for a scholarship to UCLA, but they questioned the wisdom of awarding the scholarship. Nora had so many household responsibilities that the teachers were afraid she might not be able to spend the required time on her studies.

Nora's memory of her senior year at Hollywood High is one of a painfully shy girl who was poorly dressed and hence retreated to the solace of her books. In one of the many twists in her life, she had dozens of elegant hand-me-down gowns from an aunt in San Francisco. These designers gowns, however, went unappreciated because Nora had nowhere to wear them and no clothes that were suitable for high school.

In a letter to Terman, Nora's father commented on her beauty. A picture in the file suggests that his assessment was quite objective. Hollywood apparently noticed and she was offered a job as an extra. She took the job because it allowed her to remain at home, meet the needs of the family, and yet earn some money. When asked about her beauty as a teenager, Nora demurred: "I was little and I was cute. I learned to act little and cute. Everyone treated me as little and cute. I had an exterior life and an interior life and they did not fit with each other at all." Although these comments are particularly relevant to Nora's life, the society typically attended to a young woman's physical attributes and social skills, rather than encouraging or appreciating the intellectual qualities characteristic of the Terman women.

Nora's childhood seemed singularly devoid of nurturing adult relationships. She retreated to her books, found peace from her chaotic home, and began her double life as a closet intellectual. Her father, a writer himself, never saw or explored Nora's interests in books or writing. Her intellect was seen more as a diabolical plot to make his life difficult. He wanted her to follow his moral strictures, perform her chores with enthusiasm, and not disrupt the household. The thought that he might develop Nora's intellectual resources never occurred to him, yet he raged to Terman that his son's intellectual talents had been overlooked.

San Francisco: Nora's First Intellectual Forays

Nora credits her aunt with saving her life when she was nineteen. The family had left Los Angeles for a summer in Yosemite. When they were ready to return, the aunt invited Nora to stay with her instead of returning to Hollywood. Nora describes this as a turning point in her life because had she returned to Hollywood, she would have continued in the brainless roles assigned to most Hollywood extras. In one of her positions as an extra, she overheard a director and a producer commenting on how pretty she was. They added, however, that her legs were hopeless. Looking back from the vantage point of six more decades of living, Nora comments that they were right. With her aunt, she moved onto a different path, one on which she began to use her intellect, not her beauty.

Despite the Depression, Nora landed a job in San Francisco with a library circulating service. The inner life she had developed, focused on books to shut out her hostile, rejecting home environment, served her well when she applied for the job. Although still in her twenties, she was extraordinarily well read and her enthusiasm for books bubbled forth. Little wonder that she attracted the attention of a sales representative. He was thirty-six, almost fifteen years her senior, and had a high school education. She described him as handsome, charming, and unmarried. In one of the few goals that she recalls setting during her life, she decided that she would be his wife.

Although Nora and her husband had a beautiful daughter, she realized quickly that the marriage was a mistake as her husband had few intellectual interests. Within months of the marriage, she saw him and his life as vapid. Her response was to busy herself with the care of her daughter and retreat to her books, reading as many as twenty books a month. When her daughter was five, Nora talked with Terman about her marital difficulties and decided to dissolve the marriage. Although women rarely divorced, and as a divorcee with a young child, she was taking significant financial risks, she felt it was the only solution. In her talk with Terman she indicated that she longed for intellectual companionship. Some of the courage for her decision to divorce undoubtedly came from her success in a variety of jobs in San Francisco. She had been promoted quickly through the librarian ranks and had jurisdiction over the collections for seven libraries. She had her own radio program in San Francisco for which she reviewed books and wrote short scripts. In 1936, she indicated on her questionnaire that she had a horrible suspicion that she would end up as a writer. In 1939, she commented that her radio work blended her penchant for writing and her dramatic skills.

Nora's years in San Francisco brought her intellectual interests to the fore. She felt compelled to divorce her husband who could not appreciate her intellect. Her intelligence was given voice in her library work, in her reviews of books, and in the dramatic scripts that she wrote. As a young adult in San Francisco, Nora had the chance to express her intellect and to be valued for those skills. But the depth of her intellectual interests remained hidden. She joined a group designed to let women voice their feelings, needs, and desires in a safe setting. She says, "My dirty little secret was not that I was having an affair, had had an abortion, had given up my child, or was a lesbian; it was that I was an intellectual. I could not even tell this group of women, all of whom were baring their private lives and feelings. My secret was so traumatic and so deeply personal and private, that I couldn't bring myself to tell anyone."

Monterey — An Intellectual Community

After Nora left her husband in 1940, she visited a friend in Carmel; stayed for the Bach festival; and found herself drawn into the artistic, intellectual, Bohemian community of Monterey. She met a marine biologist, thirteen years her senior, who had an abiding interest in enjoying life. Hap introduced Nora to postimpressionist art, classical music, scientific research, current writing genres, and John Steinbeck. The impact was profound. She described a moment, sitting in a restaurant with Hap, discussing art, surrounded by baroque music, in which she burst into tears because of the intense pleasure of discovering music by Monteverdi and poetry by Robinson Jeffers. Among the artists and writers, ideas were traded like currency, and she was entitled to have ideas and express them. Further, the unconventional atmosphere and the Cannery Row high jinks that flowed from that atmosphere made Nora feel safe in expressing her ideas more openly. She moved in with Hap and became part of a group that included John Steinbeck. She also began a very successful column for a local Monterey paper.

Hap had allowed, by virtue of his stature and interests, Nora's intellect to peek out from the veils of her childhood. She felt comfortable and accepted by the community. However, Hap did not personally encourage her intellectual growth except by introducing her to the community. He wanted "domesticity, dinner at six and a complete woman." Still, Nora's personal growth in this setting was obvious. She embraced a variety of avant-garde causes, including racial tolerance, and brought "vigorous leadership and dynamic conviction" to her work for these causes. She had fun, engineering a meeting between Henry Miller and a woman by suspending the woman from a barn beam. She wrote, achieving considerable notoriety and success through her own column in a local newspaper. She found other intellectual outlets—a glossary she completed for a marine biology text received special mention in one of the reviews. She edited a doctoral thesis. The freedom of the community allowed her to explore and develop.

Some of the spark went out of Nora's life when her daughter was diagnosed with a brain tumor. While she cared for her daughter, her relationship with Hap deteriorated. The moment her daughter died, Nora left Monterey and began a new relationship. What she took from Monterey was a heightened sense of awareness of her writing talents and an appreciation for an environment that encourages people to play with ideas.

Israel — Fulfilling Intellectual Promise

Nora had met her third husband at Stanford. He was on sabbatical and was planning to return to Palestine in a few months. In a momentous decision, she left Monterey and accompanied him to Palestine. She described the tumult of the moment: "I had supported several Zionist causes and there was tremendous fervency among the Jewish community about the formation of Israel. I was allowed entry into Palestine as a journalist and sailed aboard a converted liberty ship. The international tensions surrounding Israel turned the cruise into a mystery thriller, with everyone suspecting his neighbors of being spies, intelligence men, and secret agents." Palestine became Israel and Nora put her newly developed writing and analytical talents to use. As bureau chief for *Israel Speaks,* English editor for *Ktavim,* and editor and writer for *Wizo in Israel,* she produced thousands of words—"some sociological and economic analysis, some lighter commentary." In addition, she began helping others polish their writing. "The international community of scientists gathered in Israel were delighted to have me help them edit manuscripts, make sure the English was correct, and then make the manuscript easier to read and more interesting." She conducted seminars in scientific writing, prepared a manuscript on the topic, and had another child. In Israel, as much as any time in her life, she found fulfillment for her intellectual skills. She carved the time for her editing and writing out of a busy schedule as wife and mother and succeeded at all four tasks. Still, her own writing took a back seat to the editing she did for others.

In 1956, when Nora was forty-five, she and her husband returned to California. Although she continued her scientific editing, the pace was reduced. She again turned to her own work. Despite years of research on ideas for at least two books, her work never culminated in a final manuscript. She wrote in 1972 that she could have been quite a good scholar and researcher. She had come to admire the academic life and the scholarly and intellectual freedom it allowed. As an octogenarian, Nora is dynamic, sometimes fiery, and definitely passionate when speaking about issues dear to her heart. Certainly the spark that is described in the Terman files, sometimes called "strong will" or "stubbornness" by her father, is very much alive in her retirement years. She still reads voraciously and broadly, reporting during an interview on recent articles she had read concerning women's issues, the situation in the Middle East, social history, chaos theory, and DNA. Her life remains full and although Nora recognizes the complexity of her life and its various strengths and weaknesses, she evaluates the totality as unequivocally positive.

Women's Paths

Drawing meaning from Nora's life requires that we examine the directions and events of her life in terms of theories and viewpoints about women's adult development. Five aspects of her life emerge that can be framed in more general terms: (a) the importance of relationships, (b) the force of serendipity, (c) discontinuity,

(d) personal attributes that altered her life, and (e) the intentional minimizing of her intellectual skills.

Relationships, Intimacy, and Commitment

Rethinking Nora's life, we can try to cast it in the various molds provided by Levinson (1978), Vaillant (1977), Gilligan (1982), and Ginzberg (1966) to describe adult development. Despite her striking writing skills and her literary bent, Nora's career never ruled her life. In fact, Nora expresses reluctance to pursue writing, partly because her father's writing success had been sporadic and the family was often financially strapped. Hence, any model of adult development that concentrates on career goals and eclipses personal development seems inappropriate as a vehicle to examine Nora's life.

Instead, her life seems better captured by the series of relationships she had and a few specific, yet notably discontinuous, decisions. In this sense, Gilligan's views of the importance of relationships in women's lives provide a more appropriate lens for viewing Nora's life. Had she remained with her first husband, her intellectual life might well have remained stunted and secretive. By aligning herself with Hap and becoming involved in the intellectual community in Monterey, she began to establish her intellectual credentials. Notice, though, that her entrée was via her beauty, which facilitated her relationship with Hap and her position with John Steinbeck.

Relationships were important throughout Nora's life, and many of the significant changes in her life were tied to changes in her commitments. In what she regarded as a major redirection of her life, she moved to San Francisco and stayed with an aunt who was a psychologist. Here Nora reaped her first rewards from the reading that had been her refuge as a preadolescent and adolescent. Nora's father had often punished her for reading, feeling that it detracted from her chores. The move to San Francisco opened up avenues of expression and lines of intellectual inquiry that were new for Nora.

Although Nora's aunt was willing to continue to serve as a surrogate mother in San Francisco, Nora took the first opportunity to leave her family of origin. She certainly was not unique in using marriage as a vehicle to lessen the influence of her family. As in many such marriages, however, Nora was so anxious to leave a difficult situation that she was less than thorough in evaluating the situation she was entering. After her marriage, Nora realized very quickly that she could not exist simply as an attractive adjunct to her husband; she needed intellectual stimulation and an avenue for expressing her intellectual interests. Little wonder that she quickly outgrew her first husband.

The move to Monterey and her relationship with Hap allowed Nora's intellectual spirit to develop. The intellectual freedom in the fun, Bohemian atmosphere of Carmel encouraged Nora to experiment with her own modes of self-expression. For the first time, she began to feel comfortable committing ideas to paper and devoting her energy to causes she endorsed. Although she blossomed intellectually, her relationship with Hap lacked the commitment she needed.

When her daughter died, she made another surprising move, following her third husband to Israel. For the first time, she found a relationship that met her needs for intimacy and provided an environment where she could achieve intellectual satisfaction. Her successes as a wife, a mother, a writer, and an editor in the environment provided by this relationship were noteworthy.

Goals, Improvisation, and Serendipity

Three strategies for dealing with life can be plotted along a continuum: At one end we have the model of setting goals and moving down life's path in a thoughtful, planned way. At the other, we have serendipitous events in control, with the player being pulled helplessly along. In between, we have persons who do not set individual goals, but who assess their life situation and improvise to establish a life path that meets their needs.

Although many men lay out their lives in some detail as young adults, describing specific goals to be attained in three-to-five-year phases, women are much less likely to set such goals (Gilligan, 1982; Locke, Shaw, Saari, and Latham, 1981). Each of Nora's primary life changes foreshadowed a different level of intellectual expression. Were these moves orchestrated to allow her intelligence to emerge or to facilitate career opportunities? She says that except for her decision to go to Israel, she often felt like a leaf drifting down a stream. Indeed, some of her decisions, like the one to leave her home in Hollywood and live with her aunt, were made on a whim. The decision to leave her first husband was, however, a thoughtful one, reached after several years of marital difficulty. Her move to Monterey was another fortuitous event. The friend that she went to visit could just as easily have lived in Santa Barbara or Berkeley.

Such serendipity frequently surrounded the career opportunities pursued by the Terman women (Tomlinson-Keasey, 1990). Because they put their husband's and children's needs ahead of their own, the work histories of these women seemed to defy planning. Economic exigencies, divorces, and a world war conspired to pull women who planned to be homemakers into the work force. The crisis atmosphere that often surrounded their job seeking meant that career planning was minimal.

Bateson (1989) described a career strategy she labeled "improvisation." Perhaps this intermediate characterization more accurately defines Nora's life. In each of her surroundings, Nora improvised a way to find personal satisfaction. The different status that evolved from her relationships with Hap and her third husband provided specific kinds of writing opportunities and she wisely capitalized on those opportunities. Like many of the capable women in the Terman study, Nora achieved a balance between the social roles dictated by the culture and her intellectual desires, and she did it with little education and minimal encouragement.

Discontinuity

Nora's life path has several sharp turns, but each one presaged a noticeable improvement in her life situation. With only an occasional course beyond high school, she became a valued editor to scientists in an academic community. Although she never achieved the goal of writing her own manuscripts, the success she achieved is a tribute to her persistence and intellect.

The discontinuities that we see in Nora's life have been chronicled in other women's lives (Bateson, 1989; Block, 1971; Gilligan, Lyons, and Hanmer, 1990). Divorce, the most obvious discontinuity in Nora's life, may represent a woman's move from stagnation to new challenge and growth (Bateson, 1989).

Gilligan et al. (1990) described a discontinuity in women's lives that results from more negative influences. In their view, adolescence poses problems of connection for girls coming of age in Western culture and defines a critical life disjunction for women. In support of such a major developmental discontinuity, one can cite the added stress women feel during adolescence (Rutter, 1986), the increase in depression (Gjerde, 1993), and the decline in self-image (American Association of University Women [AAUW], 1992). Jack Block (1971) in his careful evaluation of lives found a similar discontinuity in the lives of adolescent females. "The most striking phenomenon is a multifaceted move toward greater interpersonal deviousness" (p. 71). Still, one can argue that this developmental discontinuity results from the culture's changing messages to adolescent women. The discontinuities referred to by Bateson and seen in Nora's life are more typically the result of geographical relocation, career moves, or changes in relationships that alter adults' life paths.

Personal Attributes

Personal attributes warrant mention in almost every model of adult achievement (Terman and Oden, 1947; Vaillant, 1977). Personal attributes differentiating women who achieve from those who are less successful inevitably involve assessments of self-confidence and the willingness to take risks (Hennig and Jardim, 1977; Sanford and Donovan, 1984). Like many Terman women, Nora reported a lack of self-confidence, a reticence or hesitancy about approaching career tasks. However, a look at her life and the decisions she made suggests that she was willing to take risks when it was necessary. Not many young women in the Terman cohort divorced while they had a young child. Fewer would have left one man to marry another and travel to Israel. The risk taking that we see in Nora appears in other women who have achieved amidst an unsupportive culture (Hennig and Jardim, 1977).

The development of confidence in her ability posed a problem for Nora and for the majority of the women in the Terman cohort (Tomlinson-Keasey, 1990). Other, more recent studies of women found similar results, "a lack of self-esteem, an inability to feel powerful or in control of one's life, a vulnerability to depression, a tendency to see oneself as less talented, less able than one really is" (Rivers, Barnett, and Baruch, 1979, p. 134). This lack of self-esteem is not limited to a few women nor is it confined to a particular period of our history or a particular age group (Sanford and Donovan, 1984). Contemporary women experience doubts about their abilities and their acceptance in a variety of career positions (AAUW, 1992; Arnold, 1993; Inglehart, Brown, and Malanchuk, 1993).

What can we learn from those women who display an easy confidence in their abilities? Successful women often point specifically to adolescence as a time when they clarified and strengthened their identities (Hennig and Jardim, 1977). During adolescence, these women waged a determined struggle against the restricted, confining feminine role others might have carved for them. Instead, with the support of their father, they continued their strong achievement orientation in atypical fields.

Minimizing Cognitive Skills

Throughout her childhood, Nora hid her intellectual predilections. Yet they were such a vital part of her person that she was forced to nurture these skills in clandestine ways. The entire society loses whenever gifted women hide their intellectual skills, are put in situations where they cannot develop or use those skills, or are discouraged by a masculine culture from trying to succeed in an "atypical" profession. Of interest in Nora's life is the fact that she was able to give fuller voice to her intellectual skills in successive environments.

Gifted and talented women continue to mask their intellects (Hollinger and Fleming, 1988). Longitudinal research reveals a consistent pattern of lowering aspiration levels and declining achievements among adolescent women who are gifted (Arnold, 1993; Kerr, 1985). The stereotypes of genius that still pervade the society perhaps contribute to the negative view of gifted women. One of the earliest stereotypes equated high levels of intelligence with emotional and social maladjustment (Lombroso, 1895). From the 1840s to the 1950s, the notion that precocious triumph would be followed by tragic collapse was prominent, even in academic circles (Sears, 1979). Although the force of some of these stereotypes has been dissipated, it is interesting that college students still believe that gifted females suffer socially (Solano, 1987). Society, the young woman, and young men often view a high level of achievement in a woman as inconsistent with femininity (Fox, 1977), and achievement in junior high and high school can be an invitation to social rejection (Hollinger and Fleming, 1984, 1985). Given the importance of relationships to women, it is little wonder that Nora, her peers, and contemporary adolescents have hidden their intellectual interests.

Although all of the Terman women did not hide their intellectual skills, it is clear that many were unable to develop those skills. In the Depression of the 1930s, many women, even those with college educations, encountered severely limited career opportunities. The Depression meant that women who were married, and thus guaranteed a means of support, were often denied jobs, even in traditionally feminine areas such as nursing and teaching. U.S. society thus funneled women into the role of homemakers.

Much has changed in the society since the Terman women were in college. However, Swiatek and Benbow (1991) reported that families still feel that educational opportunities are more important for gifted men than they are for gifted women. In their study, gifted boys who had been accelerated in school attended colleges with a median rank of twenty-third in the country. The gifted girls who had been accelerated attended colleges with a median rank of 180. Among gifted students who were not accelerated, median rank for the boys' colleges was 46; for the girls' colleges, 299.

A description of the life paths of adult women must confront the complexity of lives in which relationships, intimacy, and commitment are a primary responsibility. It must allow for discontinuity in the flow of women's lives and recognize that serendipity and improvisation are substitutes for goal setting when the woman's life path is not clear. A description of women's development must assess personal attributes that differ from those of men and that have an impact on career directions and further development.

Given the above, an acceptable model for women's development can hardly resemble the stair steps of progressive occupational attainment offered by Levinson (1978) and Vaillant (1977). A possible alternative is a circle radiating outward from the woman to include relationships, career involvement, and family responsibilities. During different periods of adult life, time commitments, activity, and responsibilities in each of these sectors might vary, and each sector might have a developmental progression of its own compared to the developmental phase of another aspect of life.

Facilitating Women's Development

In examining women's lives, it is instructive to ask how Nora's situation could have been altered to actualize her intellectual skills. Empowering women, removing obstacles to their success, recognizing the critical importance of relationships to their lives, and allowing for discontinuous events would help women who would like to contribute their skills to the society.

Empowerment

Personal empowerment may be uniquely important to the facilitation of intellectual growth for young women simply because it counters the pervasive cultural messages about the importance of physical appearance. Having a father who makes it clear that you are appreciated for qualities that go beyond the superficial and physical may be particularly salutary for women's intellectual development. Nora's father not only ignored the talent and predilections that should have been obvious to a writer, he disparaged them. Nora's teachers in high school described her promise and mentioned her for a scholarship, but decided against taking a chance on her. Nora's aunt was the only person who attempted to help by enticing Nora away from the Hollywood scene. Beyond that, Nora seems to have made her own way.

Women in the Terman era who pursued intellectual interests often had particular encouragement from their fathers. In fact, in Hennig and Jardim's study (1977) of managerial women in the 1950s, the women CEOs were always first born, typically the only child, and reported close, empowering relationships with their fathers. The fathers encouraged their daughters in a variety of venues. Further, the daughters were allowed to see and experience many facets of the father's life.

One can speculate about the mechanisms behind the father's particular influence. Were daughters of such fathers particularly likely to pursue a career and actualize their intellectual potential because their fathers demystified particular career paths? This is certainly a possibility. One pharmacist's daughter reports serving as a cashier for her father at an early age. She pursued a career in biology. An attorney's daughter remembers many visits to the courthouse and courtrooms as a child. She felt comfortable becoming an attorney. The daughter of a famed scientist grew up with scientific visitors from around the globe. She became a researcher of note in her own right. Even Nora knew about writers from her father. When a father demystifies a career, he shows his daughter that successful individuals in the occupation possess a range of talents and abilities. In doing so, he makes the career more approachable.

Perhaps the father's effect is more diffuse and should be seen as providing an opportunity for self-growth. Being encouraged by their father may help daughters define themselves and their abilities accurately. Such empowerment may also help daughters pursue both "typical" and "atypical" professions.

Both of these mechanisms could operate in a woman's life to mediate and explain a father's influence. Certainly, Nora had no nurturing, no encouragement, no empowerment, and no sense that her intellect was valuable. Still, even in her life, the occupation of writer was demystified, and Nora's familiarity with that career could well have directed her interests.

Other individuals or institutions might provide women with similar empowerment. Brothers, grandfathers, uncles, and husbands all empowered some of the Terman women. Here, too, Nora drew a blank. She was estranged from her brothers early in life. Female role models, when they exist, can demystify careers, but they are not as convincing when it comes to certifying the acceptability of developing your own intellect. Nora experienced little mothering. Only her aunt helped by offering her refuge. As I understand Nora's life story, this help turned out to be critical to Nora's intellectual development.

Recognizing the Importance of Relationships, Commitment, and Intimacy to Women's Lives

Recognizing the importance of relationships, commitment, and intimacy to women's lives as a way of facilitating women's development will require major restructuring of our society (O'Farrell and Harlan, 1984; Schroeder, 1989). The women of the Terman sample had much to offer society, and like Nora, they contributed in ways that fit with their circumstances. But listen carefully to their voices and you will hear that they did not find the structure of the world amenable to their skills. Here is Nora's comment when asked about her flaws: "I procrastinate, probably because of some basic uncertainty which leads to super-sensitivity and inferiority feelings." Simply recognizing women's hesitancies and their need for reassurance would keep many competent women from becoming discouraged. Nora suggested that her most appealing traits were her "fierce energy and her friendliness." Like many women, her social skills and her commitment to relationships could be turned into a positive force in career development and intellectual achievement. Nora noted that she refused to enter the career contests that depended on "aggressiveness and manipulation." Perhaps Nora's words allude to the differences in the way men and women contemplate and pursue their lives.

A curriculum that allows women to learn in a less competitive, more cooperative environment produces women who as high school students are more likely to pursue science (Dresselhaus, 1992). At the college level, Dresselhaus urged universities to make women feel welcome in physics, chemistry, engineering, and other disciplines. Women benefit from peer group and networking programs that provide them with information, guidance, and reassurance that they can succeed.

Organizers of professional training and career development programs need to recognize that if women are to participate in, enjoy, and succeed in their chosen field, ways have to be found to allow family goals to be met (Baruch, Biener, and Barnett, 1987). Although women in career positions initially brought attention to family concerns, men have relished the opportunity to deal with their own family-based stresses. Continued societal attention to family leave policies and flexibility in career strategies will encourage women to bring their talents to scientific and professional arenas.

Removing Societal Obstacles

The obstacles that Nora had to overcome are seldom mentioned in adult models of development. For women, many of these obstacles are cultural and invisible. Several times Nora was told that she could not be taken seriously, she was too cute. Her beauty also provided an entrée to relationships and social settings in which her intellect could then be expressed.

The intractability of the male orientation in particular fields remains. Even successful women report feeling excluded from office networks in areas like law and architecture (Milwid, 1982). In 1986, the National Research Council concluded that women's occupational choices and preferences did not account for the continued occupational segregation by sex; such barriers resulted instead from personnel practices that made advancement difficult and from stereotypes about women's proper roles and traits (Reskin and Hartmann, 1986).

Permitting Discontinuity

Instead of an orderly stepwise progression in a career, McGuigan (1980) envisioned women's adult development as "a braid of threads in which colors appear, disappear, and reappear" (p. xii). Such a model captures some of the discontinuity in women's lives that Bateson described. Allowing women with major discontinuities in their lives to compete in fields that currently have continuous career paths will require more flexible and inclusive policies than have previously existed. Medical school, for example, now offers women the opportunity to share postgraduate training. It takes these women longer to complete their studies, but it allows them to retain a family life. Governments, businesses, and other major institutions must adjust their programs to make it easier for women to follow a flexible life course that intermingles work, education, and family commitments (Giele, 1982).

Conclusions

Nora's intellectual growth radiated from the relationships she developed. Her first husband was uneducated and lived a life devoid of intellectual stimulation. Her second husband was a scientist who embraced all aspects of life and played in an intellectual community. Nora's third husband was a world-renowned researcher whose entire life revolved around intellectual questions. Nora's life and the intellectual opportunities open to her were delimited by these relationships. Could she have developed independent opportunities and pursued a goal as a writer or researcher? Perhaps, but few of the Terman women did (Terman and Oden, 1947, 1959). Instead they learned to create their opportunities out of the situations and relationships that defined their lives.

Serendipity, improvisation, and lack of goal setting were hallmarks of Nora's life and the Terman women generally. Ill-defined goals still characterize career aspirations of adult women. Very few women develop personal career goals and pursue them in a single-minded way. Their focus on relationships precludes the pursuit of clearly defined goals. Instead, women wait for serendipitous events that provide an opportunity for them to use their skills or else improvise in the situations available to them.

Nora hid her intellectual proclivities for years. Was this characteristic of intelligent women in her cohort and do we see similar behaviors today? Certainly, the women in Nora's cohort were schooled in the importance of relationships. Becoming a wife was the most frequent life goal mentioned when these women were in their mid-twenties. In accomplishing this goal, these bright women were often coy, were careful not to intimidate, and were eager to please. If this meant that they did not flaunt their intellect, it was probably a sensible decision.

The achievements of gifted women are constrained by their culture, their opportunities, their relationships, and the complexity of the lives they lead. This was true of Nora and was generally true of the women in the Terman sample. It remains true, to a lesser degree, of contemporary women. Could Nora have written a book that would have competed with some of John Steinbeck's works? Could she have pursued a research project that would have yielded answers to unsolved questions? She certainly had the cognitive ability. And the success she enjoyed with a high school education was impressive. What she lacked was education, encouragement, empowerment, and opportunities to develop those skills in ways that were compatible with a stable relationship and the family she desired.

Acknowledgments

This chapter derives from information originally collected by Lewis M. Terman and maintained in the archives at Stanford University. Hence, I owe a special debt to Robert Sears, Albert Hastorf, and Eleanor Walker of Stanford University for helping me gain access to the data. In addition, I must thank "Nora" who opened her life to scrutiny to help us better understand women's lives.

Notes

1. Names have been changed to protect privacy.

References

American Association of University Women. (1992). *How schools shortchange girls: A study of major findings on girls in education.* Washington, DC: AAUW Education Foundation.

Arnold, K. D. (1993). Academically talented women in the 1980s: The Illinois Valedictorian project. In K. D. Hulbert and D. T. Schuster (Eds.), *Women's lives through time: Educated American women of the twentieth century* (pp. 425–440). San Francisco: Jossey-Bass.

Baruch, G. K., Biener, L., & Barnett, R. C. (1987). Women and gender in research on work and family stress. *American Psychologist, 42*, 130–136.

Bateson, M. C. (1989). *Composing a life.* New York: Plume.

Block, J. (1971). *Lives through time.* Berkeley: Bancroft.

Dresselhaus, M. S. (1992, November 15). Setting Barbie straight is a start. *Davis Enterprise,* p. A-9.

Eccles, J. S. (1985). Why doesn't Jane run? Sex differences in educational and occupational patterns. In F. D. Horowitz & M. O'Brien (Eds.), *The gifted and talented: Developmental perspectives* (pp. 251–295). Washington, DC: American Psychological Association.

Erikson, E. (1950). *Childhood and Society.* New York: Norton.

Fox, L. H. (1977). Sex differences: Implications for program planning for the academically gifted. In J. C. Stanley, W. C. George, & C. H. Solano (Eds.), *The gifted and the creative: A fifty year perspective* (pp. 113–138). Baltimore: Johns Hopkins University Press.

Giele, J. Z. (1982). Women in adulthood: Unanswered questions. In J. Z. Giele (Ed.), *Women in the middle years* (pp. 1–35). New York: Wiley.

Gilligan, C. (1982). Adult development and women's development: Arrangements for a marriage. In J. Z. Giele (Ed.), *Women in the middle years* (pp. 89–114). New York: Wiley.

Gilligan, C., Lyons, N. P., & Hanmer, T. J. (1990). *Making connections.* Cambridge, MA: Harvard University Press.

Ginzberg, E. (1966). *Life styles of educated women.* New York: Columbia University Press.

Ginzberg, E., & Yohalem, A. M. (1966). *Educated American women: Self-portraits.* New York: Columbia University Press.

Gjerde, P. (1993). Depressive symptoms in young adults: A developmental perspective on gender differences. In D. Funder, R. D. Parke, C. Tomlinson-Keasey, & K. Widaman (Eds.), *Studying lives through time: Approaches to personality and development* (pp. 255–288). Washington, DC: American Psychological Association.

Grossman, H. Y., & Chester, N. L. (1990). *The experience and meaning of work in women's lives.* Hillsdale, NJ: Lawrence Erlbaum.

Gustafson, S. R., & Magnusson, D. (1991). *Female life careers: A pattern approach.* Hillsdale, NJ: Lawrence Erlbaum.

Heilbrun, C. (1988). *Writing a woman's life.* New York: Norton.

Hennig, M., & Jardim, A. (1977). *The managerial woman.* Garden City, NY: Anchor.

Hollinger, C. L., & Fleming, E. S. (1984). Internal barriers to the realization of potential: Correlates and interrelationships among gifted and talented female adolescents. *Gifted Child Quarterly, 28,* 135–139.

_____. (1985). Social orientations and the social self-esteem of gifted and talented female adolescents. *Journal of Youth and Adolescence, 14,* 389–399.

_____. (1988). Gifted and talented young women: Antecedents and correlates of life satisfaction. *Gifted Child Quarterly, 32,* 254–259.

Inglehart, M., Brown, D. R., & Malanchuk, O. (1993). University of Michigan medical school graduates of the 1980s: The professional development of women physicians. In K. D. Hulbert & D. T. Schuster (Eds.), *Women's lives through time: Educated American women of the twentieth century* (pp. 374–392). San Francisco: Jossey-Bass.

Kerr, B. A. (1985). *Smart girls, gifted women.* Columbus, OH: Ohio Psychological.

Levinson, D. J. (1978). *Seasons of a man's life.* New York: Knopf.

Locke, E. A., Shaw, K. A., Saari, L. M., & Latham, G. P. (1981). Goal setting and task performance: 1969–1980. *Psychological Bulletin, 90,* 125–152.

Lombroso, C. (1895). *The man of genius.* London: Scribner.

McClelland, D. (1975). *Power: The inner experience.* New York: Irvington.

McGuigan, D. G. (1980). Exploring women's lives: An introduction. In D. G. McGuigan (Ed.), *Women's lives: New theory, research and policy* (pp. i–xii). Ann Arbor: University of Michigan, Center for Continuing Education of Women.

Milwid, M. E. (1982). *Women in male dominated professions: A study of bankers, architects, and lawyers.* Unpublished doctoral dissertation, Wright Institute, Berkeley.

O'Farrell, B., & Harlan, S. L. (1984). Job integration strategies: Today's programs and tomorrow's needs. In B. F. Reskin (Ed.), *Sex segregation in the workplace: Trends, explanations, remedies.* (pp. 267–291). Washington, DC: National Academy Press.

Reskin, B., & Hartmann, H. (1986). *Women's work, Men's work: Sex segregation on the job.* Washington, DC: National Academy Press.

Rivers, C., Barnett, R., & Baruch, G. (1979). *Beyond sugar and spice: How women grow, learn and thrive.* New York: G. P. Putnam.

Rutter, M. (1986). The developmental psychopathology of depression: Issues and perspectives. In M. Rutter, C. Izzard, & P. Read (Eds.), *Depression in young people: Developmental and clinical perspectives* (pp. 3–32). New York: Guilford.

Sanford, L. T., & Donovan, M. E. (1984). *Women & self-esteem.* New York: Doubleday.

Schroeder, P. (1989). Toward a national family policy. *American Psychologist, 44,* 1410–1413.

Sears, P. (1979). The Terman genetic studies of genius. In A. Passow (Ed.), *The seventy-eighth yearbook of the National Society for the Study of Education* (pp. 75–96). Chicago: University of Chicago Press.

Solano, C. H. (1987). Stereotypes of social isolation and early burnout in the gifted: Do they still exist? *Journal of Youth and Adolescence, 16,* 527–539.

Swiatek, M. A., & Benbow, C. P. (1991). Ten year longitudinal follow-up of ability matched accelerated and unaccelerated gifted students. *Journal of Educational Psychology, 83,* 528–538.

Terman, L. M., & Oden, M. H. (1947). *Genetic studies of genius: Vol. 4. The gifted child grows up.* Stanford: Stanford University Press.

_____. (1959). *Genetic studies of genius: Vol. 5. The gifted group at mid-life.* Stanford: Stanford University Press.

Tomlinson-Keasey, C. (1990). The working lives of Terman's gifted women. In H. W. Grossman & N. L. Chester (Eds.), *The experience and meaning of work in women's lives* (pp. 213–240). Hillsdale, NJ: Lawrence Erlbaum.

_____. (in press). Tracing the lives of gifted women. In R. Jenkins-Friedman & F. D. Horowitz (Eds.), *Life-span research on gifted and talented children and youth.* Washington, DC: American Psychological Association.

Vaillant, G. E. (1977). *Adaptation to Life.* Boston: Little, Brown.

PART FIVE

Lives in Contrast: Comparative Case Studies

(Courtesy Radcliffe College Archives.)

17

Difference, Desire, and the Self: Three Stories

ARLENE STEIN

COMING OF AGE at a moment when U.S. society was in a period of great social ferment, when gender and sexual norms were being publicly contested, the women of the baby boom, who reached adolescence and young adulthood during the 1960s and 1970s, found themselves poised between two different accounts of lesbianism. The dominant account conceptualized lesbianism as a medical condition or psychological aberration and constructed the lesbian as an isolated individual divorced from her social context. An emergent account considered lesbianism to be "a lifestyle choice linked with a sense of personal identity, a product of multiple influences rather than traceable to a single cause" (Krieger, 1982).[1]

As part of a project on generational differences in lesbian identification, I collected the life stories of twenty-five women who constructed lesbian identities between the late 1960s and the mid-1970s. In 1991, the year most of the interviews were conducted, the women ranged in age from thirty-three to forty-seven, with an average age of forty-two. I wanted to gain a sense of the relationship between the social category "lesbian" and the variations among women who identified with that category at a particular historical moment when the meaning of lesbianism was highly contested. I also wanted to trace the trajectories of the women's identities over time.

My interviews revealed that lesbian-identified women of the baby boom tended to share a strong belief in the value of claiming a lesbian identity, but that the *meaning* this process had for individuals varied. "Coming out" provided individuals with a "progress narrative" that served to legitimate and order the lesbian experience, but the process of identification was a heterogeneous one.[2]

To some women, becoming a lesbian meant "coming home," reengaging with what they believed to be their authentic self, and acknowledging the desires they had long embraced in secret. It permitted them to adopt a surface identity as a lesbian to match the deep sense of difference they already possessed.[3] To others,

Come out!! poster. *(Photo by Peter Hujar, from the personal collection of Jim Fouratt.)*

coming out meant "discovering" their lesbianism. For these women, desire was often not the primary determinant of a lesbian identification; their deep identification as lesbian was preceded by an identification with lesbianism as a sociosexual category. For still others, women whose sexuality was relatively fluid and inchoate, becoming a lesbian meant solidifying both personal and social identities simultaneously. Illustrating these different meanings, here are the stories of three lesbian-identified women of the baby boom cohort.

Barb Yerba: "Just the Way I Am"

Forty-two-year-old Barb Yerba was born in 1949 to a lower-middle-class Italian family in New York. She thinks of herself as straddling the "old gay" and "new gay" worlds because she had same-sex experiences before the late 1960s when the lesbian/gay movements expanded the social space open to lesbians and gay men: "I was sort of an old lesbian. To be an old lesbian meant you were out before feminism. I wasn't out to anyone but myself. But I knew when I was eight years old. I probably knew much earlier." Barb experienced desires for other girls early in life, acting upon these desires in isolation, often thinking that she was "the only one." She thinks of herself as having been a tomboy. "I never played with dolls and hardly ever played with girls. I wore boys' clothes at age eight or nine." At fifteen, Barb had a first sexual experience with another girl. It was 1962. At the time, she had no words to describe her feelings.

As an adolescent, she was vaguely aware of the existence of other lesbians, though unaware of the existence of an organized subculture. In recent years, she has made a hobby of collecting lesbian pulp novels, the dime-store fiction sold during the 1950s and 1960s, featuring lurid covers and such titles as *Odd Girl Out* and *Strange Sisters*. These tales of lust, intrigue, and secrecy, of being young and confused and a social misfit remind her of her own adolescence, of "being young and out of control, having all these feelings, and having no place to go to talk about them." Being a lesbian, she says, was a "long stream of unfinished business." Like the characters in her pulp novels, she says, she felt a mixture of fear and exhilaration: "I felt the very same kind of dichotomy. On the one hand, I felt at peace with myself emotionally. This is home. There's this quote from *The Price of Salt*. 'Nobody had to tell her that this was the way it was supposed to be.' This is home after all these years. I knew that this was what I wanted, but I knew that it was a really bad thing." She feels that she has always been a lesbian, that it was not at all a matter of choice. To become a lesbian, she simply "discovered" what was already there.

Barb's first girlfriend "turned straight" after a few years. "She repressed all that stuff." But Barb couldn't. "I never had any doubts." In high school, Barb befriended Lore, the first "flesh-and-blood" lesbian she had ever met. One day, Lore looked Barb in the eye and said: "You are a lesbian." At the time, Barb says, she scoffed at the allegation, "but it planted some sort of seed." Yet claiming a lesbian identity in a social sense, beginning to self-identify as a member of a stigmatized group, was not an easy task. She was sent to a psychiatrist, who told her that she had "trouble relating to people" and prescribed tranquilizers for her to take. Through her teens and early twenties, Barb had a series of relationships with women, but never claimed a lesbian identity in a public sense—until a particular incident provided the catalyst for her coming out.

In 1970, while in college, she was living with a girlfriend and several other people in a communal house in upstate New York. One morning, she awoke to hear her roommates discussing whether the presence of Barb and her girlfriend were "warping the household." That was, she said, "the straw that broke the camel's back." Soon after, Barb became involved with a radical lesbian political group. Her first meeting, in 1971, was "like the messiah had come." "There were all these people who were like me. They were all my age. They were lesbians. I quickly realized I was a feminist as well as a lesbian." Becoming a feminist meant that she could begin to think of her lesbianism in positive terms. It also meant that she could think of her femaleness and her lesbianism as compatible, rather than conflicting. It gave her a sense that she could have a social as well as a personal identity as a lesbian. Barb says that she would be a lesbian regardless of these historical changes, but she imagines that she would have been forced to lead a far more secretive, far more unhappy life.

Barb's narrative exhibits many elements of the "dominant" account; she sees her lesbianism as an orientation that was fixed at birth or in early childhood. Adolescent girls vary in the extent to which they know their desires. Some are not at all aware of sexual feelings, heterosexual or homosexual, whereas others, like Barb, are deeply conscious of them.[4] Writing of her experiences as a therapist, Tolman (1991) noted that girls who are aware of their sexual feelings early on often experience their adolescence as a period in which their embodied sexual desire is simultaneously elicted and denigrated by the dominant culture. One can imagine that lesbian desires typically find no reflection in either the dominant culture or within adolescent peer groups (Zemsky, 1991). Indeed, as we have seen, Barb experienced herself as virtually alone in her desires, having no one to discuss them with. She talked about "knowing" she was a lesbian very early on, by age eight, even before she had words to describe her feelings.[5]

Barb identified her desires for girls and women at a relatively early age and felt these desires to be powerful and unwavering. When I asked Barb why she is a lesbian, she replied, "it's just the way I am." Indeed, she found the question itself rather curious. Barb sees her adolescent experiences of difference and her eventual homosexuality on a continuum. Her personal identity as lesbian, she says, was never really in question. As she grew older and began to affiliate with the lesbian community, these connections gave her a social identity as well, a sense of direction and purpose that went beyond the self and a way to counter some of the stigma in the dominant culture. She spoke of the important role that the lesbian community played in allowing her to normalize her sexuality.

But the fact that she experienced her lesbian desires early in life has played a formative role in shaping her sense of self and the meaning her lesbianism holds for her. Indeed, her identity account resembles the "old gay" account, insofar as the experience of secrecy and stigma looms large for those who spent their formative years "managing" their stigma, carefully determining which parts of the self they would reveal to others. (Recall Barb's comments that she felt like an "old gay" woman because she had lived much of her adult life in the closet.)

Because of these experiences, like women of an earlier cohort, Barb tended to accentuate the differences between herself and heterosexual women, viewing lesbians and heterosexuals as two distinct categories. She thinks of lesbianism in essentialist terms and believes that the only "real" lesbians are "born" lesbians— women like her who have little choice in the matter of their sexuality.

Margaret Berg:
"Coming Out Through Feminism"

Margaret Berg had always thought of lesbianism as something that was involuntary; it was an orientation that one either did or did not "have." But when she was in her early twenties, she became aware of the possibility of constructing her own sexuality and electing lesbianism. As Margaret describes her history, she was one of those women who "came out through feminism."

She grew up in Brooklyn, New York, a red diaper baby, the daughter of Jewish leftist activists. To be a woman in the 1950s and 1960s, even a middle-class white woman, she said, was to grow up with the profound sense of oneself as a second-class citizen. Margaret spoke of the fact that she had to feign underachievement in school in order to catch a husband. She said that she experienced her heterosexual relationships as largely unsatisfying. "I had all the feelings about men that we all had—we thought they were like zombies. I felt that I took care of all the men I was involved with. I felt like I was much stronger than they were. I felt like I gave much more than I got." She recalls, "we were growing up in a world that was so invalidating of women. I straightened my hair, I was ambivalent about being smart, my physics teacher told my parents: she's doing fine for a girl."[6]

The women's movement emerged in the late 1960s to structure this alienation and to situate it in the context of women's oppression. Margaret compares her exposure to feminism in 1969 to coming out of a cave. Feminism, she said, was "the most exciting and validating thing that had happened in our lives." It allowed her and others to resolve the dissonance they felt between cultural codes and subjective experience (Ginsburg, 1989). Within the context of the movement Margaret developed an analysis and vocabulary for these feelings and began to see her problems in gendered terms for the first time. She began to believe that she had devalued herself as a woman and underestimated the importance of her female relationships.

Because of their growing idealization of other women, made possible by feminism, women like Margaret withdrew from primary relationships with men. This was less a conscious decision than the product of the growing separation between men's and women's social and political worlds, at least among the young, predominantly middle-class members of what was loosely called the "movement." At the time, she was romantically involved with a man, but as her women friends became more and more central, he became more peripheral. With time, she recalls "most of my friends were women, all of my friends were feminists, men were not part of my life. It was all very seamless."

When Margaret became involved in her first lesbian relationship, she said, "the only gay women I knew (and *we* wouldn't call ourselves gay) were my friend and myself." Margaret met a woman, Jennifer, who eventually moved into her apartment. The world they traveled in was that of liberated sexuality and free use of drugs. There was, she says, "a real sense of barriers breaking." She was drawn to Jennifer as a kindred spirit, an equal. "There was a certain reflection of myself I found in her." Margaret recalls that Jennifer had "much more self-consciously identified homoerotic feelings," whereas hers were more about sexual experimentation and rebellion.

In an effort to try to make sense of her feelings and to find support for them, Margaret began to attend a women's consciousness-raising group devoted to discussing questions of sexuality. Practically overnight, through the influence of gay liberation and lesbian feminism, Margaret's feminist consciousness-raising group transformed itself into a coming out group. In that group, Margaret was socialized into the lesbian world. She began to think of herself as a lesbian and call herself one. "There was a normative sense about discovering women and male domination and how disgusting men could be. Not to be a lesbian was stupid, masochistic."

> Something called "lesbian consciousness" developed in our heads. It's hard to reconstruct just how the process occurred. We talked about "coming out" every four or five weeks. That term started having more and more ramifications as our lives changed. Not just making love with a woman for the first time—but every new situation where you experienced and/or revealed yourself as gay …

Within the context of a coming out group, Margaret carved out a place for herself within the lesbian subculture. Earlier, coming out had referred almost exclusively to the process of disclosure. But now women who had never experienced themselves as deeply and irrevocably different, but who shared a sense of alienation from gender and sexual norms could also claim lesbian identities by developing "gay consciousness." In the discourse of lesbian feminism, feminism and lesbianism were conflated. Lesbianism was revisioned to signify not simply a sexual preference, but a way for women to gain strength and confidence, to bond with other women.

But the political strategy of coming out to others as a means of establishing unity often had the contradictory effect of making differences *among* women more apparent, and the tension between identity and difference within the coming out group soon became apparent. Margaret describes the "experiential gap" separating women who were "entering a first gay relationship" and those who were "coming out of the closet" in her coming out group.

> One woman was quite involved with a man and left almost immediately—it was never clear exactly why she had joined the group, except that she felt good about women. Another woman pulled out because she felt there was a "bisexual" orientation to the group. … Her "coming out" was very different from the rest of ours. She wasn't entering a first gay relationship; rather, she was coming out of "the closet," entering a gay community and acquiring pride in an analysis of who she is. … There was a real experiential gap between her and the rest of the group. We had no understanding of the bar scene, of role-playing, of the whole range of experience of an "old

gay." I'm sure a lot of this inexperience translated into moralistic arrogance—we were a good deal less than understanding when she called her lovers "girls."

Here we see a clash of cultures and two different visions of lesbianism: the old dyke world, which valorized gender roles, and the emergent lesbian feminist culture, which rejected gendered coupledom in favor of the communalized sensuality of the group circle dance.

> We all went to our first gay women's dance together. I was very scared by a number of older women dressed sort of mannishly. Not scared that they'd do anything to me, but wary of being identified with them. I was very relieved when a group of women … showed up and we all danced together in a big friendly circle. That was my first exposure to a kind of joyful sensuality that I've come to associate with women's dances. Looking around and seeing a lot of gay women enjoying themselves and each other helped me let go of a lot of my fears and validated the possibilities for growth and pleasure in the relationship with J.

The old gay world conceptualized lesbianism as desire; the new gay world reconceptualized it more diffusely as woman identification. Margaret sees the differences primarily in generational terms, evidencing the extent to which other distinctions may have been less salient at the time. For younger women, becoming a lesbian was a matter of developing "lesbian consciousness," developing a personal sense of self as lesbian. For these women, *becoming* a lesbian, developing a personal identity as a lesbian, was not really in question, but *living* as one, developing a social identity, was. But these differences were not solely intergenerational; they also divided women of the baby boom cohort.

Margaret grappled with figuring out her place in the lesbian world. Coming out, she acknowledges, is "an incredibly hard process." She alludes to the conflict between the dominant essentialist model and an emergent constructionist one.

> Coming out is an incredibly hard process; many women think there's some magic leap into gayness—that you suddenly lose all fears, doubts, heterosexual feelings. Others are afraid that they weren't "born gay." Come-out groups help women deal with all of those feelings. The existence of the Lesbian Mothers' Group brought home to us that women are not born lesbians; that women who were both wives and mothers could decide to live with and love other women.

After feeling some doubts about whether or not she herself was "really" a lesbian, Margaret concluded that even seemingly gender-normative women—wives and mothers—can be lesbians.

Her story suggests that some women used the discourse of coming out to claim authenticity and gain membership in the lesbian world. Clearly, this was a very different path to lesbianism from that taken by women whose personal sense of self as lesbian was not really in question, for whom coming out meant coming out of the "closet." If women such as Barb thought of their lesbianism primarily as internally driven, for Margaret and other "elective" lesbians, the adoption of lesbianism as a social identity often preceded the consolidation of lesbianism as a personal identity. Unlike Barb, Margaret did not trace her lesbianism to early childhood experiences or have the experience of being "not heterosexual" early on—even if she expressed alienation from heterosexual gender norms. She reported that her sexual interest in men was often conflicted, motivated more by accommodation to male needs and social expectations than by her own desires.

Margaret also differs from Barb in her high degree of self-reflexivity, rooted at least in part in her more middle-class background. In general, she framed her lesbianism as the development of "lesbian consciousness"—a political rather than a sexual choice to be involved with women rather than men.[7] Because of her history, Margaret holds the belief that any woman can choose to be a lesbian. However, she recognizes that there are different "types" of lesbians, women with greater and lesser degrees of choice.

Joan Salton: "It's an Emotional Thing"

Forty-six-year-old Joan Salton grew up in the Midwest, the daughter of school teachers. She describes herself as a tomboy as a child. "I was always interested in the things that boys did, not really interested in playing with dolls, the whole works." She remembers herself as a "horny kid" who was interested in sexual experimentation and had sexual experiences with boys at an early age. She became sexually active with boys at age sixteen and with girls at eighteen.

Like many girls her age, she gained her early knowledge of lesbianism from pulp novels and from the literature of psychopathology. She remembers the images she found in books in the library.

> I suppose the people they talked about in those books were much less weird than the descriptions made them out to be. They were really distorted, looking at things under the microscope without any perception of what the person under the lenses was feeling. I didn't relate to that stuff, but I knew all of the words—dyke, lesbian—and I knew it meant me.

Early on, Margaret had what she describes as "better" sex with men than with women. But with women, she says, she felt a "depth of emotion" that she "couldn't feel with men." When she reached her early twenties she began to call herself a lesbian, even as she continued to have affairs with men, though she did not consider them to be "serious." Becoming involved with men, she said, was "sexually possible but emotionally not": "There are some people for whom being a lesbian means something real different. For me it is a passionate lust for women, emotional intensity I feel only with women." Still, along the line, Joan acknowledges, she made certain choices. "I dumped a guy who really loved me and who I had great sex with, and ... for a long time afterwards, I sort of regretted it, because after that I had a really hard time finding a woman with whom I had such good sex. But I knew that I couldn't love him. I didn't feel anything for him emotionally." With time, her fragile sense of lesbianism became more solidified, and she came to have little interest in heterosexuality. This coincided, not coincidentally, with the rise of the gay liberation movement, in which she became public as a lesbian, first as an early gay liberation activist, then as a lesbian feminist.

She recalls that "it was a time of great social ferment. There was a tremendous amount of feeling behind it. It was a time of connecting a lot of ideas with a lot of feelings." It was about affirming identities that were despised by members of the dominant culture and throwing them back in their faces. For Joan, lesbianism was always at least in part about the rejection of social norms—both inside and outside of the lesbian subculture. "There's a part of me that always wants to throw things in for shock value and stir them up a bit." She was a renegade of sorts, even within the movement; once she had an affair with a gay man, another gay liberation activist. Her rejection of the norms of the movement was motivated at least in part by a recognition of the partiality of sexual identifications. Joan was always very conscious of the fact that her own desires do not conform neatly with binary sexual categories, homosexual and heterosexual.

When asked whether her lesbianism is a choice, Joan replied, "yes," adding, "but I'm not straight." Joan feels that her lesbianism is a choice insofar as she could choose to deny what she "really" felt. She could choose to be with men if she wished to fit in, but she has made a choice that fitting in is less important that being "who she is."

> What's choice? Is choice what makes you happy? No, I am not a born lesbian. I know I was able to have okay relationships with men, and good sex with men. I also know that nothing compares to being with a woman, emotionally or sexually. So is it a choice? I don't know. …Maybe for me [lesbianism] was eighty percent internal compulsion in a certain direction, and twenty percent choice, and maybe for other people it is half and half or something.

She is not a lesbian like other women are lesbians, insofar as she was not "born" one, she says. Yet she sees herself as more sexually driven to women than many women who call themselves lesbians, particularly many who came out in the context of feminism. Indeed, she was involved with "one of those women" through the 1970s and was sexually dissatisfied for a long time. Whereas lesbianism was for Joan about passionate sexuality, for her girlfriend, she said, it was about bonding with other women. "It was about making a domestic relationship, making a life together where neither person dominated the other. It was about having a more equal relationship at home where one could be comfortable and not feel squashed by the other person."

As we saw earlier, Barb described her personal identity as lesbian as preceding her affiliation with lesbianism as a social category, whereas Margaret said the opposite: Her affiliation with the lesbian category preceded her consolidation of a sense of "deep" identity. For Joan, separating out the personal and social aspects of lesbian identification and isolating which "came first" is impossible. She talked about her lesbianism in terms of elements that were chosen and elements that were not, and she remained conscious of a disjunction between "doing" and "being," between engaging in homosexual acts and claiming a homosexual identity.

Joan's lesbianism is a choice insofar as acting upon her desires and claiming a lesbian identity are chosen, since originally she experienced her desires as being at least partly fluid and changing. But at the same time, she is cognizant of the fact that her adoption of a social identity as a lesbian "organized" these desires, diminishing her earlier bisexual inclinations. She began the process of identity formation with a sense of sexual difference that was relatively inchoate, embracing a lesbian identity with some uncertainty, seeing it as a strategic act rather than as a firm expression of who she "is."

Making Sense of Accounts

Barb, Margaret, and Joan each represent an alternative account of lesbian identity. Although certainly not an exhaustive sample of different ways of "being" lesbian, their stories illustrate how lesbian identification presented a solution, a symbolic resolution of a problem each woman faced at a particular historical moment.

For Barb, becoming a lesbian meant that she could affiliate with the social category lesbian, disclose that affiliation to others, and build a social world around the desires she had for so long kept private. For Margaret, becoming a lesbian was largely a matter of developing a personal sense of self as lesbian to match her affiliation with lesbianism as a social category. She did not have a closet—a subjective sense of herself as highly deviant—to overcome; she was not highly driven toward women in a sexual sense. Finally, Joan combined elements of both Barb's and Margaret's stories. Like Barb, she began the process of identity formation with a sense of sexual difference, but she differed from Barb in that her sense of difference was initially relatively inchoate and unformed. She recognized homosexual desires relatively early, but these coexisted with heterosexual desires. Joan saw her embrace of the social category lesbian as a strategic act, motivated at least in part by her deeply felt desires for other women, rather than as a firm expression of who she "is."

Through interaction with other self-identified lesbians and by gaining access to different accounts, women formed a sense of personal and social identity. These accounts were derived from the dominant culture and from lesbian/gay subcultures. A woman coming of age in the late 1960s and early 1970s had access to a wider array of different accounts and ways of being a lesbian than women from earlier cohorts, when sexual knowledge came almost exclusively from the medical discourse. However, this does not imply that all individuals had an open-ended ability to reconstruct themselves as they pleased (Vance, 1992). Indeed, each woman brought to the coming out process a sense of self that was already partially formed.

Individuals' early experiences of difference or similarity in relation to the dominant heterosexual culture figured prominently in their narratives. Their feelings of difference were often related to the age at which they became conscious of their desires for other girls and women.[8] The early-developing lesbian, such as Barb, seemed to incorporate a greater sense of "differentness" within her sense of self.

Margaret and other later-developing lesbians were often very conscious of this difference, whether or not they named it as such.[9] They were also conscious of how they differed from women who had come out before feminism and gay liberation. "Old dykes," particularly those who were very visibly butch, symbolized for them what they might become if they shunned heterosexuality, but they also embodied a kind of protofeminism, a willingness to go against the social grain.

Coming out can thus be conceptualized as two distinct but overlapping processes: the development of a personal identity as lesbian, or *individuation;* and the development of a social identity as lesbian, or *disclosure* (Davies, 1992). Most interpretations of the period in question focus on the process of disclosure, assuming that the person is fully individuated before disclosure occurs. But for many women, as I have shown, the process of individuation follows disclosure. For others, individuation and disclosure occur simultaneously, each influencing the other.

What these life stories reveal, to quote Jay and Glasgow (1990), is that "the word lesbian is not an identity with predictable content ... it is a position from which to speak" (p. 6). Individuals bring to the process of sexual identity formation a sense of self that is at least partly formed, and they use the available accounts, or repertoires of meaning, to make sense of this self. These images, or accounts, are themselves historical constructions. As women construct their identities, they study those around them, selecting images to emulate or reject, fitting themselves into the lesbian world(s).

Notes

1. Plummer (1981) called the first account the "orientation" model and the second the "identity construct" model; they are also referred to, respectively, as essentialist and constructionist conceptions of homosexuality. Faderman (1991) wrote that lesbians of this generation were divided between the "essential" and "existential" varieties, glossing over the complex ways in which individuals utilize elements of both accounts that I hope to show.

2. So pervasive among women of this age group was this narrative structure that when I started out an interview by asking individual women how they would describe their sexual identity, most responded by launching into their "coming out" story, which typically began with early childhood, and moved chronologically through time to the present. On the confessional mode of sexual narratives, see Plummer (in press); on progress narratives in lesbian feminist literature, see Zimmerman (1990).

3. I have adapted the concepts of "surface" and "deep" identities from Arlie Hochschild's (1983) work on emotional labor.

4. There may be some correlation between lesbian identity and gender identity insofar as "butch" or more masculine-identified lesbians were less likely to see their sexual identities as being elective than feminine-identified women. But the reasons for this are unclear. Is it because "mannish" lesbians were more "essentially" lesbian in orientation? Or is it because butches were the most identifiable lesbian figure since they stood out, often from an early age, and were more apt to be labeled lesbian by family members and other authority figures? For whichever reason, or combination of reasons, gender inversion is a symbolic

marker of lesbianism and a warning to women who step out of their prescribed roles that the taint of lesbianism will follow them.

5. Zemsky (1991) cited studies that indicate that the mean age for women to recognize and pronounce (at least to themselves) that this sense of difference and disquiet has something to do with lesbianism is approximately fourteen.

6. For a sense of how dominant cultural norms shaped the lives of teenage girls in the 1950s and how girls resisted these norms, see Breines (1992).

7. However, Rich (1980) and Kitzinger (1987) questioned whether lesbianism can ever really be a free "choice" or individual sexual "preference" under a system of compulsory or normative heterosexuality.

8. This would seem to imply the necessity of "bringing the body back in," acknowledging that bodily sensation and function play a role, albeit one that is always mediated by culture and subjectivity (Vance, 1992). In this sense, I depart from the tradition of interactionist studies exemplified by Ponse (1978) in which the importance of physical experience is downplayed.

9. See, for example, Burch (1993).

References

Breines, Wini. 1992. *Young, White and Miserable: Growing Up Female in the 1950s*. Boston: Beacon.

Burch, Beverly. 1993. *On Intimate Terms*. Urbana: University of Illinois Press.

Davies, Peter. 1992. "The Role of Disclosure in Coming Out Among Gay Men," in Ken Plummer, ed., *Modern Homosexualities: Fragments of Lesbian and Gay Experience* (pp. 75–83). London & New York: Routledge.

Faderman, Lillian. 1991. *Odd Girls and Twilight Lovers: A History of Lesbian Life in Twentieth Century America*. New York: Columbia University Press.

Ginsburg, Faye. 1989. "Dissonance and Harmony: The Symbolic Function of Abortion in Activists' Life Stories," in Personal Narratives Group, ed., *Interpreting Women's Lives* (pp. 59–84). Bloomington: Indiana University Press.

Hochschild, Arlie. 1983. *The Managed Heart: Commercialization of Human Feeling*. Berkeley: University of California Press.

Jay, Karla, and Joanne Glasgow. 1990. *Lesbian Texts and Contexts: Radical Revisions*. New York: New York University Press.

Kitzinger, C. 1987. *The social construction of lesbianism*. Newbury Park, CA: Sage.

Krieger, Susan. 1982. "Lesbian Identity and Community: Recent Social Science Literature," *Signs, 8*, 91–108.

Newton, Esther. 1984. "The Mythic Mannish Lesbian: Radclyffe Hall and the New Woman," *Signs, 9*, 557–575.

Plummer, Ken. 1981. "Homosexual Categories," in Ken Plummer, ed., *The Making of the Modern Homosexual* (pp. 53–75). Totowa, NJ: Barnes and Noble.

————. in press. *Telling Sexual Stories in a Late Modern World*. New York: Routledge.

Ponse, Barbara. 1978. *Identities in the Lesbian World: The Social Construction of Self*. Westport, CT: Greenwood.

Rich, A. 1980. "Compulsory Heterosexuality and Lesbian Existence," *Signs, 5*, 631–660.

Stein, Arlene. 1989. "Three Models of Sexuality: Drives, Identities and Practices," *Sociological Theory, 7*, 1–13.

Tolman, Deborah L. 1991. "Adolescent Girls, Women and Sexuality: Discerning Dilemmas of Desire," in Carol Gilligan, Annie Rogers, and Deborah L. Tolman, eds., *Women and Therapy,* Vol. 11, Nos. 3/4, 55–70.

Vance, Carole. 1992. "Social Construction Theory: Problems in the History of Sexuality," in Helen Crowley and Susan Himmelweit, eds., *Knowing Women: Feminism and Knowledge.* London: Polity.

Zemsky, Beth. 1991. "Coming Out Against All Odds: Resistance of a Young Lesbian," in Carol Gilligan, Annie Rogers, and Deborah L. Tolman, eds., *Women and Therapy,* Vol. 11, Nos. 3/4, 185–200.

Zimmerman, Bonnie. 1990. *The Safe Sea of Women.* Boston: Beacon.

18

Personal Choices
in Political Climates:
Coping with Legal and
Illegal Abortion

SHARON GOLD-STEINBERG

I didn't get completely undressed; there were tools inserted into my vagina. I was in pain immediately. It took about fifteen minutes. And I was blindfolded again (while in labor), taken by car to meet my boyfriend who was waiting in a nearby motel— where I had extreme cramps for about twelve hours. Then I expelled the fetus in a toilet. I never stopped bleeding.

—Marissa, illegal abortion in 1962

I changed clothes, was taken into the operating room, given a general anesthetic. ... Woke up in recovery room with nurse in attendance. After a while I dressed and went home.

—Janette, legal abortion in 1971

THE DECISION to have an induced abortion is a personal one, but the actual experience of the abortion is very much shaped by social factors. Laws and institutional policies, the availability of emotional support, and the meanings that individuals and their communities attach to the procedure all affect what is involved in women's coping with abortion. The two accounts in the epigraph illustrate how different legal and illegal abortion can be. Marissa described a tale of violation; Janette elaborated the steps of a medical event. The stories of two other women, Nancy, who had an illegal abortion in 1963, and Carol, who legally terminated a pregnancy in 1976, will be described more fully in this chapter. A comparison of their experiences helps to capture the significance of the social context in defining the tasks of coping with abortion.

I had the opportunity to meet Nancy and Carol while completing my doctoral dissertation on women's coping with legal and illegal abortion. As part of this study, I asked seventy-two women who had had either a legal or a "back alley" abortion between 1962 and 1978 to complete an extensive questionnaire about their experience. The survey contained many forced choice answers, but also asked for narrative accounts of the women's abortion experience and their thoughts on a number of pertinent issues. Finally, I interviewed several women (including Nancy and Carol) in more depth about the context of their life in which this event occurred. Each category of data proved to be an important source of information about how the social or political climate influenced women's coping with the personal choice to end a pregnancy. A brief review of the findings from the questionnaire data—which included a content analysis of the women's narrative accounts of their abortion experience—provides a useful context for appreciating Nancy and Carol's stories.

Quantitative data from the survey clarified ways in which women's experiences of legal and illegal abortion did and did not differ. A "group portrait" emerged from this analysis. Women who had an illegal abortion, on average, experienced higher risks for medical and emotional complications than women in the sample who had a legal abortion. In addition, more women from the first group sought psychotherapy to help them cope with their abortion experience. Women who had had an illegal abortion remembered being more anxious both before and after their procedure and acknowledged greater continuing anger about their experience. Women who had an illegal abortion did not recount feeling any more ashamed or guilty about their decision than did women who had a legal abortion. Regardless of the legal status of their abortion, women in the sample generally felt politicized by their experience. Most reflect back periodically on their decision to terminate a pregnancy, but usually without regret. Most felt that their abortion secured important opportunities for them in educational, career, or personal growth.

Content analysis of the women's narrative accounts of their abortion experience yielded significant findings about the quality of the women's memories of this event in their life. In general, the women's stories were vivid, regardless of whether the abortion they had was legal or illegal. Most of the women recounted their experiences with much detail. They remembered and described sounds, smells, the quality of pain, and the words others spoke to them on the day of the procedure. One woman recalled eating doughnuts afterward, others described the noise of the machinery or the feel of someone holding her hand as a gesture of support.

Although the stories of women from both groups did not differ in vividness, the imagery and language contained in the accounts diverged. For instance, women who wrote about an illegal abortion more often used graphic language (e.g., named reproductive organs or described bodily processes such as bleeding or vomiting) than women who described a legal abortion. In addition, the illegal abortion stories more often described an act of penetration (as in Marissa's story), though some kind of instrument must have been inserted vaginally regardless of the legality or illegality of the procedure. Women who had an illegal abortion also referred more often to a recalled command or perceived need to maintain secrecy or silence about their operation. There was an additional trend for women who had an illegal abortion to use passive language to describe being told to undress or lie on a surface for the procedure rather than to use active verb constructions to emphasize their choice to undress or to put their feet in stirrups.

Alyssa's recounting of her illegal abortion in 1966 includes many of the kinds of details common in the illegal abortion stories:

> I got into the room and he had me take my pants off and put on a gown. He explained what he was going to do. I laid on the bed while he did whatever it was. It really hurt [cramping] and I was crying. He told me to be quiet so no one would hear me. After he was done, I got up and left. I could hardly walk because it hurt so much.

Compare the tone of this story to that of Lucia, who had a legal abortion in New York State in 1970:

> Nothing unexpected occurred. I remember being counseled as to options, being examined, and being informed as to the procedure itself and what to expect in the weeks following it. It was not as painful as I perhaps anticipated and I had no complications. I do remember being somewhat surprised that only a local anesthetic was administered. The major difficulty I encountered was getting an out-of-state prescription filled when I returned to college.

Although Lucia anticipated and encountered some difficulties, a feeling of relief is also communicated by her story: "It was not as painful as I perhaps anticipated and I had no complications." In contrast, Alyssa's story conveys a stronger tone of pain and fear. Content analysis of the narratives in fact revealed that although women in the two groups included a similar number of words indicating tension or discomfort, the women who had an illegal abortion used fewer words suggestive of relief. It seemed the discomfort of the women who had a legal abortion was at least partially offset by relief, whereas the tension felt by the women who had an illegal abortion was less mitigated by relief.

Overall, the analysis of the stories revealed that women's abortion experiences were memorable and poignant (as suggested by their vividness) regardless of their legal status. Women could recount experiences fifteen to twenty-five years in the past and provide compelling, precise, and often visceral detail. However, the tone of these vivid memories differed markedly. Legal abortion stories conveyed a sense of remembering a significant medical procedure, perhaps resembling memories of other surgeries or reproductive events. In contrast, the illegal abortion stories read more like tales of anticipated exploitation.

A Case Study Approach

The questionnaire responses and written narrative accounts provided much rich data, but I was eager to talk with women in more depth about their experiences. I viewed the interviews as an opportunity to learn more about the challenges and struggles of women's lives that are not always well documented. I also saw it as a chance to ask participants about their understanding of dynamics and issues that were intriguing or puzzling in the questionnaire data. Finally, the interviews allowed me to appreciate individual women's choices in the context of their own life histories. I conducted interviews with seven women and recount the stories here of Nancy and Carol. Both were college students when they learned they were pregnant, one before and one after the legalization of abortion.

Nancy

When I met Nancy, she was in her late forties. She was married and had two daughters, one of whom was adopted. She owned a successful and creative business near Chicago. Nancy seemed both nervous and eager to talk with me about her abortion experience. She requested we meet and talk in a diner. During the interview, she appeared to struggle with ambivalence about how much she wanted to remember and feel about these past memories. She looked to me to help her gain insight into this past event, but at the same time was guarded about letting me interfere with the construction of these memories she had held on to for more than twenty-five years.

Nancy's story is illustrative in the anxiety she recalled about finding someone to perform an illegal abortion in 1963 and the many worries she harbored about what could happen to her in the process. In addition, she offered important insights about the kind of social support her friends were or were not able to offer her.

Nancy was nineteen years old in 1963. She was a senior at a Midwestern university when she found out she was nearly three months pregnant. An earlier pregnancy test had yielded a false negative result, confronting her with what she understatedly termed "a time crunch." She flew to New York where her boyfriend lived, and they began searching for someone to perform an abortion before the end of her first trimester. However, her first weekend trip to the east coast was unsuccessful. Nancy's family physician was unwilling to provide a referral and instead informed Nancy's parents, against her will, of her condition. Nancy felt betrayed and outraged, but focused on her search. After going door to door in a certain neighborhood in Trenton, New Jersey, Nancy and her boyfriend went to Manhattan. They had heard of a transient hotel where a man performed abortions. Nancy recalls:

> We went up to the room, they asked me to pass them the money and my boyfriend wanted to see the place, and they wouldn't let him in. And they let me in and it just, it looked dreary. It looked really really dirty. It was just like a dirty table in the middle.

... I mean but this was real seedy and the fact that they wouldn't let him in. ... He just almost broke down the door and dragged me out of there. That was very scary.

Nancy had confronted the fear she could die if this person had been allowed to operate on her. Luckily, Nancy had the benefit of her boyfriend's support to leave a potentially dangerous situation. However, the weekend was over and she needed to return to college.

Nancy's network of friends at college had knowledge of two reputable people who performed abortions on occasion in the the Midwest and in Pennsylvania. They knew of another Midwestern doctor with a reputation of being cruel and who did not use anesthesia. Nancy said she "stayed around with a crowd of sexually active people, or people [who] were very supportive." Even so, she was unable to arrange an abortion near where she was living, so she returned to New York the following weekend. Her boyfriend had found a private physician who would do the procedure in his office. Nancy elaborated:

> It was weird. I don't think that we had all the money. It was $500, and I think that we maybe had $200 or $100 with us. He went in and he examined me and he dilated me. And he said he would finish it when I came back with the money. And it was painful. That, I mean the dilating, was very, very painful. And I came back the next day with the money and he gave me anesthesia ... and gave me antibiotics, and I remember that. And I had no adverse effects. He was ... arrested later on. Years later. I guess somebody had died and then they turned him in or something like that.

This news confronted Nancy again with the recognition that she could have died in an attempt to end her pregnancy.

Nancy had returned to college on a thirty-nine-dollar U.S. mail flight and was picked up at a small airport by supportive friends in a borrowed car. The support of friends who helped her get to the East Coast and the caring of her boyfriend enabled her to obtain an abortion and to feel she was not alone. Nancy made clear that there was a limitation on the kind of support she could receive at that time, however. Although her mother was somewhat sympathetic (and told Nancy stories about her grandmother having had abortions), she was not a "useful" resource at that time because she had no connections to people who performed abortions.

The time pressure and the focus on finding an abortion quickly circumvented Nancy's being able to reflect on her decision and its emotional meaning to her. She knew she was ambivalent. Pregnancy had been reassuring in a way: She now knew she could get pregnant despite her mother's difficulties in conceiving. The prospect of a baby to love was compelling. Despite her mixed feelings, Nancy claims it was not a difficult decision: "At least in my experience it wasn't such a difficult decision because I really never felt that I had any options. At the time, for my own survival, I had to do that." Elsewhere, she added, "the program [of my life] was not one that was going to allow me to stop college." In addition, she was aware that single parenthood was not a socially accepted choice at that time. In her interview, Nancy advocated for options counseling for women considering abortion:

> And I also believe real strongly, one thing that I never had, and I don't know if it would have helped, but it is counseling, in such a way maybe, maybe there ought to be somebody at the door before that person is sent home to force her to cry. To force her to breathe, to force her to experience the moment, the trauma that has happened and then let her get on with her life. I mean to really just, you know, have it be real supportive. Because I don't think it's a light thing.

She went on to say:

> I want people to have the time and the atmosphere where they can really just explore alternatives and come to the conclusion that this is best for them. ... Without thinking oh, it's illegal, it's dangerous, ... where am I going to get the money, all those other considerations which are totally diverting from ... [what's going on inside].

Although Nancy recognized that in some sense it was adaptive for her to set her feelings aside at the moment to expedite the actions she wanted to take, she explained there is a legacy now of sadness—a sadness that might have been resolved more easily had she been able to experience her emotions as the event was happening. She concluded, "it's really sad to have an abortion, really, really, sad."

Nancy noted that her sadness, in part, is also a retrospective one. There were losses involved in Nancy's decision to abort her first pregnancy and she later experienced pregnancy losses at a time when she did want to conceive. After giving birth to one child, she experienced a miscarriage and an ectopic pregnancy. She subsequently adopted a second child. Nancy was fortunate that she did not experience immediate medical or psychological complications. However, she does wonder if her abortion experience contributed somehow to her later fertility difficulties.

It is for the sake of her daughters now that Nancy is a prochoice activist. She has concluded that her decision to abort in the past was a highly personal one; her commitment now is a political one. Nancy's political beliefs and emotions are closely intertwined, both about abortion and about her general political outlook. Although Nancy was sad about her own abortion, she was angered by the idea that her daughters might have to deal with illegal abortion someday. Nancy wanted to assure that her daughters and women of their generation will not have to confront the obstacles and suffering she did in finding an abortion. Near the end of the interview, she insisted, "You just can't permit abortion not to be legal, you just can't. And in the event that that happened, I would absolutely be part of any kind of movement for an underground and for setting it up."

For Nancy, the legacy of illegal abortion was one of unresolved grief. Although she had a strong support network of people who offered financial resources and some access to information, the time crunch for obtaining her abortion obscured her ability to attend to the emotional consequences of her decision. Her adamant prochoice stance in the present reflects not only her sadness, but her anger as well.

Carol

Carol was thirty years old when we met. She was working in a women's health center and brought much spunk and incisiveness to her work there as a nursing aide and as an activist. She was open in our discussions and offered information not only about her abortion experience but also about the insights she had gleaned about the politics of women's health issues from her work experience.

Carol's story provides a useful comparison with Nancy's account. Both women were college students at the time of their abortion. Both felt they made the only choice they could—and without the benefit of their family's support. Carol, like Nancy, experienced some humiliation in the process of seeking an abortion even though abortion was legal in 1976. For both women, having an abortion became a formative experience in terms of their political commitments.

Yet Nancy and Carol emphasized different themes in their interviews. Nancy's story revolved very much around the difficulties of obtaining an abortion and the fears of what would happen to her in the process. In contrast, Carol's story focused more on the emotional meanings of the decision to her and the feelings brought up by each aspect of the experience. Although these differences in emphasis certainly reflect something about the personalities and life experiences of these two women, they also help to illustrate how the legality or illegality of abortion structured what issues they had to, or had the luxury to, confront.

Carol was seventeen years old and in her first semester of college when she discovered she was pregnant:

> I realized that I had missed my period, and I had begun having morning sickness, nausea and light headedness. I didn't tell anyone. I was scared and panicky. I went to an OB/GYN for a pregnancy test and a pelvic exam. My OB/GYN was about seven and a half months pregnant at the time. When she said that I was about "eight weeks along," I felt embarrassed and guilty. She asked me if I was okay and I said yes. I asked her about abortion and she said that she didn't do abortions but gave me the phone number of a crisis center that could give me referrals. When I left, I went into the bathroom and cried.

It is important to understand Carol's life circumstances at the time she became pregnant. Carol had applied to and attended college against the will of her father and stepmother (her mother had died when Carol was ten years old). Carol was the first person in her family to go to college and had worked from the age of fourteen to save money for college. In addition, her grandmother gave her money for books. She became pregnant as a result of her first sexual relationship, with a man who was involved in a long-term relationship with another woman. Like Nancy, she felt that abortion was a choice for her own survival. For Carol, choosing abortion preserved her independence:

> My life would be completely different had I been forced to continue the pregnancy. I came from a very dysfunctional family. If I had been forced to continue the pregnancy, it would have been almost impossible for me to get out of and away from them. Being able to have a safe, legal abortion may have saved *my* life. I had the

chance to find people to help me work out the hurts I had incurred from years of emotional, physical, and sexual abuse. Had I continued the pregnancy I think that my chances of healing myself would have been small, I may have continued the cycle with a child that I was forced to give birth to. Choosing abortion was the first step out of the cycle.

As well as wanting to separate from her family, Carol opted for abortion because she felt ill prepared to care for a child. She explained, "I could barely take care of myself and I had no idea about how to take care of a baby. I mean I tried to help raise my sisters when my mom died. And when you're a kid you don't know how to do that. I just felt I wouldn't know to do it."

It was relatively easy for Carol to find a clinic to perform an abortion, but she was surprised by the way she was treated there. In the early years of legal abortion, options counseling was not routine, and none was provided to Carol. In addition, prior to an educational session about the procedure, Carol described how everyone was given birth control pills:

> There was a variety of ages in this group, there was a woman who was in her forties, and there was me, and a thirteen-year-old, and people in their twenties, and everyone got a package of birth control pills and everyone opened it at the same time. And everyone took the first pill. It was very humiliating. I mean now that thinking back about how humiliating that would be for everybody and I just did it because I just thought, well I have to do this.

Although Carol was able to obtain an abortion within a week of learning she was pregnant, she, like Nancy, received little help from others in processing the emotional impact of these events. Carol came from a family in which feelings were not addressed or tended to. It was two years before Carol spoke with a friend or her younger sisters about her experience. When she did, it was to help them appreciate their options and to not feel so alone in their reproductive choices as Carol did. In part because Carol easily located abortion services, she did not have to turn to others in the way that Nancy had to seek the contacts and financial backing of friends.

Both Nancy and Carol described a heartfelt desire to spare other women the pain they experienced in having an abortion, but Carol believed having an abortion contributed to her development of a feminist ideology as well as to a passionately held prochoice stance. Carol came to recognize that, "if I can't control what I want to do with my body and if I can't make that decision then I'm not going to be able to control anything else." Implied in Carol's statement was the awareness that abortion had been illegal just a few years previously. Experiences at college—with peers and in women's studies courses—helped to consolidate Carol's identity as a feminist and activist. Since graduation, she has worked in two women's health centers. She has developed skills both in counseling and in political action.

Looking back at the impact her abortion had on her development, Carol concluded, "I am sure there are some losses that I have because I had to terminate a pregnancy, but ... the losses would have been much greater had I continued the pregnancy." For Carol, who has not chosen to have a child since her abortion, the loss was one of not knowing firsthand the experience of pregnancy and childbirth. The gains have been in the areas of personal growth and survival and in greater assertiveness about the times and ways she chooses to be sexual.

Conclusions

These stories, along with the data from the larger study, attest to the significance of having had an abortion in these women's lives. Regardless of legal context, confronting an unanticipated pregnancy can be highly stressful. Choosing to have an abortion can become an important event in a woman's reproductive history. It also may lead to new political awarenesses. One woman in the study who had an illegal abortion said: "I felt oppressed as a woman. It was one of the first real incidents of harm done to me by a system not made by me." Another participant in the study, who had a legal abortion, explained: "It made me more aware of the necessity for women to always have this option legally available to us. ... It made me think more about women's situations at these times as well as men's. It strengthened my feminist beliefs." Though most women in the study did not feel that having had an abortion changed their life per se, many indicated that it enabled them to pursue important goals. One woman articulated this feeling well: "It simply allowed me to continue my life rather than not continue my life."

Despite these similarities, the legal and social context of abortion determine the range and acceptability of options available to women, such as the feasibility of single parenthood, the necessity of self-induced abortion attempts, and the shame associated with pregnancy outside of marriage. It also structures the tasks with which women must cope in seeking an abortion. For Nancy, finding someone to perform an abortion eclipsed any opportunity to emotionally process the event as it was happening. She needed to involve friends in the process, but did not have the luxury to rely on them for emotional support. In contrast, Carol's ease in obtaining an abortion meant she did not have to consult friends. Though she felt alone, she had more opportunity to process the meaning of the experience to her.

Most significant, the legal context of abortion influences the safety of the procedure. Illegal abortion presented women with more fears and dangers; it also confronted them with the possibility of exploitation. Two statements from the questionnaire data cogently summarize a central theme that emerged from this study. Both of these women wrote of how they understand their experience of legal abortion to be unique from illegal abortion. One concluded, "I was scared only about the pain. I was *not* scared that it was going to 'go wrong.'" The second woman's statement crystallizes the issue: "It was safer, cheaper, easy to find, less frightening and followed up better. Society in general was more accepting. I was able to cope better emotionally. It was an experience, not a trauma."

19

Struggle and Strength in the Lives of Two Lesbian Priests

BRIAN W. LITZENBERGER

IN 1969, IN A BAR in Greenwich Village in New York City, a riot took place that changed the course of the lives of lesbians and gay men in the United States. In 1974, in a church in Philadelphia, eleven women were noncanonically ordained to the priesthood in the Episcopal church—an act that changed the course of the lives of many within the Episcopal church. These two events, though dramatic, signify transitions that are the results of years of ferment. Not solitary acts, radical in their design but isolated in their genesis, the Stonewall riot and the ordination of the Philadelphia Eleven are moments in which we are able to see in relief some of the forces that have affected the lives and identities these events involved.

For one group of people, these two events have been central to their life narratives. These two historical moments exemplify the kind of struggle for place and position in society, the church, and the self that has been central to the life of many ordained lesbians in the Episcopal church. The prominence of these events suggests many questions about the women who participated in them and about their experiences, motivation, hopes, and struggles. The drama of these events highlights pressures previously unseen by many; it also highlights the strength and commitment of the women who participated in these actions.

The work that is presented in this chapter is an exploration of the lives and struggles of two women who are both lesbians and ordained priests in the Episcopal church. I interviewed these women in 1988 and 1989 as part of a study on homosexuality in the Episcopal priesthood. In the interviews, we focused on the development of their identities as spiritual and sexual people. We discussed their struggles to understand themselves as these elements of their lives became increasingly salient, potent, and conflictual to them. We talked about their struggles and their triumphs. In their stories I found pain and sacrifice, but also surpassing strength. I have chosen here to write about these particular two women because

The first ordination of Episcopal women in Philadelphia, July 1974. *(Photo by Brad Hess; courtesy Suzanne Hiatt.)*

their stories seem to complement each other particularly well. Though the two women are distinctly different, the similarities between their lived experiences are striking. Through a discussion of both of them, a clearer sense may emerge of what it means to be both a lesbian and a priest.

I became interested in these women's lives at a time in my life when I was thinking a great deal about identity politics and the psychology of marginalization. Through this research, I became interested in the experiences of those who are triply marginalized as gay, as women, and as priests. I was particularly interested in gaining an understanding of the ways in which these women navigated their seemingly conflicting identities. The focus of the interviews became an attempt to understand these differences and the difficulties that they engendered in both the internal and external worlds of the women. As I discuss in this chapter, I became interested in questions about their adaptations and compromises: How did these clearly successful women navigate what I assume to have been hard times to arrive where they are today?

It is clear that these women lead radical lives. Their lives are radical acts in a society within which the coexistence of lesbian and priest as identities within one woman is contradictory at best. As these women live, they challenge the stereotypes of lesbians and priests that function to bind them, judge them, and force them to defend their existence and rights. Through this chapter I hope to highlight the ways in which these women have challenged and been challenged by these stereotypes.

As I approach this chapter now, I am struck initially by questions about my position as observer and auditor of these women and by the differences and similarities between our identities. These relationships became a part of our conversation, for I began each interview with a discussion of some of the personal, political, and intellectual reasons with which I had come to this research. As the discussion continued, our similarities and differences became increasingly apparent. In an effort to maintain the integrity of their meanings, I asked both women to review this chapter. What follows includes their revisions.

The Episcopal church plays a central role in the lives of both of these women. Its attitudes and policies on women's ordination and homosexuality have influenced the environment and cultures within which they have lived. Although women may now be ordained in the Episcopal church, the journey to reach this point has been long and the fight to end sexism in the church is far from over. The battle for women's ordination to the priesthood may be traced back in the United States at least to the late 1960s, but it was not until the early 1970s that women began to organize to try to effect a change in the establishment. The first action took place in 1973 when women raised the issue at a national convention of the Episcopal church. Women's ordination was defeated by a technicality. The same year five women presented themselves to the bishop at St. John the Divine in New York City and were rejected. Eleven women, later to be referred to as the Philadelphia Eleven, contacted four inactive bishops, and in the full and proper manner of the Episcopal church, were ordained to the priesthood in Philadelphia on July 30,

1974. These ordinations caused a wave of controversy within the church. An emergency meeting of the House of Bishops (the governing body of bishops) was called. At this meeting, the assembled bishops pardoned the bishops who presided at the ordinations but forbade the ordained women to function as priests: Men 1, Women 0 (Hiatt, 1983). The next General Convention was not held until 1976. By this time support was so strong and there were so many women vocally present that it was no longer a matter of the women of the Episcopal church asking to be ordained, it was women proclaiming their existence and rights. They were heard, and women were finally allowed to live the professional lives that they felt God was calling them to live (Maitland, 1983).

The church's position on homosexuality has remained ambivalent. In 1979, the church published the Episcopal Church Guidelines for Ministry. These guidelines state that priests are expected to conform to church teachings on marriage, fidelity, and chastity (not a requirement for the priesthood). The guidelines note that there are "many human conditions, some in the area of sexuality, which bear upon a person's suitability for ordination" (Sherwood, 1987, p. 87). This point has been used by many to prevent gay people from being ordained. A letter in opposition to the rule was signed by forty-eight bishops, but the guidelines have not been revised. Because the Episcopal church is divided into dioceses directed by largely autonomous bishops, the degree to which homosexuality is accepted in any given church depends to a great extent upon the diocese and its bishop. Some dioceses are notoriously intolerant and others are notoriously accepting.

Liza

The first priest I interviewed is a white woman now in her early fifties. I'll call her Liza. She lives in a major metropolitan area in a diocese that has been known over the years for its liberal politics. She has been ordained for over ten years, but it has taken her nearly that long to secure a stipendiary position. She currently holds two part-time positions in churches where she serves as a priest. One of these positions is unpaid. Liza is also training to work in a business position to put some of her other talents to use—a transition she described as having "finally reconciled to making some real money." She holds four graduate degrees in the humanities and one in divinity.

I met Liza at one of her job sites where she had finished for the day. She bundled up in a navy-blue down coat and we left to find somewhere to talk. Her answers to my questions and questions of my questions reflected both her intelligence and her wit. When we talked about difficult times in her life, she was forthcoming and direct. I was quickly impressed with her as someone who had weathered well the transitions in her life. Although there had been rough spots, she appeared to regard them as evidence of her capacity for growth, even as times when she felt herself come closer to God. Her faith in God and in herself permeated her narration. This strength and its development is what I understand to have allowed her to survive and achieve an exceptional level of competence.

Liza realized she was a lesbian during the summer between her first and second years of college, "when I fell disastrously in love with somebody who was not terribly interested in me. And that sort of ... told me what was going on because ... she was gay." These feelings served as a turning point for Liza. "I suppose that was my great ... awareness of myself, and not a terribly happy one because of being connected with this disastrous unrequited love affair. But on the other hand it did make a lot of things make sense—a lot of ways in which I had never felt that I fit anywhere."

Liza was raised in the Episcopal church. When asked when she remembered first thinking about choosing a religious vocation, she recalled meeting a great-aunt at the age of eight or nine years. This aunt had been working as a missionary in an orphanage in Asia for twenty-five years and was a mythological figure in Liza's family. Meeting this woman changed her life. She remembered having been "sort of uncomfortable with the Episcopal ladies" in her home church and thinking that this woman from Asia "wasn't just mythology" and perhaps she too could find her vocation within the church. At the age of thirteen she remembered scouring the library of her prep school to find out more about Episcopal nuns. She discovered that there were orders in existence and began to correspond with women in them. These early contacts with other religious women gave her both the vision and the incentive to pursue a spiritual future for herself.

Reflected in her discussion of coming out and hearing the call to the priesthood is the understanding that, for Liza, this process involved both discovering that which was unknown and naming that which was already known. In this process, the external world and the internal world became increasingly consistent through the use of language and the notion of vocation. It was a process of self-discovery through which both her sexuality and her spirituality and their interconnectedness and centrality to her identity were articulated. A major part of her coming out process happened on a Native American Reservation in the Southwest, during which time she read about the Stonewall riot in New York City and asked herself: "What am I doing trying to foster indigenous ministries on Indian Reservations when my own people are having their own little revolution?" She returned to the large city to become more active in the ferment. Liza "started living with a college roommate that I had had a sort of tentative experience with toward our senior year and that's when I came out politically, got very involved politically, and then in the early seventies, I was back in the Episcopal church." This involvement fostered important relationships for her. "The priest whom I was working with and a man who had been a Dominican brother suggested independently of each other on the same day that I consider going to seminary and applying for ordination, and in a sense, that was a sort of coming out because it made a lot of things fall into place."

Liza made clear to me the extent to which others' values and pressures affected her internal reality. The discontinuity between the messages she was getting from the church and from society and her developing sense of her internal world created a battle in which the internal lost. The resultant difficulty—"hives of the soul"—illustrates both the degree to which this discontinuity pressured her to question her fundamental beliefs and the emotional pain she was experiencing. Looking back over her life, Liza remarked, "I don't think I was ever uncomfortable with my sexuality—how I acted it out sometimes has not been the greatest, but that was more of a dislike of myself rather than of myself as a lesbian. … I see any problems I've had with sexuality as being related to acting out problems with myself rather than because of problems with being gay." When asked about problems with being gay, she responded that the only time she experienced problems was "shortly after I became a Roman Catholic, which I did in my late teens, and just the real awful banging my head against the church's teachings, which at that point was worse than now. At least now you can occasionally find a sympatico cleric, but in those days, forget it." Alone in a denomination that she felt called her spiritually and denied her physically, she began to question herself. "That sent me into a real bout of what we call scruples. Not so much because I thought my sexuality, per se, was wrong but because I was really no longer sure of what sin was. … Awful disease scruples. It's kind of like hives of the soul."

Liza moved on with her life. She returned to the Episcopal church, then applied to and attended seminary. Liza approached her bishop about being ordained and he brought it up with the diocesan standing committee, who decided that "the time was not yet ripe for somebody who was really up front and openly out to go through the process." She sought ordination in another diocese where she was ultimately denied ordination as well. This incident served for her as an example of the kind of difficulty with which the church presented her. She was up for ordination at the same time as a man who had been convicted of murdering his wife. "Well, that's a really funny story when you think that they accepted him and he was ordained and I was turned down, until you start thinking, 'What does that say about how the church thinks about women?' The other thing of course was that he had repented of his sin and I had not. I was unwilling to admit that I had committed one, at least that particular one." Faced with clear messages from the church that the way she loved was sin, she protected herself from feelings of self-condemnation.

As she continued with her life, refusing either to lie or to deny herself her sexuality or her spirituality, the force of the external barrage increased. This force became in fact so strong that she began to accept its message. After having been denied ordination in the second diocese, Liza returned to the first diocese and sought ordination again. This time the process went forward without anyone addressing her sexuality, "probably because at that point everybody knew and thought that there was no point in asking. … I was priested in the late seventies with another woman at a church up the street and the shit hit the fan, essentially." Liza experienced a backlash, the magnitude of which she had not expected. "I had been very open and up front and out during the whole process and actually got a lot of good mail too. … It wasn't just all the bomb threats and hate mail … but there was a period of two years in which I was virtually unable to answer the telephone myself." When set upon with such vehement opposition, part of her gave in and accepted the message—so many couldn't be wrong. In this way the external conflict became internal. "I just couldn't stand it and … I probably internalized a lot of the hate that was directed at me and really was in a very bad depression for a long time. And got myself involved in a few things (including a five-year relationship) that were awful, really very awful and very self-destructive." One of the "bad things" was alcohol. Along with her depression, Liza fought a battle with alcoholism. "But a couple of years ago I finally … I've been going to AA for about five years off and on. It finally took and Christmas Day will be my second anniversary."

One of the underlying notions in this description—the most difficult time described in Liza's narrative—is that living a double life is the only way to avoid such controversy and pain. Living openly as a lesbian and a priest, Liza challenged the system, challenged people's conceptions of "priest" and "lesbian," and experienced the pain of their hatred in an internal, personal way. For the lesbian who feels the call to the priesthood, one clear message is: If you want to be in the church, you need to feel comfortable being in the closet.

Liza understands there was a twofold function to her use of alcohol. In a gay culture that was centered around the bar scene, alcohol functioned as an escape both symbolically and physically from oppressive heterosexual culture. At the same time, it functioned to deaden her negative feelings about herself, and in that she was deadening herself, her alcohol use reflected a collusion with the oppression of the dominant culture. Thus working through her relationship with alcohol became closely related to working through her relationship with the church and God. Getting sober was a focal part of her development as she grew to become more in touch with her feelings. "In the last two years I have … gotten to know myself better and have been more insistent on being myself to other people, instead of being this construct that was what came out in the ordination process, you know that was sort of 'lesbian designed by Mattel.'" Thus, instead of complying with the expectations of others, she grew to know and accept herself. As with dealing with the church's and society's oppression, facing and accepting her own problems have been important steps toward becoming the person she wants to be. In describing who she feels she is now, Liza said, "You know, this one is not as perfect, but it's human, and that's harder to deal with, but I wouldn't want to be any other way."

Being in supportive relationships has also been a focal part of Liza's development and a part of her life in which a great deal of growth has taken place. Supportive relationships are also what helped her to make it through the process of getting sober. Liza "got left in the lurch two and a half years ago," but is now in another relationship. About her current relationship, she said, "It's not the dyke drama of my previous relationship. God, I've had enough of that!" She has had to look carefully at her relationships and wonder why she found herself getting into intense and dependent relationships. Along with her relationship with alcohol, her relationships with her lovers paralleled the difficulties that she was working through. Her current relationship is one she described by saying, "fidelity doesn't have to be strangling." Part of this realization is that "I'm a middle-aged woman who actually likes living alone."

The difficulties she experienced with alcohol and intimacy may have stemmed as well from the lack of support that she felt from her family. Like her use of alcohol and her intimate relationships, Liza's relationships with her parents have gone through many changes as she has come to terms with herself. During her college years, when she was coming out to herself, her family was "monstrously unsupportive." She described her father as "one of those people who, when he got angry, simply got colder and colder and you know there's a point at which, when the temperature drops so low, that it burns just as bad as fire. Frightening man when he got angry." She explained her father's anger: "Because of his own, I suppose, sort of sexist, old-fashioned upbringing, he really found lesbians a bigger affront than gay men. He liked intelligent women, but he couldn't stand the thought of an autonomous woman and so that was a serious problem." Her father died before they could be reconciled.

"My mother, on the other hand, after having gone through a 'How have I failed?' and hauling me to shrinks and all of the usual stuff, after my father's death—I don't know, part of her will remain unreconciled forever, but the other part of her has been really pretty neat about it." Liza spoke fondly of a process of reconciliation that she and her mother went through: "That was … her own coming to terms with herself, not as an … adjunct to a man but as a person in her own right. … At the age of seventy-four she's actually using all four of her own names, instead of using my father's name, and since she still lives in the Southeast, that's pretty unusual." Liza addressed her communications with her mother: "There are things that I don't talk about with her, but she is now pretty supportive. … Maybe she's figured that the relationship with me is more important than screaming about whom I'm with. If the person I'm with is nice, it doesn't necessarily matter too much the gender."

When Liza was in seminary she became friends with a collection of gay men who were also students. She remarked, "It's really funny though, because a lot of the gay men at seminary were very anti–women's ordination and yet they and I became friends because, to me, it was a nondebatable issue and so I wasn't bothered with confrontation, you know? 'I'm here, folks. So let's chill out and if you enjoy Mozart, so do I.'" Her social life involved going to gay bars with these men and they would pick up someone but she would go home alone. In contrast, the parishes with which she is affiliated and Alcoholics Anonymous now serve as sources of many supportive friendships.

Working as a priest is "absolutely central" to Liza's life, but her understanding of what this is has evolved over time. "One of the things I am learning more and more is to listen to people and let them tell me what they need and listen to God to see how I can help them, finding not answers but directions." She has grown to recognize that working as a priest does "not anymore have anything to do with social status." Part of what she has come to accept is that if she continues to live in the city where she currently lives, she will probably never be a rector of a parish.

She understands that because she was one of the first lesbians to be ordained in the church she became "a symbol at the very beginning of my priesthood. There are people who won't let that die—the myth overshadows the woman." She went on to add, "It's interesting that working as a priest is not the problem, it's getting into that official structure of approval." Trouble getting hired for a paying position has not kept her from working, and her work is multifaceted. Liza directs retreats, works as a spiritual director, volunteers for social concerns, "joys and delights" in teaching, and preaches. She described preaching as one of her gifts, and as this activity has become more important to her, her prayer life has also grown in what she calls a necessary symbiosis. She has realized "over and over again, that what happens in the mass is really the center of my life—that incredible intimate contact between God and people." Her current approach to her work as a priest is both to facilitate that intimacy and to "get out of the way and let it happen."

Liza has developed an increasingly clear sense of the being of God and what that means for her. Earlier in her career, she felt her relationship with God to be "naively open." During her adolescence, she talked with God "rather simply. It had a zen quality to it: being with God and being able to talk with God freely." She described her relationship with God, at its nadir, as "adversarial." This was after she left the Roman Catholic church and was coming out. "For a long time it was largely ... feeling an absence or a knowing, not only that there was a relationship there, but feeling really, a lot of times, that as soon as I started feeling close that I was sort of thrown back out in the cold again." Liza described that transformation of her relationship with God as "God working through basic common sense."

There were two major realizations that occurred for her. First, she grew to realize that the act of penance (asking forgiveness for sins) was not about punishment but growth. Prayer became less "mechanical" for her as she also realized that "God had created me with the being that I am and it was up to me to be the best person given what I was created with." This was a "fairly simple, blunt realization" that allowed her to experience her relationship with God as consoling—a relationship that she could enjoy. As an example of the closeness Liza now feels with God, she recounted the following series of events: "I was on retreat a few weeks ago. It was really kind of wonderful. It was like spending a whole weekend—which I usually do as a silent retreat—spending a whole weekend just really resting in God and feeling really, very much love, absolutely right." She found a sympatico cleric: "I went in to my patron and I said, 'I don't know how I can deal with this.' He said, 'Relax and enjoy it and consider anything that takes you out of it as being demonic.' I thought, 'Alright, I'll give it a try.'" Her second realization involved discovering that she was angry at God for a church that she couldn't change. Developing a positive relationship with God involved examining her anger and redirecting it. A great deal of this anger is anger that she has toward the church and her diocese for not having hired her earlier.

Making realizations about her sexuality, spirituality, alcoholism, and relationships and their interrelations has been the largest set of tasks in the development of her current identity. This has been painful and difficult and there are still times when she thinks: "Yeah, the real world is still out there and even I have to exercise … some real discretion [which] needs to be balanced with a desire not to go back in the closet. So the kind of coming out to myself and the world as me, which is different from the image, is a hard thing but fun and I like it." Liza made it clear here that she chooses pain over anesthetization. She understood that she made a decision to change. "I anesthetized myself to the pain for years, and I don't want to do it anymore. I mean, there are times that I would love to, but I just … made the basic decision that that's not how I want to exist. I'd rather live my life even when it hurts." In doing this, she gave precedence to an experiencing of the world and God that is based on her internal senses, however painful that may be at times, rather than accepting an external reality mass-produced "by Mattel" that asks her to deny herself certain feelings so that she fits in better.

In many ways, the process Liza has gone through may be described as "coming out" not just as a lesbian, but as a person living a radical life, claiming her existence and its validity. One of the difficulties of her existence is that it exposes the frailty of the stereotypes of lesbians and of priests. In many ways, the oppression she feels is a social force protecting these stereotypes. This oppression pushed her toward going back into the closet, toward alcohol, toward destructive relationships, and ultimately, away from God. By rejecting this course, Liza changed the direction of the force and shifted the burden of responsibility back on to the society from which it came, claiming integrity for herself, however unsettling it may be for others.

Melanie

The second priest I interviewed for this study is a white woman in her mid-thirties. I'll call her Melanie. She is the rector of a parish in an inner-city neighborhood of a major metropolitan area with a focus on urban ministry. The parish uses an inclusive-language service and the congregation includes a large proportion of lesbians and gay men. I met Melanie on a busy weekday in the church office, which was bustling with people. She pulled herself from what appeared to be three different conversations to give us some time for a cup of coffee and a conversation—with only a couple of interruptions. She often thought out loud, careful to clarify what I was asking and what she was saying. Amid all of the bustle, she appeared relaxed and focused, comfortable talking about her experiences. In many ways, Melanie seems to understand her development as a process of seeking wholeness—a complete experiencing of herself as a multifaceted, individuated, and integrated woman.

One of the first salient moments for Melanie in this process came when she was a sophomore in high school. She was raised an Episcopalian and had been closely involved in her church. She was caught by the police smoking marijuana in the church parking lot. One of the priests from the church rode with her to the precinct office and during this ride asked her if she had thought of being a priest. At the time, women weren't being ordained in the Episcopal church. For Melanie, this story illustrates the way that she believes that God touches people through their worst and most shameful moments. A similar illustration came in her senior year of college when her father and grandmother (who had lived with the family all of Melanie's life) both died and her mother had a nervous breakdown. With ten dollars, her car, and her dog she arrived in the city in which she now lives. She found work and it was at this point in her life that she heard God again. Having been a religion major in college, she had always known that she was interested in people's souls. After four years of working in the city, she decided to enter seminary and pursue a path to the priesthood.

Another important moment was when she came out in high school. "I suppose the initial moment for me was when I was seventeen, in high school, and became involved with a woman who was ten years older than I. ... I knew that there was something different from the way that I looked at other women than ... my friends." She described coming out with "three other friends in my high school and we all, more or less, came out together actually, which was, I think, unusual. ... It wasn't ... this solitary angst experience: it was a group of us who were claiming our identity." The cultural timing of this was important. "It was the late ... sixties and so that was all ... part of the ferment, part of the fun ... exploring ourselves. ... At the time I don't really remember thinking, 'Oh, my God, ... I'm gay and this is an awful thing.' It was more like, 'This is an exciting possibility.'"

She recalled her parents, particularly her mother, being supportive of her being a lesbian: "I remember telling her and ... she said, 'Well, I sort of suspected that.' And I said to her, 'Well, why didn't you say anything to me?' and she said, 'Because I was waiting for you to tell me.' Which I remember struck me; it was good." Her father died when she was a senior in college and she didn't remember ever telling him in any formal way until the summer before her senior year. She didn't feel as though they ever had the chance to explore it.

As she began the process of ordination, Melanie had a conversation with her bishop in which she came out to him and they discussed her sexuality. "He wanted to explore that with me ... in terms of how I handled my sexuality—that was the issue for him not ... the gender choice." When she graduated from seminary there was a position she wanted at a parish in a nearby state. The parish discovered that she was gay. "They really wrestled with whether or not to hire me, and ... to their credit, ... they didn't just slam the door in my face, they really spent some time wrestling it through as a community and decided that they weren't ready." She described her reaction to this rejection. "That was pretty devastating but I didn't come out of that experience feeling embittered or like they were awful. ... It was like ... they weren't ready." She reflected on how out she is in her current position. "I guess you could say that there are many people ... who know that I'm gay. ... I don't particularly hide it, but I don't particularly stand up and say it either. I mean, when it's appropriate, I share that information, if it's going to be useful to what's happening at the moment. ... I haven't really experienced a lot of discrimination."

Melanie had been single for a period of four years ending shortly before this interview. This solitary experience resonated with her desire to feel whole. For her, attaining a feeling of wholeness is related to wrestling with feelings of dependence, or seeking in another what she hopes to find in herself. Realizing this has shifted the way that she understands her desire for intimacy with women, and she finds herself experiencing her sexuality as less rigidly focused on women. "There is a way in which I have been trying all my life to find my own womanhood by making love to women and in the end ... no other person can really make me whole." She was in a relationship with a woman at the time of the interview whom she described as being her opposite. This comparison allowed her to talk about what it means to her to be whole as a woman: "She's ... at home in her own body and in her own house and that's quintessentially what it means to be a woman really."

Knowing that she seeks in another what she wants for herself clearly does not preclude that seeking, but increases Melanie's understanding of herself. This change in self-conception essentially reframes her behavior so that although she may still be attracted to women who are different from her (perhaps more "womanly" to her), she has changed her expectations and her understanding of the desires that motivate the attractions. She refocuses the search for her "womanhood" on herself: "I can feel myself wanting the quality that she has and so that part of my desire for her sexually is that, if I make love to her, ... I'll somehow get that quality in myself." There is pain in this understanding: "I've realized that ... there's a way in which it's painful to keep reenacting a scenario that's ultimately bringing no fulfillment of the desired goal. It's like trying to get it in the wrong place." She distinguished this wish from reality: "The reality is that I won't get that quality in myself unless I spend time in my own house ... being alone and discovering who I am and ... cooking or, ... the phrase I use is, 'taking care of my own hearth.' All of us need to ... take care of our own hearth and—that's sort of the domestic, internal, care-for-ourselves side."

This process of realizing that she needs to find in herself that which she has been seeking in others has been paralleled by a similar shift in her work as a priest. Melanie has gone from "wanting to save" her church "in a narcissistic way" to "letting go of my need for the parish to be anything other than what it was called to be." Through this change in her relationship with her parish community (learning how to "get out of the way"), she has allowed others to "interact more directly with the spirit of God." She described a moment in a church meeting in which she altered the agenda and instead of pushing the others to change in ways that she felt they should, she began affirming the strength that she saw in front of her. Instead of seeking a spirit that existed outside of the community, the congregation found the spirit that existed within it. As a group, the people began to acknowledge the ways in which they were whole: a multicultural community with diverse backgrounds and interests. As Melanie became more confident in herself, she became less controlling of the congregation, and it became freer to grow and develop and become whole itself.

In seeking wholeness and becoming more connected with God, she has become more flexible and less controlling of her own identity, less dependent upon the external identity cues of language to support her, less rigidly connected to a reified conception of "lesbian." "I wouldn't say that I'm … a 'lesbian' any longer. … It's not quite true. … I'm still involved with women and love them and … I don't really know where I'm headed, but I'm not so …, 'Alright, this is who I am for the rest of my life.'" This flexibility came as somewhat of a surprise to her. "I never would have thought that this would be happening. … When I came out when I was seventeen and, really, all through my early twenties and early thirties, it was …, 'Well, I'm just going to be this way for the rest of my life.' And so it's sort of amazing [to] realize that something else might be in store for me." Living with this ambiguity has its own difficulties. "I don't know that … that 'me' is what's in store for me. I really don't. I have to be careful not to presume. I'm … in a waiting period in my life in which I don't know what's next. But I have been consciously attempting to give up the need to … make love to somebody to feel worthwhile."

Asking what she wants and where she is looking for it is centrally related to the development of her relationship with her body. As with her relationship with God, her relationship with her body was more distant than she allowed herself to understand. One way she kept the awareness of this distance out of her consciousness was to abuse alcohol. Melanie described recognizing her alcohol abuse as an act of faith in which she had to cast "my fate into God's hands and so it felt like a kind of baptism in which I was really relinquishing my need to control things because I could not understand but I knew that I had to go this way and that there was no way out and that God was leading me there and I had to surrender … and it took years." She also understood her journey in theological terms. "I started at the crucifixion and then … the sobriety was the resurrection and then came … back to incarnation and then you … go through them all over again."

There was a fundamentally important moment that occurred during the summer after she made her decision to become sober: She took up bicycle riding. "I went to all these different places. … I … visited friends. … One night I just went into the woods and took off all my clothes and spent the night in the woods and then, another day, I rode my bike up … a huge mountain and … what would happen was that I discovered that I had a body and … in a very tangible way." As baptism is an experience of acknowledging the presence of God in her body, these moments were experiences of acknowledging her own presence in her body. "It was a phenomenal … It was as if there was this … chasm [that] had been … closed. … I just knew that I … was a physical entity and, therefore, I knew that I had a place on the earth and, you see, therefore, I knew that I existed in some complete way."

Melanie distinguished these experiences from simply doing things with her body, experiencing the world with her body. This was a new type of union for her, "That I had just never experienced before, … and I'm a fairly physical person. … I have always been, but misplaced, and so it was … like finding some truth. And so my preaching changed and I … had a sense of my own incarnateness. It was a dis-

covery of a whole new dimension of my physical reality ... and that changed me."
What is also important here is that, for Melanie, this moment was both intensely
physical and intensely spiritual. She was able to experience her incarnateness spiritually. For Melanie, this moment was also emblematic of a new understanding of
interpersonal boundaries and her own potency. "In other words, that a woman,
when she has really found herself, can give birth to new life." As with her relationship with God and her community, she acted in a way to control these relationships, as alcohol controlled her body. It was through relinquishing that kind of
control that she began to see that she already had much of what she had been
seeking and was more whole than she had thought.

This embodiedness and understanding of connections between her feelings
about herself and her desires for others are intertwined with her feelings for and
about God. She believes that "the spiritual life begins with the way of the flesh ...
and so, for me, the two, that is the sexual and the spiritual, are absolutely united."
Becoming in touch with her body and her inner self "is the way in which I'm
going to hear God. ... I hear God through other avenues, but at each step ... I've
had to ... come to a point where nobody could take it for me. ... It was up to me."

This internal development is juxtaposed with a daily routine that is hectic, invigorating, and full. Working as a parish priest she has devoted herself to working
through her church in the large community addressing issues of homelessness
and housing, urban famine, and AIDS. The source of the strength for this work
has grown from the strength of the community of the parish; for Melanie this cul-
minates in the celebration of the eucharist. She described this as being "where it
all comes together. ... You're really gathering people at a table and in some sense
you're ... throwing a party. You're inviting people to eat and be together, and in
that event of sacramental eating ... in one level you're ... doing dishes and cooking ... and you're really ... also asking God to fill you and the community." It becomes clear here that the changes in her expectations of others have paralleled
changes in her expectations of God. What she cannot get from others she asks for
from God.

Asking from God is also complicated, and as she has changed, her relationship
with God has evolved. "I've continually worked on trying to let go of, how I really
want God to ... be the perfect parent and accept God as other." In this acceptance
of God as "other" she has also faced the task of accepting this other uncondition-
ally and without questions.

In this face-off with God Melanie has also had to face her desire for control of
her life. "Even though I don't quite have all the answers, I don't need to have all
the answers. I don't have to control everything to see and make sure if everything
is alright before I can take the risk and ... then there's no risk." This is not the first
time that Melanie has experienced this: "That's how it felt when I quit drinking
too and so I really have to accept that God is other than me and that God is really
the being of the universe and that I am a piece of that so that my needs and wants
and desires aren't the center of the universe. ... Each time that happens, then the
next time gets easier and I trust that God is leading me."

This is not to say that stasis or passivity is what Melanie is seeking. For her, "trying to discern how God is speaking to me is a very important way in which I try to live, you know, with integrity, and it's always a struggle and it's full of a lot of tension and it's full of a lot of sacrifice and it really is a fucking bitch." This "struggle" and "tension" is also about growth and development. "There's a point at which to stay safe for too long means that ... you're not really continuing to turn out or to grow and the only solution to that is to continue to try to address people to open up the fears and be up front about them, rather than deny them, and ... just try and preach the gospel and live it."

For Melanie, discerning the nature of wholeness and its genesis is the focal concern of understanding her development. In the process of moving toward a deeper sense of this she had to reassess her relationships to others, alcohol, herself, and God. In this process, she found it necessary to turn over to God the very desire to be the sole agent of change in her life. To do this, she has needed to grow to understand the origins of her feelings about herself and the ways in which she feels that she is not complete and the ways in which she is complete but has kept herself from knowing it. With this understanding, she has become more able to let go of the associated negative feelings and less dependent on finding that which she seeks in others. She has become more accepting of herself spiritually, emotionally, and physically and less dependent on others' evaluations of her—more able to accept others' reactions to her as other and separate. In describing this process as "seeking wholeness," Melanie encapsulates its nature, source, and goal. The forces that acted in her life against her functioned to fragment and disperse her sense of herself, and it is from this point that she has had to develop her self-awareness and esteem. She grew to understand that her efforts to control these feelings hindered her and prevented her from feeling and living as a complete person.

Discussion

Melanie and Liza's stories are different in many ways. Melanie is fifteen to twenty years younger than Liza. They grew up in different parts of the country, had different families, and came out at different times. Liza called herself an introvert and Melanie called herself an extrovert. Their problems have also been different. Although both fought battles for sobriety, Liza's fight was also about depression. Melanie described a turning point of discovering her body and a new sense of her incarnateness. Whereas Liza's response was to internalize hateful messages, Melanie dissociated herself from the body for which the messages were meant. The differences in their experiences and personalities and our conversations helped me to understand more fully the unique natures of their lives. These sometimes striking differences also underscore some even more striking similarities.

Although their stories are distinct and different, Melanie and Liza both found ways to access an inner strength. Each was able to understand the conflict between her sense of herself as a lived being and the perceptions of others. Faced with this dichotomy, each found the ability to foster and support this inner sense of herself. This occurred in periods of deep introspection and through a strong faith in God, but in each case, introspection was in part spurred on by crisis. Liza's depression and Melanie's dissociation both represent periods of intense pain. In each case it was their relationships that saved them—with those whom they loved and with God. Through these relationships they learned to see and reclaim the parts of themselves that they had rejected.

This process of restoring their sense of themselves as connected and loved through their relationships to themselves and others gave them the strength to overcome the pain and difficulty of facing a world that not only did not want them to exist but told them that they did not exist, that their lives were an impossibility. Finding this strength took years—a process of continually attempting to reconcile their internal reality with an external world that at times equated their sexuality with sin and pathology. As in the Stonewall riot and the ordination of the Philadelphia Eleven, Melanie's and Liza's battles with alcoholism, depression, dissociation, and bigotry were radical acts expressing their demand that the system, not they, change: Melanie and Liza were reacting to a system that functioned to keep them in a safe, limited, and understood place—as either lesbian or priest but not both.

Melanie and Liza were fortunate to find jobs that they loved, but their church, their families, and their societies gave them messages that they couldn't be both lesbian and religious. From bomb threats to unwelcoming congregations, these messages asked them to separate themselves. For Liza, the separation occurred between that which was allowed out to be seen and that which was kept closeted. The part of herself that was able to accept herself was separated from the part of herself that at times believed the messages that were heaped on her. Melanie separated from her body, fragmenting herself and feeling, for example, she was unable to "take care of her own hearth." In the end, both found wholeness and integrity in separating not from themselves but from the parts of society that demanded that they separate. In so doing, they became freer to act in the world and relate to God and choose the existence that suited them—the existence that they felt that they were called to live.

References

Hiatt, S. R. (1983). How we brought the good news from Graymoor to Minneapolis: An Episcopal paradigm. *Journal of Ecumenical Studies, 20*(4), 576–584.

Maitland, S. (1983). *A map of the new country: Women and Christianity.* London: Routledge & Kegan Paul.

Sherwood, Z. O. (1987). *Kairos: Confessions of a gay priest.* Boston: Alyson.

20

Meanings and Uses of Marginal Identities: Social Class at Radcliffe in the 1960s

JOAN M. OSTROVE & ABIGAIL J. STEWART

IN THIS CHAPTER we will explore how social class-based worldviews influence women's understanding of their own marginality and their strategies for coping with it. Because we live in a society in which everyone is stratified according to social class, class plays an important role in how we live our lives and how we define ourselves—both in our individual minds and as actors in a material world. Drawing on both questionnaire and interview data from four women who have participated in Stewart's longitudinal study of graduates of the Radcliffe class of 1964 (see Stewart, 1978, 1980; Stewart and Salt, 1981; Stewart and Vandewater, 1993, for more complete descriptions of the sample), we hope to understand more about the importance of class background in the lives of Radcliffe women. The participants in the study were never asked about social class; this chapter therefore draws on class-based constructions that arose spontaneously throughout their participation in the research.

Marginality

By "marginality" we refer specifically to the ways women experience being different from their peers, or cohort. Women may be marginal because they do something that is statistically atypical for their cohort (e.g., do not have children); because they are members of a group that is systematically denied power and privilege in U.S. society (e.g., the working class, lesbians); or because they have the psychological experience of never fitting in anywhere, of being without a niche, or of feeling unique. Of course, each of these ways of being marginal is probably quite different, although they may also have some features in common (see Frable, Blackstone, and Scherbaum, 1990). In addition, although marginality is often equivalent to a lack of privilege, it is not always so. For example, being a member of the upper class, which may be statistically atypical and may carry with it certain aspects of being an outsider, does not represent a lack of privilege. One of our tasks in this chapter is to explore the ways in which—for individual women—membership in a particular group does and does not relate to the psychological experience of feeling marginal and the extent to which being or feeling marginal is avoided, resisted, or celebrated.

Examining marginality is important for a number of reasons. First, it is relatively underexplored as a psychological construct, although it has been studied throughout this century by sociologists (Dickie-Clark, 1965–1966; Kerckhoff and McCormick, 1955–1956; Stonequist, 1937/1961; see Frable et al., 1990; Haber, 1982; Mayo, 1982, for exceptions in psychology). Second, the concept of the margin is one that has prominence in the work of some contemporary feminist scholars who are concerned with the relationship of the "margin" to the "center" in the production of knowledge (see, e.g., Anzaldúa, 1987; Brown, 1989; hooks, 1984, 1990). These scholars, along with feminist standpoint theorists who use a slightly different epistemological perspective (Collins, 1990; Harding, 1991; Smith, 1987), make the claim that studying those who have been systematically denied access to power, taking them seriously, and theorizing from their perspective will inform our knowledge of "the center" (dominant society) in new and important ways. We hope that an exploration of the lives of "marginal women" will shed light on the psychological study of social class.

Social Class

The role of social class background as a potentially marginalizing factor in women's lives has not received much attention in psychology. Working-class women are beginning to receive more attention in psychology and other fields (Luttrell, 1988, 1989; Susser, 1988), and it is increasingly recognized that their lives are not the same as those of women from the middle class. Even so, little attention appears to have been paid to the psychological experience of women who are raised in the working class and move into an upper-middle-class world via higher education (see Higginbotham and Weber, 1992, for an important exception examining the subjective experience of social mobility among Black and White women). How is the reality of having a different class background from most other people in this environment experienced? When we recognize that "class" is not relevant only in the lives of working-class and poor women, we can also ask the following questions: What is the experience of higher education for women who come from very privileged class backgrounds? What about women from the middle class? How might class consciousness be awakened or refined in the context of an elite women's college? It is particularly important to provide a nuanced analysis of social class in the lives of the women from Stewart's Radcliffe sample. Although women who graduated from Radcliffe were undeniably privileged by virtue of

Radcliffe students participating in student government.
(Courtesy Radcliffe College Archives.)

their education, they have generally been assumed to have had a similar, privileged, class background before entering Radcliffe. This assumption not only renders invisible the experiences of women who came from working-class backgrounds, but also homogenizes the differences among privileged backgrounds.

We are particularly interested in women's consciousness of social class at Radcliffe as a way of examining how women from different class backgrounds do and do not use class as a lens through which to understand and potentially change their worlds. Class consciousness, however, has not been fully studied as a psychological phenomenon in the United States (as compared, particularly, to Great Britain, for example; see Morris and Murphy, 1966, for a useful analysis of class consciousness in the field of sociology). When social class identity is studied (Blau and Duncan, 1967), it is not often studied among women (see Munson and Spivey, 1983, for a rare examination of the relationship of class and self-concept, although not directly covering class identity; see also Luttrell, 1988, 1989; Susser,

1988, for sociological studies of working-class women's consciousness), whose class identities are seen as complicated by the uncertain role of a husband's work and income in determining their wives' class identity (Vanneman and Pampel, 1977). This rationale for excluding women from studies on class ignores the possible importance of an earlier (preadulthood) development of class consciousness (Steedman, 1986; Yeskel, 1989), in addition to making the erroneous assumption that all women have husbands. This example also points to the methodological problem of the measurement of social class—variously determined by income, education, occupation—an important issue, but one that we will not address in this chapter (see Ehrenreich, 1989; Higginbotham and Weber, 1992, for further discussion of this issue).

Using information about parents' educations and occupations and the kind of secondary school the women attended, we estimate that approximately 15 percent of the women in the Radcliffe class of 1964 were raised in working-class families; of the remaining women, about half were raised in the middle class and half in the upper class. Of course, social status had important implications for the material aspects of the women's daily lives both as they were growing up and as they lived their lives at and after Radcliffe; here, though, we are interested in exploring the psychological meaning of these social class markers.

We hope to make a case for the importance of class background and class identification in women's lives, not because, as we shall see, it is always articulated as such by the women, and not, obviously, because it is an unchanging aspect of the women's lives, but because it provides a useful framework for understanding how some women negotiate and resist marginal identities. We begin by exploring the life of a woman who was raised in a working-class family, then turn to a woman with an upper-class background, and end with two women from middle-class families in an effort to address some of the complexity surrounding class identification that is stereotypically absent among members of the middle class.

Working-Class Consciousness

In her important work *Landscape for a Good Woman,* Carolyn Steedman (1986) developed a rich analysis of two women's lives in working-class England. Her biography of her mother provides a vivid and complex understanding of the politics and the psychology of "longing" among working-class women who dream of a different life that could be theirs "if only ..." It is this wish for another life, often characterized by resentment, that organized the working-class consciousness of Steedman's mother's life. The case we will discuss provides a useful contrast to Steedman's analysis, providing us with the opportunity to explore class as producing not a complicated politics of longing, but rather a complex and potentially contradictory politics of resistance.

Carla Ehrlich[1] grew up in a working-class, primarily Catholic neighborhood in a large East Coast city. Her father, who "ran a very tight financial ship" at home, worked throughout her childhood and early adulthood as a university campus public safety official. Her mother was employed as a food service worker in a college dining hall while Carla was between the ages of thirteen and nineteen. Her father began college on a scholarship, but left after two years because he lost the scholarship and needed to help his family earn money. Her father's college experience was an unusual one for her neighborhood, as was his love of books. The Ehrlich family home was filled with books, which Carla describes as "not a typical working-class experience." Carla's understanding of the complicated nature of her working-class family's relationship to the world of the educated elite obviously had early origins.

In addition to her family's class background (which, as we shall see, led to her feeling marginal at Radcliffe as well as to the emergence of her feminist consciousness), there are two other childhood experiences that may have contributed to Carla's having to manage a sense of marginality—in particular of having experiences that were different from those of her peers—early in her life. The first, which served as an explanatory framework with which Carla understood many childhood events, was that her mother was agoraphobic—she had a fear of open, especially public, places. The second was her parents' mixed religious and ethnic marriage: Her mother was Catholic and her father was Protestant, and they had different ethnic backgrounds, too.

Carla's mother's agoraphobia began with a panic attack when Carla was ten years old. Although the agoraphobia was not totally incapacitating until Carla was nineteen, Carla saw her mother's increasing passivity and dependence (especially financial) as having been an important (negative) model for shaping her own identity and worldview. In addition, her mother's need for psychotherapy to help with the agoraphobia was a source of tension concerning money in her family, as her father was extremely reluctant to pay for the therapy. Carla explained the intersection of her mother's agoraphobia, her understanding of gender and sex roles, and her class background in the process of her identity development:

> One of the messages I got out of that [the negotiation of finances to pay for therapy for agoraphobia] was [my mother's] extreme dependence in the marital relationship. ... I was very aware as a kid of my mother ... cheating on the grocery budget to buy the girdle (which my father thought was a ridiculous thing to buy), and going with her while she made her weekly layaway payments and things like that. So I think two things came out of that for me. One is that you need your own money. Whatever you do, don't get yourself stuck in a dependent relationship. ... It's not that I hoard my money, but [it's] the whole notion of being trapped.

The rejection of financial dependency on men became an important aspect of Carla's resistance to middle-class gender roles.

Carla also discussed how her worldview and some of her political stances related to her experiences with Catholicism. Although she was raised Catholic, Carla described her parents' mixed marriage as contributing to her somewhat marginal relationship to Catholicism: "My parents were a mixed marriage in those days; she was Catholic and he was Protestant. He was not an active Protestant, but at the time that they married the Catholic deal was you couldn't marry in the church, you had to marry in the rectory; and you had to promise to raise the children Catholic, so I was raised Catholic. But I went to public school, I didn't go to parochial school, and I went to church." Not only did Carla have a "physically marginal" relationship to Catholicism (being raised Catholic but not going to parochial school seems to have been important), but she also described herself as having had a "crisis of faith" and a deep sense of disillusionment because of what she saw as the discrepancies between ideology and practice in religion from the time that she was entering adolescence. Although she was committed in many ways to the ideals of Catholicism, she was also distressed by what she saw as a lack of living up to those ideals among the people at church and found herself very much caught between ideology and reality:

> [It was] nice to have the idealism, that level of commitment that you can serve people, that was great. But, when I was about thirteen or fourteen, well, earlier on, gradually it began to dawn on me that there were things that didn't quite fit. I mean you're supposed to be pious and worshipful and people in church would be coughing all the time during the sermon. … I underwent a real crisis of faith when I was about thirteen. I was very depressed, really depressed, I cried a lot, wrote gloomy poems.

First Carla worked out some compromises for herself, but eventually she stopped going to church. As she said, however, "The problem with that was that I was really quite devastated because the ideals were gone, the special relationship was gone."

Carla connected her idealistic commitment to the civil rights movement to the ideology of Catholicism and to her social class background. During college, Carla was exposed to students who were participating in the civil rights movement. She herself, however, was not active in the movement for reasons having very much to do with class: She could not afford to take trips down to Washington, and she was wary of the motivations of the other college students who "weren't serious enough for me. … They were going to drink and they were going to party and they were wondering who else was going and these were not noble reasons for participating in my humble mind, you know, for participating in a political movement." From her earlier experiences with the Catholic church, however, she "already had an idealistic bent that I didn't know how to operationalize." The public sentiment about civil rights and courses she took that exposed her to Richard Wright and James Baldwin, combined with that earlier idealism, led her to a commitment to the importance of civil rights. After graduating from Radcliffe she lived in a Black community and taught at a Black institution in the South, which she described as among the high points of her young adult years. Her choice of career also stemmed from her interest in "multiethnic situations."

In the course of Carla's transition to life at Radcliffe and to life immediately beyond Radcliffe, religious and political ideals were not the only values being tested. Her class consciousness was sharpened and articulated, perhaps because it was such a valuable tool for evaluating her Radcliffe experience. This period of her life also highlights the relationship of class consciousness to Carla's feminist consciousness. Carla's sense of class emerged in her recollection of being intimidated by the "articulateness" of some of her classmates. She also described an experience in which an instructor "could not deal with the gap in knowledge between the public school graduates and the private school graduates in his class" and ended up only teaching to one part of the class. This experience, combined with one of sexual harassment and a false accusation of cheating, all in her first year at school, led her to feel "a bit harassed" during that time of transition. This is a time when Carla felt she was obviously different from her classmates, that she was not as well prepared academically as they, and that she had to work extra hard to prove herself.

Carla's feminist consciousness was also linked in complicated ways to her working-class consciousness. Rather than first learning about the oppression of women through publications such as Betty Friedan's *The Feminine Mystique* (1963), she saw Friedan's arguments as vindicating her own understanding of the relationship between men and women that she had developed earlier:

> The women's movement [made a big impression] largely because (and this is going to sound a little arrogant) I anticipated all of those arguments independently on my own just before they opened. ... I knew that I was kind of a deviant in that I never could understand why people thought women would be happy to find their identification through their husband and children. ... I want people to be ... interested in me for me. I don't want people to talk to me because I'm Mrs. So-and-so or because I'm So-and-so's mother. ... I had a working-class background where the husband and wife's spheres were pretty delineated and the wives were recognized in their own right. ... It's true that they might have been recognized as "mothers," but ... they weren't identified as an extension of the husband. So I didn't go through that bit where you've-got-to-have-a-man-to-have-your-identity ... and yet as I got older and moved in more middle-class circles in college I was exposed to that kind of thinking. And I found it repulsive that anybody could buy into that kind of line.

It is clear that Carla's class background and class consciousness provided her with a mode of resistance to middle-class expectations about gender roles. At the same time, there exists a tension between this resistant stance toward middle-class gender roles that is generally grounded in her working-class background and her resistance to being dependent, especially financially dependent, that is particularly grounded in her understanding of her working-class mother's experiences described earlier (see Stewart and Ostrove, 1993, for further discussion of working-class women's stances toward gender roles and feminism).

It was this politics of resistance via class consciousness that was particularly characteristic of Carla's "working-class" strategy for managing marginality. Carla used her working-class background and her working-class experiences as ways to resist societal (middle-class) expectations about, for example, entertaining guests:

> A cocktail party? ... Unthinkable! never had these. ... These were "ha ha ha" things! I think part of that is also because from my mother I absorbed a real strong ... resent-

ment and suspicion of WASP culture … which also starts to merge with middle-class culture. So there was the class aspect and there was the ethnic aspect. That's not a crowd that I'd really want to move with, and it's not that I'm afraid that they won't accept me, it was that this is not the group that you want to get mixed up with.

Carla's "politics of resistance" that has such a clear working-class ideology sur-rounding it is in marked contrast to Steedman's (1986) "politics of envy/longing." Notably, however, both Carla and Steedman had an acute sense of children as burdens that they attribute to their observation of working-class mothers. Carla chose not to have children of her own (although she is a noncustodial stepmother to her second husband's children, who were almost adults when she married). She said in 1974 that "although my mother was an excellent mother to me and my brother, it was also clear that she regarded having had children as the major rea-son her own life was so limited." In 1986 she said (in contrast to Steedman, who had the sense from her mother that she and her sister were in fact burdens),

> Never did I get the sense that my brother and I were personally obstacles. I mean I was very confident of both my parents' love, but the sense that as an objective factor, kids make the woman's life much more complicated, and I did not want to be dependent. … But anyway, to not have kids, … is of course deviant, particularly growing up in a Catholic neighborhood. … There seems to be a certain middle-class romantic image about kids, pretty little four-poster beds with Raggedy Ann dolls and whatnot. Well, I grew up as I said, in a double triple-decker with triple-deckers stacked along and ev-erybody was having babies, I mean it was the fifties and they cried all the time and people yelled all the time. … [Children] intrinsically can be nice but they trap you, they foreclose lots of options to you, they make you dependent.

Carla's resistance to doing what society expects, such as having children, was clearly linked, again, to her working-class background. It is her resistance to soci-etal pressure and to the trappings of middle-class niceties that appear to ground her strong sense of who she is in relation to others. This sense of self seemed to develop out of resisting, or reworking, the sense of unpreparedness and "differ-entness" that her working-class background forced her to confront when she en-tered Radcliffe. Her clear convictions, fostered by what she learned growing up working class and developing a resistance to middle-class life, are demonstrated nicely in the following:

> *The Feminine Mystique* came out when I was nineteen, so whether I was married or not really wasn't an issue yet, or had kids, wasn't an issue. So by the time those were real issues, you know, the discourse was much broader. So I wasn't deviant, but in my mind early on I knew "Geez, I'm interested in going a path that people seem to think …" And I didn't think there was anything wrong with me, but I kind of wondered why other people … didn't pick up that they were going an unwise route.

Later in her life, Carla's sense of "doing fine" and "being fine" was derived from what she called her "frame" for comparing herself to other people. In contrast to her husband, a son of Jewish immigrants who although very successful in his own career, compares himself to others and says "I'm not this or I'm not that," Carla described herself as "much more laid back, because in a sense I think it's not that I've been striving to anything, but rather that I've been trying to avoid being dragged down by certain things." After a long period of not finding a tenure-track academic job, she finally found one that is satisfying in almost every respect. In taking her life as a whole, Carla found it useful to have a comparison group that was grounded in where she had been rather than where she was going, and she recognized that it was not necessary for her to "compare up":

> Well heck, I'm doing fine. So I don't have the money, I don't have the career status, I don't have the same number of books, I never will. But that's fine, I want to do a good job, I want to be responsible, I want to educate people, I want to add to the total sum of knowledge. You know, all of this academic crap. But I also want to be a human being, where I can relate to other people—I can be polite in the grocery store, and I can let cars go in front of me, because my life isn't one hectic deadline after another.

Carla's life was clearly shaped in important ways by her class background and by other marginalizing experiences. It is obvious too that class provided an organizing function in her own account of the formation of her ideological identity. For this working-class woman who attended Radcliffe, class served as a marginalizing experience in both negative and positive ways—by heightening a sense of unpreparedness during her transition to Radcliffe, but also, especially as she continued into adulthood, by providing her with the tools to resist "middle-class traps" in a way that allowed her to live her life in a way that she felt was truly "human."

In an effort to explore further the role of class background in shaping experiences of marginality, we now turn to the life of a woman who entered Radcliffe from a very different social position than did Carla.

Marginality and Upper-Class Consciousness

There is little research on upper-class women. However, Ostrander (1984) and Daniels (1991) demonstrated how upper-class women actively work to maintain their families' class privilege. Both of these studies focused on women who remain in the privileged social class within which they were born and eventually married. But what of those who renounce, or try to renounce, their class privilege—a group that was, perhaps, unusually visible during the 1960s on campuses of elite colleges like Radcliffe? In a thoughtful exploration of her own class background, Sturgis (1988) suggested that the definitions of "upper class" in elite environments are varied:

> To some, "upper class" means simply "rich"—having servants, summering in Europe, living in a house that could pass for a museum. By such a standard, the details of my life are upper middle class: prestigious private girls' school, a degree from an

Ivy League university, not having to work for my education, a family summer place on Martha's Vineyard, dancing school, music lessons, and horse shows.

But being upper class is more than a matter of money, though money counts. (p. 8)

In defining herself as a "daughter of the upper class," Sturgis pointed out that "Upper class means a certainty of belonging, an assumption of one's importance in the world." Because she descended from an "old Boston family," and was directly related to the men who created the U.S. history she was taught in school, she must accept an identification with the upper class.

In college, Sturgis described herself as "existing uneasily between the New Left and the antiwar movement," and thereby as "downwardly mobile," but still privileged by virtue of her education and her background. She pointed out, though, that it was really through feminism that she found an "initiating spark" that allowed her to understand racial, ethnic, heterosexual, and class oppression; and it was through exploration of the details of her complex intersecting identifications that she discovered that she could not deny her privilege. "Downward mobility," then, is not fully possible, according to her analysis. "I do not trust privileged white men who are radical or gay because it is too easy for them to pass from outsider to insider at the first sign of trouble. There are women who do not trust me for the same reasons, who would not trust me if they knew where I came from" (p. 12). Sturgis hoped to hold on to her "marginal" position as an outsider who could "pass" but chooses not to, despite her recognition that there was always a "temptation to give up or sell out" (p. 12).

Sarah Turner came to Radcliffe from almost exactly the same kind of family Sturgis described, and her life course trajectory is similar in many ways, too. Sarah's father's family was "indirectly related" to a famous and wealthy U.S. family, and possessed both inherited wealth and a sense of noblesse oblige. In an interview in 1989, she recalled, too, that in boarding school she was told "you are very privileged people and you absolutely have to make a difference in this world, you can't just sit back and enjoy it." Moreover, her mother and father "underscored" that message in their communication to all of their children. In Sarah's case, the message was eventually reshaped from the noblesse oblige of upper-class culture to a sense of responsibility more characteristic of certain left-wing intellectuals.

I was always the smart one in the family, so I think I was expected to do something intellectual; I was supposed to do good in an intellectual way. But the message was … not specific in the sense of you must become a teacher or you must do this kind of volunteer work. It was much more of a general sort of "the purpose of life is to achieve, get good grades, be respectable, and then turn over all your advantage to the less fortunate."

Themes of a somewhat ambiguous class position (because her family's financial resources did not equal their reputation, influence, and lineage), social responsibility (vs. noblesse oblige), and being "the smart one" recurred in many periods in Sarah's life. She went to boarding school in the 1950s with a lot of really rich girls. I had a slight scholarship because my father hadn't made it yet ... and the family money wasn't worth—there wasn't that much of it. So I was a slightly scholarship student, and I was the smartest person there. Me and four other girls, we were self-consciously intellectual, we were self-consciously concerned with meaning and purpose—you know, we thought we were terrifically much smarter than everybody else. So in that sense I was a rebel in boarding school. I was intellectually superior to all those rich, stupid girls with nice clothes.

This "rebellious insider" role was one that had a history in her family. Her grandfather had retired from his profession at age forty, because styles had changed and he preferred not to adapt himself to changing tastes. Similarly, her father was deeply involved in a movement within his field that eventually became institutionalized, but was initially viewed as "radical."

At Radcliffe, Sarah first operated within Harvard's "preppy world—social clubs and 'final clubs' [Harvard's fraternities]." She reported that "at the end of my sophomore year I left that world behind, pretty consciously. I decided those people were boring and not interesting, and ... in my junior and senior years, I ended up mixing it up with some sorts of Bohemian types, mostly through the men I was involved with. ... I was beginning to sort of move out, move away."

This separation from the group associated with her class background may have been related to some of the painful aspects of her experience of Radcliffe in the more academic realm, but she didn't connect these experiences at the time. Much later, she realized that at Radcliffe she had only been exposed (for example) to male writers in her American Literature courses; she also realized that "On a deeper level, which is much more complicated, there was this pervasive sense of 'you're part of this but you're really not'—this constant double message. Looking back with the feminist lens, I realize what that was, but at the time I just didn't understand." The specific ways in which Sarah felt "not really part of this" included the exclusion of women from Harvard's undergraduate library, Lamont: "I never thought anything about not being able to go to Lamont library. I just always felt inferior." She linked this sense of exclusion within this exclusive environment to having been a "smart girl." As she put it, "I always thought I was sort of—until I got to Radcliffe, I thought I was smart for a girl. When I got to Radcliffe I didn't even think that anymore, 'cause everybody at Radcliffe was smart for a girl." Painful as Sarah Turner's experiences of marginality and feelings of inferiority were, they provided her (like Sturgis) with a basis for empathic connection with others' experience of class-based and race-based oppression.

During her senior year in college, Sarah met her eventual husband—a leftist activist who also had come from a wealthy background. Through him, Sarah became increasingly involved with a variety of community organizing efforts and social change organizations. She also became a teacher and began to work on progressive curricula. Sarah felt that "I got out of that period of time an ideology about this society which is really fundamental—it goes very, very deep. ... I still sort of think that if you're not part of the solution, you're part of the problem." Although Sarah retained this core ideological commitment from her early years, she later felt that "the only way that I could be a committed socialist was by not being myself, on some level." In contrast, feminism offered her a more adequate ideology.

Sarah felt that both her commitment to social change and her sense of personal empowerment, as well as a sense of female inadequacy, were developed and nourished in her marriage. Thus, gender politics continued to create tension and a sense of "something missing" in her worldview.

> Somebody important would have had to give me permission to be like that [activist and committed]. My husband was somebody important who gave me permission to be like that. ... He said to me once when we were first married—he made some kind of putting off comment, and I said, "Do you think you're smarter than I am?" and he said, "No, I don't think I'm smarter than you are." And I said, "Do you think you're right more often than I am?" and he said, "Oh yeah, definitely!" And I said, "How come, if I'm just as smart as you?" And he said, "I'm more revolutionary than you are." And what I remember about that was feeling resentful and completely accepting that that was true.

Later, in the 1980s after her marriage ended, when she had completed a doctorate and was teaching college, Sarah joined a "feminist study group." It was in the context of that study group that she rethought her experience at Radcliffe, as well as her marriage. She realized that her exclusion from full acceptance at Radcliffe was connected to her exclusion from being "right." "Years and years of not being right because I wasn't revolutionary enough—it turns out to actually be part of the same thing—it was the gender thing." In the course of developing her feminist consciousness, Sarah said she found an "explanatory framework for my past as well as my present experience." It is both "something I can share and something that I can use to make sense of my own life and of the world." For Sarah, an important aspect of her discovery of feminism was her discovery of a feminist community:

> [Where I teach] there has been a community of people ... who have been both intellectually and personally able to sort of verify our own experiences of the world as we were going through it. So, for example, you could begin to notice things like who talks in faculty meetings, and then you could go and say to a female colleague, "Did you notice ... ?" And she'd say, "Yes, I counted—ten men spoke for every one woman." Or the much more subtle level, like the way the discourse happens in groups, in the classroom. Not only have I gotten a lens to look at my experience, but that lens has been validated and it's been sort of worked through within the context of the community.

By midlife, then, Sarah Turner had developed her own sense of herself as a "rebellious insider," but not in her original social class—in her adopted class of academics. She had to some extent left the world of her rearing behind—in her circle of friends, her "lifestyle," and her child-rearing values—and had committed herself to a politics of social change rather than the ameliorative work of upper-class women. But her evolving socialist feminist perspective did not permit or require her to deny her background; instead it "tries to ground people in particular contexts and respects the meaning-making that people have to do." Her children attended elite colleges, but they had gone to public schools through high school, and one was involved with social change efforts on her own. Sarah herself headed the efforts to transform the curriculum at the college where she worked and played an important intellectual role in shaping the theory and practice of feminist teaching there. Her career as a feminist academic allowed her to remain "marginal" to mainstream academics, but also to play a leadership role and participate in a community of people who shared her commitment to change. Aspects of the small group of four smart girls at boarding school and the larger groups of "beatniks," community organizers, and inner-city teachers she worked with later were in some ways reflected in Sarah's midlife commitments; she remained special by virtue of being "smart" and committed to social change. But she had found a basis for this marginal identity that allowed her to connect with others in egalitarian and affirming ways while bringing together her personal experience and her social commitments.

For Carla Ehrlich, identification with working-class values and culture (as well as with other marginal identities) provided a source of strength in resisting the middle-class culture she faced at Radcliffe. For Sarah Turner, exposure to socialist ideology at Radcliffe (and an enduring sense of marginality as a "smart girl") helped support her rejection of upper-class values and her exploration of feminism. If it is true that middle-class women are unlikely to develop class consciousness (see DeMott, 1990), class should not be related to middle-class women's experiences of marginality, however. We turn briefly to the lives of two women who illustrate the complicated nature of class identification within the middle class and highlight the ways in which even women with middle-class backgrounds manage marginal identities in ways that reflect their class experiences.

Middle-Class Women:
Complexities of Class Consciousness

We have stated that the development of an explicit class consciousness among members of the middle class is unusual or at least poses particular challenges. DeMott (1990) contended that the population of the United States is

> composed not of classes but of men and women of the middle united as strivers and self-betterers. The mind of the middle isn't absorbed with the subject of class, doesn't engage ceaselessly in placing itself and others, and lives without detailed maps of social difference. But those in concord with this mind aren't without conceptions of themselves and others in social terms. ... The people in question know, for instance, that as men or women of the "middle class," only with an effort of will—only by contrivance—can they imagine themselves to BE members of a class. Normally they feel themselves to be solid individual achievers in an essentially classless society composed of human beings engaged in bettering themselves. (p. 43)

Rose Gardner came to Radcliffe from a solidly middle-class, Midwestern family. Her mother owned a fabric store, and her father was a depot agent for a major Midwestern railway. Her parents also built and owned their home. In her description of her childhood, Rose did not use social class as a category for identification or for comparison with others in the community. In addition, class was not a part of her conscious representation of her experiences at Radcliffe, nor did it play a part in other descriptions of her life. *Not* using class as a mode of analysis may be thought of as very common among members of the middle class—Ehrenreich (1989) argued that at least until the 1980s the middle class in the United States was "a class which is everywhere represented as representing everyone" (p. 4), thereby making an identification as a distinct class quite difficult. In fact, it is not surprising that it is Rose Gardner, a woman from the middle class, who said that she felt she "belonged at Radcliffe"—a marked contrast both to Carla Ehrlich's alienation connected to being from a working-class background and to Sarah Turner's complicated gendered and class-based stance toward Radcliffe.

Rose Gardner's sense of "belonging" at Radcliffe does not necessarily indicate participation in a community, though; instead, it may reflect her sense of fitting in with the larger climate of values. Because what is particularly striking about Rose is her strong sense of her own individuality—an important part of "hegemonic American culture" (Ortner, 1991, p. 171) that probably most often emerges in the ideology of "the middle class"[2] and is prominent in the Harvard/Radcliffe environment. Although Rose defined herself in terms of many "marginal identities," she did not describe herself as particularly *group* identified, preferring instead to stress her uniqueness from others. In 1979 she wrote: "I am an alcoholic, although I have been sober 8 years, a former drug addict, a former smoker, a sometime Lesbian, a person who suffers from agoraphobia, depression and quasi-schizophrenic episodes. I have health problems. These facts are a motive that moves through my life along with my delight in living, in loving, in art, literature and science (and gardening)." Rose identified herself in terms of a number of "marginal" groups, but she did so in a decidedly unpoliticized way, stressing individualism rather than group identification. Her strategy for managing these marginal identities is not to ally herself with a particular group or mode of analysis, but to emphasize her individual uniqueness, a strategy that may in fact have much to do with her class background.

Rose's career path also reflected the achievement of a decidedly unique individual. She worked hard to carve out an employment life that provided both a way to earn a living and a way to satisfy her personal and intellectual interests and commitments. In combining different types of writing with various consulting opportunities, Rose's career reflects the efforts of one unwilling, here as in other aspects of her identity, to settle for established categories.

Nina Jacobs also managed marginal identities in ways that seem decidedly "middle class," though quite different from Rose Gardner's. Nina, like many apparently middle-class people, came from a mixed class background, which may in part account for the fact that class was quite present in her analysis of Radcliffe and in the way she described some aspects of her life. Her mother was raised in a poor, rural setting and worked as a teacher before her marriage and after Nina was in high school; her father came from a downwardly mobile wealthy family and worked as a university professor throughout Nina's life. Notably, Nina appeared to have learned early on that "it's not necessarily a great opportunity to … marry up."

In her retrospective account of Radcliffe, Nina also highlighted the downside of moving in an elite world: "It [Radcliffe] encouraged me to be competitive, defensive, a master of one-upmanship, and generally fostered many objectionable traits in my personality which I have since had to grow out of." She also acknowledged, however, the value of the academic life and the happiness she derived from being an "educated person."

Nina used class relatively frequently in her evaluation of certain situations she encountered in her life, but it seemed not to have been a source of personal or political identification for her. She did not see her class membership as setting her apart from others or as giving her a particular group membership. She did, however, see her son as having benefited from being a "white upper-middle-class child." Additionally, there was a period in the early 1970s during which Nina was very poor. Although she described herself as always being a frugal person, her frugality "was most extreme at that period because it was a matter of necessity. … And I think that's an experience a lot of people from my class at Radcliffe never had." It is apparent that class is an important category of analysis for Nina in some situations—perhaps due to her mixed class lineage; it is neither as absent as it was for Rose Gardner, nor does it have the broad explanatory power it had for Carla Ehrlich and Sarah Turner.

Like Rose Gardner, Nina Jacobs did not seem at all group identified in any politicized way. However, in contrast to Rose's stress on her uniqueness from others, Nina did not view her "marginal identities" as setting her apart from most other women, even when in some objective sense they did. Even as a young single mother after her early divorce at age twenty-seven in 1970, Nina did not see herself as "marginal." In the town where she lived, she felt that so many of her peers were divorced that it was a rather normative experience for her son to come from a single-parent family. Of her recognition of the inequality of marriage, she said: "You had the feeling other people were feeling the same thing. … Certainly you had the sense that there were other people, other women out there, you weren't alone."

Through our inclusion in this discussion of two middle-class women who differ from one another as well as from the women discussed earlier, we have expanded our look at the ways in which class background may or may not shape the worldviews of educated women. The two middle-class women we have presented here appear to have characteristically middle-class perspectives on their own "marginality"—one sees herself through a highly individualistic lens and stresses her uniqueness from others; the other manages to see the many other women who are in similar positions, highlighting that there are plenty of "other women out there" living similar lives.

Conclusions

In this chapter we have attempted to identify some different ways in which social class provides a worldview and influences the management of marginality in the lives of four college-educated women. Obviously, the realities of the past and current hierarchical class structure in the United States have important material ramifications for individuals. In addition, we have shown that characteristic worldviews based on class background shape women's understandings of their lives. For Carla Ehrlich, who was raised working class, class was a salient organizing principle and provided a context for understanding a variety of marginalizing experiences she had in her life. Even more, it provided her with an analytic tool that gave her leverage in resisting middle-class culture. Sarah Turner's class consciousness, in contrast, resulted in efforts to disengage herself from her privileged class position. Her commitments to socialism and later to feminism in turn provided her with the structural tools to understand and work to change systematic oppression, as well as to reevaluate her own experiences of marginality at Radcliffe/Harvard. In contrast to these women, both of whom transformed their class identifications into tools for analyzing and changing their own and others' situations, the women from middle-class backgrounds linked their class consciousness with other, potentially marginalizing experiences and life outcomes by emphasizing individual uniqueness, in one case, and connecting her situation to what many other people around her were doing, in the other. In both cases, class consciousness did not include a sense of belonging to a well-defined class-based *group* within a larger social system. It may be the ubiquitousness of middle-class culture and the assumption—or wish—that "we are all middle class" that makes it difficult for middle-class people to find meaningful identification as members of a distinct class. Thus, it may be the absence of *group* consciousness that often appears to indicate a lack of *class* consciousness among middle-class individuals (see P. Gurin, Miller, and G. Gurin, 1980; P. Gurin, 1985).

On the other hand, it is interesting to note that although Carla Ehrlich and Sarah Turner eventually experienced aspects of their social class backgrounds as marginalizing them at Radcliffe, they had other formative experiences of marginality as well (Carla Ehrlich from her mother's agoraphobia and her parents' mixed marriage; Sarah Turner from her sense of being a "smart girl"). It is unlikely that social class background alone would produce the sense of marginality that these two women felt at Radcliffe. Many upper-class girls probably felt comfortable with the class-based social life that Sarah Turner rejected in her first year. They might thereby share with middle-class women a sense of fitting in and being "like" their peers. Some girls from working-class backgrounds may have aimed more for acceptance in middle-class culture, rather than adopting Carla Ehrlich's resistant stance toward it. In this case, too, wishing to "fit in" may preclude development or maintenance of class consciousness. We do not, then, claim that material social class situation translates simply or directly into particular class consciousness. Instead, a variety of personal, family, and community experiences together help shape an individual's sense both of belonging in some groups and of marginality. In turn, under some conditions—but not automatically—class consciousness and a sense of marginality may together become a tool for understanding one's own life, as well as the power relations pervading both personal relations and the larger society. It may be that the social change movements that both Carla Ehrlich and Sarah Turner experienced as part of their lives at Radcliffe were a critical factor in legitimating their understanding of power relations as pervading their own lives (see Stewart, 1994, for a discussion of the meanings of the women's movement in their lives).

We have seen in this chapter that for Carla Ehrlich, it was a working-class consciousness and sense of marginality that provided tools for her resistance of middle-class gender norms and middle-class culture more generally. For Sarah Turner, in contrast, upper-class consciousness and a sense of marginality provided tools for resistance of a life of noblesse oblige. After Radcliffe and at midlife, both became tenured professors at equivalent universities—members of the academic class. Superficially, their lives are very similar. Nevertheless, Sarah Turner remains the daughter of a distinguished New England family, and Carla Ehrlich never forgets that she has "been trying to avoid being dragged down by certain things." Both privilege and deprivation have left traces in their lives—not only in the forms of their resistance, but also in the focus of their struggles. The most important thing about Carla Ehrlich and Sarah Turner, though, may be their sense of determination, optimism, and hope about those struggles. We need to know much more about the circumstances under which social class and marginality are transformed into useful tools of resistance and self-definition, as well as when they are experienced as confining, constraining, and irresistible forces of exclusion.

Acknowledgments

We are grateful to the four women who shared their lives with us for this chapter; they have been wonderful colleagues. We are also grateful to Lillian Cartwright, Rosie Ceballo, Carol Franz, and Wendy Wiener for helpful feedback on earlier versions of this chapter.

Notes

1. Names are pseudonyms chosen by the women, in consultation with us. Identifying details have been obscured to protect their privacy.

2. Ortner (1991) suggested that "middle class" itself may not even be a "class term," but may rather "mean a general allegiance to the nation and to large, overarching values like freedom and individualism" (p. 188).

References

Anzaldúa, G. (1987). *Borderlands/La frontera: The new mestiza*. San Francisco: Aunt Lute Books.

Blau, P. M., & Duncan, O.D.D. (1967). *The American occupational structure.* New York: Wiley.

Brown, L. S. (1989). New voices, new visions: Toward a lesbian/gay paradigm for psychology. *Psychology of Women Quarterly, 13,* 445–448.

Collins, P. H. (1990). *Black feminist thought: Knowledge, consciousness, and the politics of empowerment.* London: Harper Collins.

Daniels, A. K. (1991). Gender, class, and career in the lives of privileged women. In J. R. Blau & N. Goodman (Eds.), *Social roles and social institutions: Essays in honor of Rose Laub Coser* (pp. 115–132). Boulder: Westview.

DeMott, B. (1990). *The imperial middle.* New York: William Morrow.

Dickie-Clark, H. F. (1965–1966). The marginal situation: A contribution to marginality theory. *Social Forces, 44,* 363–370.

Ehrenreich, B. (1989). *Fear of falling: The inner life of the middle class.* New York: Pantheon.

Frable, D.E.S., Blackstone, T., & Scherbaum, C. (1990). Marginal and mindful: Deviants in social interaction. *Journal of Personality and Social Psychology, 59,* 140–149.

Friedan, B. (1963). *The feminine mystique.* New York: Dell.

Gurin, P. (1985). Women's gender consciousness. *Public Opinion Quarterly, 49,* 143–163.

Gurin, P., Miller, H., & Gurin, G. (1980). Stratum identification and consciousness. *Social Psychology Quarterly, 43,* 30–47.

Haber, G. M. (1982). Spatial relations between dominants and marginals. *Social Psychology Quarterly, 45,* 219–228.

Harding, S. (1991). *Whose science? Whose knowledge? Thinking from women's lives.* Ithaca: Cornell University Press.

Higginbotham, E., & Weber, L. (1992). Moving up with kin and community: Upward social mobility for black and white women. *Gender and Society, 6,* 416–440.

hooks, b. (1984). *Feminist theory: From margin to center.* Boston: South End.

_____. (1990). *Yearning: Race, gender, and cultural politics.* Boston: South End.

Kerckhoff, A. C., & McCormick, T. C. (1955–1956). Marginal status and marginal personality. *Social Forces, 34,* 48–55.

Luttrell, W. (1988). The Edison School struggle: The reshaping of working-class education and women's consciousness. In A. Bookman & S. Morgan (Eds.), *Women and the politics of empowerment* (pp. 136–156). Philadelphia: Temple University Press.

_____. (1989). Working class women's ways of knowing: Effects of gender, race, and class. *Sociology of Education, 62,* 33–46.

Mayo, C. (1982). Training for positive marginality. *Applied Social Psychology Annual, 3,* 57–73.

Morris, R. T., & Murphy, R. J. (1966). A paradigm for the study of class consciousness. *Sociology and Social Research, 50,* 248–313.

Munson, J. M., & Spivey, W. A. (1983). Relation between social class and three aspects of self-concept: Actual, ideal, and egocentric self. *Journal of Social Psychology, 119,* 85–94.

Ortner, S. B. (1991). Reading America: Preliminary notes on class and culture. In R. G. Fox (Ed.), *Recapturing anthropology: Working in the present* (pp. 163–189). Santa Fe, NM: School of American Research Press.

Ostrander, S. (1984). *Women of the upper class.* Philadelphia: Temple University Press.

Smith, D. (1987). *The everyday world as problematic: A feminist sociology.* Boston: Northeastern University Press.

Steedman, C. (1986). *Landscape for a good woman: A story of two lives.* London: Virago.

Stewart, A. J. (1978). A longitudinal study of coping styles of self-defining and socially defined women. *Journal of Consulting and Clinical Psychology, 46,* 1079–1084.

———. (1980). Personality and situation in the prediction of women's life patterns. *Psychology of Women Quarterly, 5,* 195–206.

———. (1994). The women's movement and women's lives: Linking individual development and social events. In R. Josselson & A. Lieblich (Eds.), *The Narrative Study of Lives: Exploring Gender and Identity Issues* (pp. 230–250). Newbury Park, CA: Sage.

Stewart, A. J., & Ostrove, J. M. (1993). Social class, social change, and gender: Working class women at Radcliffe and beyond. *Psychology of Women Quarterly, 17,* 475–497.

Stewart, A. J., & Salt, P. (1981). Life stress, life styles, depression and illness in adult women. *Journal of Personality and Social Psychology, 40,* 1063–1069.

Stewart, A. J., & Vandewater, E. A. (1993). Career and family social clock projects in a transitional cohort: The Radcliffe class of 1964. In K. Hulbert & D. Schuster (Eds.), *Women's lives through time: Educated American women of the twentieth century* (pp. 235–258). San Francisco: Jossey-Bass.

Stonequist, E. V. (1961). *The marginal man: A study in personality and cultural conflict.* New York: Russell & Russell. (Original work published 1937 by Scribner).

Sturgis, S. J. (1988). Class/Act: Beginning a translation from privilege. In C. McEwan & S. O'Sullivan (Eds.), *Out the other side: Contemporary lesbian writing* (pp. 7–13). London: Virago.

Susser, I. (1988). Working-class women, social protest, and changing ideologies. In A. Bookman & S. Morgan (Eds.), *Women and the politics of empowerment* (pp. 257–271). Philadelphia: Temple University Press.

Vanneman, R., & Pampel, F. C. (1977). The American perception of class and status. *American Sociological Review, 42,* 422–437.

Yeskel, F. (1989). You didn't talk about these things: Growing up Jewish, lesbian, and working class. In C. Balka & A. Rose (Eds.), *Twice blessed: On being lesbian, gay, and Jewish* (pp. 40–47). Boston: Beacon.

21

A Struggle That Continues: Black Women, Community, and Resistance

ELIZABETH R. COLE

HISTORICAL ACCOUNTS of the African-American struggle against systems of op-pression are characterized by the theme of communities as sites of resistance and refuge and as sources of nurture and power. Indeed, civil rights activists in the Student Non-Violent Coordinating Committee (SNCC) repeatedly invoked the ideal of the "beloved community" to describe their goal of bringing about societal transformation based upon Christian ideals of justice and brotherly love (Carson, 1981). The idea that one belongs to a community is a powerful and sustaining one; it transcends the social and temporal isolation inherent in models that presume human existence to be essentially individual. Nevertheless, in a society character-ized by alienation and injustice, the celebration of community and the attendant values of solidarity and interdependence often precludes serious inquiry into the ways in which existing communities generate and sustain political action. When viewed from the standpoint of women's experience, it is clear that in contrast to the ideal of the political community that prefigures a just society, communities engaged in progressive political struggle are influenced significantly by the mores and norms of the larger cultures from which they spring. This chapter describes two successive generations of African-American student protest movements at the University of Michigan, based on the accounts of two women who played key roles within them. Their experiences demonstrate the specific ways in which community not only gives rise to struggle, but also shapes its course; the form that struggle may take is to a large extent prefigured by the existing social rela-tions within the community.

Political protest among Black students at the University of Michigan has been characterized by a self-conscious sense of lineage and community. Between 1970 and 1987, three "generations" of African-American students came together at different times to build protest movements seeking essentially the same goals: increased recruitment, enrollment, financial aid, support services for Black students, and later, all students of color.

In spring 1970 at the University of Michigan, a coalition of Black student organizations led a ten-day strike, virtually shutting down the university. The activists, calling themselves the Black Action Movement, or BAM, mobilized a multiracial coalition of student groups and support staff whose efforts forced the university administration to reach a settlement with the BAM negotiating team (Davis, 1991).

Five years after the BAM strike, a group of African-American students staged a two-day sit-in to protest that enrollment targets for minority students had not yet been met. Conscious of the lineage of their struggle, the group named itself the Black Action Movement II. Unlike the earlier movement, BAM II was unable to obtain a negotiated settlement with the administration.

The third generation of the antiracist movement at the University of Michigan was sparked by a series of racist incidents including the distribution of White supremacist fliers in dormitories and a campus radio broadcast of racist jokes in early 1987. In response, students formed a multiracial organization called the United Coalition Against Racism (UCAR) and marched on the administration building to present a list of demands similar to those brought in the earlier actions. Not satisfied with the response, the students formed a second organization with the goal of recruiting more Black students to the current wave of protest, taking the name BAM III. These groups asked the national leader Jesse Jackson to come to Ann Arbor to aid them in the negotiations. In the glare of the national media attention Jackson brought with him, a settlement was reached (Davis, 1991).

Cynthia Stephens was the only woman student on the negotiating team of the original Black Action Movement. Now a judge of the third judicial circuit court in Wayne County in her early forties, Stephens graciously found time to meet with me in her schedule that at the time included campaigning for a seat on the state court of appeals and parenting her five-year-old child. The week we met, she had to juggle her calendar after falling behind because she had spent an afternoon with Anita Hill.

I met her in the chambers of her Detroit courtroom. The impressive setting was matched by Stephens's own poise and stature. She spoke freely and at length about the movement, but had less to say about her own thoughts and feelings during her experiences, noting, "My late adolescence, early adult years were primarily experiential and not reflective. You know, I was there, I was doing that because it was what I should be doing now. I didn't usually spend hours pondering it. I just did it."

At the time of the BAM strike, Stephens was in the second year of her formidable undergraduate career. She came to the university when she was sixteen, wrote for the student newspaper, the *Michigan Daily,* served as the vice president of the Black Student Union (BSU) as well as of her sorority, and completed her degree in political science in three years. She described herself at the time as "having a fairly strong sense of self": "I had a sense of individual power, I did not feel vulnerable to forces, had a sense of my responsibility to protect myself, did not perceive aggression as a negative concept, still don't. ... I perceived myself to be capable." Nevertheless, Stephens went on to attribute her own activism in the BAM strike, at least in part, to the milieu of Black students and the wider Black community at the time.

African-American students at the university, she argued, were a fairly homogeneous group. Generally, the Black students at Michigan were not the first in their family to go to college. And although most of their parents were underemployed relative to their educational achievements—"you had a college degree to work at the post office"—the students had had instilled in them "fairly entrenched middle-class values, and an expectation that the world for us was limitless."

Moreover, the Black students were tightly knit as a group. "We knew everybody, we even knew the five guys who belonged to White fraternities." The majority of these students had come to the university directly from several of Detroit's best high schools. "Most of us had known each other, or knew somebody who knew. ... The Black middle class isn't but so big still." Because of the small size of the community, men and women were linked to one another through current and former dating relationships: "The majority of the people dated somebody and would break up with that person and date someone else." Similarly, same-sex relationships were also tightly knit, cemented not just through informal friendships, but also more self-consciously through fraternities and sororities. "I joined a sorority because I decided—it was a conscious decision on my part—that I needed to form some bonding relationships with some sisters. It wasn't like I wanted to wear [the sorority's colors]. I mean I enjoyed being in the sorority, I participated on the national level and all of that, but the principal moving force was that I believed that I had the means to form some bonding relationships—I'm sure that I didn't put it in that kind of language—with other Black women."

The culture of this small and cohesive community lent itself to political action. Among the African-American students there was an expectation that students would participate in activities relevant to the larger community; Stephens described activism as the "presumed norm": "We didn't call it PC [politically correct], but there was in fact a politically correct way in which persons responded to the environment."

Stephens's role in BAM grew out of her leadership role in the Black Student Union, albeit in a way that recalls the "women's work" performed by women in other social movements of the time (Cable, 1992; McAdam, 1992; Thorne, 1975). Whether purposely or not, Stephens was able to transform the secondary role relegated to her by the (male) rest of the BSU leadership into a position of real power:

> I was the person who kept track of things, and so ... there were all these meetings and people would go to the meetings and come back and say "what happened?" And so,

ultimately I compiled the BAM demands [presented to the university administra-
tion]—not necessarily authored them—but compiled them. A couple of them I just
threw on there and they didn't argue with me because they hadn't kept records and
no one really knew. And I did, and they figured "Stephens keeps the records, we'll
trust her." ...

But, I was there principally, I mean, yes, I was the vice-chair [of the BSU], but I was
there because I kept the records and because I compiled the demands and when they
decided to have a strike, in the middle of a meeting, it was like, "we have to have some
demands," so—I went home and typed them up. ... Not really exciting or glamorous.

At every level, Stephens characterized the organizational structure of the BAM
movement as subject to the social structures preexisting among the students at
the Michigan campus. Just as Stephens's leadership role was constructed along the
lines of traditional gender-appropriate behavior, among the rank-and-file participants of the strike, women made a disproportionate contribution to the mundane
tasks that made the strike effective. Women carried out the work that is not seen,
such as organizing the strikers, and the work that is not remembered, such as
walking the picket lines. Indeed, women's efforts in the strike were so unremark-
able in their workaday nature that they were essentially invisible to the group's
leadership; when I contacted one of the male BAM negotiators to ask him for
names of women students involved in the BAM strike, he told me that Cynthia
Stephens was the only woman involved. In contrast, Stephens describes the dynamics of the strike itself in this way:

While the University of Michigan had far more Black male students than Black
women, if you had good pictures of the persons who were seen walking the picket
lines, etcetera, it was principally women. And I'm not talking about who was at the
front making noise, I'm talking about if you had to have a picket line every day, it's
like "OK, who's going to take the early morning duty? We'll get the women from Alice
Lloyd [dormitory]. ..." And I think that it was that role that allowed anything else to
happen, so ... I have no thing about whether they were leaders up front or not. People organized their dorms, that's leadership.

Charles Payne (1990) made a similar observation about women's participation
in the civil rights movement in 1962–1963 in the Mississippi delta. He argues that
just as the work women do to maintain life, caring for families and homes, is devalued, unpaid, and invisible, the work that women do to maintain social movements "is effectively devalued, sinking beneath the level of our sight" (p. 165). In
BAM, this gender-stratified division of labor extended to the bargaining table:

CS: And even during the process of negotiations, frankly, it was the guys talking to
each other across the table, and if you had something to say, you ... had to be ...
a pushy broad. And I found that within the confines of meetings that were not
public, they were more than willing to listen to anything I had to say, but that
when it came to public meetings, that the probability is that [particular men]
would be talking, even if you had to hand them notes. I don't mean that un-
kindly to any of them.

EC: Why do you think that was—the difference between public and private?

CS: Because there was also an ongoing conflict within the Black community about the issues of which way the "-isms" go. What do you do with sexism as it relates to the struggle against racism? Which is predominant? How do they interact? And that's a struggle that continues.

Stephens suggested that to have a voice on the negotiating team she was required to step outside her prescribed gender role in a way that was socially censured; she was regarded as a "pushy broad." Moreover, the distinction she made between the public and private behavior of the men on the negotiating team indicates that even in the role of a protest movement negotiator, her male peers expected that she limit her contributions to the private (i.e., domestic) sphere.

Stephens alluded to the fact that the question of which way the "-isms" go, the relative privileging of the struggles against racism and sexism, is historically a contested one in African-American communities. This controversy has been engendered at least in part by claims made by White policymakers that Black women's alleged dominance over Black men, rather than racism or institutional systems of discrimination, is to blame for the plight of Black Americans and their families generally (Giddings, 1984). Nevertheless, the dynamics of this internal struggle are significant to the meaning of the movement, both for those who participated in it and for those students in successive generations who took the name BAM for their own antiracist movement, as I will discuss later.

Stephens seemed somewhat reluctant to discuss her personal reactions to the gender hierarchy within BAM, waiting for me to ask her to elaborate and answering my questions only cursorily. She suggested that other women involved in the movement were also angry, yet this collective anger was never discussed publicly. Instead, it was most often expressed in the context of personal relationships. Just as the organization was constituted out of preexisting relationships, conflict within the group, based on group interests, could be dissipated through these relationships, specifically heterosexual relationships: "But the prior social relationships did have a lot to do with how folks interfaced within the nature of the political struggle, definitely, but the one-on-one relationships I was talking about were between people who were dating each other or used to date each other, or stuff like that, I'm talking about that kind of interpersonal conflict."

During the interview, Stephens reminded me at several points that the BAM strike lasted only ten days; in this sense, BAM was less a movement than an event. The coalitions that formed among BAM and other student organizations, such as the predominantly white SDS, were for a single purpose and for a brief time. BAM itself, forged from existing relationships between individuals and groups, was grounded in the community; conflict, like lightning, could travel down through the organization to be absorbed by the relationships that constituted its foundation.

When I pressed Stephens to talk about how her student political involvements affected her, she looked back at her experiences in BAM with the perspective of twenty years. She weighed the benefits of participation against the very real personal risks that activists assume; she noted that student protesters at neighboring Eastern Michigan University had been tear-gassed by the county sheriff. But what Stephens took from her experiences in the movement seems to center around the struggle as a community endeavor: "It gave me some organizing experiences that were fairly incredible, and some access to some people whom I value significantly in my life to this day." Even when discussing the sense of efficacy that the movement's success engendered in the participants, she emphasized the collective nature of the struggle: "I did not have any illusions that we had succeeded wildly, but relative success, and success in first participating in a unity of African-Americans ... working with others, builds an expectation that that is possible, and an expectation that one has some level of power, as opposed to powerlessness, and so I think that was helpful."

Stephens views her future with an awareness of the realities of the changes aging can bring: "I have become concerned that as I get older, my perspective may be colored by personal caution far more than it needs to be." Although she is still quite politically active, her perspective on politics seems tempered, perhaps by time. I asked her whether she still considered herself an activist and when she answered positively, I asked her what that meant to her. She answered: "That means that I am an individual who perceives that I have a responsibility to do more than my job, that part of my belief—in terms of how you cope with your environment and retain some reasonable level of sanity—is to attempt to organize against those things that are dangerous to you and your community, to protect yourself against those who you cannot stop, and in the worst case, just scream real loud."

Stephens's statement conveys in a very few words the connection she experiences between identity and community. As an activist, she feels a responsibility to act on behalf of her community; at the same time, she views her commitment to action as a personal coping strategy, preserving her own well-being.

In many ways, the struggle that Stephens waged, both as a part of the membership of BAM I and within the organization, was revisited seventeen years later by the United Coalition Against Racism (UCAR). Kim Smith, my second informant, joined UCAR early in its history. Now in her late twenties and completing her last year of medical school, she is still active with the Ella Baker–Nelson Mandela Center for Anti-Racist Education, the resource center that grew out of the UCAR demands. She generously agreed to meet me in an Ann Arbor cafe the day after her board exams. I was first introduced to Smith by an episode of the PBS series "Frontline" concerning racist incidents on college campuses and student responses to them. The program included footage of Smith, then an undergraduate, assertively challenging then–UM president Shapiro, as well as clips from an interview in which she dispassionately recounted events of the strike. Smith's own description of herself, as a person who is "vocal" and "in the front of things," is not far from this characterization: "I think that people see me as a person who says what I think. It's not always true, but I think in a political sense it's true, I say what I think. And that sort of stems from, I guess, the way that I was raised and a certain amount of confidence that I have in what I have to say being important, so I guess that's what I mean by being vocal. And as I got more involved in UCAR, that came out." The only woman leader in the movement interviewed in that "Frontline" episode, Smith appeared on television as a formidable figure, with the kind of solemn, single-minded commitment we expect from crusaders for justice. In person, she told me her story with warmth, humor, and animation. Her commitment to struggle was always present in her narrative, but not in the stern or moralistic manner presented in the "Frontline" episode.

Smith told me that UCAR developed out of an existing student group, the Free South Africa Coordinating Committee (FSACC). When a series of racist incidents took place on the campus early in 1987, the group redirected its efforts to protesting racism locally, its membership grew, and it took the name UCAR, the United Coalition Against Racism. Although UCAR was founded by Black students, from the beginning, it was the intention to build a more broadly based, multiracial organization. This position eventually engendered conflict between UCAR and certain Black student organizations; in response, BAM III was formed by students who desired a solely Black organization.

Like Stephens, Smith describes her initial exposure to and recruitment into the activist organization as occurring through a social network. She traces her initial involvement with the movement to her housemate at the time, Lannis Hall, who chaired the minority commission of the university student government. Smith had watched the depth of her friend's involvement indirectly and read accounts of the emerging movement; she was recruited to activism only when she came into closer contact with women active in the struggle, observing their commitment firsthand:

> I didn't really understand, or necessarily feel a part of it. ... And so I was slow to get involved in the first few weeks. ... And then as things got more and more heated, and then when there was the sit-in, then I felt absolutely obligated to be there, for one to support Lannis, because I knew that she was there, in the midst of all this. Number two, because if there were students that felt strong enough to sit in, I knew that there was something I was missing, so I felt like I needed to know more of what was going on. So I went to the sit-in, and that motivated me to know more. And I started to find out more, and started to meet more of the people involved and talk to them. ... Those people started me to thinking more, and talking more, and I sort of got pulled in from there and there was no turning back.

In contrast to Stephens's description of BAM, Smith's narrative of UCAR emphasized the organization's continuity and longevity. The events that gave rise to UCAR were only the beginning. Unlike BAM III, which Smith described as short lived, the students in UCAR continued working to address the issues that launched the movement in winter 1987 during the relative calm of the summer and into the following academic year. As the excitement of the events of the winter died down and the group refocused its energies on study groups and teach-ins, women came to predominate in the membership. Just as Stephens recounted becoming the author of the BAM I demands because no one else had kept notes,

Smith recalled that the changes in UCAR's leadership occurred at least partly by default:

> **KS:** Some of the men started stepping away for whatever reason. Some of it was dis-agreement, a lot of it was sexism, some of it was people are students and they're busy. … As the summer went on and as the fall started the next year, it really had become more women. So at that point there was maybe ten people, maybe six or seven women [on the steering committee]. So there was a big shift over the sum-mer, and then, as the fall came back, then people who had left for the summer came back and couldn't really deal with the new involvement.
>
> **EC:** When you say people, you mean men?
>
> **KS:** Yeah.

Stephens's experiences suggest that women in the first BAM were effectively kept in traditional gender roles via unspoken conventions and that gender con-flict was essentially absorbed through existing relationships. In contrast, from early on there was tension between UCAR and BAM because of UCAR's nontra-ditional approach to organizing students, including the prominence of women in the group and their openness to Whites, gays, and lesbians. Smith describes the reactions of BAM III members: "And why were there White people? Why were there gay and lesbian people? Because at the sit-in there were signs that said some of everything [e.g., antiracist, antisexist, and antihomophobic messages], which was typical of UCAR. Even early, UCAR was the type of group, I think, that peo-ple felt comfortable in regardless, you know, White folks included, so that was definitely a source of tension."

Over time, this tension escalated into open hostility from men in the commu-nity, particularly members of the Black Student Union (BSU) and former mem-bers of BAM III, centering on issues of gender and women's leadership. Several male leaders of other Black student organizations wrote to the *Michigan Daily*, publicly denouncing UCAR. Smith described the letter as a "vicious attack": "It said that we were dealing with too many issues, too much focusing on sexism, and homophobia and all of that … something along the lines of we were attacking Black men." Privately, men who had been in BAM III verbally abused men in UCAR "as having no 'balls'—they had been castrated by us [their women col-leagues]."

The sexist attacks culminated in winter 1988 during a protest organized by UCAR to challenge racist statements made by a university dean. Members of UCAR had been working to organize the rally since the previous fall. Their plan-ning appeared to have paid off; they marched the crowd to the university admin-istration building to confront the dean directly, and there Smith announced they would sit in, occupying the facility for the night. "Everybody said 'Yeah! We're gonna stay!' So then we just took off and spread throughout the whole floor and starting sitting down. And so it went great! And we were happy with how things went. It was really going well, people were in rooms and [teaching assistants] were bringing their classrooms and it was just great, it was really great."

That night, several Black male students came to the building, led by a man who formerly belonged to UCAR and who had a history of conflict with the group's leaders. "He just sort of walked in and walked up to the front and started attacking us, just started ranting and raving about stuff, 'what were we doing?' and said all these terrible things. ... He just started saying we didn't need to be up in here protesting, 'your mommas didn't send you over here to protest,' and all this stuff." Smith felt that this attack, as well as similar ones made the next day at a Martin Luther King Day rally "took the air out of these kids, a lot of freshmen who had sat in for the first time, feeling empowered, he just totally, you know, made them feel very conflicted. And he attacked UCAR. And that put us on our heels." These attacks led UCAR to set aside plans to attempt to occupy the administration building a second time. Smith later discovered that before the harangue at the sit-in, the group of men had clandestinely taken several male members of UCAR aside to encourage them to contest the women's leadership: "They just were having a little tirade about all these bitches running this thing. ... They just had a little pow-wow, these men."

Whatever the personal motivations of the man who led these attacks, it is no accident that he was able to mobilize sexism both within the group and in the wider community to slow UCAR's momentum. The success of this tactic demonstrates just how contested the question of "which way the '-isms' go" continued to be in Black communities, including among the students on the Michigan campus. Internally, UCAR was not immune to these attacks: At times the members debated trying to recruit more men to halt the criticisms, despite their principled misgivings about this strategy. "And we knew that it was screwed, but it was a question of politics versus strategy, and strategy says that we need to have more men around ... so that people can't believe what they say. But even to that degree it was buying into it, all these stupid sexist criticisms of the group being led by women."

Similarly, Smith recounts that at another point the "outspoken" women in UCAR were labeled lesbians in an attempt to silence them and discredit their work. Although their first reaction was to deny the allegations, upon reflection they realized this response was homophobic; instead they challenged their critics, asking "So what if we are—does that mean you can respect us less? ... What's your point?"

The intensity of the resistance that the women-led UCAR met from other Black students not only resonates with Stephens's contention that "the issues of which way the '-isms' go" is indeed a "struggle that continues" in the Black community, but also suggests that the failure to resolve these issues not only limits the scope and vision of liberatory struggles, but also actually impedes antiracist movement. Given this context, the history of UCAR is all the more striking for the group's ability to collectively forge an ideology connecting racism to other systems of oppression (especially sexism) and to put that ideology into practice, both as activists, and in the context of the lived community of the group; the members' resistance to the tactics of those who attempted to discredit them by labeling them lesbians is a case in point. The theme that emerges from Smith's reflections on UCAR, both before and after the actions of the winter months of 1987–1988, is the very real connection among friends who share a common purpose and vision and whose friendship is deepened over time through their shared struggle. Although UCAR was constituted in response to acts of hate, in a tangible sense its strongest tool was the connection shared among the members of the group and their collective love for and commitment to the community.

BAM I, as described by Stephens, was effective because of the students' ability to quickly mobilize existing relationships into a working coalition; UCAR was notable for the nature of the community that it built over time through political struggle. According to Smith, UCAR developed into an organization with the capacity to challenge and transform not only the university but also the political consciousness of the individuals who worked within it. Her description of the power of the community to effect change is dramatic:

> Each year more and more people would come, two or three people would come into the community, and you could see them be changed by it, you could watch them be changed by it. You had people who would come in, then in months you would see the way they addressed things be *changed*. You would hear men, hear their language change, the way that they referred to women. You would hear people who came into the group with real strong beliefs about sexuality issues grow out of that. ... It was great because we would challenge one another on those issues. And I think that everyone who came through the group changed.

Perhaps because she is closer in time to her experiences, or because of her sustained involvement in student activism, Smith evaluated her experiences as having affected her more deeply than did Stephens. "I probably couldn't even know all of the ways that it changed me," she said; indeed, it seemed clear to me that her political commitments had become the lens through which she viewed much of her life. For example, Smith considered her career to be a direct extension of her politics. Although she had long planned to pursue medicine, her political experiences clarified her desire to work in the Black community and to work with AIDS patients. Moreover, it directed her interest toward public policy as a way to extend the scope of her work: "I did a master's degree in public health because I want to have an impact in medicine beyond the individuals that I can care for." For Smith, her identity as an activist is far more salient than her professional identity:

> I still see being a physician as only what I do, and not my life. I always will be involved in political organizing as long as I can find something to do and find some people who are willing to do it with me, and I don't think that's usually going to be the case [with physicians]. I think what it's done is made me conscious of what I do with my career, because I think you can't go and be a Wall Street business person and then go organizing in your part time. I think that it's made my decision of what to do with my life politically oriented.

Like Stephens, Smith underscored the meaning of the friendships she shared within the activist community and the impact these relationships had on her, personally and politically:

I definitely developed [political consciousness] through UCAR, and it's not even just through the UCAR movement. It was the community of people that we developed and the fact that we would talk about politics and read about politics and teach each other and learn from each other all the time. ... I can still say the people that I worked with are the people that I trust in the world, and those are the people that I feel like are going to be making the right decisions. They're the people that I would want on my side, regardless.

The narratives of Smith and Stephens both contain striking accounts of the sense of community among activist groups, extending horizontally through the connections between friends and colleagues. At another, more subtle level, it is also clear that this sense of community extended vertically as well, connecting the activists to kindred individuals and groups whose struggle predated (and perhaps presaged) theirs. The members of UCAR felt strongly identified with an earlier activist group, the Student Non-Violent Coordinating Committee (SNCC), an organization on the front lines of the civil rights movement. Reading Clayborne Carson's (1981) book about the group, UCAR members identified with the women in SNCC who had faced many of the same struggles against sexism internal to the organization that UCAR members had themselves confronted. Smith spoke of these earlier activists with admiration. She and other UCAR members attended a conference on SNCC hoping that they could meet these women and share with them their common experiences of sexism within antiracist movements; however, they were disappointed: "They were very protective, they wouldn't really talk about it. ... It was very clear, they wanted to make it look like everybody was one big family, but I think it was clear that women in leadership had to deal with a lot from the men. And we wanted to learn more about that. ... And you could just tell by them talking, just hearing them speak that they were bad in their day, and they still are bad, and they didn't let men push 'em around too much."

The reticence of the SNCC women echoes Stephens's reluctance to discuss her own reactions to sexism within BAM I. Moreover, Smith's assessment that "they wanted to make it look like everybody was one big family" underscores the point that communities, like families, may collectively choose not to address certain internal issues to protect the group, but these efforts may ultimately be self-defeating.

Vincent Harding (1991) argued that it is through community that people actually experience the connection between generations; in concrete ways, through culture and shared historical memory, communities function to "link those who have already gone by in the struggle with those who are yet to come" (p. 19). Speaking with Smith and Stephens, I was very conscious of the continuity of their struggle. Although the two had never met, they each had played key roles in different eras of student protest at the University of Michigan, and thus shared a type of lineage. For Smith and Stephens, the meaning of this connection was complex.

In contrast to her feelings about the SNCC activists, Smith recalled that she did feel a connection to the BAM I protesters, "but then when I met some of the BAM

I people it put a damage in that link." A former (male) BAM I activist visiting the campus had been critical of UCAR for not having the word "Black" in its name, for not taking the name BAM III. Smith was frustrated with his response, feeling that it was wrong for him to reproach politically active students when he was removed from the political situation on campus. Nevertheless, Smith did feel a connection to the earlier movement based on their shared concerns: "A lot of our UCAR demands were based on some of the BAM demands from 1970, so I did feel that link, and I did feel it was a continuation of that struggle, and I didn't feel that we necessarily needed to name ourselves BAM III to be continuing that struggle."

Similarly, Stephens felt a connection to the UCAR and BAM III activists, a connection that was more felt than acted upon. Watching the incidents of the third wave of Black student protest at the university unfold, Stephens was "livid," both because this new generation of students had to continue the struggle that she and her classmates had spearheaded, albeit without the benefit of the support and wisdom of those who had gone before, and because it was evident that within that struggle, young women continued to be subjected to the same internal mechanisms of sexism that Stephens herself had faced.

> The conditions that were leading to the protest shouldn't have been going on, and we [the BAM I alumni] should have been more proactive from the outside in reaching student leaders and saying, "What's going on?" BAM III, however, was very instructive to me, to the extent that we had a predominantly male Black Student Union (BSU) and a female UCAR, and I found that amazing, and have to this day said, that if I had three minutes in my life I'd love to sit down and talk to people about it, because it was the expression, to me, of the conflict that I went through in 1969 and 70. And I went "Darn, yeah, I know how that happened." I was up on campus on the Martin Luther King Day celebration before [the administration] finally decided to close the university [and thus officially recognize the holiday in response to student protest]. I came up to speak, and I got a chance to briefly talk to the young sister from UCAR and the young man from BSU—it was like déjà vu. …

In many ways, the split that Stephens observed between BAM and UCAR did reflect the same themes of sexist exclusion and division that she had encountered as a student activist. At the same time, Smith's account suggests that the split indicated that the UCAR activists had taken the next step in the struggle that Stephens began. Not only did UCAR activists identify the power of competing "-isms," that is, racism, sexism, and homophobia, to divide a community, but they also fashioned a political analysis that explained the ways that these forms of oppression are interdependent and worked to put their ideology into practice, both through their political struggle and within the community they developed. By building an organization to address the goals of a diverse constituency, UCAR was able to harness diversity as a source of solidarity, rather than allowing difference to drive the group apart. Unfortunately, the vision of truly collective struggle that drove UCAR simultaneously served to divide UCAR from other groups and individuals within the Black student community at the university. The struggle to resolve the potentially competing issues of racism, sexism, and homophobia, both in ideology and in practice, is indeed a struggle that continues.

*   *   *

For many reasons, Black communities are often described by the metaphor of the extended family. This construction taps the idea of lineage and of continuity across generations, as well as speaking to the value placed on family relations among a people whose family bonds, including those between parent and child, husband and wife, were systematically denied recognition and respect during centuries of enslavement. The metaphor of the community as family is telling; it alludes to many aspects of community life that are rarely discussed. Just as feminist scholars have used the standpoint of women to understand the implications of conventional Western family arrangements (for example, Hartmann, 1981), women's experience in antiracist movements reveals the complexity of the Black community as a site of political struggle.

The experiences of Smith and Stephens in two generations of student protest at the University of Michigan suggest a variegated model of community. At the most basic level, their stories demonstrate the ways that communities, that is, networks of interconnected relationships, can mobilize individuals into political struggle, which can in turn strengthen those relationships that make up communities. As well, their narratives suggest the power of collective struggle to change individuals in ways that endure across the life course; thus, political activism may be understood not only as a mechanism of social transformation, but also as a catalyst for individual growth and development.

On another level, the relationship that Stephens and Smith shared across time, even without ever having met, as well as the relationship between the women of UCAR and those of SNCC, illustrates the ways in which identification with a community situates individuals and groups historically; among African-Americans, political struggle is given meaning, at least in part, by a felt sense of continuity with those who have come before and those who continue the struggle. Thus, activism is a tangible manifestation of a felt connection to others through current relationships within the community and to generations that went before as well as those that are yet to come.

Smith's and Stephens's experiences within the Black student movements also suggest that there is a less positive side to community. Their parallel encounters with sexism within activist communities suggest that even in visionary social movements, communities are as likely to be prefigured by the larger societies surrounding them as they are themselves to prefigure a new social reality. This phenomenon is not limited to antiracist movements; Giddings (1984) chronicled the similar history of racism within the women's suffrage movement. What these case studies make clear, however, is that just as the strengths of existing communities may be mobilized in the service of political struggle (see Morris, 1984), that struggle will also bear the imprint of the weaknesses of that community. For activists in both BAM I and UCAR/BAM III, their political struggle with external authorities was hampered by internal contradictions and divisions that had not been adequately acknowledged or addressed. Moreover, the very cohesiveness of the community that may facilitate its political mobilization may also conspire to silence these divisions; like family members keeping a secret, Stephens and the women activists of SNCC preferred not to discuss the ways that they had been excluded from their own movements by their brothers and comrades.

Much has been made of the power of Black communities to support and sustain their members in daily existence, active resistance, and collective political action. When we yield to the temptation to romanticize the ideal of community, however, we lose the opportunity to understand the textured nature of community as it is lived. We obscure the mechanisms through which community may be a radical force, making a collection of individuals more powerful than the sum of its parts through relationships, as well as the ways in which community may be conservative, limiting our struggles by enforcing an unexamined set of norms and customs. Just as the lives of women so often complicate the neatness of dualistic models (Fine, 1992; S. Harding, 1991), the lives of Smith and Stephens reveal that these two aspects of community exist side by side; neither is a truer depiction.

Smith's experience in UCAR suggests that recognizing difference within communities, incorporating the needs of diverse interests within the group into the organization's praxis, is necessary to resist the potentially explosive power of internal differences to divide a community. At the same time, UCAR's practice represents only a partial resolution of this conflict; the resistance that UCAR met from other groups and individuals within the Black student population at the university illustrates how difficult it is for social movements to transcend issues that are unresolved in the base communities from which they are constituted. Taken together, the case studies suggest that to generate social change, progressive social movement organizations must struggle both with external entities of power, as well as internally, among the membership and in the base community. Otherwise, communities are as likely to oppress as to liberate.

References

Cable, S. (1992). Women's social movement involvement: The role of structural availability in recruitment and participation processes. *Sociological Quarterly, 33,* 35–50.

Carson, C. (1981). *In struggle: SNCC and the Black awakening of the 1960s.* Cambridge, MA: Harvard University Press.

Davis, H. V. (1991). From colored to African-Americans: A history of the struggle for educational equity at the University of Michigan and an agenda for the pluralistic multicultural university of the twenty-first century. In H. V. Davis (Ed.), *Sankofa: The university since BAM: Twenty years of progress? Conference report* (pp. 30–51). Office of Minority Affairs, University of Michigan.

Fine, M. (1992). *Disruptive voices: The possibilities of feminist research.* Ann Arbor: University of Michigan Press.

Giddings, P. (1984). *When and where I enter.* New York: Morrow.

Harding, S. (1991). *Whose science? Whose knowledge?: Thinking from women's lives.* Ithaca: Cornell University Press.

Harding, V. (1991). Community as a liberating theme in civil rights history. In A. L. Robinson & P. Sullivan (Eds.), *New directions in civil rights studies* (pp. 17–29). Charlottesville: University Press of Virginia.

Hartmann, H. (1981). The family as the locus of gender, class and political struggle: The example of housework. *Signs, 6,* 366–394.

McAdam, D. (1992). Gender as a mediator of the activist experience: The case of Freedom Summer. *American Journal of Sociology, 97,* 1211–1240.

Morris, A. D. (1984). *The origins of the civil rights movement: Black communities organizing for change.* New York: Free Press.

Payne, C. (1990). Men led but women organized: Movement participation of women in the Mississippi delta. In G. West & R. L. Blumberg (Eds.), *Women and social protest* (pp. 156–165). New York: Oxford University Press.

Thorne, B. (1975). Women in the draft resistance movement: A case study of sex roles and social movements. *Sex Roles, 1,* 179–195.

22

Lessons from Lives

CAROL E. FRANZ, ELIZABETH R. COLE,
FAYE J. CROSBY, & ABIGAIL J. STEWART

ONE OF THE PROMISES we made for this book has been delivered on in all the chapters before this one—the promise of exploring women's lives in their diversity and distinctiveness, one by one. In this chapter we will show how the lives in this book have collectively fulfilled two other promises: that these lives can contribute to developing better personality theory and that they can shed light on methodological and epistemological problems that plague our field. We offer this account of what we have learned to encourage others to teach us other lessons we have not yet articulated.

Learning About Personality

The complexity and significance of identity emerge distinctly from the life stories that are retold and interpreted in these pages. As a construct, identity has been widely explored in psychological literature. Most discussions of it have been concerned with the process of individuation of a separate self—for instance in the development of the capacity for autonomous action, and commitment to values or even an occupation (see, e.g., Erikson, 1950/1963; Gould, 1978; Kegan, 1982; D. J. Levinson, Darrow, Klein, M. H. Levinson, and McKee, 1978; Vaillant, 1977). Separateness is emphasized, connectedness minimized. For Erikson, for example, childhood and adolescent years were ones of increasing individuation and separation. He downplayed the role of close relationships in that individuation process: The person gained the capacity to be intimate following establishment of identity. Typical treatments of identity formation such as Erikson's, then, set up a false dichotomy between the self and others and a false sense of structure instead of process. So prevalent is the notion that self can exist separate from others that even those like Carol Gilligan who are sometimes embraced as the harbingers of a new feminist approach in psychology argue that women should develop the capacity to put their own interests ahead of the interests of others. Gilligan (1982) suggested that some women do achieve a mature cognizance of interdependence:

> Questioning the stoicism of self-denial and replacing the illusion of innocence with an awareness of choice, they struggled to grasp the essential notion of rights, that the interests of the self can be considered legitimate. In this sense the concept of rights changes women's conceptions of self allowing them to see themselves as stronger and to consider directly their own needs. (p. 149)

The case histories in *Women Creating Lives* make plain what some feminist theorists (Franz and White, 1985; Miller, 1976; Steedman, 1986, among others) have also noted: Identity is, of necessity, characterized by the nature of one's relations with others. The ideal of the autonomous and wholly individuated self is chimerical. Because human survival and existence are necessarily relational, so are human sentience and selfhood. As these women rise to the interpersonal, survival, and political opportunities, burdens, and challenges that they encounter through chance and circumstance, they simultaneously create themselves as unique individuals and as constituents of relational networks. They stake a claim for their own well-being and that of their families, and sometimes, together, they confront the larger systems that constrain them. Across the cases, women of widely divergent backgrounds, dispositions, and personal and material resources all struggle for the common goal of creating meaningful lives. These case studies, by taking the lives of women as the starting point for an exploration of identity, reveal the figure of the individual clearly embedded in social relationships and historical context; the self is both constituted and constitutive of context and relationship.

Conceptualizing Identity

Identity, as it emerges in these pages, is characterized by many facets—two of which are immediately evident. On the one hand, identity (i.e., how the woman experiences herself) sets each individual apart as distinct from every other. Simultaneously, interconnection is the foundation of identity (i.e., how the woman describes herself). These two facets exist not as mutually exclusive poles, but instead as two faces of the same coin. It is not the case that a person is at one moment somehow separate and at another somehow connected; rather, at every moment, what makes the individual unlike any other individual—to herself and to others—is that she has a unique constellation of relationships to other people.

The authors in this volume make use of different metaphors to describe identity as both grounded in agency and embedded in relationships; they often choose the language of the women themselves. For example, Schulz uses a Navajo woman's phrase "stealing yourself," to explain the woman's decision to resist the marriage arranged by her parents and marry her lover. Similarly, Litzenberger suggests the complex meaning of "coming out" for the lesbian priests he interviewed; this process entailed not only revealing one's sexual orientation to others, but also, less obviously, the ongoing process of exploring, understanding, and accepting one's self. Almost paradoxically, Layton's reading of the pop star Madonna exemplifies this theme. At the same time that Madonna tries to destabilize the very notion of identity in public, her insistence on "making her life her work" glorifies identity, in whatever form, as an expression of self that is within the control of the individual.

Other case studies emphasize aspects of self-definitions grounded in communion. Paul's chapter, for example, makes clear that women's relational networks may be an important resource for personal development; in those relationships, aspects of identity may be explored and personal needs may, under the best circumstances, be flexibly met. Similarly, Tomlinson-Keasey shows how over the life course of a gifted woman, relationships impeding personal development might be abandoned and new relationships sought to support and facilitate growth.

Taken together, the chapters by Cole and Ceballo focusing on African American women active in struggles for civil rights vividly illustrate the dialectical relationship between identity's aspects of individuation and connection. In Cole's chapter, women for whom political beliefs were highly salient to their life choices talked of how these commitments grew out of their involvement and identification with the needs of their base communities. Through networks of friendships, in keeping with their own values and skills and those of their activist peer groups, the women Cole studied were drawn into and chose to be involved with student movements. In retrospect, they felt that these commitments not just to ideas but also to their communities extended into their personal and occupational choices.

Mary, Ceballo's case subject, gradually developed political consciousness and anger in the course of her extensive professional contact with White society. Mary established herself as a social worker after a childhood filled with difficulties often softened by people—family and friends—who cared deeply about her. At midlife, when she read of the political movements far removed from her in the deep South, she chose to travel across the country to participate in this struggle and has continued her activism over many years. For her, political participation was almost wholly a personal choice, which she understood to be relevant primarily to her personal values and development. The women in both of these chapters constructed identities at various points in their lives based around a powerful felt connection to social groups. However, Cole's and Ceballo's readings of the women's lives also suggest that very similar activities may represent different aspects of identity for different women.

Recognizing Power in Relationships

The cases in this book show that relationships are not only about connection or even identity. They illustrate the complex ways in which relationships and networks of relationships, such as families, involve power: power expressed both as oppression and empowerment. Grossman and Moore explicate the complex ways in which power, gender, and sexuality combined in one woman's experience of sexual abuse in her family. Each relationship, as well as the set of family relationships taken together, is portrayed as complicated. For example, Grossman and Moore write, "Susan voiced several views of her father in the course of the interviews. First, she noted his abuse of her sister. ..." Yet at the same time she said "My father was ... the saint. My father ... walked on water." Finally, they point out that according to "a third perspective on the father," he was "a passive witness who failed to protect his children from the mother's abuse, who both sided with the mother and also was verbally abused by her." No one of these perspectives is selected as correct; instead, all of them reflected the dynamic power relationships in Susan's family.

Cartwright illuminates the force field of love and power in the multigenerational home in which her pioneering woman physician, Natalie, was raised. This field, in turn, had many implications for identity constructions: Although her maternal grandparents' home was a "safe haven for Natalie," the necessity of returning to "her parents' home and reestablishing her dependency on them was conflictual for [her mother] Irene." Natalie's mother and grandmother were still locked in an ongoing personal struggle. Her "grandmother, playing the role of the Russian matriarch from whom all decisions and decrees concerning children and home emanate, disagreed with her [Irene's] child-rearing practices. Natalie believes that her mother's difficulties in separating from her grandmother made Irene determined that her children be independent, self-assertive, and strong. In looking backward, Natalie notes ruefully: 'She did her job too well.'" For Natalie, then, as perhaps for many people, identity construction took place in a network of relationships that was also a network of power relations.

Overall, the authors of the cases in this book have acknowledged individuation and connection as aspects of identity and explored their textured links. In doing so, they allow us to recognize and discuss the centrality of relationships (broadly defined) in many women's lives without essentializing women as having "a different voice" or exiling women to some imaginary "private" world, immune from social/political forces. Thus individuation/agency and connectedness/communion are not dichotomous constructs; instead, lives are seen in the complex interplay of both—an interplay that includes power relations.

Context: Resistance and Resilience

The power of context in shaping the chances and choices of a life is described in these chapters alongside and sometimes against identity. In each of the life stories contained here, community and history provide the grist for identity.

In his discussion of the life of Karen Horney, McAdams observes that in some respects we are all "thrown" into social, historical, and political circumstances beyond our control. The challenge of identity is to make meaning—to improvise—from the positions that are our lot. Ostrove and Stewart illustrate the myriad ways that socioeconomic class determine material and social conditions; however, they simultaneously demonstrate the disparate ways that different individuals understand, respond to, and even resist, similar conditions. Many chapters illustrate how a particular historical moment, intersecting with a moment in the life course of an individual, shapes the resulting personality. This conjunction of person and time is depicted in Gold-Steinberg's case studies of women's experience of legal and illegal abortion and its long-term consequences. Franz shows how one woman who came of age during the sixties used that time as a touchstone in later difficult times:

> Lydia saw numerous specific life choices as based on her identification with her 1960s cohort: her determination to teach disadvantaged kids and live in blue-collar towns, her search for a community (rather than remarriage) that would provide emotional support for herself and [her son] and allow her autonomy, her decision to move to Israel, and her motto that "one must make one's own choices."

In her account of women's self-definitions as lesbians, Stein emphasizes the influence of the social context. For the "baby boom cohort," Stein suggests that lesbian self-constructions are sometimes experienced primarily as a recognition or discovery of a "deep" sexuality and at other times as a political and social "choice," often connected with feminism. Comparing two cases, she concludes:

> For Barb, becoming a lesbian meant that she could affiliate with the social category lesbian, disclose that affiliation to others, and build a social world around the desires that she had for so long kept private. For Margaret, becoming a lesbian was largely a matter of developing a personal sense of self as lesbian to match her affiliation with lesbianism as a social category. She did not have a closet—a subjective sense of herself as highly deviant—to overcome; she was not highly driven toward women in a sexual sense.

In this account, as in others, the author makes clear how the intersection of a particular period in history with individuals' personality development made a difference in identity constructions as well as coping strategies and the life course.

Nagata explores the impact of a different context as she recounts a young Japanese American woman's experience first of persecution and discrimination after Pearl Harbor and then of internment in a "camp," beginning in 1942. As Nagata writes, "it is clear that the camp experience had pervasive impacts"; she quotes Sachi Kaneshiro's account: "I'm sure the whole experience made me lose self-esteem. ... I became an ex-prisoner or an ex-criminal. It created a lot of self-doubt ... feeling unworthy, feeling like we deserved what we got ... feeling very timid about going into places where you may not be welcome."

Over time, Sachi found ways of overcoming some of these effects. After participating in a creative writing class, she wrote a book-length account of her experience in internment. She said of this process, "the more I wrote about my experience the less painful it became." Moreover, public events provided some relief as well. In 1988, with passage of the bill to apologize for the internment and attempt redress through payment of $20,000 to each surviving internee, something shifted for Sachi. She said, "it really did help. I used to think, we went through all this and nobody knew about it and it's going to happen again. But I just feel now there's too much documentation to allow it to happen again."

In a chapter that similarly explores the intersection of political trauma and individual development, Espin examines how a young Latin American girl survived her emigration during a revolutionary period, an emigration that entailed loss of both her parents and her country. Like Sachi, V. sometimes felt that "I deserve everything that is happening to me!" Nevertheless, also through writing—in this case to her former teacher—V. explored her feelings and eventually found a profession and established her own family. She reflected back on those days from middle age and suggested that the correspondence she maintained with her former teacher was "decisive in my life."

Consistently, the women in these chapters meet challenges with courage and strength; they overcome obstacles posed by their personal history and the larger social history. Individually, their efforts to create meaning in their own lives represent a profound resilience. Through their own efforts, these women improvise, create, construct, steal, and lay claim to their selves. At times, they are even able to join with others in struggle, moving beyond the goal of personal survival to resist the social constraints that limit their life chances and choices.

The chapter by Lykes, focusing on the life and life choices of a Maya woman exiled from her home by a civil war that has continued for over three decades, suggests the complex relationship between individual resilience and resistance to systems of oppression. After loss of a close cousin in the conflict, Maria Izabel decided, "I am going to do what is necessary." She left her country and spoke out internationally about what was going on at home. Eventually, she found a way to return home, to work within her own community, with and for women. That choice was born out of her experience working for her people outside the country, with increasing political sophistication as well as increasing loneliness as an exile and refugee. Throughout the trauma and suffering she experienced as an individual and the Maya people suffered more generally, Maria Izabel affirms that "I define myself as giving all that I can give, all that is within my possibilities and capacities," while also affirming that "I identify myself with this community. ... I recognize myself as Maya inasmuch as I am part of the community." Identity is clearly grounded here in community and shapes both personal resilience and efforts to resist oppressive social circumstances.

Learning About Research on Lives

These case histories tell us not only about personality, but also about how we study it. The authors of the chapters in this book have aimed to answer some or all of these questions: (1) How does the individual woman experience her "self"—her identity? (2) How does the individual woman experience her life—that is, what is the context in which she finds herself? and (3) How do others experience her—that is, how does the perspective taken on a life influence the story told? This is not the first time these questions have been asked!

Kluckhohn and Murray (1953) are often cited as pointing out that there are ways in which a person is like all other people, like some other people, and like no other person (p. 53). Traditional nomothetic research has focused on how people are like all or some other persons. The picture that emerges from that research is, as White (1975) remarked, often caricature rather than portrait: "Scientific study has achieved its triumph chiefly with the fixed, the repetitive, the unrealistic, and the unspontaneous in human relationships" (p. 20). White suggested that the idiographic approach (using case studies) is the only way to discover individuality or to focus on growth. At the same time, through exploration of a single case, hypotheses about how and why this person is like some and all other persons can be developed. Perhaps most important, differences that matter—differences in social structural position, personal circumstance, culture—are not erased in the service of producing an understanding of the "average." We do not believe that one approach should be used to the neglect of the other; however, exclusive reliance on the nomothetic will, as Allport (1942) warned, lead us down "chimerical paths."

Another epistemological question arises from these chapters: Is there a connection between feminist research strategies for the understanding of human behavior and the use of case studies? Are feminists more likely than other researchers to value case studies? Do feminists conduct more case studies than other "behavioral scientists"? Do they do better case studies?

On the one hand, there may be no essential link between feminism and case histories. As noted in the introduction, a number of men not particularly identified with feminism (Allport, 1942; Dollard, 1935; Murray, 1938; White, 1966) were strong advocates for the idiographic approach early in the history of psychology. The inverse is also true: Many behavioral scientists who justifiably call themselves feminists have never written a case history and have no intention of ever writing one. But although feminists may be neither more nor less likely than other researchers to perform a life history, those feminists who do undertake a life history are likely to do so in some ways that are distinctive. Although nonfeminist psychologists have used the case method and have produced cases of women, they have often reflected antifemale biases. Thus, one contribution of a feminist approach is to offer alternatives to the portraits of women a more misogynist psychology has painted: women as pathological, inadequate, and different in ways that reflect deficiency. In bringing the details of women's lives to the foreground, our eyes can be opened to new ways of seeing the person—for instance, what appears as pathology to one psychologist may be creative forms of resilience to another.

Some other features of feminist case studies are articulated by Belle, Hornstein, and Stewart in their chapters in this volume. Through these authors' reflections on their attempts to study women's lives from a feminist stance, as well as from the many examples in the other chapters, we learn about how to do good case studies of women. Belle reveals the very different lived realities that exist among women within the single census category of the poor, mother-headed household. She reminds us that biases—whether from stereotypes or from our own life positions based on our own advantages—hinder our ability to see "individual women confronting specific life circumstances and grappling with them in specific ways." It is apparent in Belle's telling of her story that foreclosed assumptions concerning the category of "poor" women would have interfered with her discoveries concerning the lives of the women she studied.

In Hornstein's deliberations about writing a life, we learn about the struggle within the writer of lives between the desire for "truth" as imposed by the all-knowing writer and "ethic of relationship" between author and subject. "What I need most from Frieda," writes Hornstein, "is proof that she existed, and I need that so badly that sometimes I worry that I have made her up." It is perhaps because she is writing as a feminist that Hornstein can say, "Why should we be less accountable for relationships with women we write about than for other relationships in our lives? If feminism risks its integrity, does it have a right to its own ground?" Throughout the book we can see other instances of accountability between researcher and researchee; for example, in many cases the women under study read and commented on their chapter.

Finally, Stewart provides concrete strategies for studying lives—strategies that if kept in mind, help to maintain the attitude toward one's subject, writing, and learning so evident in the words of Belle and Hornstein. In brief, Stewart advises that we not accept the status quo as researchers, that we look for what's been left out, and analyze our own role or position. She highlights the benefits of stepping outside the limits of the dominant mind-set; from the stance of the marginalized it may be more possible to recognize agency in the context of social constraint and not to make assumptions about similarities—or differences—between the sexes without first using the concept of gender as an analytic tool. A feminist strategy for studying lives pushes the researcher/writer to examine ways in which gender both defines power relationships and is constructed by them and leads to analysis of other aspects of social position. Finally, to the extent that our theories about a unitary self reflect cultural and social organization, Stewart reminds us that we need to avoid the imposition of a unified self on the women whose lives we study.

By focusing specifically on women, feminist case studies allow certain types of life issues to become more salient. Gender opens out other structural categories. Thus, to the extent that feminists are currently voicing concern over how we do science—studying poorly or underresearched groups, challenging traditional psychological theorizing, discussing how the researcher and participant are in relationship with each other, and simply following up the call for case studies by doing more case studies—there is a particular relationship between feminism and doing case studies.

Reflections

The case studies in this book illustrate, as perhaps a series of nomothetic studies could not, the complex interweaving of person and situation, of individual and society, and of instrumental action and circumstance. By beginning to fill one "gap" in personality theory—the lives of individual women—we can see the extent to which nomothetic studies tend to decontextualize the person and thus cannot grasp "the person in personality" (Carlson, 1971). Across the diversity of racial, ethnic, and socioeconomic status as well as of personal inclination, sexual orientation, and historical circumstance represented in these chapters, women's lives emerge as wholly contextualized. That is, the women in these accounts are not helplessly manipulated by circumstance, but neither are they fully individuated from it; they actively make meaning in their lives given the context in which they find themselves. These meanings change over time. Identities are shaped through relations to others, whether in friendship, family, community, or even a particular birth cohort. Similarly, acting on the world does not occur in isolation; virtually all accomplishments occur through the efforts of many—it is hard to think of a goal as being reached through the exclusive efforts of an individual. The converse is also true: there is no communion devoid of agency.

The chapters in this volume suggest that it is the precise nature of these relationships that differs among individuals. However, across the chapters, we see the common experience of constructing individual lives in relation to others and to circumstance. From the life histories in *Women Creating Lives,* we see that concepts such as identity can be reframed to avoid false dichotomies between self and other. That reframing also applies to the researcher and the researched; they, too, exist in relation to each other. As the feminist sociologist Ann Oakley (1981/1990) put it, "personal involvement [in research] is more than just a dangerous bias—it is the condition under which people come to know each other and to admit others into their lives" (p. 58). Moreover, by admitting the women in this volume into our lives, we have begun to shape new knowledge and theories of personality—knowledge that cannot be separated from the relationships that generated it.

References

Allport, G. W. (1942). *The use of personal documents in psychological science.* New York: Social Science Research Council.

Carlson, R. (1971). Where is the person in personality research? *Psychological Bulletin, 75,* 203–219.

Dollard, J. (1935). *Criteria for the life history.* New Haven: Yale University Press.

Erikson, E. H. (1963). *Childhood and society.* New York: Norton. (Original work published 1950)

Franz, C. E., & White, K. W. (1985). Individuation and attachment in personality development: Extending Erikson's theory. *Journal of Personality, 53,* 224–256.

Gilligan, C. (1982). *In a different voice: Psychological theory and women's development.* Cambridge, MA: Harvard University Press.

Gould, R. (1978). *Transformations: Growth and change in adult life.* New York: Simon & Schuster.

Kegan, R. (1982). *The evolving self: Problem and process in human development.* Cambridge, MA: Harvard University Press.

Kluckhohn, C., & Murray, H. A. (1953). Personality formation: The determinants. In C. Kluckhohn, H. A. Murray, & D. M. Schneider (Eds.), *Personality in nature, society and culture* (pp. 53–67). New York: Knopf.

Levinson, D. J., Darrow, D. N., Klein, E. B., Levinson, M. H., & McKee, B. (1978). *The seasons of a man's life*. New York: Knopf.

Miller, J. B. (1976). *Toward a new psychology of women*. Boston: Beacon.

Murray, H. A. (1938). *Explorations in personality*. New York: Oxford University Press.

Oakley, A. (1990). Interviewing women: A contradiction in terms. In H. Roberts (Ed.), *Doing feminist research* (pp. 30–61). London: Routledge & Kegan Paul. (Original work published 1981)

Steedman, C. (1986). *Landscape for a good woman: A story of two lives*. London: Virago.

Vaillant, G. E. (1977). *Adaptation to life*. Boston: Little, Brown.

White, R. W. (1966). *Lives in progress: A study in the natural growth of personality* (2d ed.). New York: Holt, Rinehart & Winston.

———. (1975). *Lives in progress* (3d ed.). New York: Holt, Rinehart & Winston.

About the Book

FROM INNER-CITY PUBLIC HOUSING to the halls of Radcliffe we see women's psychological lives unfold in this collection of fascinating case studies. Unlike clinical cases, the focus of these life histories is not on psychopathology. Instead, the authors recreate the lives of a broad spectrum of women: Old and young, rich and poor, straight and lesbian, and women of different races and ethnicities find voice in this volume. By studying each woman in the context of her background and circumstances, the contributors reveal the psychological complexities that are unique to each person and, at the same time, the relationships between psychological development and gender.

In these histories, we see challenges and suffering—and growth, coping, and resilience. We witness the varied struggles of women who enter male domains to become physicians, intellectuals, and celebrities along with the multiple coping strategies of those who have lived in political turmoil, survived sexual abuse, suffered tremendous losses, or chosen abortions. This collection also takes us to sources that are too often silent. For example, the relationship between the spiritual and the sexual is explored in the lives of two lesbian priests. Layers of identity are revealed in the story of a Japanese American woman who was interned during World War II. And the study of two black activists' political involvement shows how a sense of community can reinforce a changing image of the self. Not only do these cases explore specific lives but they also address those general issues that are important to the ethical, unbiased, and sensitive study of women's experiences.

Women Creating Lives offers a feminist approach to studying women's psychological development and reveals elements of class, culture, and gender that are often left unexplored. Thus, through the study of individual lives, it helps to balance the group focus of mainstream psychological research. What emerges is a fuller picture of the way personality develops in the context of daily life.

About the Editors and Contributors

DEBORAH BELLE is associate professor of Psychology at Boston University. She edited *Lives in Stress: Women and Depression* and *Children's Social Networks and Social Supports* and co-edited *The Mental Health of Women.* She has been a William T. Grant Foundation Faculty Scholar in the Mental Health of Children and was Evelyn Green Davis Fellow in Psychology at the Bunting Institute at Radcliffe College in 1992–1993.

LILLIAN K. CARTWRIGHT received her Ph.D. from the University of California at Berkeley in 1970. Her research interests include the adult development of women; health psychology; and program planning, development, and evaluation. She maintains a private practice in adult psychotherapy in San Francisco and is a member of the clinical faculty at the University of California, San Francisco School of Medicine.

ROSARIO CEBALLO is a doctoral candidate in Clinical and Developmental Psychology at the University of Michigan. She has received the Graduate Certificate in Women's Studies and won the 1993 Dorothy Gies McGuigan Award for the best essay in Women's Studies. She also won the Oleshansky Research Award in Psychology. Her research interests focus on the impact of poverty on children and families, children's resilience to stressful life events, and women's social support systems.

ELIZABETH R. COLE received her bachelor's degree from Boston University and completed her doctoral work in Personality Psychology at the University of Michigan. She is currently an assistant professor of Psychology and African American Studies at Northeastern University. Her research focuses on the relationship between women's political attitudes and behaviors and their cognition about the self in the context of the political world. Her most recent work concerns the midlife political involvements of African American and White women who came of age during the social transformations of the late 1960s and early 1970s.

FAYE J. CROSBY is a researcher and educator. Since receiving her Ph.D. in 1976, she has taught at Rhode Island College, Yale University, the University of Waterloo, the J. L. Kellogg Graduate School of Management, and Smith College, where she is professor of Psychology. She is the author of numerous articles and chapters both in scholarly journals and books and in the popular press. Her most recent books include *Juggling* (1991), and coauthored with Susan Clayton, *Justice, Gen-*

der, and Affirmative Action (1993). She has served as president of the Society for the Psychological Study of Social Issues (SPSSI).

OLIVA M. ESPIN, Ph.D., is professor of Women's Studies at San Diego State University and part-time Core Faculty at the California School of Professional Psychology. She has published on psychotherapy with Latinas, immigrant and refugee women, women's sexuality, and other topics. She recently co-edited *Refugee Women and Their Mental Health: Shattered Societies, Shattered Lives.* Her book *Power, Culture and Tradition: The Lives of Latina Healers in Urban Centers in the United States* is forthcoming. She received a Distinguished Professional Contribution Award from the American Psychological Association in 1991.

CAROL E. FRANZ is visiting assistant professor at Williams College, Williamstown, Massachusetts. She received her B.A. degree (1980) in psychology from Gordon College and her Ph.D. (1988) in psychology from Boston University. She was a postdoctoral fellow at the Henry A. Murray Research Center at Radcliffe College, at which time she followed up the Sears, Maccoby, and Levin sample at age forty-one. Her primary interests lie in adult personality development—especially that of midlife women—and in the use of idiographic and nomothetic techniques in psychology.

SHARON GOLD-STEINBERG, Ph.D., is a clinical psychologist currently completing a postdoctoral fellowship in Child and Family Therapy at the University of Michigan Center for the Child and the Family. She is also a lecturer in the University of Michigan Department of Psychology and teaches courses on Marriage and the Family and Socialization of the Child. Her research interests focus on women's sense of self and politicization and factors affecting women's physical and mental health. Her dissertation research investigated women's coping with legal and illegal abortion.

FRANCES K. GROSSMAN is professor in the Department of Psychology at Boston University with primary responsibilities in the Clinical Psychology Doctoral Training Program. She is also a clinician with a specialty in treating adult survivors of childhood abuse. She is married and has two college-age children, one at Oberlin and one at Earlham.

GAIL A. HORNSTEIN is professor of Psychology and director of the Five College Women's Studies Research Center at Mount Holyoke College. She has written widely on identity and intimacy in women's lives, on qualitative methods, and on the history of U.S. psychology, psychiatry, and psychoanalysis. Her current project traces the development of psychotherapy as a treatment for psychotic disturbance through a case study of Frieda Fromm-Reichmann (1889–1957) and Chestnut Lodge in Rockville, Maryland (founded 1910).

LYNNE LAYTON holds a Ph.D. in Comparative Literature and in Clinical Psychology. She is a clinical instructor of Psychology at Beth Israel Hospital, Harvard Medical School, and lecturer on women's studies at Harvard University. She is also on the faculty of the Massachusetts Institute for Psychoanalysis and in private practice in Brookline, Massachusetts. She is co-editor with Barbara A. Schapiro of *Narcissism and the Text: Studies in Literature and the Psychology of Self* and is currently writing a cultural biography of Madonna.

BRIAN W. LITZENBERGER is a graduate student in Clinical Psychology at the University of Michigan. He is also working toward a Graduate Certificate in Women's Studies and is a psychology intern at a clinic that focuses on adult outpatient psychotherapy. His research focuses on identity construction and development. He has published on primary nurturing fathers and sibling abuse.

M. BRINTON LYKES, Ph.D., is associate professor in the School of Education at Boston College. Since 1983 she has worked with Guatemalans, extending earlier work on the self and social individuality and developing community-based mental health responses with and for survivors of war and state-sponsored violence in Guatemala. She is a co-founder and active participant in the international Network in Communication and Scientific Documentation in Mental Health and Human Rights and is currently collaborating in a four-country action-research project on the psychosocial and cultural effects of organized violence on children and adolescents.

DAN P. MCADAMS, Ph.D., is professor of Human Development and Psychology at Northwestern University. He is the winner of the 1988 Henry A. Murray Award from the American Psychological Association for personality research and the study of lives. He has written widely on the topics of identity and the development of the self, adult personality development, generativity, and intimacy. His most recent book is entitled *The Stories We Live By: Personal Myths and the Making of the Self* (1993).

ROSLIN P. MOORE is director of training of the Trauma Clinic, which is affiliated with Massachusetts General Hospital. She is an instructor at Harvard Medical School and has an independent practice in Newton, Massachusetts. The training of mental health professionals is one of her main interests. She is married and has two sons in high school.

DONNA K. NAGATA is associate professor of Clinical Psychology at the University of Michigan at Ann Arbor. She received her doctorate from the University of Illinois at Urbana-Champaign. Her major research interests focus upon the intergenerational impact of the Japanese American internment, Asian American mental health, and family interaction.

JOAN M. OSTROVE is a doctoral student in Personality Psychology and has completed the Graduate Certificate in Women's Studies at the University of Michigan. She was the recipient of a Research Partnership Award from the university to study the intersection of social history and women's personality development. Her current research examines the psychology of social class, specifically the role of class background in shaping individuals' lives.

ELIZABETH L. PAUL is assistant professor of Psychology at Trenton State College in Ewing, New Jersey. She earned her Ph.D. in Personality Psychology at Boston University and was on the staff at the Henry A. Murray Research Center at Radcliffe College. Her primary research interests focus on young adult intimacy development, personal relationships, and gender.

AMY SCHULZ worked for several years on women's health issues in the community. She returned to graduate school in sociology to strengthen her understanding of processes that perpetuate social inequality. She has completed her dissertation, an examination of changing ideologies of race/ethnicity and gender through analysis of U.S. Indian education policies and women's experience of and strategies for managing these changing policies and practices through the life stories of Navajo women.

ARLENE STEIN is visiting lecturer in Sociology, University of Essex, England. She received her Ph.D. from the University of California at Berkeley, where she wrote a dissertation on lesbian identities. She teaches courses on the sociology of gender and sexuality, as well as media and culture, and the sociology of the United States. She recently published the popular anthology *Sisters, Sexperts, Queers: Beyond the Lesbian Nation* (1993), and has contributed to such publications as *Sociological Theory* and *Socialist Review* and to such anthologies as Joan Nestle's *The Persistent Desire* and a forthcoming anthology on social movements and cultural politics.

ABIGAIL J. STEWART is professor of Psychology and Women's Studies at the University of Michigan. She is currently director of the Women's Studies Program there and has collaborated with colleagues in that program on two edited volumes now in press: with Anne Herrmann on *Theorizing Feminism: Parallel Trends in the Humanities and Social Sciences* (Westview Press); and with Domna Stanton on *Feminisms in the Academy*. Her research interests include longitudinal study of women's lives and personalities and the meaning of social-level events and structures in individual lives.

CAROL TOMLINSON-KEASEY is currently vice provost of Faculty Relations at the University of California at Davis and professor of Psychology. In both of these capacities, she is able to trace the lives of individuals. As a professor of Psychology she conducts research on the lives of talented individuals. As an administrator dealing with faculty, she offers practical, applied insight into the lives of academics. She received her doctoral degree from the University of California at Berkeley in developmental psychology and has often taken a life span view in her research.

Index

Abortion, 74
  counseling, 268
  illegal, 5, 7, 263, 264–268
  legal, 5, 263, 264–265, 269–271
Abuse, 153, 154
  emotional, 74
  physical, 4, 73
  sexual, 4, 7, 14, 71, 73, 74–75, 77
  survivors of, 4, 71–81, 270
Achievement, 202, 208, 227, 228, 242
Activism, 5, 7, 28, 30, 90–92, 213, 214–215,
    216, 218, 221, 223, 268, 270, 277, 299,
    301, 309–322, 327
  pacifism, 12
Adolescence, 5, 6, 12, 21, 159–161, 173–174,
    187–197, 237, 251, 310
  See also Young adulthood
African-Americans. See Blacks
Agency (Control), 4, 12, 21, 128, 138–139,
    143, 145, 154, 155, 162, 163, 164, 165, 167,
    168, 328, 333
Alcoholism, 42, 73–74, 79, 206, 279, 285,
    288
  sobriety, 279, 285
Archival research. See Methodology
Assimilation, 128
Authenticity, 55, 151, 255
Autonomy, 5, 20, 121–122, 132, 135, 153–154,
    176, 185, 207, 217, 221, 293

BAM. See Black Action Movement
Belle, Deborah, 3, 7, 331
Biography, 52, 53, 54–57, 58, 62, 63, 64,
    65(n2), 145, 147, 157–158
Black Action Movement (BAM), 310–316
Blacks, 5, 40, 48–49, 83–94, 294, 309–322.
    See also Consciousness, race; Race;
    Racism
Brittain, Vera, 4, 12–13, 14, 15–17 (photos),
    21–23

  class, gender, and race consciousness of,
    28–29, 30
  concepts of gender of, 24–25
  friendship with Winifred Holtby, 13, 14,
    17 (photo), 24, 27, 28
  life in Great Britain, 24, 26, 27, 28
  marriage to George Catlin, 16 (photo),
    18, 19–20, 25–26
  as mother, 27, 30
  relationship with brother Edward
    Brittain, 15 (photo), 18
  relationship with parents, 22
  social class of, 27–28, 30
  Testament of Friendship, 13
  Testament of Youth, 12
  as World War II nurse, 22, 23 (photo)

Cartwright, Lillian K., 5, 6, 7, 328
Case studies. See Methodology
Ceballo, Rosario, 4, 6, 7, 327
Childhood, 79, 83–84, 98–99, 129–131, 208,
    215–216, 229–232, 251
Civil Rights Movement, 7, 84, 89–92, 155,
    294, 312. See also Black Action
    Movement; Southern Christian
    Leadership Conference; Student Non-
    Violent Coordinating Committee;
    United Coalition Against Racism
Class. See Social class
Classism, 49, 86, 295
Cole, Elizabeth R., 5, 7, 327
College, 45, 117, 135, 217, 267, 269
  Howard University, 84, 87
  Radcliffe College, 5, 289, 291, 294–305
  University of Michigan, 146, 309–321
  See also Education
Communion, 4, 5, 20, 162, 163, 164, 167,
    168, 327, 333. See also Intimacy;
    Relationships

341